GOVERNMENTAL PROBLEM-SOLVING

AMERICAN POLITICS RESEARCH SERIES

GOVERNMENTAL PROBLEM-SOLVING

A Computer Simulation of Municipal Budgeting

John P. Crecine

UNIVERSITY OF MICHIGAN

RAND MᶜNALLY & COMPANY • Chicago

AMERICAN POLITICS RESEARCH SERIES
Aaron Wildavsky, Series Editor

For
MY PARENTS

PREFACE

The work reported in this book is a systematic study of an important set of organizational phenomena. Nearly every public sector organization participates in some form of budgetary decision process. The decisions emerging from this process are primary (and in many cases the only) inputs to the organization's planning process and typically provide the foundations for its control and evaluation mechanisms. Budgetary decisions are perceived as important policy decisions by members of the organization and are a (if not *the*) way of allocating scarce organizational resources.

The process of public budgeting is not only important as the primary governmental resource allocation mechanism in our society, it is also representative of the entire class of decision and policy formation processes found in non-market organizations. Non-market organizations typically do not have the several clear and concrete environmental cues and informational inputs provided to an organization functioning in a market environment. Governments must, in the absence of consistent and unambiguous environmental (external) information, rely more heavily on internal, bureaucratic decision criteria and on a system of mutual expectations within the governmental organization.

The basic research strategy employed consists of a systematic investigation (through interviews with participants) of the micro elements of the budgeting decision system (individual decision-makers). Guided by the rigor and discipline of a computer simulation methodology, the study aggregates decision elements to obtain a comprehensive, consistent model of the entire system. The macro system so obtained provides the focal point for the discussion of many questions central to the concerns of organization theory, political science, sociology, psychology, and economics. The formal, computer-simulation model is an internally consistent, unambiguous theory of an important public sector decision process and, as such, allows for the systematic manipulation of theory elements and for the unambiguous drawing of conclusions from theory premises.

My own work with data from other cities and on the budgeting process in the Department of Defense, and work by others in the areas of non-defense budgeting in the federal government and budgeting in state and county governments, argues strongly for the existence of commonality in governmental budgeting processes. The structure of the model presented in this book and the study findings would seem to provide a useful foundation for a positive theory of public resource allocation processes and for their study in other settings. In that spirit, a complete listing of the computer simulation programs comprising my model of municipal budgeting is found in the appendix.

Finally, I hope the methodology utilized here, in the study of a system of decision-making involving repetitive decisions with numerical representation (dollars), will provide a partial guide to those wishing to study (model) the making of non-numeric and non-repetitive policy decisions. The similarity of my findings and those of others studying individual cognitive processes and decision-making, involving the manipulation of non-numeric concepts, suggests that such a development is feasible. I hope this book makes it seem desirable.

John Patrick Crecine

Ann Arbor, Michigan
September, 1967

ACKNOWLEDGMENTS

The original version of this work constituted my doctoral dissertation at the Graduate School of Industrial Administration, Carnegie-Mellon University. My greatest debt of gratitude is to my dissertation committee. Not too long ago I made the *outrageous* statement to a friend that, given my interests and research area, "my doctoral committee was better than any other one that could be assembled in the world today." On reflection, I can say that statement really wasn't so outrageous after all. In fact, I am willing to argue strongly for it. I could win most arguments by merely mentioning Herbert Simon, the chairman. I doubt if there is anyone who is a better source of ideas. Equally important, he has always been accessible. Otto Davis, as a critic, has helped me sharpen my thinking on a number of issues. As my valued friend and colleague, he offers the kind of general encouragement which is of crucial importance. Timothy McGuire subjected most of my statistical techniques to the same high standards he applies to his own work (with less success in my case, however). For a long period of time the remaining, official member of the committee, Richard M. Cyert, has provided general support and encouragement that has been more important that he realizes. Providing access to the University of Pittsburgh computation center when the alternatives were unproductive, is one example. I would be especially remiss if I did not acknowledge the influence and encouragement of the man who introduced me to the 'non-casual' study of political phenomena, James G. March, an initial member of my committee. I feel extremely fortunate to have had the advice and counsel of this group.

In a study of this nature, success (or the opportunity for it) is largely dependent on those individuals studied. Individually and collectively, the decision-makers encountered in this study merit a great deal of thanks. In Detroit city government, Al Teague of the Budget Bureau spent many productive (from my standpoint) hours with me and readily supplied necessary data. Alfred M. Pelham, former controller of Detroit and of Wayne County, graciously shared his experience with me. Also very helpful in Detroit were Richard Strickhartz, controller at the time of the study, and Bob Queller of the Citizens Research Council.

In Cleveland, James A. Norton, president of Greater Cleveland Associated Foundations kindly provided access to the necessary information. Edward Knuth (director) and Ralph W. Muntz in the Department of Finance were very cooperative.

In Pittsburgh, I was exceedingly fortunate in being able to speak freely with the mayor, the Honorable Joseph M. Barr. The mayor's executive secretary, Aldo Colautti, provided me with several hours of productive conversation and generously allowed me to browse through the department request files. David Craig, then city solicitor and presently director of public safety, also provided me with a great many favors and valuable information. Calvin H. Hamilton, former city planning director (now city planning director in Los Angeles), has, during the period I have known him, provided me with a great deal of insight into the workings of government, as has Richard K. Guenther (formerly with Pittsburgh's City Planning Department). Without the willingness of these men (and a large number of their colleagues) to provide necessary background and information, this report would not have been possible.

The computer work for the dissertation has been conducted at the Carnegie-Mellon University (G-20 and 7040), the University of Pittsburgh (IBM 7094), and the University of Michigan (7090). The experiences at these four installations have taught me to appreciate deeply the conditions found at the University of Pittsburgh (and acknowledge the assistance of Ted Van Wormer) and at the IBM 7040 installations at Carnegie-Mellon.

Any research effort of the nature presented here is dependent on the generous financial assistance of various parties. I gratefully acknowledge the support, at various times, of the Ford Foundation, the Richard D. Irwin Foundation, Carnegie-Mellon University and, recently, the Institute of Public Policy Studies at The University of Michigan.

I would also like to thank Rand McNally and the editor of this series, Aaron Wildavsky, for enabling this work to be published. The excellent reader provided by Rand McNally will recognize most of his valuable suggestions in this final version.

The physical task of preparing and reproducing this document was enormous. Without my very able and dedicated typist, Miss Judy Brunclik, deadlines would not have been met and my work would have been increased substantially. Miss Brunclik was invaluable. Miss Rosemary Conte also deserves special thanks for helping ease the load. To Mrs. Betty Henry, who unsuspectingly volunteered to reproduce and assemble the initial version of this report, goes my deepest thanks. The assistance of Mrs. Doris Waco, who very ably typed the final version, is gratefully acknowledged. Mrs. Sybil Stokes provided invaluable assistance in preparing the manuscript for publication.

Some prime motivators, in an empirical sense, should not go unrecognized—those people who kept asking, "When are you going to finish?"

J.P.C.

TABLE OF CONTENTS

Table of Contents

Table of Contents

LIST OF TABLES

LIST OF FIGURES

List of Figures

GOVERNMENTAL PROBLEM-SOLVING

CHAPTER I

Introduction

EXISTING PROPOSITIONS or theories dealing with how municipal budgetary decisions are made (vs. how they ought to be made) are ambiguous and conflicting.[1] They are ambiguous largely because empirical testing has not been undertaken for the few theories that are well-enough formulated to be so tested.

Based on the need for research, this study investigates the decision process surrounding municipal operating budgets for city governments in large metropolitan areas—cities with populations of over 500,000 located in metropolitan areas of over 1,000,000 population, or roughly twenty-one areas in the United States.

The model central to this study is expressed in the form of a computer program that describes the municipal budgetary decision process. The model, constructed from observations taken in three large metropolitan governments (Pittsburgh, Detroit, and Cleveland), consists of three sub-models—the first replicates the formulation of departmental requests for the mayor's office, the second formulates the executive (mayor's) budget request, and the third duplicates the adjustment in the executive budget by the city council or legislative body which approves final appropriations. While consistent with many observations of federal and state budgetary procedures, the model is applied here only to municipal budgeting.

[1] Theories of the expenditure side of municipal resource allocation are few. While the fields of public finance, municipal decision-making, and political science are far from empty, there is a tremendous preoccupation with the revenue side of municipal resource allocation with a corresponding neglect of municipal expenditures. As Thompson points out in *A Preface to Urban Economics,* "Literally, public expenditures and public services are typically cast as exogenous variables—even as constants —that are extraneous to the proper study of local public finance." W. R. Thompson, *A Preface to Urban Economics* (Baltimore: Johns Hopkins Press, 1965), p. 256.

IMPORTANCE OF MUNICIPAL FINANCE

Urban centers are important. With roughly 70 per cent of the population of the United States found in urban areas,[2] the affairs of urban governments should hold a great deal of interest and importance for most people. Local government expenditures account for over one-quarter of total government expenditures. When expenditures for national defense and international relations are excluded, over half of the remaining expenditures are those of local governments.[3] And, the trend for both level and per cent of total government expenditures by local governments is upward. These expenditures help provide for such everyday items as hospitals, police and fire protection, streets, sewers, parks, schools, libraries, water, welfare, airports, public housing, and the like. In addition, the resources utilized in these ventures represent diversions of resources from other potential activities on the part of individuals, corporations, other governments, etc. The point is not a controversial one—local government is important, as is local government finance. The importance is primarily because of the day-to-day effects it has on the behavior of individuals and groups.

To say that local government is significant is, perhaps, too general a statement. We first stated that urban centers were important because of the number of people found in them and then went on to say that local government and local government finances are important. Just what does 'local government' mean with respect to an urban center? For example, within the Chicago, Illinois, standard metropolitan statistical area (SMSA), there are 1,060[4] local governments.[5]

Most of these governments have some powers of taxation and represent such diverse (politically, legally, and geographically) and overlapping units as school districts, townships, counties, municipalities, utility districts (water, power, sewage, etc.), urban renewal authorities, and the like. Usually, when we speak of 'government' in Chicago, we are referring to the city of Chicago, not the other 1,059 local governments in the area. This is not because the city government represents the most people or the

[2] U.S. Department of Commerce, Bureau of the Census, *Statistical Abstract of the United States: 1963* (Washington: Government Printing Office, 1964), p. 20.

[3] U.S. Department of Commerce, Bureau of the Census, *Census of Governments: 1962: Compendium of Government Finances* (Washington: Government Printing Office, 1963), p. 32.

[4] U.S. Department of Commerce, Bureau of Census, *Census of Governments: 1962: Governmental Organization* (Washington: Government Printing Office, 1963), p. 12.

[5] "A government is an organized entity which, in addition to having governmental character, has sufficient discretion in the management of its own affairs to distinguish it as separate from the administrative structure of any other governmental units." *Census of Governments: 1962, op cit.,* p. 15.

largest area (Cook County does), but because, in most urban or area-wide affairs, the city of Chicago is the dominant force—either 'officially' or through the unofficial political mechanisms operating in the Chicago metropolitan area.[6] The central city or core city in any urban area tends to be the focal point of that area's governmental activities in practice and for that reason constitutes the most important governmental unit. Again, this point is not particularly controversial (which is not to say that the central city *should* be the dominant force—merely that it is). It follows, then, that the most important local government finances are those of the central city. We will study the largest portion of the central city finances —the operating or general fund expenditures.

Reasons for Studying the Budget

Because budgets represent planned or expected expenditures and reflect commitments on the part of the organizations involved, they tend to be self-confirming.[7] Thus, the primary determinant of expenditures in a particular period is *planned* expenditures for that period. Inasmuch as the municipal budget is also a control device (no expenditure may be made unless authorized in the city's annual appropriation bill or in some municipal ordinance), all actual expenditures must be made within the confines of the budget. The budget represents an upper bound on municipal expenditures as well as an expenditure target. The budget represents a series of constraints, within which other operating decisions must be made.

Given the characteristics of budgets, one important way to study the process of allocating municipal government resources is to study the municipal budgetary process or the process of planning resource allocation. This is precisely what we intend to do.

We plan to study, in detail, only the operating or general fund budget (including both revenue and expenditure plans) of city governments. There are two primary justifications for this limitation. First, the evidence indicates that the decision procedures surrounding the operating or general fund budget are largely independent of the capital budget and fixed expenditure items (pensions, etc.).[8] And second, data on the capital budget-

---

[6] See Edward C. Banfield, *Political Influence* (New York: The Free Press, 1961), for examples of the city of Chicago's dominance in area affairs.

[7] R. M. Cyert and J. G. March, *A Behavioral Theory of the Firm* (Englewood Cliffs, N.J.: Prentice-Hall, Inc., 1963), pp. 33, 111-113.

[8] As is pointed out in later discussions (see p. 22, 22n), although operating considerations *may* have constituted a significant consideration in the original capital decision, for purposes of current operating budgets, the capital decision is taken as given and results in automatic adjustments (usually several years after the original decision). For purposes of analyzing the change in the operating budget from time t to $t + 1$, previous capital decisions appear to be largely independent decisions.

ing process are not available and significant decisions are infrequent. Capital budgeting decisions provide for independent but automatic changes in operating appropriations. Hence, the effects of capital decisions should show up as deviations in our model and provide a measure of the appropriateness of treating the decisions as independent.

Characteristics of the Budgetary Process

The formal budgetary process consists of three stages.

First, the heads of a city's operating departments are asked to submit budget requests for the approaching fiscal year. These consist of dollar requests for each separate account in existing department appropriations. For instance, the City Planning Department may have appropriations (authorization to make expenditures or to otherwise obligate municipal funds) for Wage and Salary, General Expenses, and Equipment accounts. In most cities, the general appropriations bill for a given year not only specifies *how much* may be spent by city government, but *who* may spend it (funds appropriated for City Planning Department usage), and *what* they may spend it on (Salaries and Wages). Each year, at budget formulation time, the responsible person in each city administrative unit must submit a detailed request for operating funds to the mayor.

Second, the mayor must put all of these detailed requests together, modified to reflect his policies, and present his recommended budget to the municipal legislative body. Unlike the requests for funds by departments, the mayor's budget must provide not only for the destination of funds, but for their origins as well. The mayor's budget recommendation must include a revenue plan as well as an expenditure plan. Revenue estimates are based on tax rates and estimated yields from these taxes. Revenues must be greater than expenditures. In nearly all cities, operating deficits are explicitly forbidden—the budget must be balanced or provide for a surplus.

Third, the council reviews the mayor's budget, makes necessary modifications in the expenditure and revenue plans, and passes the appropriations bill allowing the city government to collect and spend money according to budgetary specifications.

We shall study this basic process. As we shall see, however, things are not this straightforward.

We have chosen to use labels like DEPT., MAYORS, and COUNCIL to describe the three primary sets of functions performed in the budgetary process. The *functions* (and hence the submodels) are generalizable to forms of government other than the mayor-council, however. In the city manager form, the city manager and his staff would correspond to the mayor's function in our model. In the commission form, the finance committee of the council would be the functional equivalent of the mayor.

Note that the budget has nothing to say about what activities shall be engaged in or about specific municipal policies. It is but one set of decisions in a hierarchy of decisions. It may have a lot to say about how many inspectors are employed in the Department of Building Inspection, but very little to say about how many buildings are inspected, the order in which they are inspected, and how strictly building codes are enforced. Budgeted dollar amounts provide many (severe) constraints on the quality of resources available to governmental units, but few constraints on how these resources are utilized.

METHODOLOGY

A brief review of the literature indicates that no 'general' theory of municipal budget-making can be deduced from the abstract characteristics or propositions found. A major reason is that many theories in the social sciences fail to specify when propositions hold and when they do not. When a theory is subjected to a quantitative test, quantification can lead to a precise, unambiguous specification of conditions under which the theory or proposition does apply and when it does not, and the empirical data can help draw attention to cases where the theory must be extended or modified. (This is one reason why a quantitative model was constructed and subjected to empirical tests.) A detailed study of the actual decision process, if properly made, will specify the decision mechanisms operating at each point in the process and will help specify conditions under which a particular behavioral proposition holds.

ORGANIZATION OF BOOK

Chapter II contains a review of theories, empirical findings, etc., that have some bearing on the actual budget decision processes found in large municipalities. This is designed to acquaint the reader with the problem area and some existing approaches. In addition, it should help place this study in its proper perspective as well as suggest relevant areas of inquiry. Chapter III presents an argument for a process-oriented investigation of municipal budgeting rather than an approach that would attempt to test models deduced from theories in Chapter II. A discussion of the advantages and rationale of a simulation model as opposed to a system of equations or statistical model will be found in Chapter III also.

Chapter IV contains an overview of the budgetary decision process and an examination of the interaction between the various submodels

(DEPT., MAYORS, and COUNCIL), the parameter estimation problems, and the relation of budgetary decisions to other decisions.

In Chapters V, VI, and VII are found separate, detailed descriptions of the three submodels, DEPT., MAYORS, and COUNCIL. Detailed verbal and non-verbal flow charts of each submodel, discussions of behavioral mechanisms, interview data, and parameter estimation issues for *all three cities* are also found in Chapters V, VI, and VII.

The computer model, consisting of three submodels, is then used to generate detailed budget estimates for every account category in every administrative unit in our three cities, in Chapter VIII. Estimates are generated for each year in the study period at each of the three decision stages: 1) department request, 2) mayor's budget recommendation, and 3) final council appropriations. Several measures of model fit are developed, applied to model outputs, and used to compare the predictive abilities of the computer process models with those of various naive models.

In Chapters VIII and IX evidence bearing on the similarity of model process to actual decision process is presented and analyzed.

An analysis of model residuals in Chapter IX is used to deal with the general questions of model fit and the linkages between the budgetary decision system and its external environment.

Chapter X is devoted to an analysis of the dynamic properties of the simulation model together with an analysis of the model's sensitivity to key parameters.

The model serves as a common language to tie together other theories and propositions related to municipal budget-making in Chapter XI. In general, the model and portions of it will support concrete illustrations of some of the constructs reviewed in Chapter II, indicate a challenge to the relevance of some, and shape meaningful extensions and modifications of others. Specifically, the municipal budgetary process will be viewed in terms of a complex problem-solving situation in an organizational environment in Chapter XI. With the budget as a problem in resource allocation, in prediction, in electioneering, and in finding solutions feasible with respect to a series of constraints, the works of Braybrooke and Lindblom,[9] Lindblom,[10] Wildavsky,[11] Simon,[12] March and Simon,[13] Cyert and

[9] David Braybrooke and C. E. Lindblom, *A Strategy of Decision* (New York: The Free Press, 1963).

[10] C. E. Lindblom, "The Science of 'Muddling Through,'" *Public Administration Review* (Spring, 1959) and "Policy Analysis," *American Economic Review* (June, 1958).

[11] Aaron Wildavsky, *The Politics of the Budgetary Process* (Boston: Little, Brown and Company, 1964).

[12] H. A. Simon, *Administrative Behavior,* 2nd ed. (New York: The Free Press, 1965).

[13] J. G. March and H. A. Simon, *Organizations* (New York: John Wiley & Sons, Inc., 1958).

March,[14] and Popper[15] seem especially relevant. In general, the model is most easily understood as a problem-solving sequence.

In Chapter XI also, the model is evaluated with respect to the budget as a 'response-to-pressure' process. The 'pressure' model of governmental decision-making is common to most political science literature. Our computer model has a great deal to say about the kind, the location, and the effect of 'pressure' applied to the system.

The model will also be considered as a reflection of the community's power structure or distribution of values. The New Haven studies,[16] Hunter's Atlanta study,[17] Banfield's observations in Chicago,[18] and the study of *Decisions in Syracuse*[19] will be compared and contrasted with our model of resource allocation for operating expenses in a community.

Finally, the implications of this behavioral model of governmental resource allocation for traditional economic approaches[20] to the same problem are revealed. The general conclusion that the problem is too 'complicated' for the rigorous, rational treatment specified in traditional welfare economics seems the most reasonable, given present technology. Lindblom's arguments, that a strategy of "disjointed incrementalism" is the only feasible one for the complex problems of public policy-making, are certainly consistent with our findings and model of municipal resource allocation.[21]

Some substantive and methodological implications of this study for political research are suggested and study conclusions are found in Chapter XII.

Finally, in Chapter XIII, some normative implications of the decision model are covered.

The appendix consists of an explanation of parameter estimation procedures, a listing of administrative units included in the study, parameter values, detailed goodness-of-fit measures, a listing of the FORTRAN II computer programs used, large model residuals, sample output, and data sources.

[14] Cyert and March, *op. cit.*

[15] Karl R. Popper, *The Poverty of Historicism* (Boston: Beacon Press, 1957).

[16] R. A. Dahl, *Who Governs?* (New Haven: Yale University Press, 1961); N. W. Polsby, *Community Power and Political Theory* (New Haven: Yale University Press, 1963).

[17] F. W. Hunter, *Community Power Structure* (Chapel Hill: University of North Carolina Press, 1953).

[18] Banfield, *op. cit.*

[19] R. C. Martin and F. J. Munger *et al.*, *Decisions in Syracuse* (Garden City, N.Y.: Anchor Books, Doubleday & Company, Inc., 1965).

[20] Although most economic theories are normative theories (how the budget problem *ought* to be solved), there have been numerous attempts to 'adapt' the theories into positive plans of behavior. See, for instance, Verne B. Lewis, "Toward a Theory of Budgeting," *Public Administration Review* (Winter, 1952), pp. 42-54.

[21] Braybrooke and Lindblom, *op. cit.*

CHAPTER II

Concepts of Budget

ATTEMPTS AT REVIEWING the literature with the purpose of 'discovering' a positive theory or description of the municipal budgeting process in the United States quickly lead to one conclusion: *little directly applicable to the problem is available.*

Most studies of municipal budgeting are attempts at specifying conditions under which it *should* be decided to allocate X dollars to Activity A instead of Activity B[1] (attempts at an 'economic-normative' theory), or are attempts to link budget expenditure items to demand-for-services variables or ability-to-pay variables in particular municipalities.[2]

The political science literature (with the exception of Wildavsky's works) has surprisingly little to say on the subject.

Works in the public administration field are generally case studies of a particular budget or a specification of the legal requirements of the budget and the formal procedures it must undergo.

The organization theory literature contains many specific references to budgeting as a control device (referring, generally, to business firms, however) but few references to the budget formulation procedure. Primary emphasis is placed on the effects of the budget—control on expenditures, pressures on workers, etc.

The implicit assumption in most sections of the literature seems to be that the budget formation process for any organization is unique to that organization and so dependent on the particular programs, goals, tech-

[1] Verne B. Lewis, "Toward a Theory of Budgeting," *Public Administration Review* (Winter, 1952), pp. 42-54.
[2] Seymour Sacks and W. F. Hellmuth, *Financing Government in a Metropolitan Area* (New York: The Free Press, 1961); also, Harvey E. Brazer, *City Expenditures in the United States* (New York: National Bureau of Economic Research, 1959).

nology, and accounting procedures of the particular organization as to defy generalization. Hopefully, this report will cast some doubt on that assumption.

CONCEPTS OF THE BUDGETARY PROCESS

Budgeting in general has received somewhat different treatments from different disciplines. Basically, treatments of governmental resource allocation can be grouped under three conceptual frameworks: 1) an internal bureaucratic process, 2) an externally determined event, and 3) an optimizing process. These frameworks are based on the decision processes implied in the works. In most of the works cited, both positive (how budgets are made) and normative (how budgets ought to be made) notions appear.

BUDGETING AS AN OPTIMIZING PROCESS

The normative theories of public resource allocation found in public finance and welfare economics are concerned, generally, with maximizing net social welfare, a community utility function, and the like. Another central concern is that of calculating community utility functions by aggregating individual utility functions. The assumptions underlying these theories are primarily two: 1) governments *(should)* attempt to maximize community utility and 2) governments *(should)* have the information to do so.[3] These notions will be of little use to us in a search for a descriptive theory of how municipal budgets *are* formulated. From the outset, neither assumption (borrowed from traditional economic theory) is satisfied. Govern-

[3] The public finance literature applicable to public resource allocation, while not constituting even a reasonable *positive* or descriptive theory of budgeting because of the informational and cognitive limits on individual decision-makers, should at least be mentioned in passing. R. A. Dahl and C. E. Lindblom, *Politics, Economics, and Welfare* (New York: Harper and Row, Publishers, 1953), and R. A. Musgrave and A. T. Peacock, *Classics in the Theory of Public Finance* (New York: The Macmillan Co., 1958), give a good cross section of works in the field which concentrate on maximizing net social welfare, community utility functions and the like and are concerned with such 'computational' problems as defining individual utility functions and aggregating them in some manner to obtain community utility functions. 'Unity functions' are dealt with by K. J. Arrow in *Social Choice and Individual Values* (New York: John Wiley & Sons, Inc., 1951). A growing number of people in the public finance and welfare economics fields are challenging the usefulness of the above approach. For a view of this controversy, see National Bureau of Economic Research, *Public Finances: Needs, Sources, and Utilization: A Conference* (Princeton: Princeton University Press, 1961). Paul Samuelson argues that it is impossible to obtain the information necessary to maximize 'social welfare' in a system having 'public goods.' See "A Pure Theory of Public Expenditures," *Review of Economics and Statistics* (November, 1954), pp. 387-389.

ments (and their officials) do not possess information about individual utility functions, let alone the information (about relationships between variables in the community) necessary to maximize some aggregate of these. Even a casual conversation with government decision-makers indicates that maximizing community welfare is neither a real nor operative goal for them.[4]

For two reasons, then, welfare economics and public finance approaches are likely to be of little help in the search for a positive theory of budgeting. First, the assumptions underlying these theories seem to require abilities no decision-maker possesses. Second, the theories were constructed for different purposes and designed to explain different phenomena than those we are concerned with. The economic branch of the literature is largely concerned either with the way decisions *should* be made or with how they are made at a more global level than that of a department or bureau in a municipality.

Lewis, a former budget officer in the Atomic Energy Commission, attempts[5] to merge the notions of marginal utility and relative values[5] in proposing a budgeting procedure that forces comparison of programs and services at the margin.[6] Pigou's objective ". . . that resources should be so distributed among different uses that the marginal return of satisfaction is the same for all of them,"[7] is "realized" in Lewis' plan through the concept of alternative budgets where

> . . . each administrative official who prepares a budget estimate, either as a basis for an appropriation request or an allotment request after the appropriation is made, would be required to prepare a basic budget estimate supplemented by skeleton plans for alternative amounts. If the amount of the basic estimate equals 100, the alternatives might represent, respectively, 80, 90, 110, and 120 percent of that amount.[8]

These alternative budgets would then allow the 'superior' to compare budgets of the various administrative units under his control by considering their marginal returns and marginal costs. By comparing the 'marginal programs' of his subordinates and accepting a portion of these programs on the basis of their relative merits, the superior reduces his problem (or, so

[4] For a similar comment on the applicability of classical economics to a theory of the firm, see R. M. Cyert and J. G. March, *A Behavioral Theory of the Firm* (Englewood Cliffs, N.J.: Prentice-Hall, Inc., 1963), pp. 5-15.
[5] Lewis bases his work on the theories of Pigou. A. C. Pigou, *A Study in Public Finance* (London: Macmillan and Co., Ltd., 1947).
[6] Lewis, *op cit.*
[7] Quoted in V. O. Key, Jr., "The Lack of a Budgetary Theory," *American Political Science Review* (December, 1940), p. 1139.
[8] Lewis, *op cit.*, p. 49.

Lewis claims) of choosing the expenditure distribution which maximizes community satisfaction to a manageable one.

Lewis' attempt to apply normative economic theories to public resource allocation is one of many in the literature. While not intended to be a description of actual behavior it at least represents a potential positive theory of budgeting.

Another departure from the traditional economic approach is found in Lindblom's work.[9] He argues that given the complexity of the real world, the multiplicity of values and goals to be considered, the difficulty in generating policy alternatives to achieve multiple goals, the lack of theory to predict consequences of policy alternatives, the lack of available information on relevant values, and the limited computational ability of the administrator in practice, the policy-maker must settle for much less than rational, optimizing decision procedures. Because of these difficulties with the ideal analytic decision model, the policy-maker concentrates on one or two of the many possible policy goals, limits the alternatives considered to those relatively few that occur to him ("most of them familiar from past controversies") and will ". . . rely heavily on the record of past experience with small policy steps to predict the consequences of similar steps extended into the future."[10] The choice of policies would involve, first, a choice among values, and second, a choice among policy instruments for achieving those values. Briefly, Lindblom's administrator is a man with limited knowledge, limited information, and limited cognitive ability, making a policy choice in an uncertain world by "drastically" simplifying the problem and making marginal adjustments in past "successful" policies to formulate current policies.[11] Lindblom goes on to argue that, in the face of uncertainty, limited information (and the "cost" of information), and limited computational ability (and the "cost" of expanding it), that incremental change—marginal adjustments of "proven" policies—is probably a very rational way to reach policy decisions.

When applied to the budget problem, Lindblom's model is similar, in some respects, to Lewis'. Departmental budget estimates, for Lindblom, would be marginal adjustments of previous appropriations (last year's

[9] C. E. Lindblom, "The Science of 'Muddling Through,'" *Public Administration Review* (Spring, 1959), pp. 79-88, and "Policy Analysis," *American Economic Review* (June, 1958), pp. 298-312, and David Braybrooke and C. E. Lindblom, *A Strategy of Decision* (New York: The Macmillan Company, 1963), pp. 61-111.

[10] Lindblom, "Science of 'Muddling Through,'" *op. cit.*, pp. 79-80.

[11] Very similar models of decision-making are found in the organization theory literature—most notably in H. A. Simon, *Administrative Behavior*, 2nd ed. (New York: The Free Press, 1965), pp. 79-109; J. G. March and H. A. Simon, *Organizations* (New York: John Wiley & Sons, Inc., 1958), pp. 169-171; and Cyert and March, *op. cit.*

budget with a small change), with the lion's share of the estimate never being reconsidered from year to year. This would correspond quite closely to Lewis' alternative budget concept where there are only marginal differences between budgets.

BUDGETING AS AN EXTERNALLY DETERMINED EVENT

A sizeable portion of the studies of governmental budgeting represents an attempt to link expenditures with community demand for services or the availability of revenue (ability of the community to pay). This linkage implies some way of translating demands into specific expenditures—i.e., some form of service standard. For example, Sacks and Hellmuth in *Financing Government in a Metropolitan Area*[12] attempt to link government expenditures in the Cleveland area to variables such as population, representing a demand for services, and a measure of community wealth (based on both personal income and real property), representing the ability to pay. Although these variables explain a portion of the differences (from about 10 per cent to 80 per cent of the variance) in per capita expenditures for various functions *between* governmental subdivisions in the Cleveland area, a good deal of the short run variation remains unexplained. The model of the budgetary process implied in this type of public expenditure study is a simple one. In the long run, the budget is merely a computational mechanism whereby demands for services (population) are multiplied by some standard of service (measured in dollars per capita) determined by community wealth per capita (wealthier communities demand higher service levels than poorer communities) to arrive at total dollars to be expended on a given community function. Thus, the municipal budgetary process, according to this long-run view is a passive instrument for translating demands into expenditures (supplies of services), where the environment (again, in the long run) provides some sort of cues and correctional mechanisms for policy-makers.

In a cross-sectional study of differences in per capita expenditure levels for similar service functions (differences in service levels or standards) in 462 cities of the United States, Brazer[13] found a great deal of variance in levels between cities, some of which could be attributed to population density and the ratio of central city population to that of the entire metropolitan area. The hypotheses tested by Brazer would imply, as did those of Sacks and Hellmuth, that budgets, *in the long run,* are determined by demands for services and ability to pay. The findings of both works suggest that, in the short run, either the concept of 'service standards' is not used in the budget formation process (assuming, of course, that

[12] Sacks and Hellmuth, *op. cit.*, p. 121.
[13] Brazer, *op. cit.*

expenditures are roughly equivalent to appropriations), different cities use different service standards (an historically generated standard, perhaps),[14] or that standards include such a wide range of behaviors as to be unimportant in the short run. In any case, a budget-making mechanism that has a set of service standards is not likely to give adequate representation of actual budgetary process in the short run.

Much of the public administration literature deals at length with so-called performance and program budgeting.[15] A budget formulated according to these procedures starts with a desired level of activity (x miles of street, y applications processed, etc.) or a program elaborated into the necessary personnel and materials and, by applying a set of unit costs ($/mile of street, etc.), ends with a dollar level of estimated expenditures.[16] The antithesis, of course, is the budget that begins with the dollar amount and then is translated into activities or programs. Admittedly, a good deal of the discussion of performance or program budgeting is aimed at converting administrators to the 'cause' and its adherents do not claim its widespread usage. In spite of this, performance and program budgeting represent a theory of the budgetary process.

The service standard—unit cost—approach to budgeting represents a force model of decision-making where the budget merely translates the sum of the forces into dollar amounts—the forces being public demand for service levels (amount of service) and service quality (cost of service). An alternative, force model of public decision-making can also be found in the literature.

Both Key and Truman imply that governmental budgets are the product of pressures on the chief administrative budget officer (mayor, in our case) exerted by a coalition of the agency making the request and interested pressure groups, combined with his ability to resist these pressures.[17] Much of the organizations literature takes a similar view.[18]

[14] The one exception to this 'lack of standards' seems to be in the field of education. Here, dollars per student per year seems to be a meaningful operating standard. In addition, public school revenues received from the state are many times tied to number of pupils. One would expect, therefore, that budgetary processes associated with education would be somewhat different than those associated with other municipal purposes.

[15] Jesse Burkhead, *Government Budgeting* (New York: John Wiley & Sons, Inc., 1956), pp. 133-182, and Arthur Smithies, *The Budgetary Process in the United States* (New York: McGraw-Hill, Inc., 1955), pp. 229-265.

[16] See C. E. Ridley and H. A. Simon, *Measuring Municipal Activities* (Chicago: International City Managers' Association, 1938) for an excellent review of concepts of municipal activity and service standards.

[17] V. O. Key, Jr., *Politics, Parties, and Pressure Groups* (New York: The Crowell-Collier Publishing Company, 1958), p. 744, and David B. Truman, *The Governmental Process* (New York: Alfred A. Knopf, Inc., 1960), pp. 428-430.

[18] For example, "There will be more conflict between units adjacent to one another in a flow-chart sense than between other units, and the conflict will center on the re-

The community decision literature, while preoccupied with the question of who *really* makes decisions in a community, uses a rather simple model of community decision-making which can easily be applied to budgetary decisions. It, too, is a force model. The vector addition of the component forces produces a resultant force which, in turn, determines policy. Dahl and his followers contend that while few individuals or groups are active and exert force (power) in any given decision, different sets of people operate in different decision areas and that community decision-making viewed in its entirety is dispersed.[19] On any given issue, however, the sum of the exerted forces determines the decision. Hunter presents an almost identical model of choice. The actors in his system are different, however. He contends that only a few in the community possess enough force (power) to have any influence on the outcome and that the same, small set of people (ruling elite) exerts its power in practically every area of community decision.[20] Applied to the municipal budgetary process, the community decision literature would imply a major role for individuals and groups outside of government in a theory of budgeting. While many social scientists view the municipal budget as the outcome of a contest[21] conducted outside the formal administrative organization of city government, others view the process as primarily a bureaucratic, administrative phenomena subject to some external constraints. Now we will turn to this class of theories.

BUDGETING AS AN INTERNAL BUREAUCRATIC PROCESS

Cyert and March have sketched a theory of internal resource allocation for business firms[22] which, with only slight modification, they claim, is applicable to other non-business organizations.[23] This theory of internal

---

source (budget is an internal allocation of resources) . . . represented in the flow. Conflict among subunits in an organization will be particularly acute with respect to budgeting and the allocation of money. . . ." March and Simon, *op. cit.*, p. 123.

[19] R. A. Dahl, *Who Governs?* (New Haven: Yale University Press, 1961).

[20] F. W. Hunter, *Community Power Structure* (Chapel Hill: University of North Carolina Press, 1953).

[21] For example, W. S. Sayre and Herbert Kaufman in *Governing New York City* (New York: Russell Sage Foundation, 1960) describe the political decision process as a contest involving seven categories of participants: 1) public officials of a city, 2) members of the government bureaucracy, 3) hierarchies of political party functionaries, 4) non-governmental groups (interest groups), 5) the press and other mass media, 6) electorates, and 7) officials of other governments. Their study suggests that these participants enter the allocation process at different points. Precisely what these points are is an empirical question and a legitimate inquiry.

[22] Cyert and March, *op. cit.*, pp. 270-278.

[23] Cyert and March, *op. cit.*, p. 288.

resource allocation is presented within the framework of the four major relational concepts found in their theory of business decision-making:

1. *Quasi-resolution of conflict* where goal conflicts are not 'resolved' by reducing all goals to a common dimension or making them internally consistent, but by viewing goals as a set of independent constraints which an acceptable policy must satisfy; by subdividing problems and delegating them to subunits thereby insuring that subunits deal with a ". . . limited set of problems and a limited set of goals," and reducing the potential for goal conflict between subunits; by using acceptable-level decision rules rather than optimization as a decision criterion (reducing potential for goal conflict); and by sequential attention to goals rather than simultaneous consideration of all goals.

2. *Uncertainty avoidance* where uncertainty is circumvented rather than faced by resorting to feedback-react decision procedures to solve problems when they arise instead of anticipating problems and planning for their solution ahead of time; and by negotiating with the environment to insure stability and predictability of the organization's surroundings through standard practices in an industry or budgets within a firm.

3. *Problemistic search* where the search for alternatives or solutions is activated by the presence of a perceived problem and depressed by a perceived solution; where the search for solutions "proceeds on the basis of a simple model of causality" based on the characteristics of the problem until failure to discover a solution forces use of a more complex model; and where search is biased and aimed in the direction of previous, successful problem solutions, existing organizational information, experience, and training.

4. *Organizational learning* where learning is perceived as the adaptation, with experience, of goals, attention rules, and search rules. Goals are changed on the basis of past experience, past goals, and the performance of comparable organizations. Attention rules are reasonably fixed in the short run but shift in the long run toward those that generally indicate satisfactory performance for the subunit involved. Search rules change slowly in the direction of success. When an organization discovers a solution to a problem by searching in a particular way, it will be more likely to search that way in future problems of the same type.[24]

Cyert and March then apply these notions to the problem of internal (to the organization) resource allocation.

[24] Cyert and March, *op. cit.,* pp. 116-125.

Consider the quasi-resolution of organizational conflict. In budgeting, . . . we expect to find that goals tend to enter as more or less independent constraints. . . . Where an allocation plan apparently meets the constraints, we expect rather loose evaluations of the accuracy of the estimates and other assumptions on which it is based. Where resource rationing is necessary, we expect two general kinds of reactions: first, a tendency to use arbitrary allocation rules that maintain the relative positions of the members of the coalition; second, a tendency to re-evaluate those estimates that are relatively difficult to defend in terms of traditional organizational practice, standard accounting procedure, or immediacy of tangible return.[25]

Applied to municipal budgeting, this seems to imply that if revenue estimates are less than departmental requests (always the case), the mayor's office will scale down requests so each department may retain the same portion of the municipal expenditure pie. Furthermore, maintenance and equipment items are most likely to be cut, because they can easily be deferred, and would not lower current levels of operations.

Discussing search behavior, Cyert and March predict "problem-oriented" search. We find request-cutting procedures are evoked by the mayor's office or the council only when total department requests exceed estimated revenues, when a department's request exceeds last period's appropriations by more than a fixed percentage, etc. They also predict search "directed by learned rules for associating search behavior with particular problems."[26] In city government there exists a set of fixed procedures, policies, etc., for deciding which requests are granted, cut, etc.

While dealing with uncertainty avoidance as applied to budgeting, Cyert and March contend that we will find extensive dependency of budgeting on standard industry and firm rules. Widely shared operative criteria will standardize decisions by permitting cross-firm comparisons.[27] Translated to the case of municipal operating budgets, this implies rather uniform budgeting procedures (decision sequences, budget forms, etc.), perhaps through 'model legislation,' drafted by various national organizations or reform groups, and a set of service or operating standards (x dollars/capita to be spent on police protection, etc.).

Finally, Cyert and March theorize that "organizational learning" with respect to budgeting will take the form of changes in goals over time, changes in the search and decision rules, and changes in the learning rules. In general, they expect a behavioral model of internal resource allocation to be heavily history-dependent. [28]

[25] Cyert and March, *op. cit.*, p. 270. (© 1963. Reprinted by permission of Prentice-Hall, Inc., Englewood Cliffs, N.J.)

[26] Cyert and March, *op. cit.*, p. 271.

[27] Cyert and March, *op. cit.*, p. 271.

[28] Cyert and March, *op. cit.*, p. 271.

What Cyert and March seem to be suggesting is that there exists a set of widely shared heuristics for solving complex problems within an organization, with "only" parameters changing from organization to organization or from problem to problem within an organization. With internal resource allocation being a complex problem for any organization, the broad outlines of the Cyert-March behavioral theory of organizational decision-making will be relevant to our problem.

The Cyert-March theory of organizational decision-making is generally consistent with the works in organization theory that take the decision and associated-decision process as the focal point in the study of organizations.[29] For this reason, it will not be necessary to consider explicitly such important (and relevant) works as Simon's *Administrative Behavior* and *Public Administration* (with D. W. Smithburg and V. A. Thompson), and March and Simon's *Organizations*.

In easily the most important theoretical work to date on a positive theory of governmental budgeting, Wildavsky's findings[30] are strikingly similar to the theories of Simon, March and Simon, and Cyert and March, relative to the organizational decision processes. A similar congruence exists between those notions relating to problem complexity and its influence on decision strategies put forth by Braybrooke and Lindblom in *A Strategy of Decision*. Wildavsky has constructed a theory of the formation of the federal budget based on a detailed description of the decision process. Wildavsky obtained the material for his theory through a series of detailed interviews with agency heads, Bureau of the Budget personnel, and congresssmen. Perhaps the most important feature of his theories, however, is the empirical verification of many of them in his work with Otto A. Davis, an economist, and Michael Dempster, a mathematician, using linear regression models of the congressional decision processes.[31]

While emphasizing the complexity of the budget-maker's problem,

---

[29] Simon advocated the "decision" as the unifying concept in the administrative process in *Administrative Behavior*, first published in 1950. This viewpoint was significantly expanded and elaborated in March and Simon's *Organizations, op. cit.* Cyert and March's work in many respects is a continuation, expansion, and elaboration of many of the notions found in *Organizations* and applied to organizational decision processes, just as G. P. E. Clarkson's book, *Portfolio Selection: A Simulation of Trust Investment* (Englewood Cliffs, N.J.: Prentice-Hall, Inc., 1962), represents a similar extension into the realm of individual decision-making.

[30] Aaron Wildavsky, *The Politics of the Budgetary Process* (Boston: Little, Brown and Company, 1964).

[31] O. A. Davis, M. A. H. Dempster, and Aaron Wildavsky, "On the Process of Budgeting: An Empirical Study of Congressional Appropriation" in Gordon Tullock, ed., *Papers on Non-market Decision Making* (Charlottesville, Va.: Thomas Jefferson Center for Political Economy, 1966) and Davis, Dempster, and Wildavsky, "A Theory of the Budgetary Process," *American Political Science Review* (September, 1966), pp. 529-547.

Wildavsky describes a series of "aids to calculation" to help the decision-maker simplify the problem and reach a decision. Some of these are:

1. Experiential budgeting—"One way of dealing with a problem of huge magnitude is to make only the roughest guesses while letting experience accumulate."
2. Simplification—Ignore complicated aspects of the problem and concentrate on those items with which decision-maker is familiar.
3. "Satisfice"—Rather than maximize, budget officials "satisfy" and suffice."[32]
4. Incrementalism—"The largest determining factor of the size and content of this year's budget is last year's budget. Most of the budget is a product of previous decisions."[33]

Wildavsky also describes two notions widely held by participants in the federal budgetary process—"fair share" and "base." "The base is the general expectation among participants that programs will be carried on at close to the going level of expenditures but it does not necessarily include all activities."[34] In other words, appropriations for a department in year $t + 1$ are "never" less than a fixed percentage of appropriations for year t. " 'Fair share' means not only the base an agency has established but also the expectation that it will receive some proportion of funds, if any, which are to be increased over or decreased below the base of the various governmental agencies."[35] Increases and decreases are to be distributed 'democratically' among the agencies.[36]

The roles of the participants cited by Wildavsky are generally those assumed by more casual observers of a bureaucracy in general and the federal government in particular: department heads ask for more than they expect, budget officials and the chief executive tend to scale down agency requests, and Congress tends to cut the executive budget.

The extension of Wildavsky's theory to municipal budgeting is fairly straightforward. If police and fire department functions are substituted for the defense functions of the federal government and if foreign policy is ignored, large municipal governments perform functions very similar to those of the federal government on the expenditure side of the ledger. The

[32] This term was originated by Herbert A. Simon, *Models of Man* (New York: John Wiley & Sons, Inc., 1957), and is similar to "aspiration level" of March and Simon and "acceptable-level decision criteria" of Cyert and March.
[33] Wildavsky, *op. cit.*, pp. 11-16. This view parallels Cyert and March's contention that internal resource allocation is "heavily history dependent" and that the budget can usefully be thought of as an elaboration of goals and policy commitments. This is also similar to Lindblom's notion of "incrementalism" as a method of dealing with complex problems.
[34] Wildavsky, *op. cit.*, p. 17.
[35] Wildavsky, *op. cit.*, p. 17.
[36] Neither the Davis, Dempster, and Wildavsky work or ours confirms the existence of this 'concept' in the behavioral sense. See measures of goodness-of-fit, p. 122 in Chapter VIII, constant-share-of-the-increase model.

roles of participants in the sequence or flow of decisions is, as a first ap-proximation, roughly similar with city department heads corresponding to agency or bureau chiefs, the mayor's office or budget department similar to the Bureau of the Budget, the mayor's function paralleling that of the Chief Executive, and that of the council corresponding to Congress.

How well Wildavsky's 'model' fits municipal budgets is, of course, an empirical question that this study will attempt to answer.

Other approaches to the study of organizations and bureaucracies that might be considered focus on role perceptions of the participants (socio-logical approach),[37] motivations,[38] "compliance systems,"[39] the informal social network, etc. All of these approaches are represented in one form or another in either Cyert and March's formulation of budgetary processes or in Wildavsky's.

Before moving on to the methodological question one other general conception of political decision processes should be cited. Banfield, in his studies of political processes in the Chicago area, perceives the area as being governed by ". . . hundreds, perhaps thousands of bodies, each of which has a measure of legal authority. . . . Altogether, these many bodies are like a great governing committee each member of which has, in matters affecting it, an absolute veto." Banfield contends there is "no communica-tion" between members of the committee, and each body "acts inde-pendently without knowledge of the others," with the result that proposed action must satisfy a series of independent constraints imposed by the bodies or committee members.[40] Applying this decision model to the municipal budgetary process means identifying the relevant members of the "committee" (individuals or groups) and specifying the constraints imposed by each "member" for budget approval. Banfield's model bears some similarity to the Cyert-March concept of goals of the participants entering the decision process as a series of more or less independent con-straints (each of which must normally be satisfied), and to the Dahl influ-ence model where the influencers must be identified for each problem area.

OVERVIEW OF THEORIES OF BUDGETARY BEHAVIOR

The above represents the general 'state of the art' relative to positive theories of municipal resource allocation. As can be seen, many of the theories are somewhat ambiguous (and perhaps open to interpretations

[37] P. M. Blau, and W. R. Scott, *Formal Organizations* (San Francisco: Chandler Publishing Company, 1962).
[38] Chris Argyris, *The Impact of Budgets on People* (New York: Controllership Foun-dation, 1954).
[39] Amitai Etzioni, *A Comparative Analysis of Complex Organizations* (New York: The Free Press, 1961).
[40] E. C. Banfield, *Political Influence* (New York: The Free Press, 1961), pp. 5-6.

different from the ones given). This ambiguity is not characteristic of a particularly good theory, however.

A second problem arises in the set of theories offered above. Many are inconsistent with each other. It is not merely the case of many blind men observing different portions of the same elephant and coming up with different descriptions—all of which are true, but only partially so. For instance, the differences between the Wildavsky, Davis, Cyert-March, and Lindblom views of the world and those implied in the works of Pigou, Lewis, Sacks and Hellmuth, Brazer, and Hunter are more than differences of degree or emphasis, they are differences in kind. *The assumption that participants in the budget-making process are passive instruments who will come up with a predetermined solution to the problem of municipal resource allocation either by following economic dictates and service demands or by following the dictates of community power figures vs. the assumption that budget-makers are organizational decision-makers and problem-solvers who structure complex problems, generate alternatives, and make choices on the basis of some criteria, is a real difference.* How might we choose between these conceptualizations?

If 'external' (to the formal government) participants and environmental information constitute important elements in the process, then:

1. References to these extra-governmental information sources should emerge in interviews of the formal participants, *or*
2. Models that consider only those 'internal' mechanisms uncovered in interviews with the formal (governmental) participants should produce systematic errors when model predictions are compared with observed budgetary behavior.

Most of the economics and public finance literature is aimed at discovering long-run forces that shape the overall distributions of municipal resources—with the hope of constructing an operational normative theory. The two expectations listed above would apply if these external forces were important in the short-run decision process. Another possibility exists. Suppose that the decision system monitors these external forces only occasionally (or *vice versa*). It might be that the decision system (or its decisions) is 'allowed' to operate within a relatively loose set of constraints imposed by the external environment. The decision system would be permitted to wander within this system of changing external constraints. If the government wanders outside these constraints, the external environment would 'step in' and correct the situation. If this were the case:

3. External decision corrections would be observed occasionally, and any model based solely on internal, bureaucratic processes would experience a sizeable error when the environment intervened to make corrections.

Thus, a model based on interviews with the formal participants in the decision process that did not have the 'external' environment as a key variable would either not 'explain' (statistically) very well or would generate significant errors whenever the external environment intervened. The relationships between short-run, internal bureaucratic models and long-run, external-environment models can be investigated through measures of overall model goodness-of-fit and an analysis of residuals. (These analyses are found in Chapters VI and VII.) Both are empirical issues involving theory validity. We now turn to the problem of constructing theories that can be subjected to empirical test.

CHAPTER III

Research Strategy

THE CHOICE of a research methodology is really a two-stage process. Before one can decide on a particular methodology, one must first decide on the scope of the problem to be examined and the general *research strategy* to be employed.

RESEARCH STRATEGY

The scope of the problem has already been examined in a very general sense in Chapter I. The expenditure side of the municipal operating budget is our problem area. The decision to separate the study of the municipal operating budget from the capital budget and revenue or tax decisions was based partially on rough empirical knowledge, and partially on the availability of data. Preliminary interviews with budget officials indicated that:

1. In the short run, only a loose connection seems to exist between the capital and operating budgets in municipal government. These connections appear to be computational in nature and to consist of the elaboration of the implications of particular capital expenditures. For example, moving several city departments from rented quarters to a new, city-owned building involves a 'legitimate' (i.e., automatic) increase in custodial costs, maintenance charges, furniture, and the like. Equally automatic decreases in rental charges are also made in the operating budget.[1]

[1] In the long run, elaborations of the capital decision process could prove to be one of the prime determinants of resource allocation. For instance, the construction of a civic center in Detroit involved more than just a facility to be maintained (the impact on the operating budget). It represented elements of a long–run urban renewal commitment as well as the desire for convention trade. These 'shocks' to the operating

2. Revenue estimates made by the city administration appear unbiased and as accurate as possible, with the estimates being corroborated by outside, 'independent' organizations. The primary connection between revenue estimates and budgeted expenditure estimates occurs when anticipated expenditures force an increase in tax rates (i.e., a change in tax policy). No changes in tax *yield* estimates to 'make the budget balance' were observed.

In a sense, the decision to limit the scope of the problem to operating expenditures leaves the study open to a charge that methodology (commitment to an empirically-based study) has limited the choice and scope of the problem.[2] This is true. This limitation appears to be a reasonable one, however, insofar as the operating budget (allocation decisions) represents a set of relationships reasonably independent from the capital and revenue decisions (level decisions) for the municipality.

Given the scope of the study, there are many ways we can proceed. One research strategy would be to take some or all of the theories outlined in Chapter II, gather information on the relevant variables, use the theories (elaborated or restated in a testable form) to make predictions, then compare predictions with real, observed behavior to arrive at a choice among theories or a specification of the conditions for a theory's applicability.

A second posssible research strategy is to construct a descriptive model of the budgetary decision process based on empirical evidence, then use the validated model as a theory[3] in its own right and/or *use the model*

---

budget in the form of capital budget elaborations can be cumulative in many cases.

By nature, capital decisions are infrequent decisions, thereby limiting the opportunity for observation. Also, access to relevant decision variables and decision-makers is largely a chance phenomenon. If the success of a research project is a function of the number of relevant variables and relationships investigated, then research on capital decisions has a low probability of success. Both the frequency (number) of observations and the probability of making a successful observation are low.

[2] "The more substantively oriented social scientists decry the tendency to study what they visualize as trivial problems with impeccable methodology, and argue that despite inadequate techniques, social scientists have more to contribute by exploring bigger and more significant problems. The new school of empiricists and methodologists responds that all scientific activity moves slowly: systemization, they say, is required if we are ever to be in a position to make an intelligent attack on many problems of great importance." David Mechanic, "Some Considerations in the Methodology of Organizational Studies," in H. J. Leavitt, ed., *The Social Science of Organizations: Four Perspectives* (Englewood Cliffs, N.J.: Prentice-Hall, Inc., 1963), p. 142.

[3] In this report, 'theory' and 'model' are used interchangeably. Generally speaking, a theory should contain statements of the relations between important variables in the system being studied—statements of the interdependencies between variables, the functional form of those interdependencies, and the structural characteristics of the system of behavior. A 'model' or 'theory' is ". . . essentially a set of assumptions from which a conclusion or a set of conclusions is logically deduced. . . . [T]he assump-

as a focal point, comparing existing theories and postulates to it in a sort of consistency test. This comparison would then serve the same function as the first strategy outlined above.

Our basic *research strategy,* then, is to examine the decision process in detail, forming a positive theory of municipal budgeting, rather than to examine the various theories cited in Chapter II. On the basis of preliminary empirical evidence, one theory or abstraction of municipal budgeting will be constructed, rather than a separate one for each municipality examined, thus gaining some of the advantages of a more general theory.

Methodology

In our discussion of existing theories of governmental resource allocation and decision-making we alluded to two problems with these theories: 1) ambiguity or the use of non-operational concepts, and 2) the presence of 'conflicting' theories with no way to choose among them because they were not stated in empirically testable form.

If we are not to be guilty of the same sins of omission, our theory must be such that it is precise and unambiguous with respect to the kinds of behavior it implies and must be stated in an empirically testable form. These two considerations are definite, self-imposed constraints on this study.

Theory Formalization

The desire to state a theory in an unambiguous form leads directly to the question of the language to be used. The language of mathematics is clearly unambiguous and is a ready solution to our problem of precision. In addition, properly constructed, a mathematical formulation of relationships and processes involved in the budgetary decisions should permit one to trace unambiguously the implications of these relationships. The implications of our theory (budget figures generated by the mathematical statement of our theory) will be in a form that permits ready comparison with observed behavior (actual budgetary decisions).

The advantages of formulating a problem mathematically are many:

a) Knowing more precisely what mechanisms or structural relationships

---

tions need not be *exact representations* of reality, but they may instead be *reasonable abstractions* of reality." (K. J. Cohen and R. M. Cyert, "The Methodology of Model Building." Unpublished mimeographed paper, Carnegie-Mellon University, 1961). In our case, this means that the abstraction of decision rules used in the model or theory must be a 'reasonable abstraction' of the decision rules actually employed as well as being capable of generating the same kinds of decisions found in reality.

are being postulated, and sometimes calling attention to the need for further clarification of the operational meaning of definitions and statements;

b) Discovering whether certain postulates can be derived from others, and hence can be eliminated as independent assumptions; whether additional postulates need to be added to make the system complete and the deductions rigorous; and whether there are inconsistencies among postulates;

c) Assisting in the discovery of inconsistencies between the empirical data and the theories used to explain them;

d) Laying the basis for the further elaboration of theory, and to deductions from the postulates that suggest further empirical studies for verification;

e) Aiding in handling complicated, simultaneous interrelations among a relatively large number of variables, with some reductions of the obscuring circumlocutions entailed by non-mathematical language.[4]

Having chosen a language (mathematics), we must pick a dialect. Many types of mathematical models exist. Systems of equations (linear and differential, to name two), statistical models (stochastic, Markovian, etc.), and computer programs are a few of the many dialects in the language of mathematics.

COMPUTER PROGRAMS AND PROBLEM-SOLVING PROCESSES

Our model will be stated in the form of a computer program. The nature of the budgetary decision process suggests such an approach. Even a superficial examination of the municipal resource allocation procedure indicates that it is the result of a *sequence* of decisions—departmental requests, mayor's executive budget, and final council appropriations. A computer program is really a collection of *instructions* executed in a *specific* sequence.

A logical question to be raised at this point is: Are the individual budgetary decision procedures repetitive? And if so, are these 'stable' decision rules applied in a regular, systematic sequence? The answer should be affirmative if the computer-program description of budgeting is to be valid. The obvious reason why repetitive procedures tend to be programmed, and *vice versa,* is that if a particular problem recurs often enough, a routine procedure will usually be established for solving it. Certainly the municipal budget is a recurrent (yearly) problem. And evidence exists that recurrent, complex problems are solved by breaking the

[4] H. A. Simon, *Administrative Behavior,* 2nd ed. (New York: The Free Press, 1965), p. 142.

global problem into a series of less complex ones, and then solving the simplified problems sequentially.

In particular, a computer-program description of the problem-solving behavior of individuals exists for a trust investment officer,[5] a department store buyer,[6] laboratory subjects solving simple problems[7] and chess players.[8]

Computer Simulation of Municipal Budgeting

Our proposed computer program will attempt to describe or simulate the behavior of many individuals—department heads and budget officers, budget officials in the mayor's office, and the council—simultaneously. But there is no reason to think that the hundred or so actors involved in the formal budgetary decision system will be any more difficult to 'program' or simulate than such individuals as, say, the trust investment officer. The difficulty, if any, will arise from the number of decisions and decision-makers in our model, and the quantity of data to be analyzed.[9]

SIMULATION AS A RESEARCH TOOL

"Simulation is a technique for building theories that reproduce part or all of the output of a behaving system."[10] In addition, some simulation models have the goal of reproducing not only the final output but also the

---

[5] G. P. E. Clarkson, *Portfolio Selection: A Simulation of Trust Investment* (Englewood Cliffs, N. J.: Prentice-Hall, Inc., 1962).

[6] R. M. Cyert and J. G. March, *A Behavioral Theory of the Firm* (Englewood Cliffs, N. J.: Prentice-Hall, Inc., 1963). Chapters VII and VIII.

[7] A. Newell and H. A. Simon, "Computers in Psychology," in R. D. Luce, R. R. Bush, and E. Galanter, eds., *Handbook of Mathematical Psychology*, Vol. I (New York: John Wiley & Sons, Inc., 1963), and "GPS, A Program That Stimulates Human Thought," in E. Feigenbaum and J. Feldman, eds., *Computers and Thought* (New York: McGraw-Hill, Inc., 1963).

[8] A. Newell, J. C. Shaw, and H. A. Simon, "Chess-Playing Programs and the Problem of Complexity," in Feigenbaum and Feldman, eds., *op. cit.*

[9] The implications of the magnitude of the problem are many. First, it should be fairly obvious that each actor in our simulation model will be described in a more abstract manner than the individual problem-solvers in most of the works cited above. Second, assumptions will have to be made which detract from the overall accuracy (i.e., completeness) of the model. For example, it will be necessary to assume that each department head in the system behaves according to the same decision model, with only parameters changing. It is obviously not practical or reasonable to interview all department heads and all parties involved in the budgetary process. Behavioral rules attributed by others to our decision-makers will have to be incorporated in the model without individual preliminary checks. The reasonableness and 'accuracy' of these necessary short cuts will, of course, be measured empirically when the model is tested.

[10] Clarkson, *op. cit.*, p. 16.

procedures, processes, and decision rules between the informational inputs and outputs (budgetary decisions). This is our task. The attempt to reproduce output and procedures will be in the form of a computer program representing the structural form of the decision process (sequence of decisions), the functional form of the individual decision rules (individual equations representing actual decision rules), and the decision parameters (values of constants or empirically determined variables embedded in the structure and functional relations of the model). Model terminology is defined in Table III-1.

The entire computer program will then represent a formalization of our positive theory of municipal resource allocation.

In addition to the advantages of theory formalization cited above, the particular kind of formalization—computer simulation—offers other advantages:

1. Since most mathematical models are intended for analytic solution, their complexity and realism must be severely limited. Computer models, however, can be made as complex and realistic as our theories permit, for analytical solutions to these models are unnecessary.[11]

2. The assumptions inherent in a computer program can be easily modified, and once the model (program) is set up, testing alternative assumptions by changing one or two relationships in the program or by varying values of parameters and noting the effects of such changes on the system is relatively easy.

Cohen and Cyert identify four categories of simulations of organizational[12] behavior:

1. "Descriptive simulation" studies of existing organizations . . . to formulate theories which explain why existing organizations have behaved in particular ways, to test these theories by comparing the observed past behavior with the simulated behavior generated by the model, and to predict how these organizations will behave in the future.

2. "Illustrative simulations" that explore the implications of a set of reasonable assumptions about organizational behavior.

3. "Normative simulations" exploring several types of organizational

[11] K. J. Cohen, *Computer Models of the Shoe, Leather, Hide Sequence* (Englewood Cliffs, N.J.: Prentice-Hall, Inc., 1959).
[12] The 'relevant' organization here includes those people involved in formulating the municipal operating budget—specifically, department heads and their chief accountants or budget officers, the budget and controller's office in some cities, those people in the mayor's office concerned with budgetary decisions, and the council. The *possibility* of 'outside' forces being involved in a systematic way (see Dahl and Hunter) is not denied, it simply was not observed.

TABLE III-1
Model Terminology

Terminology	Translation	Examples
Model Structure	Sequence of Decisions and Application of Decision Rules	1. Department Estimates 2. Mayor's Budget 3. Final Council Appropriations
Functional Form of Decision Rules	Mathematical Relationship Representing Decision Rules Rules: A. Budget Request is Based on Last Year's Appropriation Plus an Increment B. Budget Increase No Greater than a Certain Per cent of Last Year's Appropriation	A. Budget Request $= (1 + a)$ $\times$ Last Year's Appropriation B. If [(Budget Request) $\geq (1 + d)$ $\times$ Last Year's Appropriation], then Budget Request $= (1 + d)$ $\times$ (Last Year's Appropriation)
Decision Parameters	Empirically Determined Parameters in Decision Rules A. Size of Increment B. Maximum Increase	A. Value of a B. Value of d

structure and design in terms of certain desired characteristics.

4. "Man-machine" simulations to train people to function better in organizational settings.[13]

Quite obviously, our study is a 'descriptive simulation' of the governmental decision process for forming the operating budget.

HYPOTHESIS CONSTRUCTION

Up to this point the implication has been that a set of hypotheses or assumptions exists and that the problem is merely one of finding a language with the desired characteristics of precision and empirical testability in which to state the assumptions. This is clearly not the case. The reason for examining the theory-language and methodological-technique questions first is simple. The methods of collecting data and formulating hypotheses about municipal budgeting depend somewhat, at least, on what is to be done with the data and hypotheses found. The decision to use computer simulation as a research tool means that relationships uncovered through interviews, etc., must ultimately be stated in a quantifiable form and that key variables for purposes of the model must have some means of being measured or calculated.

The basic research strategy was covered briefly in Chapter I:

1. Preliminary unstructured interviews,
2. Construction of preliminary model—uncovering inconsistencies in interview data and highlighting missing sets of relationships not discovered in preliminary interviews,
3. Re-interviews (structured and unstructured) to cover model deficiencies found in steps 2 or 5,
4. Construction and modification of computer model on basis of 3,
5. Examination of model's output (If 'satisfied,' move on to step 6, if not, recycle through 3 and 4.),
6. Examination, for regularities, of cases where model fails to explain behavior.

A first, reasonable step to discover how a municipality allocates resources and operating funds is to *ask* the decision-makers (those charged with official responsibility for the decisions) how they arrive at their decisions or budget estimates. This is clearly a reasonable way to proceed unless one believes that a widespread conspiracy exists within a city government and that the formal decision-makers ('puppets') will conceal or be unaware of the presence of the 'real' decision-maker or 'power behind the throne.' The researcher's task is to ask questions in such a way that a

[13] K. J. Cohen and R. M. Cyert, "Simulation of Organizational Behavior." Unpublished mimeographed paper, Carnegie-Mellon University, 1964, pp. 7-8.

realistic and complete theory can be formulated. Failure of the researcher to construct a realistic description (model) of the decision process will become apparent when the hypotheses derived from the interviews are subjected to empirical tests. One need not worry about the methodology being *inherently* misleading.

Data Collection

We are attempting to reproduce the budgetary decision processes. This means that the majority of our decision data will be part of the public record. Specifically, the mayor's budget recommendations to the council and the final appropriations of the council are available in public documents. Unfortunately, departmental request data are sometimes not kept or must be assembled by the researcher. Some cities, however, publish departmental request figures as well (in our study, Detroit publishes departmental request data, Cleveland keeps it on file for four or five years, and Pittsburgh keeps it for one year only and in an unassembled form).

What other data are relevant will of course depend on the kind of model we construct and the relevant variables in the model. We will defer discussion of this portion of the data until the model itself has been presented.

BUDGET CATEGORIES

One other item remains to be covered in this section—the choice of budget categories. This involves two questions:

1. The method of dividing the budget into administrative units: Should the Department of Public Safety be considered as one or should it be broken down into its component bureaus—police, fire, building inspection, etc.,?
2. How finely should one divide the account categories within administrative units? Should salaries and wages be treated as one category or should a separate category be established for administrative salaries?

They are both answered rather pragmatically. Because the model is a behavioral one, the answers rest in the assumptions that administrative units are treated differently and expenditure items are treated differently (Salaries and Wages is treated differently from Equipment). The appropriateness of the assumptions depends on the model's ability to 'explain' and predict decisions. *Prima facie* evidence of a real cognitive differentiation of administrative units and account categories can be found in the accounting systems of the government involved. For example, where the budget for the Bureau of Streets and Highways appears separately from that of the Bureau of Sewers and Sanitation in the final appropriations bill, even though both are in the Department of Public Works, it is reasonable to assume the two bureaus' budget estimates were processed differently by the various decision-makers. Similarly, the fact that Expenses and Equipment are separate, summary-line items in the final appropriations bill more than likely reflects a real, cognitive differentiation on the part of decision-makers. The component budget decisions were defined on this basis. More on this matter will be considered in Chapter V.

SUMMARY

In the quest for a positive (behavioral) model of municipal resource allocation we have:

1. Decided to concentrate on a semi-independent portion of the problem—general fund or operating expenditures,
2. Chosen mathematics as the language to describe the allocation process,
3. Proposed a computer program as the particular kind of mathematical description to be employed,
4. Designated the computer abstraction of the decision process to be the focal point and organizing device for our discussion of alternative and related theories of bureaucratic and political decision-making, and
5. Assumed that empirical verification was the objective to be attained in model construction.

We now turn to the formal model of municipal resource allocation.

CHAPTER IV

Overview of Model

OVERVIEW OF DECISION PROCESS: DESCRIPTION OF PROCEDURES

FIGURE IV-1 ILLUSTRATES the information flow in the municipal budgetary decision process in the three cities examined—Cleveland, Detroit, and Pittsburgh. This general sequence of decisions is common to mayor-council municipal governments. Decisions made at any stage in the revenue (level)–budget (allocation)–expenditure (actual operations) sequence provide constraints for decisions at following stages in the sequence.

Strictly speaking, the decisions flow through the network with surprisingly little feedback.[1] Estimates of revenue and surplus are 'unbiased.' There was no evidence in any of the three cities of any altering of the anticipated-funds estimate because of the expenditure decisions.[2] The only adjustment of the estimate occurs as the result of policy decisions on new taxes or tax rates by the mayor's office or as the result of a better estimate of yield being available.[3] The estimate of the expected yield from a tax is not

---

[1] Although much information is exchanged, most of it represents attempts by the mayor's office to keep other parts of the decision system informed on developments. To the extent that this information leads to changes in behavior, there is surprisingly little feedback.

[2] One possible exception exists in the 1960-61 and 1961-62 budgets for Detroit. The incoming mayor (in 1962-63) accused the outgoing administration of "overly-optimistic" revenue estimates for the 1960-61 and 1961-62 budget periods, leaving the new administration with high operating deficits. *Minutes of the Common Council, City of Detroit,* 1962, Detroit, Michigan, April 10, 1962, pp. 754-755.

[3] In some areas tax rate changes are affected by changing assessed valuations instead of legal rates. In these instances revaluations are policy decisions.

FIGURE IV-1

Overview of Decision Procedures

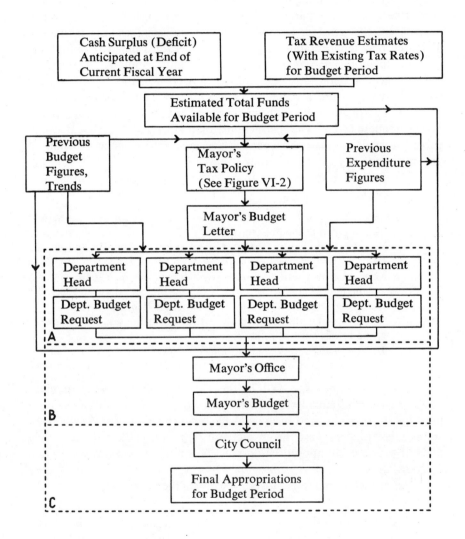

altered. The revenue estimate is taken as a 'given' by the mayor's office and by our model.[4]

An estimate of funds available for expenditure in the coming budget period is calculated on the basis of estimated revenues for the coming budget period and anticipated cash surpluses at the end of the current budget period. By comparing the current year's budget totals plus known expenditure changes (for example, increases in social security payments, increased maintenance and custodial personnel for a new public building near completion, etc.) with the available-funds estimate, the mayor's office forms a general impression of the budget—whether it will be tight or loose, whether new revenues are needed, etc. The mayor then sends a letter to department heads with instructions for filling in their department budget request forms. The instructions, or budget guidelines, sent to department heads are reasonably explicit and reflect the revenue-expenditure picture for the city quite accurately.

The following are excerpts from executive budget letters in each of the three cities:

Cleveland—. . . your requests for salaries and wages for the year should be computed at the present rates of pay.

Detroit—We find that in the past comparatively few changes in the Personal Services section were requested by the departments. It is assumed that a similar situation will prevail in the 1964-65 budget . . . the figures appearing in the '1963-64 Budget Allowance' column have been duplicated in the 'Departmental Request' column.

Pittsburgh—In arriving at your departmental estimates, the following ground rules must be followed:
1. Your 1965 total requests should be lower than your 1964 appropriations, and in no instance, higher than 1964 appropriations.

Using guidelines specified in the mayor's budget letter, previous budget figures and (to a lesser extent) past expenditure data as explicit inputs, the department head formulates his *regular departmental request*. In some cities,[5] any request for an increase of a noticeable (2-5 per cent) amount over current appropriation must be submitted via a *supplemental budget request*.[6]

Departmental requests (together with supplemental requests or unu-

[4] In all three cities investigated, the mayor's office attempts to corroborate the city's revenue estimates with like estimates from outside, independent sources. In all cases great attempts are made to get accurate revenue estimates.
[5] Pittsburgh and Detroit in our sample.
[6] There is evidence that even though Cleveland does not require a supplemental request as such, the portion of a request that exceeds current appropriations is processed by the mayor's office in much the same way that supplemental requests are processed in Detroit and Pittsburgh.

34

sual increases) are then transmitted to the mayor's office where a preliminary estimate of the total operating budget is made (excluding supplemental requests). The estimate of total expenditures is then compared with estimated available funds for the budget period. If a surplus is indicated, a general salary increase is considered for inclusion in the budget along with increases in various departmental appropriations or special programs of the mayor. If the preliminary expenditure estimate and anticipated funds figures are close, a slight tax increase (either a rate or 'coverage' increase, or a new tax) may be considered, small cuts may be proposed to bring revenues and appropriations into line, or portions of some supplemental requests may be granted. On the basis of the mayor's tax policy and wage policy, a final budget is prepared (with revenues always greater than expenditures as specified by law for the municipalities investigated)—after conferences with department heads where they are allowed to argue for their supplemental requests or to protest minor cuts. This budget is then transmitted to the council with the mayor's budget message outlining, in detail:

1. General economic picture for the region,
2. Revenue estimates and reasons for changes from the previous year,
3. Changes in expenditures from the previous year,
4. A list of deserving programs or projects that could not be included because of lack of revenue.

The council, in virtually every case, approves the mayor's budget almost exactly as submitted after a series of public hearings where interested parties plead their cases (usually for increased expenditures for some purpose or a decrease or elimination of a tax).

FORMAL MODEL CHARACTERISTICS

Scope of Model

The formal computer model will consider explicitly three decision processes: 1) departmental requests as formulated by the various department heads in city government, 2) mayor's budget for council consideration, and 3) final appropriations as approved by the council. These three processes are indicated by areas A, B, and C in Figure IV-1 (p. 33). The outputs of the departmental-request submodel are inputs to the mayor's-budget submodel and outputs of the mayor's submodel are inputs to the council appropriations submodel. (For convenience, these submodels will be referred to as the DEPT. model, MAYORS model, and COUNCIL model.)

The outputs of each submodel correspond quite closely, in number and level of detail, with the actual outputs (or decisions) of the municipal budgetary process. In the model, each department included in the general fund or operating budget has requests for appropriations for each of two to five standard account categories—depending on the city involved. For example, the model will produce—at each of the three stages of the decision process—the following dollar estimates for each administrative unit:

Cleveland		Detroit		Pittsburgh	
Personal Services	} $X	Administrative Salaries	} $X	Administrative Salaries	} $X
		Non-Adm. Salaries		Non-Adm. Salaries	} $Y
Materials		Materials,		Materials,	
Supplies		Supplies and	} $Y	Supplies and	} $W
Expenses	} $Y	Expenses		Expenses	
Equipment		Equipment and	} $Z	Equipment	} $U
Repairs and		Repairs		Maintenance	} $Z
Improvement				Special	} $V

Forty-four to sixty-four departments and administrative units are involved in each of the cities examined, with units having estimates for two to five accounts. About 128 to 220 decisions are produced at each of the three stages of the model, for each year tested, in each of the three cities examined.

At this point, one might legitimately ask two important questions: 1. Why are accounts categorized in the manner indicated? 2. Why is dollars the unit of resource allocation rather than men, number of street lights, etc.?

Both questions are crucial ones for a normative theory of budgeting. In a positive theory, however, the answers are the same and rather straightforward. People interviewed in all three cities think and talk in terms of dollars; they differentiate (at least in interviews) expenditures in terms of the same categories that the city's accounting system uses. Apparently, dollar amounts provide the relevant reference points for dealing with the conceptual framework provided by the city's accounting system.[7]

SUBMODEL INTERDEPENDENCE AND FEEDBACK

In the diagram of general information flow for the process in Figure IV-1 (p. 33), the only feedback provided occurs through past budgetary

[7] A legitimate question would be: Why was a city's accounting system designed around a particular set of account categories? But this, however interesting, is beyond the scope of this study.

decisions and the mayor's budget letter. This is not literally true. Informal communications certainly do exist between areas A, B, and C in the diagram.

Communications between department heads and the mayor's office (A and B) tend to center around feeling out which supplemental requests are likely to be approved, etc. The mayor's office generally just reinforces the impressions and guidelines set down in the budget letter to department heads. If a tax increase is in the offing, this is communicated to department heads (which results in slightly increased requests).[8] A series of executive budget hearings or review sessions are held before the mayor's budget is submitted to the council. In reality, these sessions are concerned with the departments' supplemental requests—an extremely small portion of the total. By the time the mayor's budget reaches this stage, most of the mayor's decisions have been made and there is very little money, if any, left to allocate. Oftentimes these sessions are used to explain to department heads just why no funds are available to grant their particular request.

Two chief budget officers describe these hearings as follows:

> The department hearings (with the mayor's office) give the department a chance to argue for its programs, but by that time, most of the decisions have been made.

> It resulted in a feeling of greater satisfaction on their part that they had been fairly dealt with. They knew what the situation was in terms of fund availability, they recognized the multiple demands that were being placed on these limited resources.[9]

The council is briefed informally by the mayor (B and C) prior to the formal presentation of the budget, but this is primarily a communication of information, not a bargaining session.[10] "Council really changes very little in the mayor's budget. There has been only one substantial change in the last twenty years. That was in '58 when council doubled a proposed 2 mill (property tax) increase and raised wages."[11] Most significant council changes in the mayor's budget seem to deal with his tax policy.[12]

Usually, little or no informal communication relative to budget requests exists between the council and department heads outside of the

[8] Aldo Colautti, mayor's executive secretary, city of Pittsburgh, October 30, 1964 interview.
[9] Names withheld on request.
[10] "He's (the mayor) the boss and what he says goes." (Name withheld on request.)
[11] Aldo Colautti, mayor's executive secretary, city of Pittsburgh, October 30, 1964 interview.
[12] The Detroit Common Council rejected a proposed meat inspection tax in 1964 ($500,000+) and in 1964 the Cleveland Council rejected a proposed general income tax.

council's budget hearings. Politically, going over the mayor's head is not perceived as wise strategy.

> We (department heads) *never* go over the mayor's head to council. It just wouldn't pay to undermine a relationship with the mayor and his staff for the sake of one 'break' in our budget for one year.

> If you want to get more money for the department, there are better ways than to try and go around the mayor's office. There are many sources of funds outside of the city government if you're just willing to search them out.[13]

As we will see again in Chapter VII, the council is not in a position to change the budget much anyway.

In summary, the municipal budget is the mayor's budget in which the mayor's policies dominate the department totals and city-wide wage and tax policies. The council and department heads have surprisingly little to say about municipal resource allocation on a macro level.

OVERVIEW OF DECISION PROCESS: FUNCTIONAL CONSIDERATIONS

The entire process can be viewed as an organized means for the decision-maker to deal with the potential complexity of the budgetary problem. The most prominent feature of the original problem, in terms of its contribution to complexity, is the externally imposed constraint of a balanced budget—which requires that, *at some level of generality*, all budget items be considered simultaneously.

Different characteristics of the decision process perform different functions which enable the system to effectively cope with (or avoid) the potential complexity of the budgetary problem.

Problem Perception and Mutual Expectations

Before proceeding, we should note that the problem we are referring to is the *budgetary problem as seen by the actual decision-makers* (department officials, mayor and mayor's staff, and council members). It is quite clear (from interviews) that the decision-makers *do not* see the problem as one of optimally balancing community resources, allocating funds among functions to achieve overall community goals, and the like.

The problem is generally considered by department heads as compiling a budget request that (1) assures the department of funds to carry on

---

[13] Department heads' names withheld on request.

existing programs as part of a continuing attack on existing problems, (2) is acceptable to the mayor's office, (3) and provides a reasonable share of any overall budget increases to the department to enable it to attack new problems (if any).

The mayor's problem is largely one of recommending a budget that (1) is balanced, (2) at least maintains existing service levels, (3) provides for increases in city employee wages if at all possible, and (4) avoids tax increases (especially property tax increases in the belief that increased property taxes cause business and industry to move from the city, reducing its tax base). If, after achieving some of the above objectives, the mayor has 'extra' funds, they will be used to sponsor programs or projects he has on the 'agenda.'[14]

The problem for the council is to review the mayor's budget recommendations and check for obvious errors and omissions. Because of the complexity and detail in the mayor's budget and lack of council staff, the council's options are limited largely to approving the mayor's budget. The requirement of a balanced budget means that a change in one expenditure category, for instance, implies a change in other categories and for other administrative units or a change on the revenue side of the bill—i.e., one change in the budget (by council) implies many changes which the council has neither time nor staff to consider.

Each of the groups participating are aware of the different perspectives of other participants and expect others to behave in a manner consistent with their perspectives. Through this system of shared expectations

[14] The presence of an 'agenda' of projects by the mayor is easily seen in the mayor's annual budget messages to council. The list is reasonably stable from year to year. For example:
  (1) 1964 Pittsburgh Budget Message—
      a. We have reached the point, it seems to me, beyond which it would be unfair to ask the municipal employee to go. I therefore propose the following wage adjustment. . . . (5 per cent general increment).
      b. . . . I was hoping to recommend the elimination of the one mill mercantile tax imposed (on) . . . wholesalers.
      c. . . . an attempt to have the cost of area-wide functions . . . shared on a county-wide level.
  (2) 1965 Pittsburgh Budget Message—
      a. A wage increase for municipal employees would be wholly justified. . . . Our executive and supervisory salaries, in my judgment, particularly need revision. . . .
      b. I am recommending the abolition of this levy (wholesale mercantile tax). . . .
      c. We would hope that Allegheny County . . . will give high priority to securing proper reassignment of public functions, particularly those that are area-wide in scope. . . .
      d. Council should be alerted to the possibility that city cash may be needed . . . to take full advantage of this program (Federal Antipoverty Program).

participants can deal with their portion of the problem without having to consider large errors in forecasting behavior of other participants.

Partitioning the Problem into Manageable Subproblems

Part of the way municipal decision-makers deal with the *potential* complexity of the municipal resource allocation problem is through their necessarily simplified perception of the problem as discussed above. Notice, also, that:

1. The operating budget is treated separately from the capital budget —as a generally independent problem. The only behavioral connection between the operating and capital budgets is the 'logical' elaboration of capital budgeting decisions in the operating budget.[15]

2. The budget is formulated within a system of administrative units (departments and bureaus) and account categories (Salaries, Supplies and Expenses, Equipment, etc.) that is extremely stable from year to year. This partial structuring of the problem permits most of the decision-makers to treat the appropriation question for one account category in one administrative unit as a (sub-) problem, separate from the overall resource allocation problem. Thus, the overall problem is transformed into a series of smaller problems of determining appropriations for individual departments.

3. As noted earlier, the revenue estimates are generally separate from expenditure estimates. That is, estimates of yields from a given tax are treated independently from expenditures. While, on occasion, tax rates may be adjusted somewhat on the basis of preliminary calculations of *total* expenditure *estimates,* in order to balance the budget, tax *yield estimates* are not manipulated to achieve a balance.

4. The fact that the decision process itself represents a division of labor between department heads, the mayor's office, and council, reflects not only the administrative hierarchy, but a set of simplifying heuristics for making a complex problem manageable.

[15] The 'legitimate' claim on operating funds by the capital budget is reflected in the following, found in the mayor's message accompanying the 1965 Pittsburgh budget:

> A big item in the Lands and Buildings request pertains to the opening and operation of the new Public Safety Center next spring. . . . There is a non-recurring expenditure of $150,000 for new furniture . . . and $91,000 is sought for maintenance personnel.

Our model does not formally include this *one-way interaction* with the capital budget, but as will be seen in Chapter IX, this particular kind of behavior will explain many of the model's deviations from actual behavior.

5. Finally, an additional simplifying policy was found in all cities investigated. The presence of a uniform wage policy[16] which maintains relative positions of employees within a city-wide civil service pay scale, eliminates the potentially complex problem of deciding wage rates on an individual basis while attempting to maintain some kind of 'similar-pay-for-similar-jobs' standard.

Governing by Precedent

Perhaps the overriding feature of the mayor's budgetary problem is the balanced budget requirement. *If* the mayor took even the majority of items in the budget under serious consideration, his task would be enormous. The requirement of a *balanced* budget *could* mean that the mayor would not only have to consider every budget item, but he would have to consider each item relative to all others. Somehow the entire level of police expenditures would have to be justified in light of the implied preemption of health department services, public works, fire department expenditures, etc. Obviously a mayor does not have either the staff, cognitive ability, or time to undertake such a study—even if the necessary knowledge and information existed.

Instead, the mayor perceives the budgetary problem as a continuing one that must be dealt with periodically (yearly). He perceives this year's budget to be basically similar to last year's with a slight change in resources available (new revenue estimates) for dealing with a continuing set of municipal problems (police and fire protection, urban renewal, public works, transportation) augmented by a small number of partial solutions to old problems. In this context, a logical way to proceed in solving the complex budgeting problem is to take last year's solution (current appropriations) and modify it in light of the *change* in available resources and the *change* in municipal problems and their available solutions, to obtain this year's solution. This, of course, means that the budget is a slowly changing thing, consisting of a series of marginal changes from previous budgets.[17] Very small portions of the budget are reconsidered from year to year and consequently, once an item is in the budget, its mere existence becomes its reason for being in succeeding budgets.

Government by precedent is an integral part of nearly all the positive models of decision-making in the literature. Cyert and March's *A Behav-*

---

[16] On some occasions we note that police and fire personnel are dealt with as a unit separate from other personnel.

[17] These notions are very similar to those of 'disjointed incrementalism' expressed in David Braybrooke and C. E. Lindblom, *A Strategy of Decision* (New York: The Free Press, 1963), and Lindblom, "The Science of 'Muddling Through,'" *Public Administration Review* (Spring, 1959).

ioral Theory of the Firm describes the use of previous solutions and solution procedures to solve new problems and is largely a model of *incremental* adaptations of economic organizations to their internal and external environment. Braybrooke and Lindblom argue that "precedent" is justified and defensible as a "rational" decision strategy. Wildavsky emphasizes the role of "precedent" as an "aid to calculation" in the federal budgetary process.

Openness of Public Decisions

A basic property of decision-making in the public sector (compared with the private) is that both ultimate decisions and decision procedures are always subject (at least potentially) to public scrutiny. This means decisions in the public sector would tend to be ones that can be defended and each particular decision (budget item) in a decision system (entire budget) should be able to stand on its own merit. In addition, decision *procedures* are also subject to public question. We would argue that the openness of public decisions encourages the use of rather straightforward methods of partitioning the budget-decision problem, the use of *precedent* as a defensible[18] decision strategy, and the use of simpler, easier to-understand decision procedures than might otherwise be found.

THE SUBMODELS: COMMON STRUCTURAL AND PARAMETER ESTIMATION ISSUES

Before describing the parts of the model in more detail and detailing the operationalizing of them, we will examine data and parameter estimation issues and problems common to all of the cities in our study.

Modification of Model Structure

In fitting the model to our three data points, several structural modifications must be made to adapt the model to a particular city's accounting system. The administrative units and account categories for each city must be defined. In general, those administrative units and account categories for which separate entries appear in the city's annual budget are defined as the administrative units and account categories in the model. It is assumed that the city's accounting system as presented in the municipal budget provides the cognitive map and problem structure for the decision-makers involved.

Inasmuch as the form of the appropriations provides a limit on ex-

[18] We would also argue that, in general, the need for 'defensible' decisions leads to more conservative decisions in the public sector than in the private.

penditures of a particular kind, the accounting system constitutes a real variable and not merely a decisional aid. A list of the administrative units we will use can be found in the appendix, pp. 254-256. The standard accounts used are found in Table IV-1. In Cleveland and Detroit, the summary categories in Table IV-1 are found in the appropriations bills. The Pittsburgh categorization is a summarization of a larger number of 'standard' account categories.

TABLE IV-1

Account Categories

Cleveland		Detroit		Pittsburgh	
No.	*Account*	*No.*	*Account*	*No.*	*Account*
01	Salaries and Wages	01	Salaries and Wages	01	Administrative Salaries
02	Other	02	Supplies, Materials	02	Non-administrative Salaries
		03	Equipment	03	Supplies, Materials, and Expenses
				04	Equipment
				05	Maintenance
NSTD* = 2		NSTD* = 3		NSTD* = 5	

* Number of Standard Accounts

The fact that various kinds of expenses are dealt with differently[19] leads to additional complexity in our model. Otherwise, the task would be simplified by dealing with *total* department appropriations, rather than breakdowns by standard account categories within departments.

One other structural consideration should be mentioned. In Cleveland, there is a January 1 to December 31 fiscal year, but the budget for a particular year is not formulated until the end of February—well into the budget period. This means, for example, that decision-makers putting the 1966 budget together would have access to preliminary totals of actual expenditures in 1965—information not available to their Pittsburgh and Detroit counterparts who formulate the budget prior to the budget period, not during it. Not all departments in Cleveland use the additional data, however, because departments must assemble and compile expenditure data themselves, through the Finance Department. Nevertheless, in the Cleveland model, expenditure data ($EXPN1_{ij}$) for the period immediately

[19] Based on interviews and the observed uniform wage policy in all three cities (indicating that at least personnel accounts are handled differently from others).

preceding the budget period is used as a data input[20] to the model (whether it is used by the department is reflected in our parameter values—see below).

Parameter Estimation: Some Common Problems

In the decision system whose broad characteristics we have just described, we have made two contentions that create problems in parameter estimation. *The first* is that participants in the system think in terms of dollars allocated to administrative units and account categories within these units. *The second* is that each group of participants (department personnel, the mayor's office, and the council) has different perceptions, expectations, etc., for different administrative units and account categories. This means, *a priori,* that each group of participants has a different set of parameters for those decision variables (accounts and administrative units) in its domain. This characteristic of the municipal budgetary process coupled with our commitment to a computer simulation model tied to real world data, places some severe demands on the data base. In particular, it forces the use of less-than-optimal parameter estimation procedures. Records of the following subunit decisions were available:

TABLE IV-2

Data Used in Model

	DEPT. *Requests*	*MAYORS* *Recommended* *Budget*	*COUNCIL* *Final* *Appropriations*
Cleveland	5 years	10 years	10 years
Detroit	7 years	7 years	7 years
Pittsburgh	1 year	6 years	6 years

The *ideal* research methodology would have included discussions with all the decision-makers (department heads and all employees dealing with the budget, employees in the mayor's office, and members of the council) involved in the formal budgetary decision process for a long enough period of time (since World War II, for example) to establish a significant statistical foundation for parameter estimates. Unfortunately, we were not afforded this opportunity. Either the data were not kept (department re-

[20] Include $EXPN1_{ij}$ in item 1 in Figure V-1b (DEPT.); item 3 in Figure VI-1b (MAYORS); and item 1 in Figure VII-1b (COUNCIL) in place of $EXPND_{ij}$ for the Cleveland models, and $(EXPN1_{ij} - APPR1_{ij})$ in place of $(EXPND_{ij} - APPR0_{ij})$.

quests in Pittsburgh and Cleveland) or the accounting system changed so significantly that analysis of the data for longer periods of time was meaningless or required infeasible amounts of time and effort to transform it into comparable time-series forms. In any case, we were forced to conduct the study with the aforementioned data.

Note also that our data represent concrete decisions—decisions of the department heads, mayor's office, and the council. Because our model parameters deal with intermediate stages in the submodel decision processes, we would prefer data from the intermediate stages for estimating parameters. Again, this is information we do not possess. We are faced with the task of estimating the internal workings of a black box using only input and output data. (For a discussion of the mathematical reasonableness of this procedure, see appendix, pp. 251-253.) Fortunately, through interviews and analysis of budgetary documents, we have some knowledge of the mechanisms inside the black box. Specifically, we have used those mechanisms in Figures V-1b (DEPT.), VI-1b (MAYORS), and VII-1b (COUNCIL) to describe the budgetary decision process found in municipal government.

Mathematically, our submodels consist of a linear function used to make some sort of preliminary calculation [item 3 in Figure V-1b (DEPT.), item 4 in Figure VI-1b (MAYORS) and item 9 in Figure VII-1b (COUNCIL)][21] and a series of constraints that the problem solution must satisfy. Generally, we shall use multiple regression analysis to estimate the parameters of the linear function, interview data, and *ad hoc* techniques to determine appropriate values for the other model parameters.

Possible Problems in Parameter Estimation

Before discussing some of the statistical problems likely to be encountered with our parameter estimation procedures, it should be pointed out that we are working with so few observations (see Table IV-2) that very little of substance can be said about the estimated values. The paucity of data, in most instances, leaves so few degrees of freedom that statistical analysis of particular parameters is made meaningless. It also lessens the value of including error terms as a formal part of our process model.[22] Our small-sample problem, although crucial, is unavoidable. This handicap

[21] The notation for particular decision mechanisms refers to model flowcharts in the text. For example, item 9 in Figure VII-1b (COUNCIL) refers to the box labeled 9 in Figure 1b, Chapter VII. Item 7 in Figure VI-1b refers to [RESID = REVEST − TBUD].

[22] The error term would refer to unpredictable or random, external events affecting the budget (civil rights riots, changes in state legislative regulations, availability of federal monies, etc.).

makes it all the more important to avoid other statistical pitfalls, however. A brief description of some of the problems associated with the preliminary-calculation parameters [item 3 in Figure V-1b (DEPT.), item 4 in Figure VI-1b (MAYORS), and item 9 in Figure VII-1b (COUNCIL)] and how they affect our estimates, follows:

1. *Autocorrelation*—One of the assumptions underlying the linear regression model is that of *serial independence*. For our purpose, this means that there is no correlation between the error in the budget estimate (based on the linear regression model) for a particular year and the error for the previous year. The errors are assumed to be independent.[23] A calculation of the Durbin-Watson *d* statistic for each parameter estimated with time-series data indicated that this is not a significant problem.[24]

2. *Heteroscedasticity*—The linear model assumes that the magnitude of the error is independent of the magnitude of the dependent variables (and normally distributed).[25] This is generally not a problem for us where we have complete data for a particular set of subunit decisions (MAYORS and COUNCIL), because observations on the dependent variable are of roughly the same orders of magnitude. However, in Pittsburgh and Cleveland we are forced to group subunits in order to get sufficient data to estimate parameter values for the DEPT. submodel. When a scarcity of data forces us to group subunits with budgets of different magnitudes together (for instance, police and building inspection) to estimate a common set of parameters, we are likely to run into a problem of heteroscedasticity (see Chapter VI, pp. 61-62) due to widely varying dependent-variable observations. In the instances where the problem is encountered (estimating the DEPT. param-

[23] John Johnston, *Economics Methods* (New York: McGraw-Hill, Inc., 1963), p. 177. Johnston also discusses a problem associated with lagged variables. Because all of our preliminary-calculation models dealing with adjustment in levels (models 11, 12, 13, and 14 for the DEPT. submodel; 21 and 22 for the MAYORS submodel; and 31 and 32 for the COUNCIL submodel) rather than changes (models 21 and 22 in the MAYORS submodel) have this problem, it is worth noting. Johnston concludes that ". . . the least-squares estimates will be biased, though if the disturbance term follows a normal distribution, they will tend to have the desirable asymptotic properties of consistency and efficiency," p. 212.

[24] O. A. Davis, M. A. H. Dempster, and Aaron Wildavsky found in their studies of Congressional budgetary behavior—"On the Process of Budgeting: An Empirical Study of Congressional Appropriation" in Gordon Tullock, ed., *Papers on Nonmarket Decision Making* (Charlottesville, Va.: Thomas Jefferson Center for Political Economy, 1966)—that the error terms were correlated in some cases and represented a norm-restoring mechanism for correcting previous errors. Durbin-Watson *d* statistics (see appendix, item III) indicate that these mechanisms were not present to a great extent in our analysis (probably due to the tighter budget constraints and the inclusion of a 'trend' term in most of our relationships).

[25] Johnston, *op. cit.*, pp. 207-208.

eters in Pittsburgh and Cleveland), we might avoid it by transforming the data. This was not done, however, because of the computational difficulties.[26]

3. *Multicollinearity*—The linear model also assumes that the independent variables are independent of one another. This problem can be avoided in two ways:

    a. Allow only one of two correlated independent variables to be in the relationship (a step-wise regression procedure can prevent much of this) at any one time,

    b. Group the two correlated variables to form a third variable.

In general, we used technique (a) to circumvent this problem.

OVERVIEW: HIERARCHIES OF PROBLEMS

Generalizing, the entire model is one of a systematic, administrative decision process. The stability of the decision system is portrayed as evolving from the restrictive revenue environment, an assumed continuity in the actors manning the system, and an implied stable or non-existent 'community power network.' The interaction of problem complexity and need for decision combined with the lack of extra-governmental reference points or standards fosters:

(1) a decision system which uses historical experience and precedent as its operating standards,

(2) a system which handles interest conflicts (high service rates, low taxes) by largely ignoring divergent viewpoints and using feasibility as the prime decision criterion,

(3) a system which handles complexity by fragmenting and simplifying the problem by assuming (implicitly) that this year's problem is nearly identical to last year's and therefore this year's solution will be nearly identical to last year's,

(4) a system that structures a complex problem, formulates alternatives and makes choices using simple decision rules.

Hierarchies of Decisions

Our model really represents a hierarchy of decisions. In this hierarchical sequence, any given decision provides the constraints for the next

---

[26] Johnston, *op. cit.*, p. 208-211. Johnston outlines a procedure for transforming the data if the linear relationship contains a constant term. Our relationships do not, however. Hence, not only would the original data have to be transformed, but so would the resulting vector of regression coefficients. This difficulty, plus the fact that the data transformation matrix was unknown for each (of many) set of data, discouraged any attempt at systematically dealing with this problem.

FIGURE IV-2
Hierarchy of Decisions

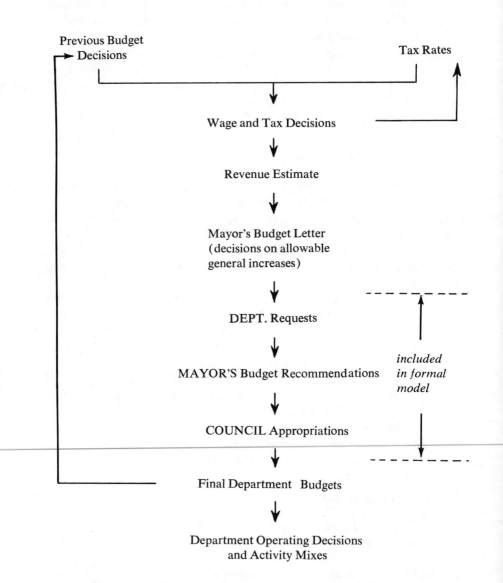

decision. The global resource allocation problem is broken into a series of subproblems. Decision processes surrounding these subproblems are separated in time and by administrative unit. The outputs of each subproblem provide inputs to succeeding subproblems as illustrated in Figure IV-2.

Thus, although *budgetary decisions* appear to have little content that might be described as political, this is not to say actual *operating decisions* are non-political.

The formal model of budgeting to be described is the result of extensive interviews with observers and participants in the municipal budgetary process. The model derived from the initial interviews was subsequently altered (marginally) by systematically examining the output of preliminary models. Additional interviews were then directed toward specific model mechanisms. Detailed descriptions of the DEPT., MAYORS, and COUNCIL submodels follow in Chapters V, VI, and VII, respectively, together with appropriate parameter estimation procedures.

CHAPTER V

DEPT. Submodel

OVERVIEW

Role of Department Head

THE ROLE of the department head is similar to that of the agency or bureau chief in the federal government as described in the Wildavsky study. His objective is to obtain the largest possible amount of funds for his department and his purposes. Just as "Washington is filled . . . with dedicated men and women who feel that government funds should be spent for one purpose or another,"[1] so are municipal governments. In general, department heads, through experience and the process of socialization in their positions, and by 'learning' that their request is likely to be cut by the mayor's office or council, tend to ask for more than they expect to get. This 'padding' of the budget is one part of a system of mutual expectations and roles. Department heads are expected to ask for more than they really need, the mayor's office is expected to cut these requests in order to balance the budget.

Context of Decisions

Another set of behavior norms for department heads found during the study is incorporated in the model. While these norms deal with things that aren't done rather than with things that are, they deserve mention. Unlike the close relationship between some agency and bureau heads and some congressional committees in the federal government, municipal departments do not go 'over the mayor's head' to the council to request more

[1] President John F. Kennedy, quoted in T. C. Sorensen, *Kennedy* (New York: Harper & Row, Publishers, 1965), p. 414.

funds for their programs or to restore cuts made in the mayor's office. No widespread system of stable relationships seems to exist between particular council members or committees and departments. Whether this is a characteristic of strong-mayor systems of government,[2] a result of the lack of a council staff to enable the council to alter the mayor's budget, or something else, is not clear. Another kind of phenomena that is *not* found is the existence of competition (in a behavioral sense) between department heads for funds.[3] Not only are department requests treated independently (as independent constraints) by the mayor's office—especially if the total revenue constraint is not particularly binding—but the departments do not perceive themselves as competing with one another for funds. " 'Conflict' among departments for funds is not a very useful way to describe the (budgetary) process."[4]

Instead the competition is perceived to be with the mayor's office[5] over the granting of funds. Much of this lack of a competitive viewpoint between departments can probably be attributed to the great differences in functions, etc., making the sorts of comparisons necessary for a competitive outlook meaningless. Widely-held municipal policies also contribute to this lack of interdepartmental squabbling. For instance, police and fire, being semi-military organizations, are either given identical pay scales and/or are grouped together into a department of public safety. The opportunity for conflict is reduced by treating these two subunits identically.

This is not to say, however, that conflict does not exist within city departments, only that it has not been observed on an interdepartmental plane. Actually, *the decisions* we are talking about *are ones setting a limit on spending for the coming fiscal year*. They are *limits on manpower, supplies, material, and equipment*. They are *not program budgets in the sense that exact activity mixes are included in the municipal budget*. In a sense, *what we are talking about is an intermediate decision. This decision provides the constraints under which decisions about particular department activities must be made*. Setting *levels* of expenditures is just one part of the

[2] Research is currently under way testing the notions in this study in the city-manager, non-industrially based municipalities of Santa Monica, Calif. and Kansas City, Mo., and should shed some light on this question.

[3] As expected in the internal-resource-allocation theory of R. M. Cyert, and J. G. March, *A Behavioral Theory of the Firm* (Englewood Cliffs, N. J.: Prentice-Hall, Inc., 1963), pp. 270-271.

[4] Aldo Colautti, executive secretary to the mayor, city of Pittsburgh, October 30, 1964 interview.

[5] For instance, in the city of Pittsburgh, the firefighters union has picketed the mayor off and on for several years in the attempt to get higher pay. Their demands and suggestions do not include notions of 'competing departments' depriving them of needed funds. Their wrath is focused entirely on the mayor's office.

department head's continuing problems. Within a given expenditure ceiling, many different activity mixes can be utilized. "Low ceilings, in short, can still permit several rooms."[6]

DEPT. MODEL CHARACTERISTICS

The role of the mayor's budget letter and the budget forms sent to the department head is a clear one. Together with the time schedule for submission of the completed budget forms, these items have the effect of structuring the department head's problem for him. Budget forms are typically sent to department heads less than two months in advance of the presentation of the completed budget to council. The department head usually has about one month before his completed request forms are due in the mayor's office.

The function of the time deadline should not be underestimated. In that there is no moratorium on the department head's problems, budget compilation represents an additional workload. In the context of a myriad of non-budgetary problems and duties, the vast majority of department heads are more than willing to accept the way the problem is structured for them by the budget forms. To do otherwise would not only involve the task of creating an alternative structure, but would place the burden of proof on the department head as far as justifying the alternative to the mayor's office is concerned.

Just how is the problem presented to the department head so as to pre-structure it for him?

Budget Forms

Budget forms [item 1 in Figure V-1a (DEPT.) and Figure V-1b, pp. 55, 58] seem to be nearly the physical constants of the universe. They are laid out as follows:

	Expenditures Previous Year (EXPND)	Appropriations Current Year (APPR1)	Request Next Year (DEPR2)
Standard Account 1	$54,321.00	$57,400.00	?
Standard Account 2	$43,219.00	$45,600.00	?
Standard Account N	$ 100.00	$ 120.00	?

---

[6] T. C. Sorensen, referring to the federal budgeting process in *Kennedy,* p. 414.

In all cases, the Actual Expenditures (EXPND) and Appropriations (APPR1) columns were filled in for the department head for each of the account categories appearing in the previous budgets. The department head's task is to fill in the blank Department Request column (DEPR2). The physical makeup of the budget forms probably has as much influence as anything in determining the department head's response to the request for budget estimates. By structuring the department head's problem, the forms 'bias' the outcome or decision in two ways:

1. They provide a great deal of incentive for the department head to formulate his requests within the confines of the existing set of accounts.

2. They provide for an automatic comparison between next year's request and this year's appropriation—which automatically determines that this year's appropriation provides one criterion and reference point for next year's request.

"The budget estimate forms call for a comparison of our proposed budget with last year's. . . . In order to come up with our estimates, we also have to look at the current year's trends to see how things are going."[7]

In addition to the standard account categories (those categories common to most departments in the city—e.g., salaries and wages, materials and expenses, equipment), each line item's historical data are listed. The level of detail in line items has its influence on the department head's decision process also. (In one city studied, one of the line items listed a $3 current appropriation for mothballs.) In general, each item separately identified in the budget (each line item) forces one historical comparison and, hence, represents one more constraint the department request must satisfy. In the face of an increasing number of constraints (increasing as budget detail increases), we would expect the department head to resort to simpler decision rules to handle this difficult problem. In addition, we would predict that the more detailed the budget (in terms of line items), because of the structure of the budget forms, the less change in requests (and appropriations) from year to year.

The need for effective budgetary control in the mayor's office, made more difficult by the presence of a small staff,[8] is met by a large number of simple, historical comparisons. This has, in many instances, resulted in a burdensome amount of detail to which busy department heads respond with little change in budget behavior from year to year.

[7] David Craig, city solicitor, city of Pittsburgh, interview, October 15, 1964.
[8] Small in relation to a similar organization in the private sector. For instance, in the city of Pittsburgh, no more than four people examine the budget in any detail. Of these four (maximum), at least one is faced with the purely physical problem of putting the budget together, checking and compiling city totals.

Mayor's Budget Letter

The mayor's budget letter always contains instructions which reinforce the structuring of the problem provided by budget forms—by requiring the department head to provide a ". . . written explanation for any change in individual cost accounts. . . . Experience for the years 1962 and 1963 is shown . . . to assist you in estimating your needs for 1965. . . . Under the heading 'Explanation of Increases and Decreases' must be explained the factors . . . which make up the increase or decrease over or under the current budget allowance as shown above on this form."[9]

The tone of the letter accompanying the budget forms (TML) has the effect of providing an arbitrary ceiling on the department's request [item 5 in Figures V-1a (DEPT.) and Figure V-1b]. If the department total exceeds the ceiling, the overage is generally submitted as a supplemental request [item 7 and 8 in Figure V-1a (DEPT.) and Figure V-1b]. In addition, changes in salary rates through raises or promotions are submitted as a supplemental request (or not at all). Supplemental requests are accompanied with a detailed explanation and are treated separately by the mayor's office—and are always on the agenda when the department head meets with the mayor's office to discuss his requests.

Much of the department head's calculations involve figuring 'what will go' with the mayor's office.[10] This calculation involves using current appropriations as a base and adjusting this amount for recent appropriations trends, discrepancies between appropriations and corresponding expenditures, and the like [item 3 in Figure V-1a (DEPT.) and Figure V-1b]. The results of this calculation are then tested to see if they satisfy the constraints discussed above. Preliminary decisions are then adjusted until constraints are satisfied and the final request is entered on the standard budget forms and sent to the mayor's office for consideration.

With the above in mind, we now turn to the formal model.

FORMAL DEPT. MODEL

The description of the formal DEPT. model is presented in two levels of detail. First, a verbal flowchart representing the decision process as constructed from the interview data is presented [Figure V-1a (DEPT.)]. The verbal flowchart can also be interpreted as an abstraction of the descrip-

---

[9] September 3, 1964 budget letter from mayor to Pittsburgh department heads, p. 2. September 12, 1963 budget letter from budget director to Detroit department heads, p. 7.

[10] Similar to Wildavsky's observations of department heads at the bottom of the decision hierarchy, in Aaron Wildavsky, *The Politics of the Budgetary Process* (Boston: Little, Brown and Company, 1964), pp. 25-31, and Sorensen's from the top of the hierarchy in the federal government. Sorensen, *op. cit.*

tions presented in the preceding portion of this chapter. A further abstraction and operationalization of the DEPT. decision process model is found in the detailed flowchart and accompanying variable dictionary, Figure V-1b (DEPT.) and Table V-1, respectively.

The non-verbal flowchart [Figure V-1b (DEPT.)] is written in sufficient detail so that a computer program can be constructed directly from it. The interested reader can compare Figure V-1b (DEPT.) with the computer program for the department request submodel (DEPT.) in the appendix, p. 298.

To aid the reader, the verbal and non-verbal flowcharts have been numbered in such a way that it is possible to move from one to the other with relative ease. In addition the number system allows reference to specific model mechanisms in the text (see footnote 21, p. 45).

FIGURE V-1a

General DEPT. Request Decision Process

1. Budget letter and budget forms received from mayor containing:
   a. current appropriations for all account categories in the department;
   b. current total appropriation; c. previous year's expenditures in various account categories; d. estimate of allowable increase over current appropriations implied from the 'tone' of the mayor's letter.

2. Trend of departmental appropriations —direction and magnitude of recent changes in amounts of appropriations in departmental account categories.

3. Department, using information from 1 and 2, formulates a 'reasonable' request for funds in its existing account categories, using current appropriations as a base or reference point and adjusting this estimate according to whether there was an increase in appropriations last year (for some accounts, an increase for the current year means a decrease for next year, e.g., equipment; for others, an increase for the current year indicates another increase next year), and the difference between last year's expenditures and appropriations.

4. Using reasonable requests calculated in 3, a preliminary department total request is calculated.

5.

4.
↓

5. Is the total department request outside the guidelines set by the mayor's office (implied from the tone of the mayor's budget letter)?

no   *yes*

6. Check to see if there are any increases in salary accounts over current appropriations.

no increase   *increase*

7. All department requests in all categories are adjusted so that any increase (proposed) over current appropriations is submitted as a supplemental request. Go to 6 to check for salary increases.

8. Make regular request equal current appropriations and put increase in as supplemental request.

9. Calculate total of regular departmental request.

10. Send regular requests and departmental total to mayor's office along with supplemental requests.

Variable Dictionary

The variables used in the formal DEPT. model are of four basic types:

  i. Model Inputs—information available to decision-makers prior to decision-making. Included is information about past budgetary decisions, expenditures, and the like, and information about the accounting system (the number of account categories, etc.).

  ii. Accounting Variables—variables used to store the results of automatic calculations made by the decision-makers, such as the total of all department requests, the difference between revenues and expenditures, etc.

  iii. Parameters—values of internally generated constraints and empirically estimated parameters used in preliminary-calculations mechanisms [item 3 in Figure V-1b (DEPT.), item 4 in Figure VI-1b (MAYORS) and item 9 in Figure VII-1b (COUNCIL)].

  iv. Intermediate Calculations and Model Outputs—Variables representing model outputs undergo a series of alterations between the start and finish of the decision process represented by a particular submodel. The initial value of a department request ($DEPR2_{ij}$) is based on a preliminary calculation [item 3 in Figure V-1b (DEPT.)]. The request is then altered according to procedures defined in the program until it reaches its final (output) value. The same variable name ($DEPR2_{ij}$) is used throughout the program to store the current value of the request. When these variables are referenced in the flowcharts or in the text, they refer to the value of a particular quantity *at a particular stage in the decision process.* In this sense, our variable names define a computer address where values are stored and not the values themselves as in most other forms of mathematics.

TABLE V-1

DEPT. Variable Dictionary

Variable	*Definition*
Model Inputs	
$APPR0_{ij}$	Final Appropriations, previous year
$APPR1_{ij}$	Final Appropriations, current year
$EXPND_{ij}$	Expenditure Total, previous year
$RMAY1_{ij}$	Mayor's Budget Recommendation, current year
TML	Tone of Mayor's Budget Letter for next budget year
$NACCT_i$	Number of Account Categories in the department
Accounting	
$TAPR1_i$	Total Appropriations (all accounts) for department, current year
$TDEP2_i$	Total requests (all accounts) for department for next budget year
Parameters	
$A_{ij}, B_{ij}, C_{ij}, D_{ij}$	Empirically determined preliminary-calculations parameters (see pp. 61-66, Tables V-2, V-3, and Appendix, pp. 259-263)
Intermediate Calculations and Model Outputs	
$DEPR2_{ij}$	Department budget request for next budget year
$DSUPR_{ij}$	Department supplemental budget request for next budget year

Note: Subscript *i* refers to a department and *j* refers to an account category within a department.

FIGURE V-1b
Formalized DEPT. Request Decision Process

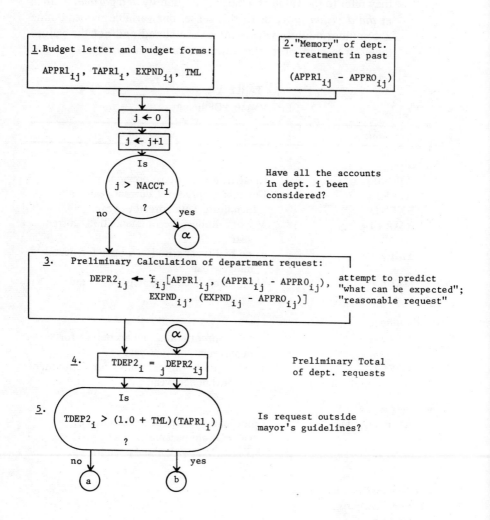

1. Budget letter and budget forms:

   $APPR1_{ij}$, $TAPR1_i$, $EXPND_{ij}$, TML

2. "Memory" of dept. treatment in past

   $(APPR1_{ij} - APPRO_{ij})$

$j \leftarrow 0$

$j \leftarrow j+1$

Is

$j > NACCT_i$

?

no   yes

Have all the accounts in dept. i been considered?

α

3. Preliminary Calculation of department request:

   $DEPR2_{ij} \leftarrow f_{ij}[APPR1_{ij}, (APPR1_{ij} - APPRO_{ij}),$
   $EXPND_{ij}, (EXPND_{ij} - APPRO_{ij})]$

   attempt to predict "what can be expected"; "reasonable request"

α

4. $TDEP2_i = \sum_j DEPR2_{ij}$

   Preliminary Total of dept. requests

5. Is

   $TDEP2_i > (1.0 + TML)(TAPR1_i)$

   ?

   no   yes

   Is request outside mayor's guidelines?

   a   b

58

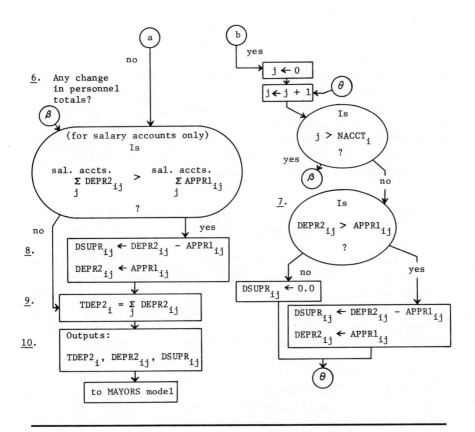

BEHAVIOR NOT INCLUDED IN FORMAL DEPT. MODEL

According to our formal theory, department budgetary behavior varies from department to department only by the relative weights assigned to previous appropriations, trends, and expenditures by the various department heads [item 3 in Figure V-1b (DEPT.)]. Furthermore, the DEPT. model contends that these relative weights are stable over time. Missing from the formal model are notions of non-regular innovation (or change) by department administrators and notions of the department as a mechanism for responding to particular kinds of complaints from the citizenry —in short, the department is perceived as explicitly responding to only the mayor's pressures. Also missing are changes in the budget requests as logical elaborations of other policy commitments—implied increases in operating budget because of capital budgeting considerations, changes in intergovernmental support for services (the classic problem in this category involves the highly volatile state-local split of welfare payments), transfer of activities to (and from) other governing units (transfer of hospital system to state or county, etc.), and changes in activity level and scope because of funds obtained from sources (Urban Renewal planning and demonstration grants, the federal Anti-Poverty Program, etc.) other than the general fund.

At first glance, the model might be said to preclude innovative behavior on the part of department heads. Inasmuch as innovation is a relative concept, operationally this allegation refers to the model's assumption that department heads vary only by the relative weights attached to previous appropriations, trends, and expenditures when calculating what the department can expect to get, reasonable requests, etc.:

$$DEPR2_{ij} \leftarrow f_{ij} [APPR1_{ij}, (APPR1_{ij} - APPR0_{ij}), EXPND_{ij}, (EXPND_{ij} - APPR0_{ij})]$$

In other words the functional form, f_{ij}, and parameters are different from department to department. These differences are enough to explain differences in departmental behaviors which, in turn, reflect stable relationships between department personnel and the mayor's office. This assumption of the model does not preclude innovative behavior. It merely states that innovation (if any) takes place within a regularly changing budget ceiling. Parameter values that lead to relatively large, regular request increases $(DEPR2_{ij} - APPR1_{ij})$ in the above relationship may represent a greater potential for innovation than do those leading to smaller increases (or decreases)—providing, of course, that a portion of the request is granted. On the other hand, the presence of a budget ceiling in the face of changing citizenry needs and pressures (precipitating a change in department goals and program needs) may force a department head to innovate to survive. Cyert and March, citing the work of Mansfield,[11] side with the former concept of innovation rather than the latter. They argue that the presence of 'organizational slack' (evidenced by budgetary increases) ". . . provides a source of funds for innovations that would not be approved in the face of scarcity but that have strong subunit support." Major technological innovations, it is argued, are not problem-oriented innovations.[12] At any rate, our model does not restrict innovative behavior. The model is, however, unable to predict or recognize the acceptance of policy innovations that result in major changes in total expenditures and appropriations.

Another objection to the model is that it may fail to deal with outside influences at all. This is particularly true if by departmental responses to

---

[11] Edwin Mansfield, "Technical Change and the Rate of Initiation," *Econometrica*, No. 29 (1961), pp. 741-766.
[12] Cyert and March, *op. cit.,* p. 279.

pressure one assumes that total (for the department) external pressure and influence is a thing that varies a good deal from year to year and that mechanisms for responding to the varying pressure would lead to irregular budget decisions. If, however, one assumes that each department has, over the years, not only 'made its peace' with the mayor's office, but with the extra-governmental environment, then the pressure-response mechanisms (i.e., constant responses to constant pressures) would also be reflected in the empirically determined model parameters [item 3 in Figure V-1b (DEPT.)]. The pressure-response characteristics of this model will be examined more fully later in the report. Again, the model does not exclude a pressure-response kind of budgetary behavior, but has a good deal to say about the nature and context of the response (and pressure).

PARAMETER ESTIMATES: DEPT.

As was brought out in Chapter IV, p. 46, we are forced to use less-than-optimal techniques to estimate parameters for functional relationships imbedded within a process model, using only data on inputs and outputs. The reasonableness of the techniques used below is dealt with more fully in the appendix, pp. 251-253.

As can be seen from Figure V-1b (DEPT.), we must specify the functional form of the preliminary-calculation relationship [item 3 in Figure V-1b (DEPT.)] and estimate the function parameters. In addition, the tone of the mayor's letter (TML) must be specified to operationalize DEPT. All other data can be found in the city's accounting records.

Preliminary Calculations: Pittsburgh

Four preliminary-calculations relationships [item 3 in Figure V-1b (DEPT.)] were tested (see variable dictionary, Table V-1) for Pittsburgh:

(11) $\quad \text{DEPR2}_{ij} = A_{ij}(\text{APPR1}_{ij}) + B_{ij}(\text{APPR1}_{ij} - \text{RMAY1}_{ij}) +$
$\qquad D_{ij}(\text{EXPND}_{ij}\ \text{APPR0}_{ij})$

Regular department request is based on current appropriations adjusted to second-guess the previous mayor-council change and overspending.

(12) $\quad \text{DEPR2}_{ij} = A_{ij}(\text{APPR1}_{ij}) + B_{ij}(\text{APPR1}_{ij} - \text{APPR0}_{ij}) +$
$\qquad C_{ij}(\text{EXPND}_{ij})$

Regular department request based on current appropriations, trends, and expenditure experience.

(13) $(DEPR2_{ij} + DSUPR_{ij}) = A_{ij}(APPR1_{ij}) +$
$$B_{ij}(APPR1_{ij} - RMAY1_{ij}) +$$
$$D_{ij}(EXPND_{ij} - APPR0_{ij})$$

Total department request—same as 11.

(14) $(DEPR2_{ij} + DSUPR_{ij}) = A_{ij}(APPR1_{ij}) +$
$$B_{ij}(APPR1_{ij} - APPR0_{ij}) +$$
$$C_{ij}(EXPND_{ij})$$

Total department request—same as 12.

Relationships 13 and 14 estimate the total department request (regular and supplemental) while relationships 11 and 12 estimate only the regular request. Clearly, with information from only one year—1965 (see Table VI-3)—we must use cross-sectional data to estimate the values of A_{ij}, B_{ij}, C_{ij}, D_{ij} in the above relationships. Having no basis for grouping departments (the *i*'s), we are left with only one reasonable alternative for grouping our data—by account categories. This is a reasonable way to group the data insofar as different types of expenditures are treated differently by department heads in Pittsburgh. The results are found in Table V-2.

As can be seen in Table V-2, there is little basis for choosing among relationships in terms of goodness-of-fit (R^2). One reasonable criterion concerns the nature of the DEPT. submodel. Because the 'preliminary request calculation' is adjusted to obtain *both* regular and supplemental requests, it seems reasonable to use either relationship 13 or 14 in the Pittsburgh DEPT. submodel.

Ideally, we would like to choose between 13 and 14 on the basis of the cognitive maps of individual department heads. Although our interviews suggested (at least consciously, and for 1965) that department heads did not attempt to second guess the mayor or blame him for past dissatisfactions with the budget, statistical considerations dictate that 13 be used in the model. The variables $APPR1_{ij}$ and $EXPND_{ij}$ in relationship 14 are of roughly the same magnitude, presenting the multicollinearity problem noted in Chapter IV, p. 47. The effects of multicollinearity can be seen in the coefficient *j* equals 3 and 4 in Table V-2.

Tone of Mayor's Letter

The tone-of-the-mayor's-letter variable, TML, in Pittsburgh has the effect of deciding the portion of the request to be included in supplementals. Anything over a *reasonable* increase must be submitted via supplemental

TABLE V-2
Pittsburgh DEPT. Submodel Relationships

Relationship 11 $\text{DEPR2}_{ij} = A_{ij}(\text{APPR1}_{ij}) + B_{ij}(\text{APPR1}_{ij} - \text{RMAY1}_{ij}) + C_{ij}(\text{EXPND}_{ij} - \text{APPR0}_{ij})$

	A_{ij}	B_{ij}	C_{ij}	R^2
All Accounts	.998	0	0	.9999
Account j = 1	.999	−.065	−6.777	.999
Account j = 2	.999	0	0	1.0
Account j = 3	1.005	.170	0	.9998
Account j = 4	1.362	−.503	1.079	.998
Account j = 5	1.0	0	0	1.0

Relationship 12 $\text{DEPR}_{ij} = A_{ij}(\text{APPR1}_{ij}) + B_{ij}(\text{APPR1}_{ij} - \text{APPR0}_{ij}) + C_{ij}(\text{EXPND}_{ij})$

	A_{ij}	B_{ij}	C_{ij}	R^2
All Accounts	.998	0	0	.9999
Account j = 1	.998	.0067	0	.9998
Account j = 2	.999	0	0	1.0
Account j = 3	1.002	.083	0	.9998
Account j = 4	.245	.476	1.062	.998
Account j = 5	1.0	0	0	1.0

Relationship 13* $(\text{DEPR2}_{ij} + \text{DSUPR}_{ij}) = A_{ij}(\text{APPR1}_{ij}) + B_{ij}(\text{APPR1}_{ij} - \text{RMAY1}_{ij}) + C_{ij}(\text{EXPND}_{ij} - \text{APPR0}_{ij})$

	A_{ij}	B_{ij}	C_{ij}	R^2
All Accounts	1.057	−.270	−.289	.9990
Account j = 1	1.015	.158	−137.848	.998
Account j = 2	1.041	−.825	−.942	.999
Account j = 3	1.037	−.167	.158	.999
Account j = 4	2.525	−.596	4.532	.967
Account j = 5	1.130	0	.210	.989

Relationship 14 $(\text{DEPR}_{ij} + \text{DSUPR}_{ij}) = A_{ij}(\text{APPR1}_{ij}) + B_{ij}(\text{APPR1}_{ij} - \text{APPR0}_{ij}) + C_{ij}(\text{EXPND}_{ij})$

	A_{ij}	B_{ij}	C_{ij}	R^2
All Accounts	1.327	−.189	−.274	.9990
Account j = 1	1.143	0	−.135	.998
Account j = 2	1.055	.207	0	.999
Account j = 3	.914	.168	.112	.999
Account j = 4	−1.993	3.945	4.511	.967
Account j = 5	1.019	1.195	0	.999

Account 1—Administrative Salaries

Account 2—Nonadministrative Salaries

Account 3—Materials, Supplies, Expense

Account 4—Equipment

Account 5—Maintenance

* Used in process model

requests. The reasonable increase was somewhat arbitrarily chosen to be 5 per cent in all cities. A sensitivity analysis of the model in Chapter X indicates this constraint is not very significant (probably because it is imbedded in the preliminary-calculations parameters). Lack of supplemental request data also forced the assumption of 5 per cent (see footnote 6 in Chapter IV).

Preliminary Calculations: Cleveland

In Cleveland, unlike Pittsburgh, we do have some time-series data for department requests. We do not have sufficient observations to justify estimating a separate relationship for each account category in each administrative unit, however. Fortunately, administrative units in the budget are (and have been for the ten-year study period) grouped by major classifications (see appendix, pp. 254-256, for a listing of units included in these classifications). The two relationships outlined below were tested for each classification, using the available department request data (1960-63 and 1965).

Relationships tested:

(11) $DEPR2_{ij} = A_{ij}(APPR1_{ij}) + B_{ij}(EXPN1_{ij} - APPR1_{ij}) + C_{ij}(APPR1_{ij} - APPR0_{ij})$

(12) $DEPR2_{ij} = A_{ij}(APPR1_{ij}) + C_{ij}(APPR1_{ij} - APPR0_{ij}) + D_{ij}(EXPN1_{ij})$

Multiple regression techniques were used to estimate the values of A_{ij}, B_{ij}, C_{ij}, and D_{ij}, and a choice was made between Relationships 11 and 12 for each major administrative unit classification, using the associated R^2 statistic. Preliminary-calculation models chosen appear in Table V-3.

Preliminary Calculations: Detroit

The estimation of DEPT. relationships in Detroit is more straightforward. Department request figures have been published since 1958 and were used in our study. Enough data were available to calculate separate parameters for each account category in each administrative unit. Again, multiple regression was used to estimate parameter values.

Relationships tested were:

(11) $DEPR2_{ij} = A_{ij}(EXPND_{ij} - APPR0_{ij}) + B_{ij}(APPR1_{ij} + C_{ij}(APPR1_{ij} - APPR0_{ij})$

(12) $DEPR2_{ij} = B_{ij}(APPR1_{ij}) + C_{ij}(APPR1_{ij} - APPR0_{ij}) + D_{ij}(EXPND_{ij})$

TABLE V-3

Cleveland DEPT. Submodel Relationships

Major Classification	Relationship Number	Account Category	APPR1 A_{ij}	(EXPN1-APPR0) B_{ij}	(APPR1-APPR0) C_{ij}	EXPN1 D_{ij}	R^2	N
General Government	12	Salaries, Wages* (j = 1)	.320	—	.653	.745	.996	65
	11	Other (j = 2)	1.198	.274	-.157	—	.948	65
Public Properties	11	Salaries, Wages (j = 1)	1.625	.782	-4.424	—	.473	55
	11	Other (j = 2)	1.045	.864	-.213	—	.9923	55
Public Service	11	Salaries, Wages (j = 1)	1.045	4.068	-.192	—	.9966	35
	12	Other (j = 2)	0	—	.737	1.023	.9917	35
Health and Welfare	12	Salaries, Wages	0	—	.487	1.110	.9992	50
	11	Other	1.108	1.574	.333	—	.9990	55
Urban Renewal	12	Salaries, Wages*	2.044	—	-1.359	-.845	.9990	20
	11	Other	1.094	3.586	—	—	.872	20
Public Safety	11	Salaries, Wages	1.026	.890	.360	—	.9993	40
	12	Other*	-.0878	—	.312	1.140	.9971	40
Finance	11	Salaries, Wages	1.039	1.002	-.080	—	.9989	30
	11	Other	1.627	-1.773	-2.701	—	.540	30
Port Control	11	Salaries, Wages	1.274	.794	-.954	—	.9962	15
	11	Other	1.003	6.421	-.221	—	.9968	15
Miscellaneous	11	Salaries, Wages	1.044	1.105	1.792	—	.9842	10
	11	Other	1.439	.895	-.081	—	.991	5

* Imprecise due to multicollinearity

(13) $(DEPR2_{ij} + DSUPR_{ij}) = A_{ij}(EXPND_{ij} - APPR0_{ij}) +$
$$B_{ij}(APPR1_{ij}) +$$
$$C_{ij}(APPR1_{ij} - APPR0_{ij})$$

(14) $(DEPR2_{ij} + DSUPR_{ij}) = B_{ij}(APPR1_{ij}) +$
$$C_{ij}(APPR1_{ij} - APPR0_{ij}) +$$
$$D_{ij}(EXPND_{ij})$$

In Detroit, 'supplemental requests,' defined (by Detroit) as any requested increase over current appropriations, are incorporated in the regular department requests for all items except salary-rate changes (caused by filling an open position, change in civil service seniority status, step-raises, etc.). This means that Relationships 11 and 13, and 12 and 14 are identical for all accounts except Salary and Wages. Relationship 13 was chosen for all accounts and all administrative units in the Detroit DEPT. submodel. Relationship 14 was eliminated because of the collinearity between variables $APPR1_{ij}$ and $EXPND_{ij}$. (See appendix, p. 259-263, for the listing or regression coefficients used in Detroit DEPT. submodel.)

We now turn to a detailed description of the next stage of the decision process and a specification of the MAYORS submodel.

CHAPTER VI

MAYORS Submodel

OVERVIEW

Role of Mayor's Office

THE FUNCTION of the mayor's office relative to the budget is to fulfill the legal obligation of submitting a balanced budget to the city council for consideration. The key word, of course, is *balanced*. Most of the problem-solving activity and behavior in the mayor's office revolves around attempts to eliminate a deficit or reduce a surplus. Like other organizations, subunit requests (stated needs) almost always exceed available resources. So, *vis-à-vis* the departments, the mayor's role is that of an economizer, cutting departmental requests to the bare minimum in lean years and keeping the cost of government under control when revenues are more plentiful.

MAYORS Model Characteristics

The decision process in the mayor's office can usefully be thought of as a search for a solution to the balanced-budget problem. In a sense, the mayor has guaranteed the existence of a solution through use of budget guidelines set up in his letter of instruction to department heads. Approximately four months before the final budget is due for council passage, the mayor obtains preliminary revenue estimates from people in city government and from an outside source. Armed with a rough estimate of money available for expenditures in the next budget period, current appropriations, and a knowledge of required and predetermined budgetary changes for the coming year, the mayor is able to make a rough guess of the total allowable increase or decrease over current appropriations. From this figure, an estimate of an allowable per cent increase (or decrease) is made and transmitted to department heads via the budget letter. (Only the output from this part of the process is explicitly included in our model, TML —tone of mayor's letter.) In most instances, then, the sum of the budget requests reaching the mayor's office represents a nearly (within 10 per cent) balanced budget.

The conversion of departmental requests to a balanced budget recommendation to council is the task of the mayor's office. Balancing techniques are:

1. Raise tax rates or add a new tax to eliminate anticipated deficit.
2. Cut lower priority account categories (maintenance, equipment) to bring expenditures into line with revenues.
3. Grant some supplemental requests to reduce anticipated surplus.
4. Eliminate an undesirable tax or reduce rates to reduce anticipated surplus.

In general, strategies 1 and 4 are used when the anticipated discrepancy between revenues and expenditures is high while techniques 2 and 3 are used if revenues and expenditures are reasonably close. The general tendency is to move toward a balance between revenues and expenditures by changing either revenue *or* expenditures, but not both. There is one exception to this. The exception involves general wage and salary increases for city employees. A minimum payroll increase (in all three cities investigated) appears to be an across-the-board 3½ per cent-5 per cent increase. Although not enough data points are available to specify the complete decision process for the mayor's wage and salary policy, a general set of necessary conditions for an across-the-board increase can be identified:

1. Very small anticipated deficit or an anticipated surplus (without payroll increase).
2. At least two years since last general salary increase.
3. Availability of an acceptable revenue source.
4. Generally rising economic conditions (low unemployment in the area and high yield from city income taxes).

The mayor's budget letter, which includes budget guidelines for department heads, has the effect of restricting the budget balancing problem to relatively small amounts so that strategies 2 and 3, above, are feasible. In any event, decisions on significant changes in tax *rates* have already been made by the time the mayor's budget letter goes out and the revenue estimate (REVEST) enters the process as an independent constraint to be satisfied.

On a very few occasions, revenue or tax *rates* (balancing techniques 1 and 4, above) are changed to bring the budget into balance, but, in the municipalities investigated, there was *no* evidence of any altering of tax *yields* to balance the budget.[1]

Our formal model does not include the part of the decision process evoked when the revenue constraint becomes so restrictive (or loose) as to necessitate a change in tax rates. This process will be discussed below, however. Tax rate decisions are made prior to the sending of the budget letter to department heads and are considered as given from that point on.

Just as the budget forms and account categories structure the problem for the department head, they also structure it for the mayor's office [items 1 and 3 in Figure VI-1b (MAYORS)]. The legal requirement of a balanced budget also structures the problem for the mayor's office—as well as partially determining its role behavior. The system of accounts and administrative units in the city together with the balanced budget requirement combine to specify the cognitive map for the decision situation for participants in the mayor's office.

Preliminary Screening of Requests

As budget requests are received from departments by the mayor's office they are screened individually [item 4 in Figure VI-1b (MAYORS)]. This preliminary screening of requests reflects particular biases and relationships the mayor's office has with individual department heads (and departments).

> Competent evaluation in the Budget Division will rather quickly discern over a period of time who the ones are that you can depend upon as requesting their basic and fundamental needs without 'fat,' shall we say. You get to know the ones who generally will ask for a heckuva lot more than they expect to get on the theory that they are going to be cut down anyway and, of course, in most big organizations . . . you'll have some that

[1] Similar findings on the unbiased nature of state revenue estimates are reported by Charles J. Goetz, "Estimates of Tax Revenue and Their Effects on Budgetary Decisions." Paper delivered at Southern Economic Association Meetings, Atlanta, 1966.

One exception to the general rule that there is no alteration of the revenue yield estimates (revenue side) to achieve balance with expenditures was found. For a couple of years in Detroit, part of the cost of governmental operations was financed through 'overly optimistic' revenue estimates which ultimately resulted in operating deficits. Those deficits (technically illegal) were then refinanced, with debt service charges for this refinancing showing up in subsequent operating budgets as deductions from revenue available for general fund expenditures. This brief 'operating practice' was quickly discontinued by a new city administration. The magnitude of the effect of this operating practice on the planning process (budgetary decision process) is unclear and is not incorporated in the formal model. The effects should show up in larger deviations of model estimates from actual decisions during particular years in the city of Detroit.

don't pay the appropriate amount of attention or place the proper importance upon the preparation of budget requests and they are then sometimes not too carefully prepared or too carefully documented.[2]

Different perceptions of different departments show up (in the model) in both model structure and model parameters [item 4 in Figure VI-1b (MAYORS)]. The interaction of the mayor's role in the budgetary process (to cut requests) and perceptions of individual departments describes the preliminary screening process.

Basically, if the department request for a given account category is less than current appropriations, an automatic, preliminary acceptance of the request is made. If the request is larger than current appropriations, a request evaluation procedure is evoked that calculates or subjectively determines preliminary appropriations figures. This subjective evaluation is represented in our model as a problem of choosing between four basic evaluation models. A particular department can evoke one of four basic evaluation models. The particular model evoked represents the cognitive map used by the mayor's office.

Evaluation of Requests

The four basic models include two which arrive at a preliminary appropriations figure by making marginal adjustments to the department request ($DEPR2_{ij}$) figures—representing departments that submit 'honest' or realistic budget estimates—and two which make adjustments in current appropriations ($APPR1_{ij}$) to arrive at preliminary recommendation figures ($RMAY2_{ij}$)—representing less realistic or honest departments.

Two of the four evaluation models estimate the change (difference) from the reference point [($RMAY2_{ij} - DEPR2_{ij}$) and ($RMAY2_{ij} - APPR1_{ij}$)] and two estimate the preliminary recommendation ($RMAY2_{ij}$) directly:

(21) $$RMAY2_{ij} = A_{ij}DEPR2_{ij} + B_{ij}DSUPR_{ij} + C_{ij}(APPR1_{ij} - APPR0_{ij})$$

Department head's request respected and adjusted by his supplemental request and current trends.

(22) $$RMAY2_{ij} = A_{ij}APPR1_{ij} + B_{ij}(APPR1_{ij} - APPR0_{ij}) + C_{ij}(EXPND_{ij} - APPR0_{ij})$$

Department head's request ignored, and current appropriations

[2] Alfred M. Pelham, former controller, Wayne County, Michigan, and former controller, city of Detroit (interview), October 7, 1964.

adjusted to reflect recent trends and overspending or under-spending in the past.

(23) $(RMAY2_{ij} - DEPR2_{ij}) = A_{ij}(DEPR2_{ij} - APPR1_{ij}) +$
$$B_{ij}DSUPR_{ij} +$$
$$C_{ij}(APPR1_{ij} - APPR0_{ij})$$

Department head's request used as a basis for calculation and changes in it are based on the magnitude of the requested change in appropriations, supplemental requests, and past changes in appropriations.

(24) $(RMAY2_{ij} - APPR1_{ij}) = A_{ij}(APPR1_{ij} - APPR0_{ij}) +$
$$B_{ij}(EXPND_{ij} - APPR0_{ij})$$

Department request ignored and change from current appro-priations based on previous changes and magnitude of under-spending or overspending in the past.

The values of the parameters $(A_{ij}, B_{ij}, \text{etc.})$ represent the relative weights given to variables in the particular model by decision-makers in the mayor's office.[3] While these weights *may reflect* real variables in the external environment (the effects of rising costs or inflation, interest groups, etc.), there is no indication that these kinds of variables ever were a conscious or significant part of the decision process. The search for possible unconscious relationships between parameter values and other external variables is beyond the scope and resources of this study.

The two 'trust' models are (21) and (23) and the two 'no-confidence' models are (22) and (24); (21) and (22) represent 'levels' calculations and (23) and (24) are 'change' models.

Table VI-1 gives the frequency of choice among preliminary evalua-tion models in the three cities. On the basis of Table VI-1 one should not conclude that the mayor's office trusts few of its departments in Cleve-land. While there is a substantial theoretical difference between evaluation models (21) and (22), in many cases both models fit the data equally well. The reason for similar fits of cognitively different evaluation models to the same data is easily seen by noting that:

(a) Department requests are highly correlated with current appro-priations, and

(b) The department-request and current-appropriations terms rep-resent much greater quantities than the other terms in models

---

[3] According to our theory, we would expect the values of the parameters to shift with a change in participants (new department head or new city administration). Un-fortunately, not enough data exist to identify these shift points.

(21) and (22), and model (21) is nearly equivalent *(mathematically)* to model (22).[4]

TABLE VI-1

Evaluation Models Used (Frequency)*—(Item 4 in Figure VI-1b)

	Trust Level (21)	No Confidence Level (22)	Trust Change (23)	No Confidence Change (24)
Cleveland	21	60	30	17
Detroit	0	3	120	49
Pittsburgh	210	19	0	0

* Evaluation models were chosen for particular account categories and departments by choosing that model with the lowest standard-error-of-the-estimate. Standard-error-of-the-estimate was used as a measure of fit, so that models with different dependent variables could be meaningfully compared.

From the preliminary screening of requests outlined above [item 4 in Figure VI-1b (MAYORS)], a preliminary budget total is compiled [item 5 in Figure VI-1b (MAYORS)]. An anticipated deficit or anticipated surplus [item 6 in Figure VI-1b (MAYORS)] is noted on the basis of the preliminary total. If a surplus is indicated, surplus-reduction routines are evoked; if not, deficit elimination procedures are evoked. Note, either one set of procedures or another is used, not both.

Surplus and Deficit Elimination Procedures

If a surplus is anticipated, several standard spending alternatives are considered in order of their priority:

1. General salary increase [items 8 to 10 in Figure VI-1b (MAYORS)];
2. Grant portion of supplemental requests [items 11 to 14 in Figure VI-1b (MAYORS)],
   a. general expense account [item 12 in Figure VI-1b (MAYORS)] first, then
   b. equipment accounts, and
   c. maintenance accounts.

[4] (21) $RMAY2_{ij} = A_{ij}DEPR2_{ij} + B_{ij}DSUPR_{ij} + C_{ij}(APPR1_{ij} - APPR0_{ij})$ if $DEPR2_{ij} = A'_{ij}APPR1_{ij}$, then
(21') $RMAY2_{ij} = A''_{ij}APPR1_{ij} + B_{ij}DSUPR_{ij} + C_{ij}(APPR1_{ij} - APPR0_{ij})$
which is nearly equivalent to model (22) if both supplemental requests and overspending are relatively small amounts.

Although the formal model includes only the above alternatives, others are clearly available to the mayor. With reasonable assurance, the first alternative considered is a general salary increase whenever a surplus is anticipated.

The model is also incomplete in the sense that some departmental priority list obviously exists for the granting of supplemental requests. Thus, the sequence in which departments are considered [the order of the i's in items 11 and 13 in Figure VI-1b (MAYORS)] is important under a revenue constraint. The model's assumption that departments are considered in the order of their account numbers is unrealistic, but not enough department request data existed to establish any other reasonable priority list.[5] A priority list of account categories does exist though and is shared by both departments and the mayor's offices. The salience of wage and salary accounts is readily discernible through interviews.[6]

If, after preliminary screening of requests, a potential deficit appears (the usual case), some routines are evoked to eliminate this deficit. One routine not evoked in the formal model, but part of the behavioral alternatives sometimes evoked in practice, is the option of raising taxes. More will be said on revenue policy.

The alternatives in the formal model are evoked in the following order:

(a) Check preliminary recommendations (checking lower priority accounts first) to see if they are within certain limits on increases —alter recommendations accordingly.

(b) Eliminate all recommended increases in non-salary appropriations, considering low priority accounts first.

(c) Uniform reduction of all non-salary accounts to eliminate deficit, if all else fails.

The order in which the alternatives are considered represents a priority list for the alternatives (in the order of their decreasing desirability). The anticipated-deficit stimulus [item 15 in Figure VI-1b (MAYORS)] first evokes a check of all preliminary mayor's recommendations to see if they represent an increase over current appropriations of more than a specified per cent (an increase roughly equivalent to the limit indicated in the mayor's budget letter to department heads). If the particular recommen-

[5] It should be noted that a substantial portion of this department priority phenomena is accounted for in the preliminary screening of requests [item 4 in Figure VI-1b (MAYORS)].

[6] As well as satisfying Harrison White's "principle of least astonishment," it is 'intuitively obvious.' 'Priority list' was suggested and confirmed by the following participants in the budgetary process: Alfred M. Pelham, former Detroit controller; Aldo Colautti, Mayor's executive secretary, Pittsburgh; Calvin H. Hamilton and David W. Craig, former department heads, Pittsburgh.

dation represents an increase over the limit (i.e., doesn't satisfy the constraint), the increase is set back to the limit and a new preliminary recommendation is calculated. Obviously, the order in which the screened requests are considered can be of crucial importance. A priority list of departments that partially determines which departments are cut and which ones are not probably exists, but here again, it is not part of the formal model.[7] A priority of account types is explicitly a part of our model, however.

The order of account sanctity for the mayor's office is identical to that of the department. This shared preference ordering[8] is as follows: 1) administrative salaries, 2) non-administrative salaries and wages, 3) operating expenses, supplies, materials, etc., 4) equipment, and 5) maintenance. The order corresponds to the postponability of expenditures with maintenance and equipment being the first to be cut (and the last to be considered for an increase in the surplus elimination routines) and salaries the last. The deficit elimination procedure is executed only as long as a deficit exists. The first acceptable alternative (balanced budget) found is adopted and search activity is halted.

If, however, the budget is examined and altered so as to keep all recommended appropriations within a fixed percentage of current appropriations, and a deficit still exists, another set of constraints is evoked and the search for a solution continues. A check is then made of the mayor's preliminary recommendations to see if there is any planned increase over current appropriations. If there is, the preliminary recommendation is altered to satisfy the constraint [items 22 and 23 in Figure VI-1b (MAYORS)]. The application of the no-increase-over-current appropriations constraint is, again, sequential. The constraint is first applied to non-standard account categories [items 2 and 24 in Figure VI-1b (MAYORS)], then to lower priority accounts [item 25 in Figure VI-1b (MAYORS)], and finally if the deficit is not yet eliminated, to salaries and wages for the departments.

If the budget is not yet balanced, the remaining deficit is eliminated by spreading a uniform cut over all non-salary and wage account categories and over all departments. One item that is never reduced from current appropriations in the usual sense is salaries and wages. The salary and wage accounts are different from other accounts in that they represent commitments to individuals currently employed. There are no mass layoffs of government employees or firings to eliminate potential budget deficits. If money is 'tight' in city hall, a freeze is placed on filling positions vacated by

---

[7] Again, the hard, departmental request data do not exist in sufficient quantities to reconstruct the departmental priority list and the soft data are unavailable. Interviewees are perfectly willing to talk about relative importances of account categories, but not of departments and department heads.

[8] Shared also with the council.

retirement, resignations, and death and on scheduled step-raises and salary increments, in order to reduce costs.

Finally, either by reducing the surplus or eliminating a deficit, the mayor's office arrives at a balanced budget.

We now turn to a detailed description of the formal MAYORS submodel.

FORMAL MAYORS MODEL

The description of the formal MAYORS model is presented in two levels of detail, similar to the DEPT. model (see Chapter V, p. 55). The computer program associated with the non-verbal flowchart, Figure VI-1b (MAYORS), is found in the appendix, pp. 299-301.

FIGURE VI-1a
General MAYORS Budget Recommendation Model

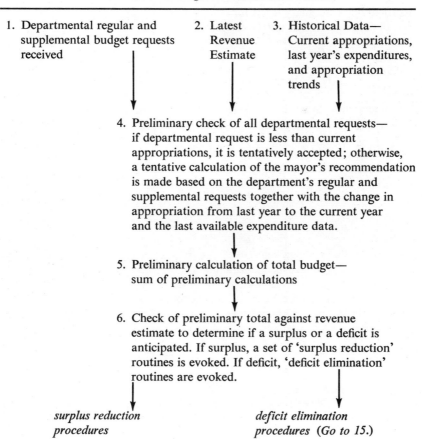

1. Departmental regular and supplemental budget requests received

2. Latest Revenue Estimate

3. Historical Data— Current appropriations, last year's expenditures, and appropriation trends

4. Preliminary check of all departmental requests— if departmental request is less than current appropriations, it is tentatively accepted; otherwise, a tentative calculation of the mayor's recommendation is made based on the department's regular and supplemental requests together with the change in appropriation from last year to the current year and the last available expenditure data.

5. Preliminary calculation of total budget— sum of preliminary calculations

6. Check of preliminary total against revenue estimate to determine if a surplus or a deficit is anticipated. If surplus, a set of 'surplus reduction' routines is evoked. If deficit, 'deficit elimination' routines are evoked.

surplus reduction procedures

deficit elimination procedures (Go to 15.)

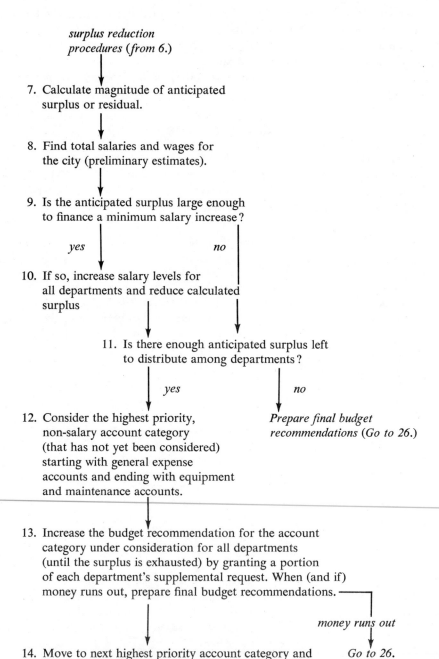

surplus reduction procedures (from 6.)

7. Calculate magnitude of anticipated surplus or residual.

8. Find total salaries and wages for the city (preliminary estimates).

9. Is the anticipated surplus large enough to finance a minimum salary increase?

yes   *no*

10. If so, increase salary levels for all departments and reduce calculated surplus

11. Is there enough anticipated surplus left to distribute among departments?

yes   *no*

12. Consider the highest priority, non-salary account category (that has not yet been considered) starting with general expense accounts and ending with equipment and maintenance accounts.

Prepare final budget recommendations (Go to 26.)

13. Increase the budget recommendation for the account category under consideration for all departments (until the surplus is exhausted) by granting a portion of each department's supplemental request. When (and if) money runs out, prepare final budget recommendations.

money runs out

14. Move to next highest priority account category and go to 12. If all categories have been considered, prepare final budget recommendations. (*Go to 26.*)

Go to 26.

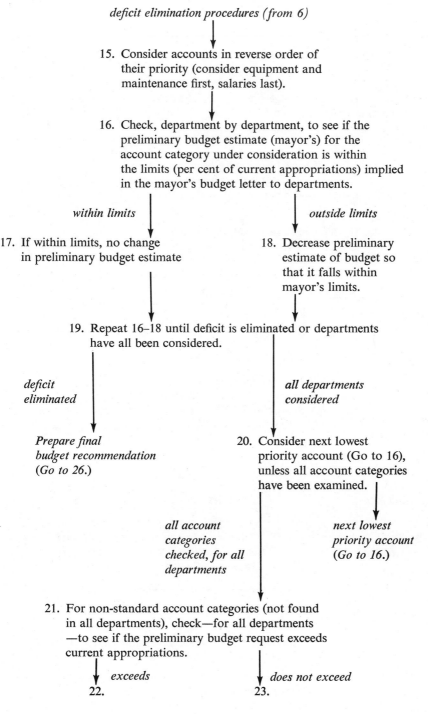

deficit elimination procedures (from 6)

15. Consider accounts in reverse order of their priority (consider equipment and maintenance first, salaries last).

16. Check, department by department, to see if the preliminary budget estimate (mayor's) for the account category under consideration is within the limits (per cent of current appropriations) implied in the mayor's budget letter to departments.

within limits

outside limits

17. If within limits, no change in preliminary budget estimate

18. Decrease preliminary estimate of budget so that it falls within mayor's limits.

19. Repeat 16–18 until deficit is eliminated or departments have all been considered.

deficit eliminated

all departments considered

Prepare final budget recommendation (Go to 26.)

20. Consider next lowest priority account (Go to 16), unless all account categories have been examined.

all account categories checked, for all departments

next lowest priority account (Go to 16.)

21. For non-standard account categories (not found in all departments), check—for all departments —to see if the preliminary budget request exceeds current appropriations.

exceeds

22.

does not exceed

23.

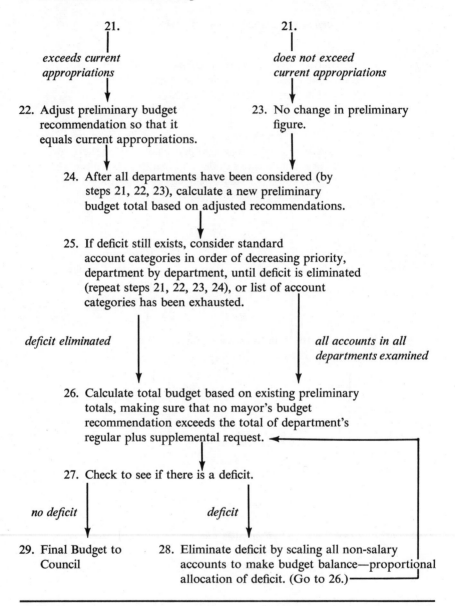

21.
exceeds current
appropriations

21.
does not exceed
current appropriations

22. Adjust preliminary budget
recommendation so that it
equals current appropriations.

23. No change in preliminary
figure.

24. After all departments have been considered (by
steps 21, 22, 23), calculate a new preliminary
budget total based on adjusted recommendations.

25. If deficit still exists, consider standard
account categories in order of decreasing priority,
department by department, until deficit is eliminated
(repeat steps 21, 22, 23, 24), or list of account
categories has been exhausted.

deficit eliminated

all accounts in all
departments examined

26. Calculate total budget based on existing preliminary
totals, making sure that no mayor's budget
recommendation exceeds the total of department's
regular plus supplemental request.

27. Check to see if there is a deficit.

no deficit

deficit

29. Final Budget to
Council

28. Eliminate deficit by scaling all non-salary
accounts to make budget balance—proportional
allocation of deficit. (Go to 26.)

Variable Dictionary

As in the DEPT. model presentation, the variables used in the formal
MAYORS model are of four types: model inputs, accounting variables,
parameters, and intermediate calculations-model outputs (see Chapter V,
pp. 55-56). Variable definitions are found in Table VI-2.

TABLE VI-2

MAYORS Variable Dictionary

Variable	Definition
Model Inputs	
$APPR0_{ij}$	Final Appropriations, previous year
$EXPND_{ij}$	Expenditure Total, previous year
$APPR1_{ij}$	Final Appropriations, current year
$DEPR2_{ij}$	Department Budget Request for next budget year
$DSUPR_{ij}$	Department Supplemental Budget request for next budget year
NSTD	Number of Standard Account Categories in city (see Table IV-1)
N	Total Number of Departments in city
$NACCT_i$	Number of Account Categories in a department
W	Number of Wage and Salary Accounts in city $(W \leq NSTD)$.
REVEST	Revenue Estimate
Accounting	
TBUD	Budget Total (intermediate values)
TSAL	Budget Total, Wages (intermediate values) and Salary Accounts only
RESID	Revenue Estimate Less Budget Total
ADDED	Cumulative Total of Supplemental Requests Granted
ZCNT	Identifies for Non-standard Account
SUMW	Sum of Wage Accounts
SUM	Sum of Non-wage Accounts
SCALE	Scale Factor for Eliminating *RESID*, Using *SUMW, SUM*
Parameters	
$D_{ij}, E_{ij}, F_{ij}, G_{ij}$	Empirically Determined Preliminary-Calculations Parameters
XLMT	Solution Criteria for Budget Balancing
GG_{ij}	Portion of Supplemental Requests Granted
XK, XL	Limits on Department Requests
Intermediate Calculations-Model Outputs	
$RMAY2_{ij}$	Mayor's Budget Recommendation for next budget year
TBUD	Total Mayor's budget

Note: Subscript *i* refers to a department, *j* refers to an account category within a department.

FIGURE VI-1b

Formalized MAYORS Budget Recommendation Model

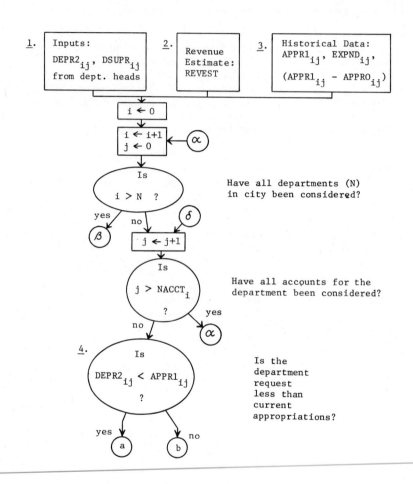

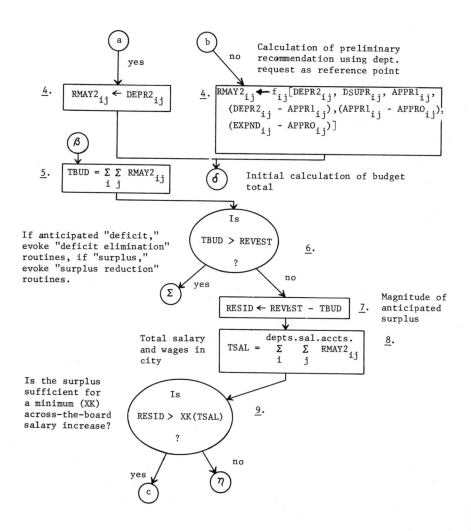

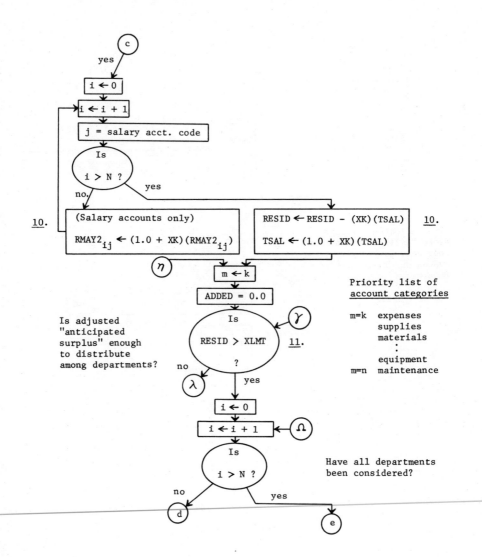

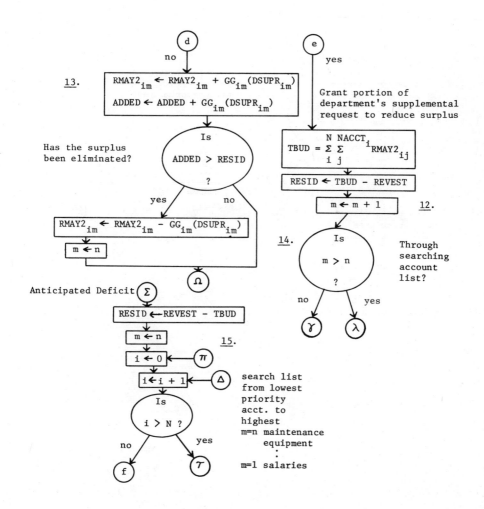

13. $RMAY2_{im} \leftarrow RMAY2_{im} + GG_{im}(DSUPR_{im})$

$ADDED \leftarrow ADDED + GG_{im}(DSUPR_{im})$

Has the surplus been eliminated?

Is ADDED > RESID ?

yes   no

$RMAY2_{im} \leftarrow RMAY2_{im} - GG_{im}(DSUPR_{im})$

$m \leftarrow n$

Anticipated Deficit Σ

$RESID \leftarrow REVEST - TBUD$

$m \leftarrow n$

$i \leftarrow 0$ π

15.

$i \leftarrow i + 1$ Δ

Is i > N ?

no   yes

f τ

no d   e yes

Grant portion of department's supplemental request to reduce surplus

$TBUD = \sum_i \sum_j^{N} {}^{NACCT_i} RMAY2_{ij}$

$RESID \leftarrow TBUD - REVEST$

$m \leftarrow m + 1$ 12.

14.

Is m > n ?

Through searching account list?

no   yes

γ λ

search list from lowest priority acct. to highest
m=n maintenance equipment
:
m=1 salaries

83

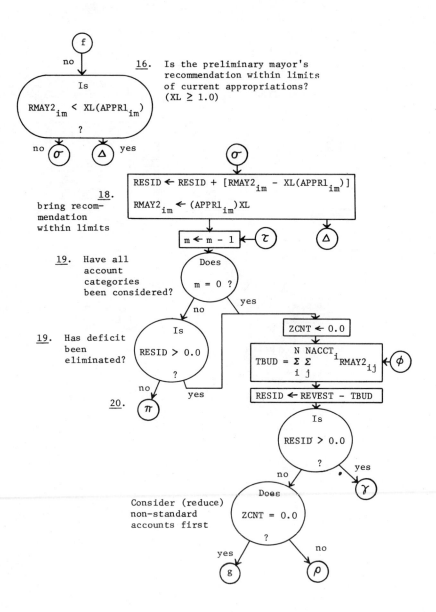

16. Is the preliminary mayor's recommendation within limits of current appropriations? $(XL \geq 1.0)$

Is

$$RMAY2_{im} < XL(APPR1_{im}) \quad ?$$

18. bring recommendation within limits

$$RESID \leftarrow RESID + [RMAY2_{im} - XL(APPR1_{im})]$$

$$RMAY2_{im} \leftarrow (APPR1_{im})XL$$

$$m \leftarrow m - 1$$

19. Have all account categories been considered?

Does $m = 0$?

19. Has deficit been eliminated?

Is RESID > 0.0 ?

20.

$$ZCNT \leftarrow 0.0$$

$$TBUD = \sum_i \sum_j^{N \; NACCT_i} RMAY2_{ij}$$

$$RESID \leftarrow REVEST - TBUD$$

Is RESID > 0.0 ?

Consider (reduce) non-standard accounts first

Does ZCNT $= 0.0$?

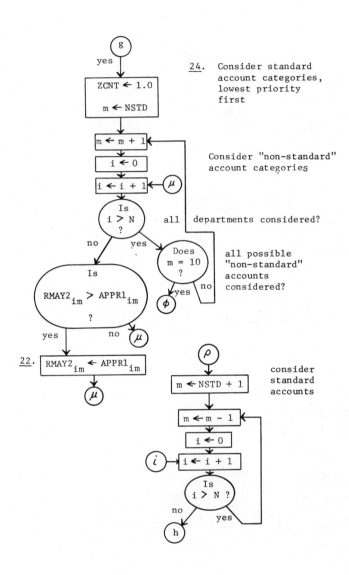

24. Consider standard account categories, lowest priority first

Consider "non-standard" account categories

all departments considered?

all possible "non-standard" accounts considered?

consider standard accounts

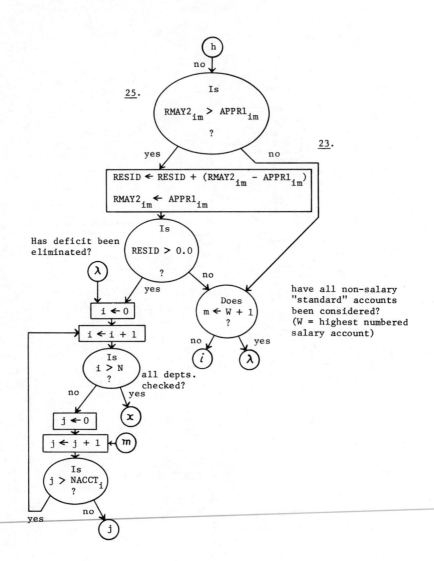

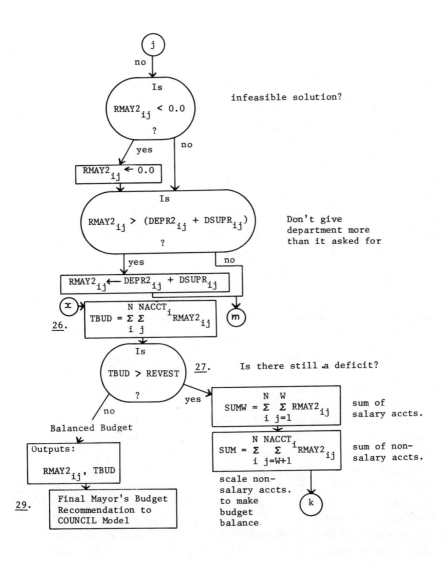

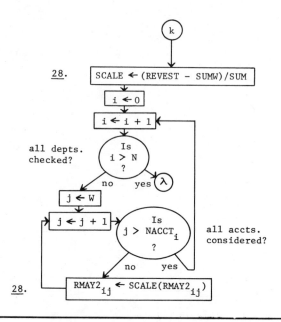

BEHAVIOR NOT INCLUDED IN MAYORS FORMAL MODEL

The mayor's decision process can be described as a series of search routines aimed at finding a feasible solution to the budgetary problem (search for a balanced budget). The sequence in which various search routines are evoked really represents a measure of the relative desirability of solution methods. As we have pointed out before, the formal model does not contain all possible search routines the mayor could evoke. MAYORS only contains those evoked most often. At the bottom of the mayor's priority list of search routines are those relating to changes in tax policy as a balancing technique. Apparently, tax policy is tied very closely to city-wide wage policy and this pair of problems is treated somewhat separately from the budgetary problem (as defined in the *observed* decision process).

Tax and Wage Policy

As we have noted previously, the mayor's tax decision (and, hence, revenue) is taken by the model as given. Our *assumption* has been that revenue decisions are substantially independent of expenditure decisions. This is not completely true, of course. While the revenue decisions could (and should) legitimately provide the subject matter for an entire study, there are some things we can say about its relationship to the allocation decisions. A look at some crude data and interviews with people included in the MAYORS submodel indicates that the primary systematic relationship between allocation and total-budget (revenue) decisions is related to general salary levels, rather than activity levels. "The 'only' time we raise taxes is to finance a pay increase for municipal employees. No tax increase—no wage increase. Of course, when we (the mayor) do decide to raise taxes, the word gets around and we find departments coming in (with their budget requests) a little higher, trying to take advantage of any leftovers."[9] A brief look at the data (see Table VI-3) indicates that there is a high correlation between general[10] wage increases and new or increased taxes. We can say little about cause and effect, however. The data also indicate the ability of uniformed police and firemen to secure differential wage increases (not possible in our model). This *could* reflect the availability of comparable salary data between cities.

As Table VI-3 indicates, additional revenues can be obtained in any of three ways.[11]

1. Increase in rate of existing taxes.
2. Expand base of an existing tax (increase assessed valuation, etc.).
3. Addition of a new tax.

There seem to be three or four requirements that any new revenue source must satisfy:

1. It must be within the limits on tax rates specified by the state government. If the alternative involves a new tax, it must be allowable under state laws.[12]
2. The additional revenue must come from those who can afford to pay, not the unemployed, retired, etc.

---

[9] Aldo Colautti, mayor's executive secretary, city of Pittsburgh, October 30, 1964 interview.

[10] The 'uniform wage policy' is part of a city-wide civil service classification system. Thus, one important way in which individuals receive pay increases is through a change in classification (promotion). Our model does not deal explicitly with these kinds of changes in wage accounts. It does not distinguish between increments due to reclassification and those attributable to new personnel.

[11] Other revenue sources do exist such as transfers of funds from other government authorities, transfer of functions to other governmental units, removal of exemption status from classes of taxpayers, etc., but these sources cannot usually provide funds in any substantial amounts.

[12] State taxation limits are not unimportant. The city of Pittsburgh has reached the point where it can no longer add new *general* taxes—it has exhausted those allowed by the state legislature—without special state legislation. In addition, rates for all taxes except the property tax are at their legal limits. The only new tax sources available are those affecting business operations inside the city limits. The mayor's belief that increased taxes on businesses would cause firms to leave Pittsburgh limits this tax source.

TABLE VI-3

Relationship Between Wages and Taxes

Year	Tax changes	Wage-level increases
Cleveland		
1955	.60 mill property tax increase defeated at polls	5% for uniformed police and fire, 3% general
1956	1.20 mill increase defeated at polls	none
1957	County Auditor increased property valuation: increased yield	10% for uniformed police and fire, 8% all others
1958	1.30 mill *reduction* offset by increased valuation	5% for uniformed police and fire, 3% general
1959	.90 mill increase	5.3% for uniformed police and fire, 3% general
1960	.70 mill reduction	none
1961	.70 mill increase	5.2% for uniformed police and fire, 3% for all others
1962-63	none	none
1964	1.20 mill increase	10% for all
1965	.40 mill increase	none
Detroit		
1958-59	slight property tax increase to offset declining yields	none
1959-60	slight property tax increase to offset declining yields	4% general cost-of-living
1960-61	none	2% increase
1961-62	small property tax increase to offset decreases in assessments	$.04/hour cost-of-living
1962-63	reduced property tax and new income tax	2% increase plus $100/year for uniformed police and fire
1963-64	none	$.03/hour cost-of-living
1964-65	small property tax reduction; more income tax available as previous years' deficits are eliminated	2.5% increase plus $140/year for uniformed police and fire
Pittsburgh		
1960	none	none
1961	earned income tax up from .5% to 1%	$2.2 M increase associated with major job reclassification plan
1962-63	none	none
1964	$10 occupational privilege tax	5% increment
1965	none	none

3. The additional revenue, if at all possible, should come from all who use the city's facilities, not just residents or property owners (i.e., increased property taxes are avoided in an attempt to get area residents to pay their share of city expenses).
4. Increased property or business operation taxes are to be avoided to keep business firms from moving out of the city.[13]

If the anticipated deficit is large enough or pressure for a general wage increase is strong enough, a new revenue source must be found that will provide additional revenues in quantities at least as great as those required by the deficit or wage increase. The decision to change the revenue source or rates results in a minimum revenue increase of about $1,000,000. Any lower deficit will be eliminated by reducing expenditures. Any substantial tax increase is usually decided upon *before* the mayor's budget letter is sent and has the effect of loosening restrictions on all expenditures. (All departments are likely to get a portion of any new tax revenue.)

For a crude outline of the decision process that appears to be evoked for tax-wage decisions, see Figure VI-2.

Priority of Departments

Another prominent omission of problem-solving behavior concerns the lack of a priority list of departments. The model assumes that the departmental priority list is ordered the same way as department account numbers. The overall importance of this faulty assumption is, of course, an empirical question. If we assume that high-priority departments are distributed randomly among all departments on the list and that deficit elimination procedures are evoked much more frequently than surplus elimination figures, then we should expect that our model would, in general, underestimate appropriations for lower-numbered departments (always the first ones to be cut regardless of actual department priority) and overestimate them for higher numbered departments. In fact, we did not observe this, indicating that the priority-effect might be reflected in the preliminary screening coefficients [item 4 in Figure VI-1b (MAYORS)].

Changes in Political Administration

The entire budgetary process model we have constructed hypothesizes a stable decision structure between and within cities, reflecting stable sets of relationships between positions and roles within the city established

---

[13] Hon. Joseph M. Barr, mayor, city of Pittsburgh, and Aldo Colautti, mayor's executive secretary, city of Pittsburgh (joint interview), February 23, 1965.

FIGURE VI-2
Mayor's Tax Decision Process

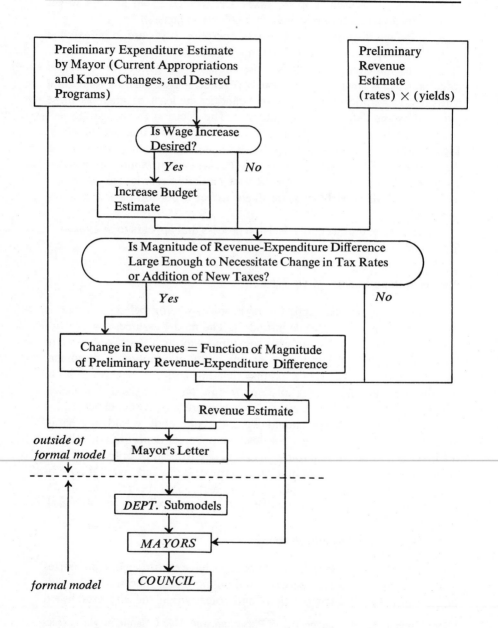

through some process of learning, reinforcement, and socialization. This assumption of stability and uniform socialization is predicated on an assumption that relatively few participants in the budgetary process change in a given period of time. One obvious exception is found when an administration is defeated at the polls. This results in a complete reordering of position occupants and relationships. The gradual socialization and learning process will no longer hold. So, we expect that the first years at the start of a new administration will produce a shift in model parameter values and a change in model fit.[14]

External Pressure

Another kind of behavior not included in the model is a response to external (to the government) pressure and constraints by the mayor. Again, as in the department models, the MAYORS model does not preclude a response to requests for services from powerful interest groups or individuals. It only postulates that the response is within the budget level for the department involved. The model, as constructed, implies that either the response to pressure is systematic and regular over the years (implying a stable system of pressure or influence in the community) and is reflected in the model parameters or it does not enter the part of the budgetary process represented by our model at all. The only case where external influence could be considered as imposing a decisional constraint is in the revenue estimate. Most systematic pressure from the business community concentrates on keeping tax rates constant, and not on particular expenditure items.[15]

The importance of these conscious omissions will be reflected in the empirical tests of the model.

PARAMETER ESTIMATION: MAYORS MODEL

In the MAYORS submodel, the primary relationship to be empirically determined relates to the preliminary screening of department requests

---

[14] O. A. Davis, M. A. H. Dempster, and A. Wildavsky, "On the Process of Budgeting: An Empirical Study of Congressional Appropriation," in Gordon Tullock, ed., *Papers on Non-Market Decision Making* (Charlottesville, Va.: Thomas Jefferson Center for Political Economy, 1966), noted a shift in models and parameters while studying the federal budgetary process, representing the Truman-to-Eisenhower switch. Although our lack of data prevented us from calculating parameter shift points, we were able to detect a shift in model fit for a new administration (see Chapter VIII).

[15] Suggested by Hon. Joseph M. Barr, mayor of Pittsburgh (November 19, 1964 interview), Aldo Colautti, mayor's executive secretary, Pittsburgh (October 30, 1964 interview), Alfred M. Pelham, former controller, Detroit (October 7, 1964 interview), and Richard Strichartz, controller, Detroit (October 6, 1964 interview).

Governmental Problem-Solving

by the mayor's office [see item 4 in Figure VI-1b (MAYORS)]. In addition the following variables must be defined and estimated: the minimum salary increase considered for city employees [XK in item 9 of Figure VI-1b (MAYORS)], the level of anticipated surplus decision-makers will tolerate without searching for ways to eliminate it [$XLMT$ in item 11 of Figure VI-1b (MAYORS)], the portion of department supplemental requests granted by the mayor's office if anything at all is granted[16] [GG_{ij} in item 14 of Figure VI-1b (MAYORS)], and the limit on departmental increases for the year [XL in item 16 of Figure VI-1b (MAYORS)]. Again, the ideal way to estimate relationships and constraints in the MAYORS submodel would be to use observations made on relevant variables at appropriate stages of the actual decision processes, over time. Obviously, these intermediate data were not and are not recorded in any form, let alone the form implied by our formal model. As in the DEPT. submodel, the only hard data we have are specific, *final* decisions made at fixed stages in the decision process (i.e., department requests, mayor's recommendations to council, and final council appropriations). (See discussion on estimation of submodel relationships, appendix, pp. 252-253.)

MAYORS Relationships: Preliminary Screening

As departmental requests are received in the mayor's office, a preliminary screening is undergone. For each department, in all three cities, four different models of the preliminary-screening estimate [item 4 in Figure VI-1b (MAYORS)] were tested:

$$(21) \quad RMAY2_{ij} = A_{ij}DEPR2_{ij} + B_{ij}DSUPR_{ij} + C_{ij}(APPR1_{ij} - APPR0_{ij})$$

Department head's request respected and adjusted by his supplemental request and current trends.

$$(22) \quad RMAY2_{ij} = A_{ij}APPR1_{ij} + B_{ij}(APPR1_{ij} - APPR0_{ij}) + C_{ij}(EXPND_{ij} - APPR0_{ij})$$

Department head's request ignored, and current appropriations adjusted to reflect recent trends and overspending or underspending in the past.[17]

---

[16] Either nothing extra is granted, or a significant portion of the supplemental request is granted. If any increase is granted, it must be 'enough to matter.'

[17] For Cleveland, substitute $(EXPN1_{ij} - APPR1_{ij})$ in all four models for $(EXPND_{ij} - APPR0_{ij})$ to reflect the availability of more current expenditure data at the time of decision.

94

(23) $(RMAY2_{ij} - DEPR2_{ij}) = A_{ij}(DEPR2_{ij} - APPR1_{ij}) +$
$B_{ij}DSUPR_{ij} +$
$C_{ij}(APPR1_{ij} - APPR0_{ij})$

Department head's request used as a basis for calculation and changes in it are based on the magnitude of the requested change in appropriations, supplemental requests, and past changes in appropriations.

(24) $(RMAY2_{ij} - APPR1_{ij}) = A_{ij}(APPR1_{ij} - APPR0_{ij}) +$
$B_{ij}(EXPND_{ij} - APPR0_{ij})$

Department request ignored and change from current appropriations based on previous changes and magnitude of previous underspending or overspending.

Time-series data and linear regression techniques were used to estimate parameters for all departments and account categories in all three cities. Parameters and preliminary-screening models used as a result are found in Appendix C. As mentioned on p. 72, models were chosen for particular account categories and departments on the basis of the standard-error-of-the-estimates. The frequency of choice of the four formulations of the preliminary-screening procedure in the mayor's office is found in Table VI-1, p. 72.

VARIABLE DEFINITION: MAYORS MODEL

Revenue Estimates

Each city investigated has a rather complex system of revenues, of which general fund revenues are only part. A city's revenues consist of contributions from several sources—property taxes, city income tax, licenses and fees, treasurer's sales, amusement taxes, mercantile taxes, interest, utility charges, rental income, assessments, etc. Funds from some sources are earmarked for specific expenditures even though listed in the general fund. Adding to the complexity of accounts is the practice of including many outside revenue sources (including those outside of the general fund, such as inter-governmental transfers, fees, etc.) in the operating budget. In the departments affected, some appropriations are charged to the general fund, others are charged to the special funds (revenue sources). This means the revenue estimate as used in our model is really a number of separate estimates. To add to difficulties, many of these separate estimates are not kept (in their original form) by the city in any systematic way. To avoid confusion and the painstaking task of separating department appropriations by funds, while still retaining the essence of the revenue constraint and balanced budget requirement, the revenue estimates used in the model consist of the total of actual appropriations for those accounts included in the model plus any surplus indicated in the council appropriation bill. The difference between this method of determining the overall revenue estimate *(REVEST)* for a year and the theoretically preferable way of using individual estimates and the total general fund revenue estimate is more one of convenience than substance. The dollar difference is relatively small and represents a large number of small, automatic, accounting adjustments that are unimportant for our purposes. The cognitive separation of tax policy and expenditures decisions discussed above makes this procedure reasonable. Revenue estimates *(REVEST)* used in the study appear in Table VI-4.

TABLE VI-4

Model Revenue Estimates

Year	Cleveland	Detroit (with Welfare Dept.)	Detroit (without Welfare Dept.)	Pittsburgh
1956	$43,100,000	—	—	—
1957	45,780,000	—	—	—
1958(–59)	43,400,000	$164,000,000	$147,100,000	—
1959(–60)	46,470,000	166,700,000	153,000,000	—
1960(–61)	48,870,000	163,800,000	149,400,000	$38,300,000
1961(–62)	51,440,000	163,100,000	156,100,000	40,350,000
1962(–63)	51,630,000	187,000,000	153,900,000	39,870,000
1963(–64)	51,260,000	174,200,000	148,800,000	39,660,000
1964(–65)	56,370,000	171,000,000	153,000,000	42,950,000
1965	57,020,000	—	—	44,540,000

Minimum Salary Increase Parameter, XK

If there is a surplus of any magnitude [item 6 in Figure VI-1b (MAYORS)], the first surplus-reduction alternative evoked is that of granting an across-the-board salary increase [items 9 and 10 in Figure VI-1b (MAYORS)]. An increase is granted if the anticipated surplus exceeds a certain per cent *(XK)* of the city-wide salary total. The minimum across-the-board salary increase is a per cent, *XK,* of total salaries. The value of *XK,* according to interviews in all three cities and recent salary increases, appears to be in the neighborhood of 5 per cent. One reason for the 5 per cent figure, of course, is the desire on the part of city administrators to make salary changes visible or significant. At any rate, 5 per cent is the figure explicitly mentioned as a target by budget decision-makers, used most often when salaries are increased, and incorporated as the value of *XK* in our model for all three cities.

Criteria for Solution to Budget Balancing Problem, XLMT

Quite clearly, while trying to balance the budget, the mayor's office does not balance it so exactly that revenues equal expenditures. Specifically, in the surplus elimination routines evoked, a limit is reached when it is no longer feasible to search for ways to eliminate the anticipated surplus [item 11 in Figure VI-1b (MAYORS)]. All this says is that part of the budget will be a *planned* surplus. This planned surplus takes the place of a contingency fund for the administration in some cities. The magnitude of this test for a feasible solution is the result of many considerations:

(a) The presence of a formal, explicit contingency fund or other sources of a budget cushion (for instance, a 'programmed' discrepancy between appropriations and expenditures);[18]

(b) The nature of the projects and programs competing for funds (In some respects the magnitude of the limit is really an estimate of that surplus level at which no desirable programs can be undertaken. The indivisibility of projects enters into this limit. If a program or project has a minimum feasible price tag, the value of *XLMT* is really a kind of measure of this minimum price. For instance, if a data processing installation can be set up for a minimum of $300,000 and the anticipated surplus is only $200,000, then it is unlikely that data processing will be undertaken in the budget.);

(c) The total size of the budget (The compilers of a $1 billion budget are likely to stop searching for ways to eliminate an anticipated

---

[18] In Pittsburgh, two budgetary rules result in a level of expenditures lower than appropriations:

    a. An extremely detailed appropriations bill coupled with the requirement that only expenditures explicitly approved in the appropriations bill can be made. The more specific the approved expenditure items, the more difficult it is to spend on the approved limit.

    b. The presence of a cash budget for quarterly expenditures with the provision that there is no carryover from quarter to quarter (if a department does not spend the money it has budgeted for an item in the third quarter, it cannot purchase that item in the fourth quarter without a special authorization). Again, this makes it more difficult for departments to spend up to their appropriation limits.

surplus much sooner than their counterparts are likely to stop putting together a $100 million budget.).

In light of the considerations above, and the difficulty of estimating their effect on the value of *XLMT,* the observed planned surpluses in the budgets of the three cities were used as a guide for determining *XLMT.* Because of the limited effect *XLMT* has in the model, no formal estimating procedures were used and a reasonable value of $150,000 was used in the MAYORS submodel in all three cities. An analysis of the model's sensitivity to *XLMT* is undertaken in Chapter X. It does not prove to be a significant parameter.

Portion of Supplemental Request Granted, GG$_{ij}$

If an anticipated surplus is encountered that is large enough to make a difference in budget preparation, one way of eliminating it is to grant a portion *(GG$_{ij}$)* of a department's supplemental request [item 13 in Figure VI-1b (MAYORS)]. The lack of data relating to departmental requests in general and supplemental requests in particular (very few supplemental requests are granted at all), forces us to use a rather simple mechanism to determine the portion granted. A compromise between the department (all) and the mayor's office (nothing granted) is assumed. It is assumed that *if* a supplemental is granted, it will equal one-half of the department's original supplemental request *(GG$_{ij}$ = 0.5)*.[19]

Preliminary Recommendation within Limits? XL

When an anticipated deficit is encountered [item 6 in Figure VI-1b (MAYORS)], the first deficit-elimination routine evoked is a check to make sure that the preliminary mayor's recommendation is within limits of current appropriations indicated by the mayor in his budget letter [equals *(1.0 + TML)* in (item 5 in Figure V-1b)]. While it is acknowledged that conditions probably change between issuance of the mayor's budget letter to department heads and the consideration of the budget by the mayor's office, the tone of the mayor's budget letter is probably a good estimate of the limits actually applied to appropriations by the mayor's office [item 16 in Figure VI-1b (MAYORS)]. The assumption used in the model was that *XL = 1.0 + TML,* for all accounts in all cities.

We now turn to a detailed description of the COUNCIL submodel.

[19] One real difficulty in estimating *GG$_{ij}$* statistically is that the supplemental requests are usually in the form of a memo to the mayor. These are not codified and included in any single document (except in Detroit) and as a result are in department and mayor's office files—and hence, unavailable.

CHAPTER VII

COUNCIL Submodel

OVERVIEW

THE MAYOR'S BUDGET (output of MAYORS) is submitted to the city council for their approval and/or alteration. The council traditionally holds a series of public hearings on various portions of the budget, but rarely makes alterations of any significance. This lack of initiative on the part of the council is largely explained in terms of the nature of demands on the council, and party control in Pittsburgh (and to a lesser extent in Cleveland). In addition, the mayor's budget really represents a broad policy where the various parts are *not* independent of one another (the balanced-budget requirement insures this). To change one portion of the budget means to change at least one other portion to compensate for the change. Commitment to a uniform wage and salary policy means that any change in any salary account (approximately 70 per cent of the budget) involving wage rates also means a major revision in the tax policy of the city. The council has neither the staff nor inclination to undertake such drastic revisions.

Role and Context of Decisions

The role of the city council is a limited one. A primary reason for this limitation is more one of cognitive and informational constraints than lack of interest. The city budget is a complex document when it reaches the council. The level of detail makes considering all or even a majority of the items virtually impossible. For example, in the Pittsburgh Department of Public Works, the Division of Incineration Miscellaneous Services account is presented to the council as shown in Table VII-1.

TABLE VII-1

Budget Complexity: Department of Public Works

1963 Code Acct. No.	Title of Account	Departmental Estimates 1964	Appropriation Year 1963	Expenditures Year 1962	Increase Or Decrease '64 Over '63
Division of Incineration					
1687 Miscellaneous Services					
B-5	Recharge Fire Extinguishers	$ 50.00	$........	$ 89.26	$.....
B-5	Extermination Service	200.00	....	....	.....
B-8	Towel Rental	25.00	....	.26	.....
B-9	Supper Money	100.00	....	....	.....
B-13	Freight and Express Charges	89.00	....	....	.....
B-17	Public Property and Property Damage Insurance	125.00	....	....	.....
B-18	Water Cooler Rental	390.00	....	390.00	.....
B-18	Power Shovel Rental	12,960.00	....	14,880.00	.....
B-18	Truck Rental for Incinerator and Bell Farm	3,765.00	....	2,295.00	.....
B-20	Waste Disposal Permits	50.00	....	50.00	.....
B-20	Demurrage on Oxygen and Acetylene Tanks	170.00	....	200.40	.....
B-20	Services, N.O.C.	275.00	....	....	.....
B-21	Test Boring, Survey and Report, for Landfills	1,000.00	....	....	.....
	TOTALS	$19,199.00	$18,199.00	$17,904.92	$1,000

The council is asked to deal with the budget at this level of detail. When we realize that, in Pittsburgh, for example, there are five or more account categories like *miscellaneous services* in each administrative unit and that there are about forty-five such units in the city, we can easily understand why the council cannot seriously consider each line item (like the $25 reference to *towel rental,* Table VII-1). The sheer volume of information to be processed limits the ability of a council, without a budget staff, to consider the budget in a sophisticated or complex manner.

Another, perhaps more important, consideration is the balanced budget requirement. If there is little slack in the budget the mayor presents to the council [item 8 in Figure VII-1b (COUNCIL)], any increase the council makes in any account category must be balanced by a corresponding decrease in another account (or by an increase in revenue). So, in the presence of a revenue constraint, the council cannot consider elements of the budget independently, as is done in Congress. Davis, Dempster, and Wildavsky found that Congressional budgetary behavior could be described extremely well using a series of linear decision rules.[1] Behavior of this nature would not be possible if the sum of the changes in budgets made by Congress were required to add to zero—i.e., if the budget had to add up to an amount pre-determined by the President. Congressmen and Congressional committees also have staffs, councilmen do not.

TABLE VII-2

Council Strategies

	Decrease Other Item(s)	*Raise Taxes*	*Lower Taxes*	*Increase Other Item(s)*	*No Other Changes*
Item Budget Cuts	—	—	C	D	E
Item Budget Increases	A	B	—	—	F
		(Only feasible or probable strategies are identified)			

Of course, there are other behavioral options open to councilmen which allow changes while maintaining a balanced budget, as shown in Table VII-2. When one considers the nature of the external pressures on council members, strategies A and B (see Table VII-2) appear most likely. All interest groups, neighborhood organizations, department heads, etc. feel that some department's budget should be increased. The pressures transmitted to council concerning the operating budget are of one kind—those advocating increases in the mayor's recommendations. The other side of the argument—curtailment of government activities—is seldom, if ever, presented to council.[2] This countervailing influence enters the decision process not at the council level, but generally through the mayor's office and in particular through the mayor's revenue estimate. At this stage

[1] O. A. Davis, M. A. H. Dempster, and Aaron Wildavsky, "A Theory of the Budgetary Process," *American Political Science Review* (September, 1966), pp. 529-547.
[2] Suggested by Aldo Colautti, executive secretary to the mayor, city of Pittsburgh (October 30, 1964 interview).

in the decision process the business community or so-called economic elite attempt to influence municipal resource allocation by either implicitly or explicitly arguing for stable (non-rising) tax rates (not yields) and hence limiting the resources available for allocation.[3] Little interest is exhibited by the business community in the exact allocation of resources (the operating budget), however. The lack of pressure for budget cuts at the council level makes strategies *C*, *D*, and *E* less likely. The use of strategy *F* assumes the mayor leaves enough slack (surplus) in his budget to allow the council the luxury of selectively increasing portions of the budget.[4] This, of course, the mayor seldom does.

From the above we can see that the role of the council is limited due both to the nature of pressures impinging on them and their lack of informational and computational capabilities (budget staff). Where the mayor and council are of the same party, the party also acts as a control mechanism. The mayor as party leader acts to reduce the council's role. The council is then forced to use the mayor's decisions as reference points for its decisions. The constraints—pressure, informational, and computational—coupled with a recommended budget with no slack to allocate, makes changing any portion of the mayor's budget extremely difficult for them.[5]

FORMAL MODEL CHARACTERISTICS

The problem is perceived by the council as one of compromising the department requests (including supplementals) with the mayor's recommendations [items 6 and 9 in Figure VII-1b (COUNCIL)] if there are enough resources available to allow this [items 4 and 8 in Figure VII-1b (COUNCIL)]. The *preliminary* decision in all cases is to accept the mayor's recommendation (decisional reference point)—[item 5 in Figure VII-1b (COUNCIL)]. If the mayor gives the department all it asks for [item 6 in Figure VII-1b (COUNCIL)]—including supplemental requests—then the mayor's recommendation is automatically accepted. If not, and *if the anticipated surplus* (revenue estimate minus preliminary budget total) *is large enough,* the department is granted an additional amount based on the mayor's recommendation, the magnitude of the

[3] The nature of pressures on tax policy may partially explain the commitment of a large portion of the city's capital budget to those projects which tend to increase the city's tax base.

[4] In Detroit, before Mayor Cavanaugh took office, it was customary, when city employees received a general pay raise, for the mayor to grant a general increase and then leave enough of a surplus in the budget so that the council could add to the pay raise and take some "credit" for it, too.

[5] Occasionally the council will eliminate a *new* tax proposed by the mayor—income tax in Cleveland, tax for meat inspectors in Detroit—but hardly ever turns down an expenditure recommendation.

mayor's cut in the departmental request, and past, actual expenditure amounts [item 9 in Figure VII-1b (COUNCIL)].

If, by chance or through the elimination of a revenue source by the council, there is an anticipated deficit, it is eliminated by successively reducing proposed appropriations to current appropriation levels [items 14 and 15 in Figure VII-1b (COUNCIL)].

FORMAL COUNCIL MODEL

Following the same format used in presenting the DEPT. and MAYORS models, COUNCIL is described below using verbal [Figure VII-1a (COUNCIL)] and non-verbal flowcharts [Figure VII-1b (COUNCIL)]. The computer program associated with the non-verbal flowchart is found in the appendix, pp. 301-302.

FIGURE VII-1a

General COUNCIL Appropriations Model

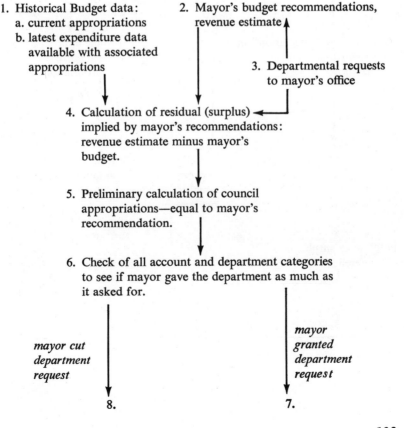

1. Historical Budget data:
   a. current appropriations
   b. latest expenditure data available with associated appropriations

2. Mayor's budget recommendations, revenue estimate

3. Departmental requests to mayor's office

4. Calculation of residual (surplus) implied by mayor's recommendations: revenue estimate minus mayor's budget.

5. Preliminary calculation of council appropriations—equal to mayor's recommendation.

6. Check of all account and department categories to see if mayor gave the department as much as it asked for.

mayor cut department request

mayor granted department request

8.

7.

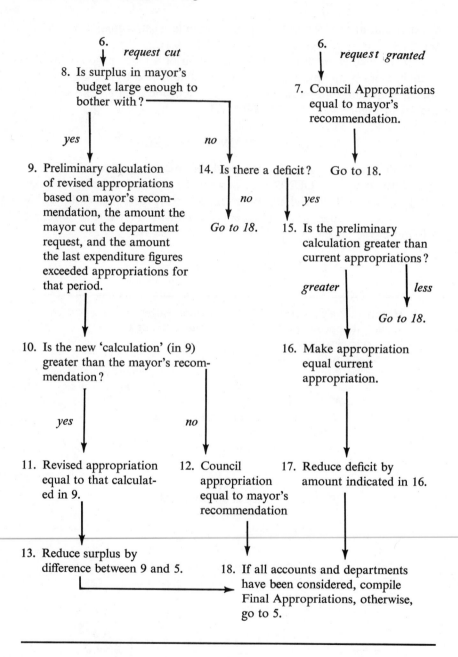

6.   *request cut*

8. Is surplus in mayor's
   budget large enough to
   bother with?

6.   *request granted*

7. Council Appropriations
   equal to mayor's
   recommendation.

yes   *no*

9. Preliminary calculation
   of revised appropriations
   based on mayor's recommendation, the amount the
   mayor cut the department
   request, and the amount
   the last expenditure figures
   exceeded appropriations for
   that period.

14. Is there a deficit?   Go to 18.

no   *yes*

Go to 18.

15. Is the preliminary
    calculation greater than
    current appropriations?

greater   *less*

Go to 18.

10. Is the new 'calculation' (in 9)
    greater than the mayor's recom-
    mendation?

16. Make appropriation
    equal current
    appropriation.

yes   *no*

11. Revised appropriation
    equal to that calculat-
    ed in 9.

12. Council
    appropriation
    equal to mayor's
    recommendation

17. Reduce deficit by
    amount indicated in 16.

13. Reduce surplus by
    difference between 9 and 5.

18. If all accounts and departments
    have been considered, compile
    Final Appropriations, otherwise,
    go to 5.

Variable Dictionary

The COUNCIL variable dictionary follows the format and general definitions found in DEPT. and MAYORS variable dictionaries.

TABLE VII-3
COUNCIL Variable Dictionary

Variable	Definition
Model Inputs	
$APPR0_{ij}$	Final Appropriations, previous year
$EXPND_{ij}$	Expenditure Total, previous year
$APPR1_{ij}$	Final Appropriations, current year
$DEPR2_{ij}$	Department Request, next budget year
$DSUPR_{ij}$	Department Supplemental Request, next budget year
$RMAY2_{ij}$	Mayor's Budget Recommendation, next budget year
TBUD	Total Budget (from mayor)
$NACCT_i$	Number of Accounts within a department
N	Number of Departments in a city
REVEST	Revenue Estimate
Accounting	
TBUD	Total Budget
RESID	Revenue Estimate less Total Budget
STOR	Short-term Memory to keep track of total changes
Parameters	
Q_{ij}, PP_{ij}, S_{ij}	Empirically Determined Preliminary-Calculations Parameters
XLMT	Solution Criteria for Budget Balancing
Intermediate Calculations-Model Outputs	
$APPR2_{ij}$	Final Appropriations for next budget year
TBUD	Final Budget Total

Note: Subscript *i* refers to a department, *j* refers to an account category within a department.

BEHAVIOR NOT INCLUDED IN FORMAL COUNCIL MODEL

As we have already indicated, constraints and the nature of the pressure on the council are such that it really has few behavioral alternatives. Those alternatives not open to the council are not included in the model. Actually only one kind of councilmanic behavior observed in the last ten years in our three cities will not be found in the formal model. The behavior occurs in those rare instances when council decides to change the tax rates (either by turning down a tax proposal of the mayor's or by increasing a tax to provide additional revenue for a particular purpose). These omissions will show up in an analysis of the model's residuals.

FIGURE VII-1b

Formalized COUNCIL Appropriations Model

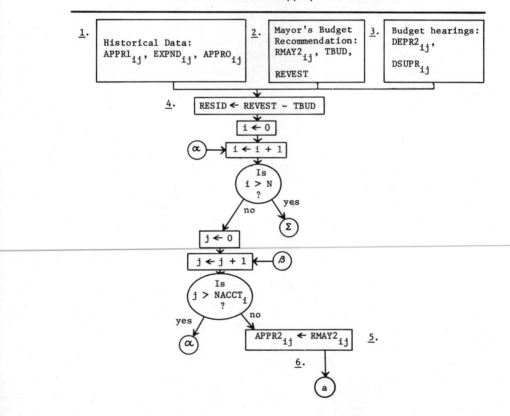

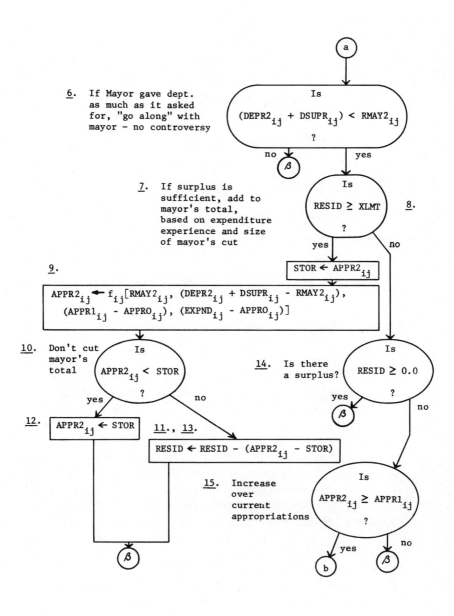

6. If Mayor gave dept. as much as it asked for, "go along" with mayor - no controversy

Is $(DEPR2_{ij} + DSUPR_{ij}) < RMAY2_{ij}$?

7. If surplus is sufficient, add to mayor's total, based on expenditure experience and size of mayor's cut

Is $RESID \geq XLMT$?

8.

$STOR \leftarrow APPR2_{ij}$

9.

$$APPR2_{ij} \leftarrow f_{ij}[RMAY2_{ij}, (DEPR2_{ij} + DSUPR_{ij} - RMAY2_{ij}), (APPR1_{ij} - APPRO_{ij}), (EXPND_{ij} - APPRO_{ij})]$$

10. Don't cut mayor's total

Is $APPR2_{ij} < STOR$?

14. Is there a surplus?

Is $RESID \geq 0.0$?

12.

$APPR2_{ij} \leftarrow STOR$

11., 13.

$RESID \leftarrow RESID - (APPR2_{ij} - STOR)$

15. Increase over current appropriations

Is $APPR2_{ij} \geq APPR1_{ij}$?

b

107

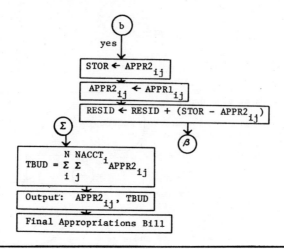

PARAMETER ESTIMATION AND VARIABLE DEFINITION: COUNCIL MODEL

Parameters for two relationships were estimated for the COUNCIL submodel:

(1) A test to see if the mayor (output from MAYORS Submodel) had left enough of a budgetary surplus for the council to consider [item 8 in Figure VII-1b (COUNCIL)]. Because of the council's lack of staff (and time) and in light of the balanced-budget requirement, the only strategies open to council are to increase appropriations in the face of an adequate surplus [item 8 in Figure VII-1b (COUNCIL)] or to decrease appropriations in light of an anticipated deficit [items 14 and 15 in Figure VII-1b (COUNCIL)]. The limit, *XLMT* defining an adequate surplus, is the parameter to be estimated.

(2) If the test above indicates an adequate surplus, the council then increases appropriations for various departments and account categories on the basis of:

a. Mayor's recommendation—$RMAY2_{ij}$,

b. Magnitude of the mayor's cut in the total departmental request—$(DEPR2_{ij} + DSUPR_{ij} - RMAY2_{ij})$,

---

[6] Because of the availability of more current data in Cleveland, overspending and underspending is calculated using $(EXPN1_{ij} - APPR1_{ij})$.

    c. Overspending or underspending by the department in the past[6] *(EXPND$_{ij}$ — APPR0$_{ij}$)*, or

    d. Current appropriations trends—*(APPR1$_{ij}$ — APPR0$_{ij}$)*.

[See item 9 in Figure VII-1b (COUNCIL) in the formal model.]

Criteria for Adequate Surplus—XLMT

The criteria the council applies to decide whether the mayor's budget recommendation has a surplus adequate to allow additional appropriations is subject to the same sorts of considerations inherent in the mayor's criterion for solution to budget balancing problems, *XLMT,* discussed earlier. Because council rarely alters the mayor's budget in any significant way and because of the similarity in the two concepts, the limit defining an adequate surplus, *XLMT,* for COUNCIL to increase appropriations is assumed to be identical to the criterion for solution to the budget balancing problem, *XLMT,* in the MAYORS submodel.[7]

Adjustment of Mayor's Recommendations

Two relationships for describing the COUNCIL adjustment process (if evoked) were tested for each account category in each department.

Relationships tested for Detroit and Pittsburgh:

$$(31) \quad APPR2_{ij} = PP_{ij}(RMAY2_{ij}) + Q_{ij}(DEPR2_{ij} + DSUPR_{ij} - RMAY2_{ij})$$

$$(32) \quad APPR2_{ij} = PP_{ij}(RMAY2_{ij}) + R_{ij}(APPR1_{ij} - APPR0_{ij}) + S_{ij}(EXPND_{ij} - APPR0_{ij})$$

The parameters *PP$_{ij}$, Q$_{ij}$, R$_{ij}$,* and *S$_{ij}$* were estimated using time-series data from Detroit and Pittsburgh and linear regression techniques. A choice between relationships (31) and (32) was made for each account category in each department on the basis of the associated R^2 statistics. In *most* cases, there was no significant difference between the R^2 statistics for models (31) and (32), and the choice was somewhat arbitrary. The results of this choice are found in the appendix, pp. 266-269 and 274-278.

---

[7] Equal to $150,000. This assumption means that the council alters the budget 'only' when the mayor's office has not used up the excess over $150,000. The net effect under these circumstances is for the council to grant a larger portion of supplemental requests than the mayor.

Relationships tested for Cleveland:

(31') $\quad APPR2_{ij} = PP_{ij}(RMAY2_{ij}) + Q_{ij}(DEPR2_{ij} - APPR1_{ij}) +$
$\quad\quad\quad R_{ij}(APPR1_{ij} - APPR0_{ij})$

(32') $\quad APPR2_{ij} = PP_{ij}(RMAY2_{ij}) + R_{ij}(APPR1_{ij} - APPR0_{ij}) +$
$\quad\quad\quad S_{ij}(EXPN1_{ij} - APPR1_{ij})$

In nearly every case, PP_{ij} equaled 1.0 and the other parameters were not significant. Because of this, PP_{ij} was assumed to be 1.0 in Cleveland for all accounts and administrative units and R_{ij}, S_{ij}, and Q_{ij} were set equal to zero.

In Chapters IV, V, VI, and VII we developed a formal model of municipal budgetary problem-solving, a set of behavioral concepts consistent with the structure of the model, and estimated parameters to fit the structure to the study cities. We now turn to the task of empirically testing the consistency of our theory with actual budgetary decisions in Cleveland, Detroit, and Pittsburgh.

CHAPTER VIII

Budgetary Model Fits

GENERAL CONSIDERATIONS

THE FORMAL SIMULATION MODEL as presented in Chapters IV-VII represents a series of interdependent hypotheses relative to the municipal budgeting process. After fitting the general model to the specific cases of Cleveland, Detroit, and Pittsburgh as outlined above, the task is now one of testing the model to see if it conforms to the real-world phenomena it is attempting to describe.

There are two kinds of questions to which we should address our decision model:

1. Does the model yield outcomes similar to the real-world phenomena it purports to describe?
2. Does the model reach these decisions using the same mechanisms as the corresponding real-world decision system?

Operationally, question (1) implies a comparison between time-series data (decisions) generated by the model (computer program) and data generated by the real decision system (municipal government). Question (2) necessitates a comparison of decision mechanisms evoked by the model (branches in the computer program) and decision rules or procedures evoked by the decision-makers in the real-world system. Operationally, question (2) raises questions like: In 1962, did both the model and the mayor of Pittsburgh check to see if the anticipated surplus was sufficient for a 5 per cent, across-the-board salary increase for municipal employees [item 9 in Figure VI-1b (MAYORS)], and did both the model and the mayor find that there was not a sufficient surplus [did model branch from item 9 to 11 in Figure VI-1b (MAYORS) instead of to 10]?

Evidence in support of the goodness-of-fit of the budgetary process model is presented in Chapters VIII and IX. Chapter VIII deals primarily with the general question of goodness-of-fit and presents evidence in support of the model's general predictive ability. Chapter IX presents much stronger evidence of fit, dealing with the similarity between real-world and model processes, rather than outcomes.

Testing the Process or Model Mechanisms

As both Newell and Simon[1] and Clarkson[2] have pointed out, an adaptation of Turing's test[3] is an adequate (and potentially strong) way of testing decision-process models. They write:

> Turing's test can be applied in stronger or weaker forms. Comparison of the (decision made by the computer model) with the (decisions made) by human (decision-makers) in the same position would be a weak test.[4] The program might have reached its decision by quite a different process from that used by humans. . . .
>
> If data are gathered, however, by the thinking-aloud technique or by other means, that indicate the process used to select the behavior, it may, and usually will, be possible to distinguish different ways of arriving at the same result. If the program makes the same analysis as the humans, notices the same traps, then we will infer, and properly, that down to some level of detail, the program provides an explanation of the human processes. The more minute and detailed the comparison between program (model) and behavior, the greater will be the opportunity for detecting differences between the predicted and actual behavior.[5]

The Newell and Simon quotation above has several implications for our goodness-of-fit problem. For municipal budgetary decision processes, the strength of the application of Turing's test varies both with the 'minuteness' and 'detailedness' of the comparison and the number of comparisons

---

[1] Allen Newell and H. A. Simon, "The Simulation of Human Thought," *P-1734* (Santa Monica: The Rand Corporation, June, 1959), pp. 14-15.

[2] G. P. E. Clarkson, *Portfolio Selection: A Simulation of Trust Investment* (Englewood Cliffs, N.J.: Prentice-Hall, Inc., 1962), pp. 56-58.

[3] Turing's test was proposed ". . . to consider the question, 'Can machines think?'" Turing proposes an "imitation game" with three players: a human subject, a machine, and an interrogator. Communication between the interrogator and other players is allowed only under conditions ". . . which [prevent] the interrogator from seeing or touching the other competitors, or hearing their voices." The object of the interrogator is to discover which player is the human and which the machine. A. M. Turing, "Computing Machinery and Intelligence," in Edward Feigenbaum and Julian Feldman, eds., *Computers and Thought* (New York: McGraw-Hill, Inc., 1963), pp. 11-13.

[4] The weak Turing's test is equivalent to: Does the decisional model yield the same decisions as the real-world phenomena it purports to describe?

[5] Newell and Simon, *op. cit.*

FIGURE VIII-1

Strength of Turing's Tests as a Function of
the Level of Detail of Model Comparisons with Actual Behavior

Strong

All Budget Line Items	Individual Submodel Decision Rules
*Standard (summary) Account Categories	Outputs of Submodels*
Department Totals Only	Final Appropriation* Totals Only
Entire Budget Total	
Total of Budgets over span of several years	Total of Appropriations during a several year period

Weak

* Comparisons used in study.

made. Figure VIII-1 indicates the relationships between the positions in the decision process at which comparisons with actual data are made, the level of detail of the decisions, and the strength of an adapted Turing's test. Naturally enough, our position is one of maximizing the strength of a Turing's test subject to data constraints.

Because resource and accessibility constraints prevented us from obtaining 'thinking aloud' or protocol data from forty to sixty different department heads in each city, from the mayors and their staffs, and from the various city councils, less direct ways of attacking the problem were used. One method, which seems particularly suggestive, involves comparing 'traps' or 'unusual situations' noticed by the mayor with model residuals. Results of this analysis are discussed and presented in Chapter IX. Another method involved comparison of model-generated data at the three submodel stages with observed decisions at these stages—DEPT. submodel output with department requests, MAYORS submodel outputs with mayor's recommended budgets, and COUNCIL submodel outputs with final municipal appropriations in our three cities. Comparing submodel with observed outputs, while not as 'strong' a test of our simulation model as Clarkson was able to use or as Newell and Simon have used to test their models of a chess player, is not a particularly weak test. Certainly, our goodness-of-fit test is not weaker (on the level-of-detail continuum) than the ones reported by Cyert and March of the department store buyer—where sales estimation decisions, actual orders, markups, sale prices, and markdowns generated by the model were compared with decisions made by the department store buyer.[6]

Before continuing our discussion of model tests, one major, but unavoidable, deficiency in the test should be pointed out. Due to lack of data (six years' in Pittsburgh, seven years' in Detroit, and ten years' data in Cleveland), following the much-preferred procedure of estimating parameters using one set of data and testing the model with another set was impossible.[7] Unfortunately, the same data had to be used for both estimation and testing. The only alternative would have been to let the 'tail wag the dog' and reduce the scope and complexity of our research task and the realism of our decision model.

Specific elaboration of the ideas presented above is called for in two areas:

1. Discussion of the exact nature of model runs,
2. Definition of goodness-of-fit measures.

Model Runs

Generally speaking, each of the three submodels (DEPT., MAYORS, and COUNCIL) defines a function which transforms input data to output data. The inputs to the next submodel in the sequence can be real-world decision inputs or they can be outputs from the previous submodel. Certainly, the model takes on different meanings dependent on the spacing of reconciliations with real-world data. If we use real-world data as inputs at each stage of the process (for each submodel), the resulting model run is an example of a one-*stage* change model. By piecing together the submodels in a different manner and letting the submodels run for a longer period and updating the input data with actual data once each period (year), we obtain a one-*period* change model.

If instead of intervening after each decisional stage (DEPT., MAYORS, COUNCIL) to obtain a one-stage change model, or after each year to obtain a one-period change model, we start the model at the beginning of our data and let it continue to run without updating until the data are exhausted, we have a simulation model in the true sense of the word.[8] The relations between the nature of model runs and data input configurations can be seen in Figure VIII-2.

[6] R. M. Cyert and J. G. March, *A Behavioral Theory of the Firm* (Englewood Cliffs, N.J.: Prentice-Hall, Inc., 1963), pp. 144-148.
[7] K. J. Cohen and R. M. Cyert, *Theory of the Firm: Resource Allocation in a Market Economy* (Englewood Cliffs, N.J.: Prentice-Hall, Inc., 1965), pp. 26-27.
[8] Cohen and Cyert in R. M. Cyert and J. G. March, *op. cit.*, pp. 312-325, distinguish between one-period change and simulation or process models as does Clarkson, *op. cit.*, pp. 17-18.

FIGURE VIII-2
Nature of Model Runs and Data Inputs

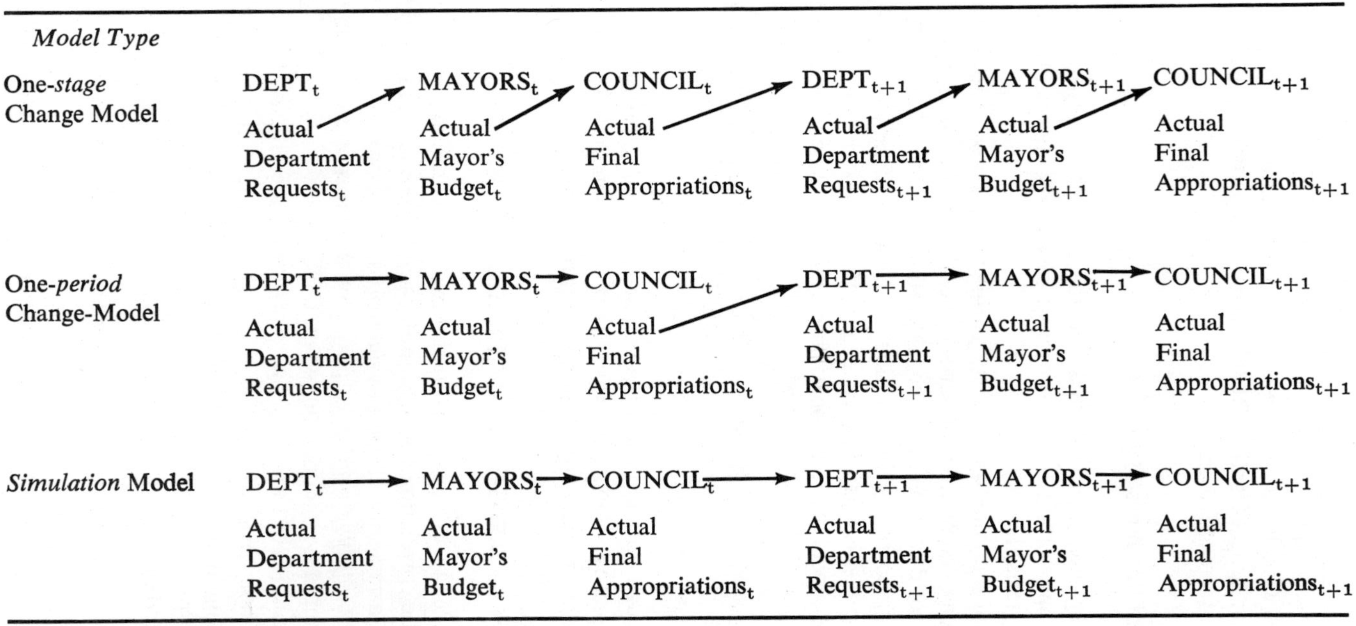

Model Type

One-*stage* Change Model

$DEPT_t \rightarrow MAYORS_t \rightarrow COUNCIL_t \quad DEPT_{t+1} \rightarrow MAYORS_{t+1} \rightarrow COUNCIL_{t+1}$

| Actual Department Requests$_t$ | Actual Mayor's Budget$_t$ | Actual Final Appropriations$_t$ | Actual Department Requests$_{t+1}$ | Actual Mayor's Budget$_{t+1}$ | Actual Final Appropriations$_{t+1}$ |

One-*period* Change-Model

$DEPT_t \rightarrow MAYORS_t \rightarrow COUNCIL_t \quad DEPT_{t+1} \rightarrow MAYORS_{t+1} \rightarrow COUNCIL_{t+1}$

| Actual Department Requests$_t$ | Actual Mayor's Budget$_t$ | Actual Final Appropriations$_t$ | Actual Department Requests$_{t+1}$ | Actual Mayor's Budget$_{t+1}$ | Actual Final Appropriations$_{t+1}$ |

Simulation Model

$DEPT_t \rightarrow MAYORS_t \rightarrow COUNCIL_t \quad DEPT_{t+1} \rightarrow MAYORS_{t+1} \rightarrow COUNCIL_{t+1}$

| Actual Department Requests$_t$ | Actual Mayor's Budget$_t$ | Actual Final Appropriations$_t$ | Actual Department Requests$_{t+1}$ | Actual Mayor's Budget$_{t+1}$ | Actual Final Appropriations$_{t+1}$ |

We shall space our real-world interventions so that our process model is run both as a one-period change model and as a simulation model, for all three cities. Goodness-of-fit measures were computed after each *stage* in the decision process (after DEPT., after MAYORS, and after COUNCIL), and for each year.[9]

Measures of Goodness-of-fit

Having attempted to maximize the strength of our goodness-of-fit tests by manipulating model runs and real-world interventions, we now turn to the tests themselves.

The most common way of subjecting process models to statistical testing has been to compare time series generated by the model with the actual time series of decisions under consideration.

This again raises the question of model verification. As Popper has argued, a model is scientifically meaningful if, and only if, it is possible to refute the model by empirical observation.[10] When is a model good enough?

> There are various degrees to which any model can fail to describe the world, however, so it is meaningful to say that some models are more adequate descriptions of reality than others.[11]

Although devising tests that confirm or refute a process model in an 'ultimate' sense is impossible with the present state of development, there are many ways we can attack the verification problem.

MEASURES OF PREDICTIVE ABILITY

Specifically, our tests will involve two considerations:

a. The correlation between model predictions and observed behavior —a measure of the *absolute* predictive power;

b. The *relative* predictive power of the process models and various alternative models and hypotheses.

Three kinds of formal goodness-of-fit tests are proposed:

1. Simple regressions of the model-generated series of decisions as a function of the observed series, to test for model bias and ability to predict;[12]

2. Modified-R^2 statistics measuring the ratio of variances explained

---

[9] In Cleveland and Pittsburgh, missing department request data prevent comparisons in those years.

[10] Karl R. Popper, *The Logic of Scientific Discovery* (New York: Basic Books, 1959).

[11] K. J. Cohen and R. M. Cyert, "Computer Models in Dynamic Economics," *The Quarterly Journal of Economics* (February, 1961), pp. 112-127.

[12] Cyert and March, *op. cit.*, pp. 319-320.

by the model relative to variances explained using alternative hypotheses.

3. Model comparisons where the predictability of three alternative, naive models is compared with that of our process models.

In addition, a less formal test of goodness-of-fit will be presented in Chapter IX involving an analysis of process model residuals. This test, by suggesting that the process models and human decision-makers both noticed the same traps or special cases in the problem-solving process, is probably stronger than the more formal measures presented here.

Absolute Predictive Ability: Regression of Predictions on Observations

The following regression equation was fitted to the decisions generated by our process models:

$$\begin{bmatrix} \text{Model Estimate} \\ \text{of Appropriations} \end{bmatrix} = a \cdot \begin{bmatrix} \text{Observed} \\ \text{Appropriations} \end{bmatrix} + b$$

A high R^2 for the regression equation will measure the power of the process models to predict well. For an unbiased model that predicts perfectly, the expected value of a is 1.0, and the expected value of b is 0.0. The results are found in Table VIII-1.

TABLE VIII-1

Regression of Model Estimates on

Observed Appropriations

$$\begin{bmatrix} \text{Model Estimate} \\ \text{of Appropriations} \end{bmatrix} = a \cdot \begin{bmatrix} \text{Observed} \\ \text{Appropriations} \end{bmatrix} + b$$

Case	a	Std. Error of a	b	R^2	n
Cleveland					
One-Period Change	.977	.001	$-\$5282$	.9980	999
Simulation	.930	.003	$\$3526$	.9933	651
Detroit (with Welfare)					
One-Period Change	.963	.007	$\$31247$	.9527	937
Simulation	.912	.009	$\$106402$	.9329	682
Detroit (without Welfare)					
One-Period Change	.984	.005	$\$7281$	.9772	918
Simulation	.971	.006	$\$29181$	.9754	667
Pittsburgh					
One-Period Change	.991	.002	$-\$28$	.9975	1002
Simulation	1.011	.003	$-\$4918$	.9955	669

The uniformly high R^2 statistics indicate that our models fit the data quite well. The simulation models, not having the benefit of the yearly corrections of model errors, have more opportunities for error. Not surprisingly, the R^2 are lower for simulation models.

The one-period change and simulation models appear reasonably unbiased except in Detroit. The peculiarities in Detroit which probably produce the bias in model outputs will be discussed later in this chapter (deficit spending, capital items in operations budget, etc.).

There does appear to be a slight tendency for the model to underestimate budget appropriations, however. There are several reasons why this would be so. One reason is because the model deals only with existing administrative units and account categories. When a new unit is created, the model will not 'recognize' it (until the next period, for one-period change models), leading to a built-in, negative bias (see analysis of model residuals in Chapter IX). Another bias is inherent in the model. The MAYORS model consists of deficit-elimination and surplus-elimination routines. The deficit-elimination routine is such that any deficit is always eliminated (ultimately, by a proportional adjustment of all non-salary accounts). The surplus-elimination routines are different, however. If the surplus is large enough, it can go undistributed. Only a small number of the many surplus elimination routines *available* to the mayor are included in our formal model. The absence of a complete set of surplus routines could bias the *total* budget estimate downward.

The. results of the regression in Table VIII-1 indicate the process model predicts well.[13] We now turn to the question of how well.

Relative Predictive Ability: Ordinal Comparisons

MODIFIED-R^2 MEASURES. The most well-known goodness-of-fit measure is the R^2 statistic[14] associated with regression analysis. Mathematically,[15] it is:

$$R^2 = 1.0 - \frac{\Sigma \, (\text{observed} - \text{model prediction})^2}{\Sigma \, (\text{observed} - \text{mean of observed})^2}$$

'Observed' refers to values of the dependent variable found in the real world. 'Model prediction' refers to the corresponding value generated by the model or hypothesis being tested. From the above, we can see that the value of R^2 is merely a measure of how much better the model or hypothesis

[13] One reason for the high statistical correlation between real-world and process model outcomes might concern the 'degrees of freedom' in the calibrated models. The identification problem is discussed in the appendix following this chapter.

[14] Also known as the coefficient of determination.

[15] John Johnston, *Econometric Methods* (New York: McGraw-Hill, Inc., 1963), p. 31.

is at reproducing the observed data than the alternative hypothesis that the observations come from random draws from a normal population. (If this is so, then the best *estimate* of the value of the dependent variable is the *mean of the observed, normal population.*)

Briefly, the standard R^2 measure was modified by substituting more reasonable null hypotheses for *observed equals mean of observed*. The null hypotheses used in the modified-R^2 statistics computed were:

i. R^2_m: observed equals mean of observed, over the study period, for the particular account in the particular department under question, rather than the mean over *all* departments and accounts.

ii. R^2_c: observed equals previous year's appropriation for the particular department and account under question.

The values of these modified-R^2 statistics must be interpreted with care. Unlike the familiar regression R^2, the bounds on the statistics are *not* zero to one. In addition, the null hypotheses included in R^2_m and R^2_c are very good predictors in their own right. In such cases, values of R^2_m and R^2_c near zero would indicate that both the process model and the null hypothesis have predicted well. The null hypothesis should be particularly relevant where the city must 'hold the line' on expenditures—during periods of constant or declining revenues.

A more detailed explanation of the nature of the modified-R^2 statistics is found in the appendix following this chapter.

ORDINAL COMPARISONS OF PROCESS MODEL WITH VARIOUS NAIVE MODELS. The literature suggests three reasonable models of the budgetary process:

A1: Constant-Growth Model

$APPR2_{ij} = a_{ij} APPR1_{ij} + b_{ij}$

where a_{ij} and b_{ij} represent growth parameters and are empirically determined using linear regression techniques;

A2: Constant-Share-of-the-Budget-Total Model[16]

$APPR2_{ij} = c_{ij} TBUD2$

where *TBUD2* is the total budget for the city and c_{ij} represents the portion of the total going to department *i*, account *j*. c_{ij} will be empirically determined using linear regression techniques;

A3: Constant-Share-of-the-Increase Model[17]

$(APPR2_{ij} - APPR1_{ij}) = d_{ij}(TBUD2 - TBUD1)$

[16] Similar to Wildavsky's concept of agency "base." "The base is the general expectation among the participants that programs will be carried on at close to the going level of expenditures. . . ." Aaron Wildavsky, *The Politics of the Budgetary Process* (Boston: Little, Brown and Company, 1964), p. 17.

[17] Similar to Wildavsky's concept of "fair share" of any increases or decreases above or below ". . . the base of the various governmental agencies." Wildavsky, *op. cit.*

where *(TBUD2 — TBUD1)* represents the total increase in the budget, and d_{ij} is an empirically determined parameter—the share of the increase for department *i,* account *j.*

As an additional test of the relative *predictive* power of our model of municipal resource allocation, the parameters a_{ij}, b_{ij}, c_{ij}, and d_{ij} were calculated for all *i* and *j,* and estimates of appropriations were generated on the basis of these three alternative models. These estimates were generated in a manner similar to the one-period change models discussed above.

The task of evaluating the *relative* predictive powers of the three alternative models and our process model is not a particularly easy one. As we will see below, the ordering of similar models on the basis of a statistical measure of goodness-of-fit is sometimes a function of the type of measure used when the models to be compared do excellent jobs of predicting.

The state of the art in testing process models is a crude one. Testing these models is, of necessity, an eclectic procedure, involving *ad hoc* measures. In the absence of any dominant statistical test, we have elected to try several. Without a panel of experts, we are resorting to a majority vote of measures. In the face of uncertainty about relevant tests, if all yield the same results, at least some confidence can then be placed in those results.

CHOOSING BETWEEN ALTERNATIVE MODELS. If it is valid to view our model(s) as generating probabilities of dollars finding their way into a particular account in a particular department, we can draw on the work of Hunt for guidelines in choosing between our model and the three alternative models, above, on the basis of predicted and observed frequencies.[18]

Hunt uses two criteria to distinguish between similar models applied to the same set of data:

1. χ^2*-Criteria*

$$\text{Min } \Sigma \left[\frac{(\text{observed} - \text{predicted})^2}{\text{predicted}} \right]$$

2. *Bayesian-Induction Criteria*

$$\text{Min } \Sigma \left[\frac{(\text{observed} - \text{predicted})^2}{\text{observed}} \right]$$

Although we would have to know something about the distributions of the simulation model output (and the real-world appropriations decisions) to assess levels of significance to Hunt's proposed goodness-of-fit criteria,

[18] Earl B. Hunt, "The Evaluation of Somewhat Parallel Models," in Fred Massarik and Philburn Ratoosh, eds., *Mathematical Explorations in Behavioral Science* (Homewood, Ill.: Richard D. Irwin, Inc., 1965), pp. 41-42.

there are no obvious reasons why we cannot use these statistics as an aid in choosing between alternative models.

In fact, the general situation under which a formal χ^2-goodness-of-fit test is appropriate is quite similar to our situation. Consider ". . . the case in sampling with replacement from a population of individuals which could be classified into k classes, a common problem is that of testing whether the probabilities have specified numerical values."[19] An appropriate test under these conditions is the χ^2 test. If we assume our resource allocation model generates *probabilities* that one dollar will be distributed to each of several departments and account categories, the similarities to the usual χ^2-situation are apparent.[20] The major difference is that we do not know the distribution of the statistics in our measures.

In operationalizing the above criteria for distinguishing between alternative models, we must take into account the fact that these measures have a tendency to break down for "rare events."[21] "Rare events" refer to the magnitude of the denominator in (1) and (2), opposite. Adjustments must also be made for the number of accounts and departments excluded as "rare events." Details of these adjustments are found in the appendix following this chapter.

GOODNESS-OF-FIT TESTS APPLIED

Summarizing the previous section, the following measures will be applied to the cities of Cleveland, Detroit, and Pittsburgh:

MODIFIED-R^2 MEASURES.
1. R^2 about the department and account mean—R^2_m
2. R^2 about previous years' appropriations—R^2_c
3. R^2 over all departments and accounts [to provide a contrast to (1) and (2)]—R^2_o

MEASURES FOR CHOOSING AMONG ALTERNATIVE MODELS.
4. χ^2-Criteria for choosing between alternative models
5. Bayesian-Induction Criteria for choosing between alternative models

All five of the measures can be used to compare the relative goodness-of-fit of the two process models and three naive models:

A1: Constant-Growth Model
A2: Constant-Share-of-the-Budget-Total Model

---

[19] Alexander Mood, *Introduction to the Theory of Statistics* (New York: McGraw-Hill, Inc., 1950), p. 270.
[20] We could also assume that the total budget is large enough that the distribution of $1 to an account and department without replacement is roughly equivalent to sampling with replacement.
[21] Hunt, *op. cit.*, p. 42.

A3: Constant-Share-of-the-Increase Model

For reasons of computational convenience, the following measures were used to rank the indicated models:

R^2_m: One-Period Change, Simulation, *A1, A2*

R^2_c: One-Period Change, Simulation, *A3*

R^2_o: One-Period Change, Simulation, *A1, A2*

Chi-squared Criteria: One-Period Change, Simulation, *A1, A2*

Bayesian Criteria: One-Period Change, Simulation, *A1, A2*

All measures except R^2_m were calculated for each year in each city.

We have already discussed how we are attempting to maximize the strength of these tests—by maximizing the level of detail of the predictions. An example of the level of detail model output can be found in the appendix, pp. 325-327. In addition, by calculating separate goodness-of-fit measures for each year, rather than obtaining one summary measure for the study period, hopefully some causes can be established for model success or failure. Possible causes that are monitored include changes in the city administration and the changing revenue patterns.

Before results are presented, note that goodness-of-fit measures were calculated for intermediate results (after the DEPT. and MAYORS submodel stages) as well as for the final appropriations each year (COUNCIL submodel output). Only the measures computed for the COUNCIL submodel output are reported here. In general, the goodness-of-fit measures calculated after the MAYORS submodel was executed are indistinguishable from the same measures for the COUNCIL output. The DEPT. submodel measures generally show a poorer fit, resulting from the paucity of data at that stage of the decision process and from imputing the same submodel structure to all departments in the study. In any event, no useful information is lost by not presenting the measures from the submodels.

Again, it would be wise to review the meanings of the modified-R^2 statistics and Hunt's χ^2 and Bayesian Criteria. As used here, values for R^2_c and R^2_m above zero indicate relatively (and absolutely) good fits for the process models. Numbers representing the Hunt-criteria have no meaning in an absolute sense—only in a relative sense. If the Bayesian Criteria measure for a process model in a given year is less than the Bayesian measure for naive model *A2, for the same year,* the interpretation is that the process model is a relatively better predictor for that year. The magnitude of the differences in the Hunt-statistics for a given year, while *correlated* with the magnitude of the relative predictive power of the two models *for that year,* are inconsistent measures from year to year. Magnitudes of differences are suggestive at best and should be ignored.

PITTSBURGH GOODNESS-OF-FIT. The Pittsburgh results are of more interest for what they do not show than for what they do show.

First, the one-period change model did not apppear to 'shift' or experience any difficulty in processing a new mayor. None of the measures associated with the 1960 budget (new mayor) appear to reflect this change in the decision system. This should not be too surprising, however. The previous mayor in Pittsburgh resigned to become governor of Pennsylvania. The out-going mayor chose (with his party's approval) his replacement. The transition was smooth and the new mayor retained the retiring mayor's personal staff and administration. In our system of stable relationships and mutual expectations, we would expect the system characteristics to change only if there was a substantial change in the actors. With a change of only *one* actor (mayor), it is far more likely that the single actor will, through a process of socialization or learning, merge with the existing system, than change the system.

Our process models (one-period change and simulation) did not do quite as well at allocating under conditions of declining revenues (appropriations) as it did at allocating budgetary increases (see Figure VIII-3). Referring to the fit of naive model *A3* (constant-share-of-decrease) to the 1962 and 1963 budgets, it is apparent that budget cuts are not across-the-board cuts. By examining Figure VIII-4 and appendix, pp. 285-287, it is apparent that the deficit-elimination procedures contained in our process model account for budget reduction procedures better that *A3*. On the other hand, *A2*'s (constant-share-of-total-budget) naive predictions are nearly as accurate as those of our process models.

As was expected (see discussion on pp. 118-119), the values of R^2_c in years where appropriations (revenues) were nearly constant (1960 and 1963) or declining (1962) are near zero. The corresponding values of the Bayesian Induction and χ^2-Criteria did not rise, however, indicating the problem is with the goodness-of-fit measure and not necessarily with the model(s).

In summary, our one-period change and simulation models perform reasonably well on all goodness-of-fit measures. Given the short study period (six years) and the fluctuating revenue picture, the total change in the budget during the period was not great. Consequently, the naive model emphasizing stability—*A2* (constant-share-of-the-total)—proved to be a slightly better predictor. Naive models emphasizing change—*A1* (constant growth) and *A3* (constant share of the increase)—did not fare as well.

CLEVELAND GOODNESS-OF-FIT. The Cleveland models performed in much the same manner as their Pittsburgh counterparts. No shift in model fit with a change in city administration was noted. Again this would be expected. The man who had been mayor in Cleveland for a number of years resigned his position to accept a Cabinet post. The vacancy was filled from

FIGURE VIII-3

Pittsburgh Model-Selection and Goodness-of-Fit Measures

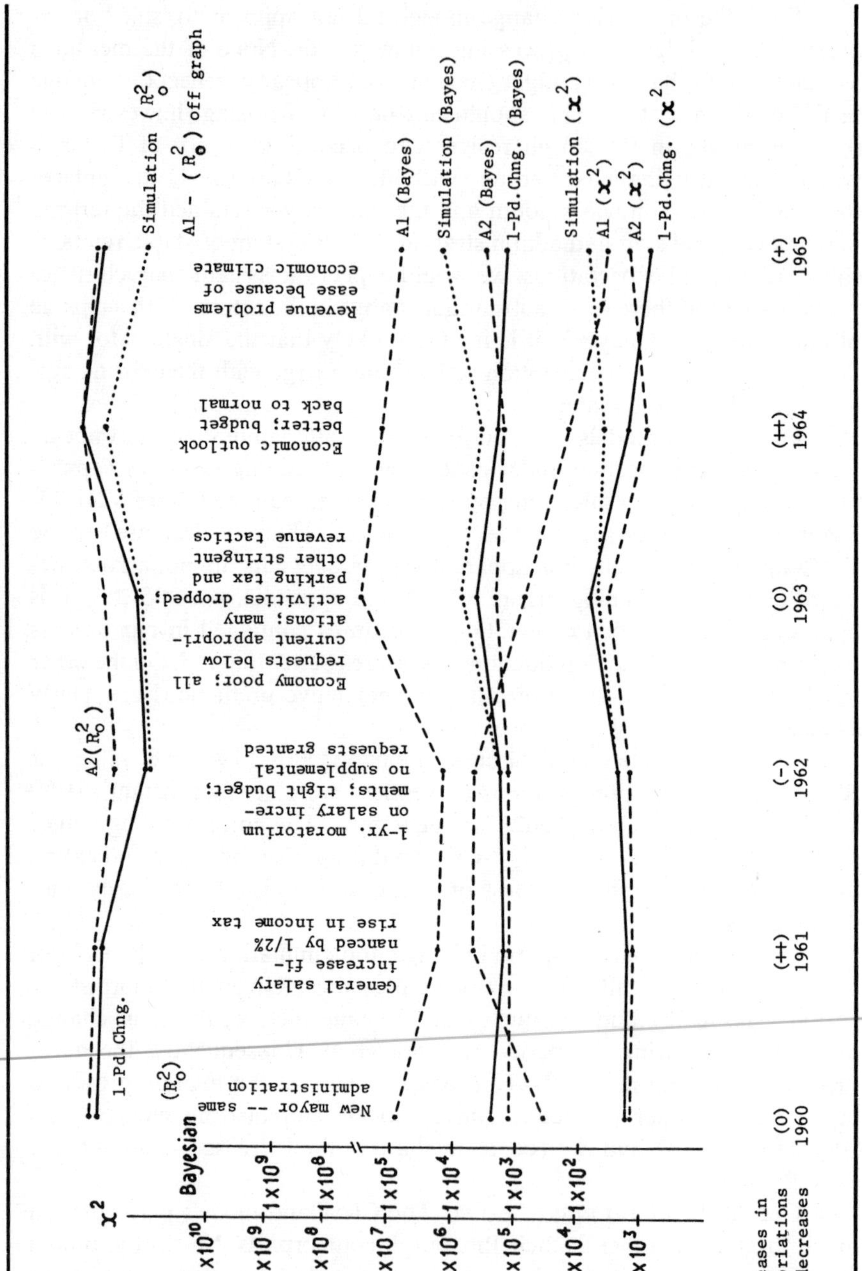

FIGURE VIII-4

Pittsburgh Goodness-of-Fit Measures
Portion of Variance 'Explained' by Model vs.
Assumption 'This Year's Equals Last Year's'

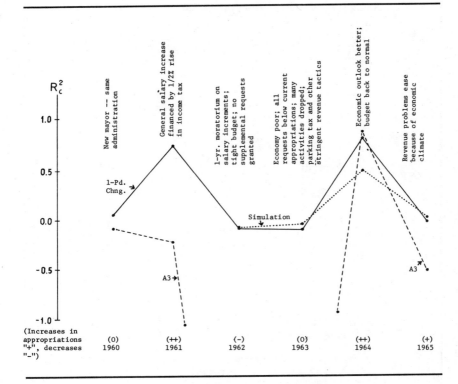

within the incumbent political party and, similar to the case in Pittsburgh, did not result in a change in the administration, only in the change of one member.

The Cleveland one-period change and simulation models appear to work equally well for revenue increases and declines (see Figures VIII-5 and VIII-6 and appendix, pp. 279-281), unlike the Pittsburgh models.

A major organization change in Cleveland city government in the study period shows up as a 'poor year' in four measures (Bayesian, χ^2, R^2_c, and R^2_o). More will be said about this policy shift in Chapter IX when model residuals are analyzed.

On the basis of predictability *only,* the one-period change model would be chosen over the naive models in nine of ten years using the Bayesian-Induction Criteria, half of the time using the χ^2-Criteria, in eight of ten years using R^2_o, and in seven of ten years using R^2_c.

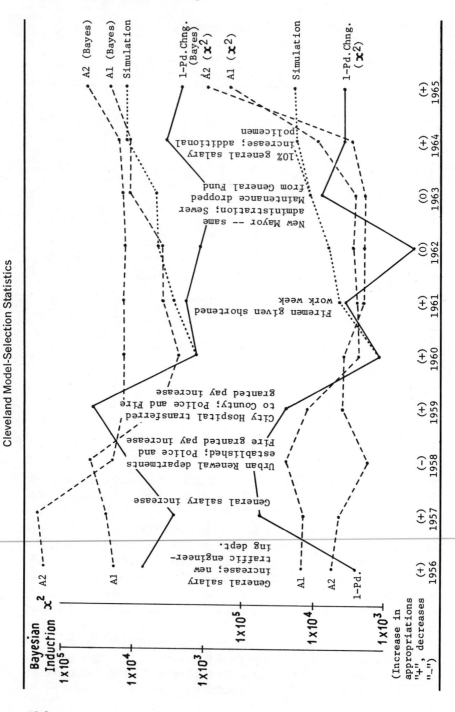

FIGURE VIII-5

Cleveland Model-Selection Statistics

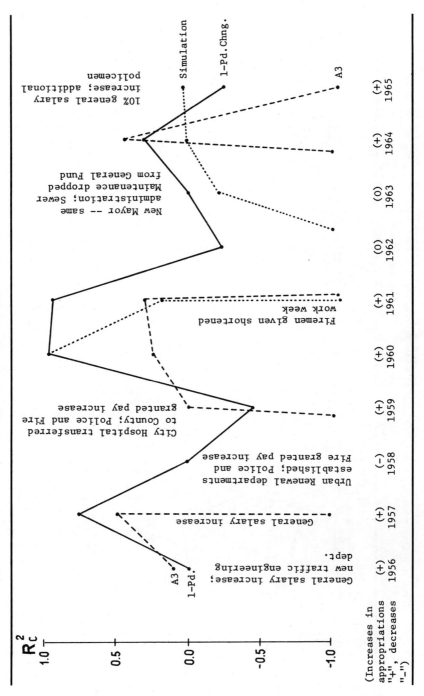

FIGURE VIII-6

Cleveland Goodness-of-Fit Measures

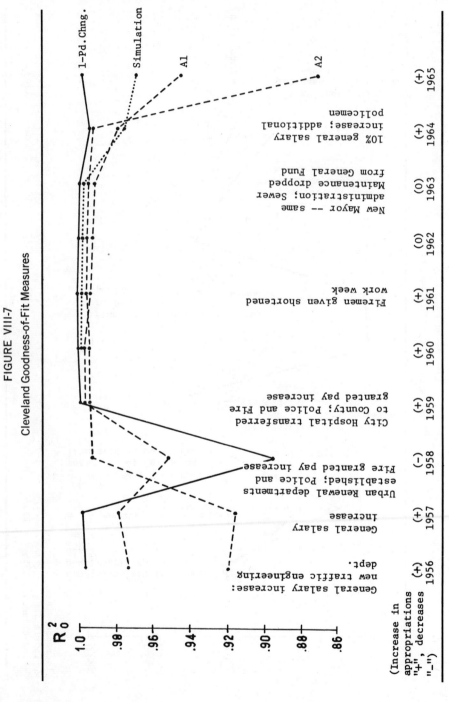

FIGURE VIII-7

Cleveland Goodness-of-Fit Measures

The Cleveland data, unlike Pittsburgh's, represent a much wider range of activities. While the study period in Pittsburgh exhibited a fluctuating revenue pattern, there was no substantial change in the budget *total* over the six years. During the ten-year study period in Cleveland, however, the total budget increased substantially. Consequently, Cleveland parameters and, hence, the Cleveland process models probably represent a better test of our theory than does Pittsburgh.

DETROIT GOODNESS-OF-FIT MEASURES. Before examining the model applications to Detroit in detail, there are some operating irregularities that will strongly influence the model fit that should be discussed.

1. *Welfare Payments*—In Detroit, both the state and city 'cooperate' on welfare payments, with each paying its share. The first portion of the seven-year study period in Detroit was dominated by the difficulties surrounding the state's share of the total. In 1957, the state unilaterally cut its share of payments from 50 per cent to 30 per cent. This caused a deficit of $6.8 million for the 1957-58 fiscal year,[22] and provided for a corresponding increase in the 1957-58 budget. Perhaps the most important outcome of this was that the 1957-58 deficit was refinanced, thus providing a precedent for deficit spending.

2. *Large Operating Deficits*—Partly due to the welfare problems above, and partly due to the economic downturn in the late 1950s resulting in inflated revenue estimates and faulty expenditure estimates (particularly on welfare needs), Detroit accumulated a general fund deficit of over $19,200,000. In addition, operating deficits in previous years had been partially financed through deferred payments to the tax-supported employees pension systems. Funds had been transferred from the pension funds to the general fund—illegally, according to a 1962 Circuit Court decision. At any rate, when a new administration took office in 1963, it was faced with a $35,000,000-plus deficit. "It was therefore necessary in the 1962-63 budget to add approximately $18,500,000 to previously underfinanced appropriations just to maintain the existing level of operations and further eliminate over-estimation of revenue in the sum of approximately $2,000,000."[23] In addition, old

[22] The city administration appeared committed to the existing schedule of welfare payments. Otherwise another response to the state-share reduction could have been to reduce *total* welfare payments proportional to the state's reduction—i.e., lower payments and blame the state government, not the city welfare department. The reduction in the state share from 50 per cent to 30 per cent was the product of an outstate, Republican legislature against the wishes of the state executive branch, controlled by more urban-minded Democrats.

[23] "Communications from the Mayor, April 9, 1963," Detroit Common Council Minutes, April 9, 1963, p. 787.

deficits had to be financed. The response was an income tax for the city.

3. *Capital Items Included in Operating Budget*—Until 1962-63, the Detroit operating or general fund budget included a series of large improvements or capital items. Subsequently, items of this nature were included in the capital budget. As a result of this account irregularity, many 'errors' are built into the model. Departments whose expenditures include a major capital item before 1962-63 will not only contribute greatly to the total model error for that year, but the department parameters, being biased, will generate faulty model estimates for other years.

The ideal way to handle the third problem would have been to eliminate large capital items from the raw Detroit budget data. Unfortunately, detailed appropriations records were not available for the earlier years in Detroit.

Insofar as the operating-deficit problem affects the planning or budgeting process indirectly most of the time, it does not constitute a problem of the magnitude presented by the capital items. Again, the effect enters *through* the revenue constraint and represents a kind of 'pad' on the revenues during the years the deficit is incurred, or, alternatively, represents an external source of funds. In the years the accumulated deficit must be eliminated (1962-63 and 1963-64) it represents a pressure to increase total revenues, and an automatic or accounting deduction from the revenue estimate. The direct effects of the problem of deficit financing were largely eliminated by our choice of revenue estimating procedures (see Chapter VI, pp. 95-96).

The welfare problem with the state can be *partially* eliminated by subtracting welfare appropriations from the revenue estimate and by not considering the welfare department in the budget. This will eliminate the direct effect of the welfare department, but will not remove the effects this externally-caused event had on the other department appropriations as mediated by the revenue constraint. Because this change did not require any recalculation of parameters, the Detroit one-period change and simulation models were run two ways: 1) with the welfare department—W, 2) without the welfare department—NW. In examining overall goodness-of-fit for Detroit, it appears, especially in the R^2_c and R^2_o statistics, that by removing the welfare estimates, we removed proportionately more variance from the actual appropriations than we did from the model errors. This causes R^2_c (see Figure VIII-10 and appendix, p. 282 and p. 284) and R^2_o (see Figure VIII-9 and appendix, p. 283 and p. 285) to be higher with welfare included than without. A glance at the χ^2 (see Figure VIII-8 and appendix, p. 282 and p. 284) and Bayesian-Induction Criteria (see Figure

FIGURE VIII-8

Detroit Model-Selection Statistics

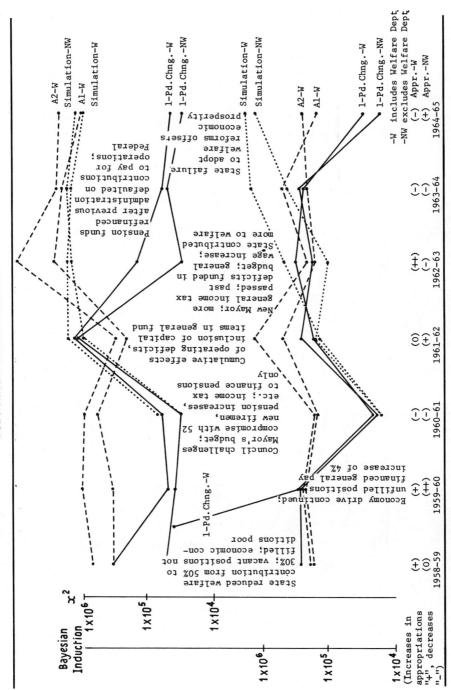

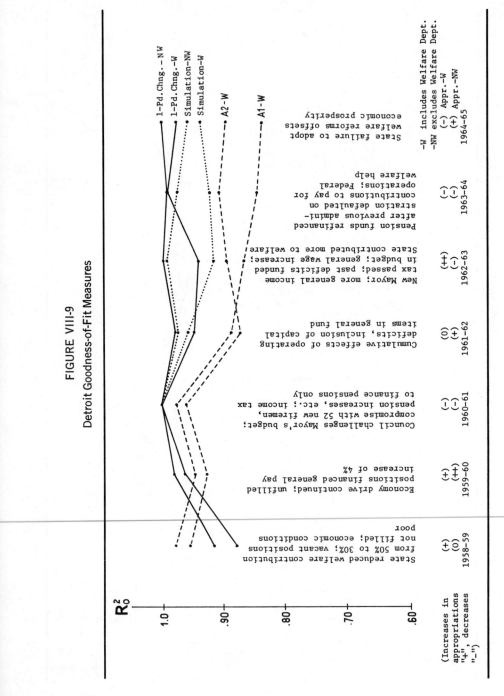

FIGURE VIII-9

Detroit Goodness-of-Fit Measures

FIGURE VIII-10

Detroit Goodness-of-Fit Measures

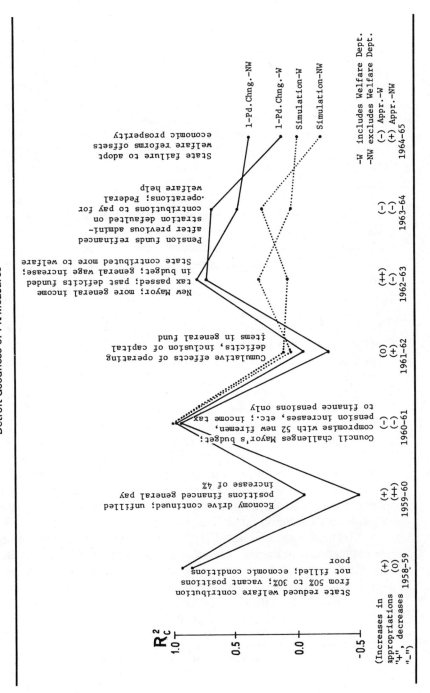

VIII-8, appendix, p. 281 and p. 283) reveals a significant *overall* improvement, however.

All of the goodness-of-fit measures seem to improve considerably at the end of the study period (1962-63 and after). Two events would seem to account for this. First, 1962-63 signals the start of the administration of a new mayor of Detroit. Contrary to the Pittsburgh and Cleveland administration changes described earlier, this change was a significant one. Not only the occupant of the mayor's office changed in this decisional coalition, but all of the key department heads and financial officers changed as well. Davis, Dempster, and Wildavsky found a similar break in model fit while examining the federal budgetary process in the change from the Truman to the Eisenhower administration.[24] A change in all the key actors in the decision system is bound to cause a significant shift in the system of interrelationships and mutual expectations characterizing the budgetary process. This shift really signals the existence of a new set of model parameters reflecting the cognitive maps and perceptions of the new participants. Unfortunately, we did not have enough data points to estimate two sets of parameters for Detroit, so this shift in real parameter values is compromised by the estimated parameters and reflected in a shift in goodness-of-fit. The other changes which improved goodness-of-fit measures after 1961-62 were also related to the new administration. They 'removed' capital items from the operating budget and eliminated the deficit-spending practice.

There does not appear to be any difference between goodness-of-fit in years of budget increase (surplus-elimination routines evoked) and budget decline (deficit-elimination procedures evoked).

Considering the problems presented by deficit spending, capital items in the operating budget, and state share of the welfare load, the Detroit models fit reasonably well. Although in many years an alternative naive model predicts as well or better, on the whole the process models (one-period change and simulation) rate much higher (see Figures VIII-8 and VIII-9, and appendix, pp. 281-285).

OVERALL GOODNESS-OF-FIT. We will conclude the discussion of the formal measures of the goodness-of-fit of our models to Cleveland, Detroit, and Pittsburgh, with the following topic: Summary goodness-of-fit measure —R^2_m (null hypothesis: individual account total for a particular year equals the mean over the study period).

Before interpreting the R^2_m goodness-of-fit measure in Table VIII-2,

---

[24] O. A. Davis, M. A. H. Dempster, and A. Wildavsky, "On the Process of Budgeting: An Empirical Study of Congressional Appropriation" in Gordon Tullock, ed., *Papers on Non-Market Decision Making* (Charlottesville, Va.: Thomas Jefferson Center for Political Economy, 1966).

we would do well to recall our previous discussion (see pp. 118-119). For a short study period or one in which revenues do not experience substantial changes, an R^2_m near zero may indicate a reasonably-good fit.

TABLE VIII-2

Overall Goodness-of-Fit Measure

$$R^2_m = 1.0 - \frac{\sum\limits_{t=1}^{nn} \sum\limits_{i=1}^{n} \sum\limits_{j=1}^{m_i} (AAPRO_{ij} - APPR2_{ij})^2}{\sum\limits_{t=1}^{nn} \sum\limits_{i=1}^{n} \sum\limits_{j=1}^{m_i} (AAPRO_{ij} - \overline{AAPRO_{ij}})^2}$$

Detroit (with Welfare Department)

One-Period Change 1958-59 to 1964-65	.1045
Simulation 1960-61 to 1964-65	−.3483
A1—constant growth	.2622
A2—constant share of total	.1069

Detroit (without Welfare Department)

One-Period Change 1958-59 to 1964-65	.0663
Simulation 1960-61 to 1964-65	−.6113

Cleveland

One-Period Change 1956-65	.9207
Simulation 1960-65	−1.527
A1—constant growth	.5311
A2—constant share of total	.2672

Pittsburgh

One-Period Change 1960-65	.4322
Simulation 1962-65	−.0256
A1—constant growth	.0000
A2—constant share of total	.6875

$APPR2_{ij}$ = model estimate, department i, account j

$AAPRO_{ij}$ = observed appropriations, department i, account j

$\overline{AAPRO_{ij}}$ = average appropriation during study period, department i, account j

nn = number of years in study period

m_i = number of accounts, department i

n = number of departments in city

As Table VIII-2 indicates, the one-period change process model explains more of the variance in budgetary decisions than does the null hypothesis that the amount budgeted to a given account in a given department equals the average over the study period for that account in that department ($R^2_m > 0$). The cumulative nature of errors in the simulation process models indicates that a study-period average is a better predictor ($R^2_m < 0$). The one-period change process model compares favorably with the naive, constant-growth *(A1)* and constant-share-of-the-total *(A2)* models.

The results of the ordinal comparisons put forth between the process models and various null hypotheses and naive models are far from clear. Although the process models win more than their share of the contests, a great deal of ambiguity in conclusions remains.

CONCLUSIONS: RELATIVE FIT OF PROCESS MODEL

Evidence obtained by regressing time series of budget decisions generated by the process model as a function of the actual series (see Table VIII-1) indicates that the process model in both its one-period change and simulation versions accurately reproduces budgetary decisions.

Ordinal comparisons between process models and alternative hypotheses indicate it is not always possible to distinguish between them. In many cases, the outcome of a comparison between models depends on the measure used, as can be easily seen in Table VIII-3. Does this mean that the naive models are just as good as the process models?

In addressing ourselves to this question, we wish to make two points:

1. The goodness-of-fit measures cited above represent a much stronger test for the process models than for the naive models.

2. One of our primary objectives has been to describe the budgetary decision process explicitly, in the form of a computer program. Our description is consistent with the budgetary data.

A computer simulation model contains a larger set of behavioral mechanisms, interconnected in non-obvious ways. Contrasted with the single-equation naive models, the process model represents a much stronger statement about the nature of the world. Parameter values estimated in the naive models *can* easily contain within them many of the decision mechanisms explicitly represented in the process models. As Holt demonstrates, the internal-consistency test implicit in measuring process model goodness-of-fit is a severe test:

> The first question to explore is how well the model fits known data. Usually the model is estimated from historical data and the use of the same set of data to test the model would appear somewhat questionable. However, two important points can be explored. First, if the model was estimated as a set of individual equations or alternatively as subsets of equations, then it may be a significant test to solve the equations as a simultaneous system. It is quite possible for the individual equations, or

TABLE VIII-3

Ordinal Comparisons Between Models

City	Criteria														
	Bayesian				χ^2				R^2_c			R^2_o			
	A1	A2	One Period	Simu-lation	A1	A2	One Period	Simu-lation	A3	One Period	Simu-lation	A1	A2	One Period	Simu-lation
Cleveland	0	1	9	(4)	0	6	4	(1)	3	6(1)	1(1)	1	1	8	(3)
Detroit—W	2	2	3	(2)	1	1	5	(4)	1	5(1)	1(4)	1	0	5(1)	1(4)
Detroit—NW	2	1	2(2)	2(2)	1	0	6	(3)	1	5(1)	1(4)	1	0	5(1)	1(4)
Pittsburgh*	0	5	1	0	0	5	1	0	1	4(1)	1(2)	0	6	0	0

Note: Numbers in cells represent number of years model had best comparative fit. Numbers in parentheses indicate years simulation model was second to one-period-change model and *vice versa.* Simulation model runs cover fewer years than the other models.

* In every comparison, *A2* and the *one-period change* model were *extremely* close. See Appendix D.

137

subsystems of equations, to fit reasonably well, but when all of the equations are solved jointly the errors may accumulate and a bad fit be obtained. Second, the parameter estimates usually are made on the basis of 'forecasting' one time period ahead. Since many applications of the model will require forecasts for a time horizon of several or even many time periods, it is important to test whether the model is capable of giving reasonably good forecasts over longer forecast spans. After the unknown endogenous variables for one time have been solved, time is advanced one time period and then the unknown endogenous variables for the following period are solved, and so on. As this process is repeated we would anticipate that the calculated values would gradually worsen. This is a severe test even when the model has the advantage of being tested against the data which was used in its estimation. Should the model fall down badly on either of these two tests, there is clear indication that further work is needed before any great confidence can be placed in the model.[25]

The process model performs well on both of Holt's tests. The accumulation of decision mechanisms and subsystems in the one-period change model does not result in a corresponding accumulation of errors, indicating the entire system is internally consistent as well as statistically explaining the data well (see Table VIII-1).

The process model when run as a simulation usually does worse than when updated annually (one-period change model). However, as can be seen in Table VIII-3, the number of times the simulation model finished second to the one-period change model again represents strong evidence for the validity of the process model.[26]

As Holt notes, these are strong tests—cumulative-consistency tests to which the naive models have not been subjected. In any event, the process models are consistent, *statistically,* with the data, even with greater opportunities for error.

In this rather complicated, *ad hoc,* and sometimes-confusing discussion of model validity, we should not lose sight of the primary objective of this research effort—to describe the *process* of municipal expenditure decision-making. There can be no doubt that the process models provide the more complete description of the decision process. Interview data and evidence presented in Chapter IX bear this out. Up to this point, our discussion has centered around *statistical* goodness-of-fit. The second mea-

---

[25] Charles C. Holt, "Validation and Application of Macroeconomic Models Using Computer Simulation," in J. S. Duesenberry, Gary Fromm, L. R. Klein, and Edwin Kuh, eds., *The Brookings Quarterly Econometric Model of the United States* (Chicago: Rand McNally & Company, 1965), p. 639.
[26] The naive models should have been run without annual up-dating of the data (as simulation models) to provide an additional comparison with the process models.

sure, similarity-of-*process,* is of importance here. In modeling most phenomena, model simplicity is highly valued. For most purposes, our naive models would be superior to the process models, *ceteris paribus, if the naive models represent a more compact way of describing the multiple mechanisms of the process models.* Stated differently, if the functional transformation in the naive model(s) is equivalent to the transformation of the process models, then the additional complexity of the process model would not be justified. As will be seen below, there is no functional equivalence.

To test for functional equivalence, we shall use naive model *A2,* constant-share-of-the-budget total, as the basis for comparison. *A2* was the only naive model that performed well on a statistical basis with any consistency and hence represents the severest test. Are there deviations in model predictions? Are the deviations systematic?

PROCESS MODEL AND CONSTANT-SHARE MODEL: TEST FOR FUNCTIONAL EQUIVALENCE. As we have seen, above, the constant-share, naive model *(A2)* predicted nearly as well as our process model. If we had to choose between the two each year, the results would be as shown in Table VIII-4. Although both predict well, investigating those cases where the predictions of the two models do not agree may prove informative. The constant-share model is illustrated in Figure VIII-11.[27]

TABLE VIII-4

Choice* Between One-Period Change: Process Model and A2

	No. of Years Model Chosen (x^2-Criteria)		No. of Years Model Chosen (Bayesian-Induction Criteria)	
	A2	Process	A2	Process
Cleveland	6	4	1	9
Detroit—W	2	5	3	4
Detroit—NW	1	6	3	4
Pittsburgh	5	1	5	1

* See Appendix D.

A question of interest to us concerns the reasons for deviations from the constant-share-of-total-budget line (slope, c_{ij}) as the revenue con-

[27] A2: $APPR2_{ij} = c_{ij}(TBUD2)$. See p. 119.

FIGURE VIII-11
Constant-Share-of-Resources (A2)
$$APPR2_{ij} = C_{ij} \,(TBUD2)$$

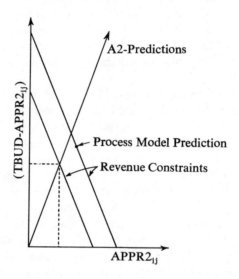

straint shifts. We shall use the Detroit[28] process and *A2* models (including the welfare department) in a rough analysis of differences in the *models'* predictions. What causes the process model to drift off the constant-share line? Does the process model describe a random walk about this line, or are there explainable and systematic deviations? The characteristics of budget-share-changes over time, for a given account category in particular departments, is covered in detail in Chapter X. At present we shall limit our discussion to major differences in model predictions. The five largest (absolute) differences were identified for each year in the study period.

Of the thirty-five model differences so identified, fifteen are attributable to the Equipment accounts in Detroit. The *A2* model yields an *average* share-of-the-budget figure. As we noted above, the Equipment account included capital items until 1962-63. This, of course, would lead to low estimates for *A2* in the early years of the study and unusually high estimates for Equipment after capital items had been dropped from the operat-

---

[28] Detroit was chosen partly because the fit of its process model, in general, is not as good as in the other cities, partly because it has complete department request data, partly because of its shift in administrations, and partly because of its fluctuating revenue experience during the study period.

ing budget. The historically-dependent process model, on the other hand, would pick up this shift in accounting practice after one year [see item 3 in Figure V-1b (DEPT.), item 4 in Figure VI-1b (MAYORS) and item 9 in Figure VII-1b (COUNCIL)]. This leads to the more general observation that *A2* should do poorly in account categories where, due to external factors, there are large shifts in budget amounts. Most of the remaining differences (non-Equipment) between *A2* and process-model predictions relate to unprogrammed budget decisions and policy shifts (to be examined in detail in Chapter IX).

Several items are *suggested* by the data in Table VIII-5 concerning the relationships of the naive model and our process model. For instance, in those cases where the differences in prediction are *large* (i.e., included in Table VIII-5), the process model is almost always the better predictor. Why? As was indicated previously, the process model is able to pick up policy shifts one year after they occur, at the latest. *A2* reacts to changes in the total budget only.

TABLE VIII-5

Differences Between A2 and Process Model Predictions

Department	Affected Account	[A2 Prediction] − [Process Model Prediction]	Model Nearest to Observed Appropriations
1958–59			
Civic Center	Equipment	− $7,332,000	*A2*
Recorders Court —Criminal	Equipment	− $6,397,000	*A2*
Police	Salaries	− $1,098,000	*A2*
Public Works —Streets	Salaries	+ $4,642,000	Process
Welfare	Expenses	+ $1,218,000	*A2*
1959–60			
Welfare	Expenses	+ $8,232,000	Both
Civic Center	Equipment	− $5,985,000	Process
Health Department —Kiefer Hospital	Salaries and Expenses	− $1,029,000	Process
Parks and Recreation	Equipment	+ $1,455,000	*A2*
Public Works— Sewers	Equipment	+ $951,700	Process

141

1960–61

Police	Salaries	− $2,224,000	Process
Public Works— Sanitation	Salaries	− $1,539,000	Process
Welfare	Expenses	+ $1,922,000	Process
Civic Center	Equipment	+ $2,698,000	Both
Public Works— Streets	Salaries	+ $5,235,000	Process

1961–62

Public Works— Streets	Salaries	+ $6,072,000	Process
Civic Center	Equipment	+ $1,530,000	Process
Welfare	Expenses	+ $1,453,000	Process
Lighting	Equipment	+ $1,150,000	Process
Public Works— Sewers	Equipment	+ $1,025,000	Process

1962–63

Public Works— Streets	Salaries and Expenses	+ $9,330,000	Process
Civic Center	Equipment	+ $1,637,000	Process
Lighting	Equipment	+ $1,505,000	Process
Public Works— Sewers	Equipment	+ $1,230,000	Process
Parks and Recreation	Equipment	+ $1,058,000	Process

1963–64

Public Works— Streets	Salaries	+ $1,217,000	Process
Welfare	Expenses	− $7,946,000	Process
Police	Salaries	+ $3,093,000	Process
Lighting	Equipment, Others	+ $2,895,000	Process
Public Works— Sanitation	Salaries	+ $2,599,000	Process

1964–65

Public Works— Streets	All	+ $1,634,000	A2
Public Works— Sewers	All	+ $3,310,000	Process
Welfare	Expenses	− $4,508,000	A2
Civic Center	Equipment	+ $2,096,000	Process
Public Works— Sanitation	Salaries	+ $2,092,000	Process

A second line of reasoning is also suggested. *A2* obviously performs reasonably well for most departments and accounts, most of the time (see Table VIII-4). When it misses, however, it appears to miss by a large amount (see Table VIII-5). *Perhaps* the better performance of our process model for these cases indicates the presence of constraints on appropriations decisions. If this is true, the above analysis indicates that our process model has succeeded in specifying at least some of these constraints.

A third and related thought is suggested by Table VIII-5. We will see that, in most instances, the large *differences* in model predictions correspond very closely to the large deviations when our process model is compared with observed budgetary decisions. (See Chapter IX, "Detroit Model Residuals," pp. 160-162). This suggests that certain irregularities are found in the budgetary process that neither the process model nor the naive models can predict well. Table VIII-5 indicates that the process model does a much better job of handling these irregularities, however. Perhaps one key reason is that through granting supplemental requests and through the trend terms in the process model, departments can experience very *different* rates of growth over time, taking advantage of revenue opportunities. An analysis of model residuals in Chapter IX indicates that the budgetary process is indeed opportunistic. To the extent that the process model captures some of this, it will behave differently from the naive models. Long-run sensitivity analysis of the model, in Chapter X, also demonstrates the ability of the process model to bring about significant reallocations of resources, unlike *A2*.

No relationship was observed between the relative predictive powers of the *A2* and process models and the magnitude or direction of revenue change or changes in administration.

Although some naive models also predicted well, few would argue that they "adequately reproduce" the decision system.[29] An analysis of differences between one naive model and a process model suggests that the two are not functional equivalents. Although there are some unavoidable statistical problems, all goodness-of-fit measures used indicate that our process model is at least consistent with the intermediate and final outputs of the real decision system.

Summary—Goodness-of-fit

The central problem inherent in all simulation processes, and in all model building as well, is that of an adequate reproduction of the real system.[30]

---

[29] Cyert and March, *op. cit.*, p. 148, make a similar point.
[30] Richard E. Dawson, "Simulation in the Social Sciences," in H. E. Guetzkow, ed., *Simulation in Social Science: Readings* (Englewood Cliffs, N.J.: Prentice-Hall, Inc., 1962), p. 13.

We have seen that our model generates the same kinds of data that the real system generates. In order to 'adequately reproduce' the real system, the model must also arrive at its appropriations decisions in the same manner as the system. The real test of our model is not how well it 'predicts' (although this is important), but how well it 'describes.' Referring to Figure VIII-1, p. 113, we can ask how well the DEPT. and MAYORS submodels performed in generating their decisions. The same goodness-of-fit measures were calculated for the DEPT. and MAYORS submodel outputs as were for the COUNCIL model.

In general, the MAYORS submodel's output fit the observed mayor's budget recommendations as well or better than the COUNCIL outputs discussed previously. This was not the case with the DEPT. submodels, however. The measures of fit were significantly worse than with MAYOR or COUNCIL outputs. For the most part a lack of time-series data for the DEPT. model dictated this.

Another indication of how well the model 'describes' concerns the roles of the submodels discussed in Chapters V, VI, and VII. The DEPT. model, with the department head as an advocate, should, if it corresponds to our role description, result in a sum-of-department-requests higher than the mayor's budget. In all three cities for all years in the study period (twenty-three observations), the model-estimated DEPT. budget exceeds the mayor's budget by a substantial amount (as did observed requests). In addition the *total* of DEPT. budgets was close to the observed *totals*. The MAYORS submodel in *all* cases produced the budget-trimming behavior 'expected' by the DEPT. submodel and observed in practice. As was expected, final appropriations produced by the COUNCIL submodel were not substantially different from the outputs of the MAYORS model. Briefly, all submodels in all cities exhibited the 'proper' role behavior.

The measures of similarity-of-process, as opposed to similarity-of-outcomes, have been crude and relatively weak. The evidence presented in Chapter IX will provide a much stronger test of *process* explanation.

> If the program makes the same analysis as the humans, *notices the same traps,* then we will infer, and properly, that down to some level of detail the program provides an explanation of the human processes.[31]

In attempting to detect direct impacts of events in the external environment on budgetary decisions, process model residuals were analyzed (Chapter IX). In attempting to associate causes with model residuals, a most important discovery was made. For nearly every budget item where the process model erred badly, the reason for the error was mentioned explicitly in the mayor's annual budget message to the city council. Very few

[31] Newell and Simon, *op. cit.*, p. 15.

budget items are mentioned in the text of the mayor's message so the correlation of model errors to explicit mention in the budget message cannot be attributed to chance. *It appears as if the process model is implicitly identifying the same set of 'unusual' cases (budget items) and noticing the same traps as is the mayor.* This, more than any other single measure, represents impressive evidence that the process model adequately describes the budgetary decision *process.*

TECHNICAL APPENDIX

Identification Problem

While we have shown our model to be a reasonably good predictor of budgetary behavior, this *may* be due to the large number of parameters we have estimated. The *order* conditions for identifiability ". . . means that the number of predetermined variables excluded from the relation must be at

TABLE VIII-6

Identification Statistics

	Cleveland	Detroit *(with welfare)*	Pittsburgh
*Observations**			
1. Department Requests	620	1204	231
2. Mayor's Budget Recommendations	1240	1204	1386
3. Final Appropriations	1240	1204	1386
Total Observations	3100	3612	2997
Less: *Parameters Estimated*			
1. DEPT. Submodel	120	516	18
2. MAYORS Submodel	346	344	687
3. COUNCIL Submodel	—	513	693
	466	913	1398
Net 'degrees of freedom':	2634	2699	1599
(If we include expenditure data used, as)			
Expenditure Observations	1240	1204	1386
Total 'degrees of freedom' including Expenditures data	3874	3903	2985

* Equal to: [(Administrative units) × (Account categories) × (Years of data)]

least as great as the number of endogenous variables included, less one."[32] For a single-equation regression model, the above indicates that one must have more data points than unknowns (regression coefficients). Little is known about parameter estimation for simulation models and other non-linear model structures. We can, however, look at some crude statistics to get an *idea* of the magnitude of any identification problem we might have. Our crude measure consists of the difference between total observations (decisions) and the number of parameters estimated from these.

As Table VIII-6 indicates, while the system is not 'under-identified,' the actual parameter values calculated suffer from a lack of data. Drawing an analogy, Pittsburgh parameter calculations are similar to calculating an average from two observations, in Detroit, from about three observations, and in Cleveland, from five. Clearly, viewed in this light, analyzing individual parameters in detail would appear to be of little value. The naive models suffer from similar afflictions.

Modified-R^2 Statistics

For the moment, let us assume that we are attempting to measure the ability of our process model to estimate final appropriations for each account category in each department within a city, for a given year. Let:

$APPR2_{ij}$ = model estimates of appropriations

$AAPRO_{ij}$ = observed (actual) appropriations

where

i = department

j = account category,

m_i = number of account categories in department i

n = total departments in the city.

In addition, let:

$\overline{AAPRO}$ = average of observed appropriations (alternative hypothesis). A direct elaboration of the R^2 measure would be:

$$R^2_0 = \frac{\sum_{i=1}^{n} \sum_{j=1}^{m_i} (AAPRO_{ij} - APPR2_{ij})^2}{\sum_{i=1}^{n} \sum_{j=1}^{m_i} (AAPRO_{ij} - \overline{AAPRO})^2}$$

Is this measure appropriate for our purposes? It depends on the precise definition of $\overline{AAPRO}$. As written, it is defined as:

$$\overline{AAPRO} = \frac{\sum_{i=1}^{n} \sum_{j=1}^{m_i} (AAPRO_{ij})}{\sum_{i=1}^{n} m_i}$$

[32] Johnston, *op. cit.*, pp. 250-251.

Our process model, hence, would be compared with the alternative hypothesis: The appropriation for a given account category in a given department is equal to the mean of appropriations over *all* departments and *all* accounts. Almost any model of appropriations would fare well under these conditions. (R^2_0 was calculated to demonstrate this fact.) What is needed, if we are to use an R^2-type of measure, is a more reasonable alternative hypothesis. Two come to mind:

1. Appropriations for a given account category in a given department equal the mean appropriations for the *same* account category in the *same* department during the study period.

   R^2 *about the department and account mean:*

$$1.0 - \frac{\sum\limits_{i=1}^{n} \sum\limits_{j=1}^{m_1} (AAPRO_{ij} - APPR2_{ij})^2}{\sum\limits_{i=1}^{n} \sum\limits_{j=1}^{m_1} (AAPRO_{ij} - \overline{AAPRO_{ij}})^2}$$

   if we are speaking of a measure for a single year, where $\overline{AAPRO_{ij}}$ = mean level of actual appropriations, department i, account j, over the study period. For the entire study period, the appropriate measure would be

$$R^2_m = 1.0 - \frac{\sum\limits_{t=1}^{yrs.} \sum\limits_{i=1}^{n} \sum\limits_{j=1}^{m_1} (AAPRO_{ij} - APPR2_{ij})^2}{\sum\limits_{t=1}^{yrs.} \sum\limits_{i=1}^{n} \sum\limits_{j=1}^{m_1} (AAPRO_{ij} - \overline{AAPRO_{ij}})^2}$$

2. Appropriations for a given account category in a given department equal the appropriations for the *same* account category and department for the previous year.

   R^2 *about current appropriations:*

$$R^2_c = 1.0 - \frac{\sum\limits_{i=1}^{n} \sum\limits_{j=1}^{m_1} (AAPRO_{ij} - APPR2_{ij})^2}{\sum\limits_{i=1}^{n} \sum\limits_{j=1}^{m_1} (AAPRO_{ij} - APPR1_{ij})^2}$$

   for a single year, where

   $APPR1_{ij}$ = current appropriations, department i, account j.

Two characteristics of our modified-R^2 measures, R^2_m and R^2_c, should be noted:

a. Unlike the R^2 statistic of regression analysis, there is *no* guarantee that $0.0 \leq R^2_c, R^2_m \leq 1.0$ holds. Bounds on the regression-R^2 statistic are inherent in the least-squares estimation procedure used in regression analysis. Our estimation procedure has no such guarantee.

b. Because of the relatively short durations of our study periods, the 'alternative hypotheses' inherent in the R^2_m and R^2_c statistics are likely to be very good *predictors* in their own right. In fact, we have argued throughout that stability and organizational inertia are key features of the problem-solving process. Consequently, *any* positive values for R^2_m and R^2_c might be regarded as a reasonable test of the *predictive* ability of our resource allocation model.

We are suggesting that because of (a) and (b), the values of R^2_c and R^2_m should be evaluated quite differently than the usual R^2 of regression analysis. Values close to zero may merely indicate that both the alternative hypotheses and the model do an excellent job of predicting appropriations. In the short run, the following alternative hypotheses may prove to be reasonably good *predictors* of appropriations.

1. R^2_m: $APPR2_{ij} = \overline{AAPRO}_{ij}$ (next-year's appropriations equals the average over the study period), or

2. R^2_c: $APPR2_{ij} = APPR1_{ij}$ (next-year's appropriations equals current appropriations).

They tell us little about the process and procedures leading to these decisions, however.

Another undesirable aspect of the measures outlined above (R^2_m and R^2_c) concerns the characteristics of these statistics in years where the revenue constraint is very tight and the 'line is held' on appropriations. In cases where a small change occurs in the denominator, any random errors occurring in our model (and, hence, appearing in the numerator) are amplified unduly. This phenomenon is easily observed by analyzing an extreme case where every item in the new budget is identical to current appropriations (or near the average for the period). This would make the denominator nearly zero and if the model produced any errors at all, the value of the statistic would approach a minus infinity. In summary, in those years where the number of budget cases are small, the R^2_m and R^2_c goodness-of-fit measures have the undesirable property of 'falsely' amplifying model errors.

In spite of these difficulties, however, the measures R^2_m and R^2_c are on the whole reasonable and should, *properly interpreted,* shed a good deal of light on our model's predictive power.

Bayesian Induction and χ^2 Criteria

We can operationalize the criteria cited on page 121 by excluding rare events from our calculations, where rare events are defined as accounts whose expected (for the χ^2-Criteria) or observed (for the Bayesian-Induction Criteria) appropriations are less than \$20. Elimination of rare events introduces another problem—depending on the model results, we can have different numbers of departments and accounts (categories) for different models. Summing over different events makes the measures for the models incomparable again. To circumvent this problem, we are introducing a second modification in the criteria. To make the criteria comparable, the statistic totals will be divided by the number of categories (departments and accounts) contributing to the sum. This average χ^2 or Bayesian-Induction total will be used as the relevant criteria:[33]

1. χ^2-Criteria:

$$\text{Min}\left[\frac{\sum\limits_{i=1}^{n}\sum\limits_{j=1}^{m_i}\dfrac{(\text{AAPRO}_{ij}-\text{APPR2}_{ij})^2}{\text{APPR2}_{ij}}}{\sum\limits_{i=1}^{n}m_i}\right]$$

for $\text{APPR2}_{ij} \geqq \$20.$

2. Bayesian-Induction Criteria:

$$\text{Min}\left[\frac{\sum\limits_{i=1}^{n}\sum\limits_{j=1}^{m_i}\dfrac{(\text{AAPRO}_{ij}-\text{APPR2}_{ij})^2}{\text{AAPRO}_{ij}}}{\sum\limits_{i=1}^{n}m_i}\right]$$

for $\text{AAPRO}_{ij} \geqq \$20.$

where $m_i =$ number of accounts in department i where
χ^2-Criteria: $\text{APPR2}_{ij} \geqq \$20.$
Bayesian Criteria: $\text{AAPRO}_{ij} \geqq \$20.$

[33] This adjustment serves much the same function as the 'degrees-of-freedom' adjustment in the formal χ^2 test. L. H. C. Tippett, *The Methods of Statistics* (New York: John Wiley & Sons, Inc., 1952), pp. 128-129.

CHAPTER IX

Unprogrammed Decisions and Policy Shifts

IF THE MODEL actually illustrates the decision process, we would expect that those decisions the process model identifies as *different* or *special* (i.e., those it cannot predict well) will correspond closely to those the real system perceives as different or special. Hence we would expect explanations of 'unusual decisions' to appear in official budget documents. We now turn to an analysis of model residuals in an attempt to further investigate the descriptive power of the model (Are certain decisions 'unusual' for both the model and the real system?) and to discover model limitations and suggest modifications or extensions.

In general, there are two kinds of budgetary change:[1]

1. Those changes resulting from the continuation and elaboration of existing policies, and
2. Those changes resulting from shifts in municipal policies.

Our model is clearly one describing changes of the first kind. It is a model of the standard procedures which result in particular forms of marginal adjustments in resource allocation from year to year. The model, as it stands, assumes the relevant decision-makers' cognitive maps of the process are stable over time (the same standard accounts and administrative units exist from year to year). It assumes that perceptions[2] of departments and administrative units by the participants are relatively stable over time (the model parameters are constants).

The model does not describe changes of the second kind—significant shifts in municipal policies. The model, however, by filtering out (i.e., pre-

---

[1] By change, we mean change in appropriations levels from one year to the next: $(APPR2_{ij} - APPR1_{ij})$.

[2] Including expectations.

dicting or explaining, in the statistical sense) incremental changes, draws attention to those items (unexplained) in the budget that are *not* marginal adjustments or elaborations of previous policies. As we have seen, the model explains most resource-allocation decisions made by municipal government—but not all.

This section will focus on the unexplained changes in resource allocation. Unexplained significant changes can be characterized in, roughly, three ways:

1. Incremental changes whose cumulative effect results in a non-incremental change or policy shift,
2. Non-incremental policy shifts,[3]
3. Significant changes in policy, not reflected in the budget.

A little reflection on the above indicates that not all large changes are changes resulting from shifts in municipal policies, and not all small changes are changes resulting from the continuation and elaboration of existing policies. For example, a significant policy shift may result from the decision to handle the city's welfare load through the welfare department, rather than have the program administered by the county or the state for a fee. The total budget cost may be nearly the same, so this significant change may never be reflected in the operating budget. On the other hand, suppose the city decides to construct an office building to house a number of departments, rather than rent office space. Once the building has been completed, several years after the initial decision, a large change is noted in the budget—a change our formal model is not equipped to handle. This change, representing an increase in personnel and building maintenance expenses and large decreases in rental expenses for the departments affected does not represent a significant shift in policy. It is merely an elaboration of a long-existing policy. The original decision to build represents a significant policy shift, however, and anticipated operating budget changes may or may not have been an important part of this capital decision. Our point is that for purposes of analyzing the 1966 operating budgetary process, the items resulting from previous capital decisions represent automatic changes in appropriations.

INVISIBLE ORGANIZATIONAL CHANGES

Before analyzing model residuals, we should examine the third major class of significant changes: significant changes in policy, not reflected in

[3] The use of the term 'innovation' has been consciously avoided in this section because of lack of a generally agreed upon operational definition of the concept. Rather, 'policy shift' will be our theoretical construct. An allocation decision represents a policy shift when either through cumulative effects of small changes or immediate effects, it brings about a significant reallocation of resources between account categories.

the budget. Naturally, because of the lack of 'hard' data, we have less to say about this class of changes than the others. That is not to say that this class of changes is either small or unimportant, however. Those policy shifts not reflected in the budget *might* be the *most significant* in terms of activities actually engaged in by municipal agencies and departments. Two important types of significant policy shifts that do not appear in the budget will be discussed: (1) Non-general fund expenditures administered by a municipal department that increase the department's effective budget ceiling and (2) Policies that alter efficiencies within an administrative unit, enabling the unit to engage in more (or less) activities and provide more services within the same budget ceiling.

Increases in Effective Budget Ceiling

Within the existing budget framework in our three cities, the revenue or balanced-budget constraint practically guarantees no dramatic increases in general fund appropriations for any department or agency. If municipal revenues were, in fact, the only source of funds for a municipality, the outlook for urban areas would be a dismal one, to say the least. However, there are other methods of funding. For instance, city planning and urban renewal functions have access to many kinds of federal monies as well as private foundation grants. In their 1965 budget estimate, the Pittsburgh City Planning Department's *total* budget (general fund appropriations plus outside sources) contained the following sources of funds:

1. Tax-based or general funds
2. Municipal bonds
3. Private foundations and public corporations[4]
4. Federal Community Renewal Program funds
5. Federal '701 Program' funds

An idea of the relative magnitudes of these items can be obtained by looking at the department's 1964 estimated revenues:

1. Tax Funds	$379,674
2. Bonds	95,378
3. CRP Funds	318,223
4. Other	7,247
Total	$800,522

Less than half of Pittsburgh's City Planning Department operations were financed through the general fund. The municipal operating budget (and our model) is clearly a very misleading document for some municipal ac-

---

[4] Homewood-Brushton Fund, and Regional Industrial Development Corporation—both of which are financed primarily with private foundation and industrial support such as T. Mellon and Sons and The Ford Foundation.

tivities. This situation is rare in municipal government, however, and can probably be attributed to a very enterprising and imaginative department head.[5] The situation illustrates a point. City operating budgets *do not always* reflect either the level or kind of activity carried on in a municipal agency.

With the influx of federal anti-poverty programs, etc., outside funding of municipal agencies should become increasingly important. The mere presence of outside sources of funds should (and does, as we shall see) encourage highly-motivated agency heads to expand their search routine to include variables and funds outside the control of the municipal government.

To the extent that outside resources become available to agency heads, our DEPT. model should be modified to include this, and 'outside funds' should be included in our MAYORS model (probably as a simple addition to total agency appropriations, unless the increase in outside funds is used to free regular department funds for reallocation to other agencies).

INCREASES IN AVAILABLE REVENUE. Another common way of securing funds from outside sources is for a municipality to persuade another governmental unit to share in the cost of some of the city's activities or to take them over completely.

Cleveland persuaded the county to take over the city hospital, Cleveland Boys' School, and the Cleveland Girls' School in 1958, freeing appropriations for other general fund expenditures.

Much of the unexplained portion of Detroit budgets revolves around Detroit's long feud with the state of Michigan over the proper share of expenses to be borne by the state in certain kinds of welfare cases. In recent years, state contributions have fluctuated from 20 per cent to 50 per cent of the total. As a result of the city's lobbying, the current contribution is 50 per cent—freeing several million dollars for other uses.

The city of Pittsburgh is engaged in a somewhat similar attempt to obtain additional revenues. Both the city and the board of education tax the property within the city. The mayor and his administration wants to keep property taxes constant to keep business firms within the city. Under these conditions, if Pittsburgh is to raise its real estate tax rate, the board of education would have to lower its rate. The city has been trying (with the knowledge and cooperation of the board of education) to persuade the state to increase appropriations to the Pittsburgh School District. Presumably, if the increase is large enough, this will permit the board of education to lower its real estate taxes. The city would then pick up the board of education reduction so that the millage total would remain unchanged.

[5] Calvin H. Hamilton, now director of city planning for the city of Los Angeles, California.

(One mill would yield approximately $700,000 additional revenue for the city.) So far, they have not succeeded.

INCREASES IN AGENCY EFFICIENCY. One way for an agency head to increase resources is to increase agency efficiency. The increase in efficiency would enable him to take on new programs and activities while still operating within the old budget ceiling. Detroit has, in effect, institutionalized this particular kind of municipal change to a degree that warrants special attention.

DETROIT'S BUDGET BUREAU—EFFICIENCY EXPERTS. The Budget Bureau in the city of Detroit is a major operating function. Using a system of budget examiners permanently assigned to a fixed set of departments, the budgeting operation literally becomes a year-round process at all levels of city government.

> The budget examiners are continually in contact with the operating departments. They attend commission and other department meetings. All departmental purchase requisitions have to be approved as to necessity by the budget examiner . . .
>
> Between budget periods, the budget examiner makes studies of departmental operating efficiency, organization, and activity.
>
> . . . During November and December, the departments prepare their budget requests and fill in the request columns on these forms. The budget examiner is in constant consultation with departments during this period.
>
> Since he is in constant contact with the department during the year, the examiner is well acquainted with departmental problems. Usually he knows well in advance about major requests, and therefore has a portion of his analysis completed before the requests come to the Budget Bureau.
>
> After completing his analysis, the examiner prepares for the Budget Director a summary of the requests, his recommendations, and a list of items upon which he could not reach an agreement with the department.[6]

If, in fact, budget examiners perform these functions in the city of Detroit, the budget examiner for a department is nearly equivalent to having a full-time efficiency expert or operations analyst on the department's staff.

Assuming the budget examiner exerts a reasonable amount of influence in departmental affairs, his presence must help to increase departmental efficiency.[7] This being so, the cumulative effects of repeated and

[6] Budget Bureau, city of Detroit, *Budget Organization and Operation in Detroit,* mimeo, p. 2-3.
[7] Others have dealt with the measurement of efficiency in public agencies with little observed success, so we shall ignore the question of the degree to which budget examiners increase efficiency. Our contention is that search for more efficient methods of operation is at least partially successful.

continuous attacks on efficiency problems, by a somewhat more detached observer than department personnel, should be considerable. Most observers familiar with municipal government in all three cities would agree that Detroit, overall, is considerably advanced in most areas of operation. The degree to which this is due to institutionalized efficiency or the considerably higher wage rates for civil servants in Detroit is not clear. At any rate, we shall have more to say about normative considerations in Chapter XIII.

One additional comment on the Detroit budget examiner system should be made. Note that most of the examiner's activity, influence, etc., is carried on *before* the department's budget request is submitted. The reader familiar with Detroit municipal government will most certainly wonder why there has been little mention of the Budget Bureau in regard to Detroit when it plays such a key role in the process. The reason should be apparent. The Budget Bureau functions primarily through its system of budget examiners. The battles between the Budget Bureau and the department head have usually been fought and settled *before* the department's budget request is submitted. The major role of the Budget Bureau is, then, embedded in the DEPT. submodel.[8]

We now turn to those policy shifts, significant changes, etc., that *are* reflected in the municipal operating budget.

VISIBLE ORGANIZATIONAL CHANGES

Our model is clearly one of incremental changes where current trends, perceptions, needs, policies, etc., are elaborated so as to arrive at future allocation decisions. Model deviations, therefore, ought to represent the

---

[8] The DEPT. submodel for the city of Detroit is surely open to criticism because of this. Ideally, two submodels should take the place of DEPT.:

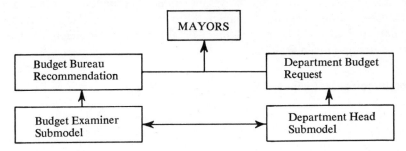

The primary reason this was not done was because the budget examiner–department head coalition could be perceived as one decision system, which in turn yielded reasonable statistical fits for DEPT. submodel in Detroit.

unusual or unprogrammed part of decisions and those items with large deviations should highlight major, unprogrammed decisions—hopefully those decisions representing policy shifts.

Incremental Change—Cumulative Nature

We are also aware of the fact that incremental changes, over time, can turn out to be major policy shifts. One example of this concerns the war-time decision of the city of Detroit to attempt to keep municipal salaries as competitive as possible with industrial salaries—the so-called *prevailing wage* rate policy.

In 1942-43, this policy represented an incremental change (needed to keep municipal positions filled in the face of war time demands for labor), as the following account indicates:

> July 1, 1941—Prevailing rate employees generally were granted an increase of 10 cents per hour.
> July 1, 1942—Salary employees were granted an increase of 10% with a maximum of $300. This was later supplemented by an additional 4.54% with a maximum of $150 as of March 8, 1943 to bring the total increase up to 15% or the so-called 'Little Steel Formula.' Prevailing rates were increased on a sliding scale of from 5 cents to 7 cents per hour.[9]

In the early 1940s, this was clearly an incremental change (in terms of the *immediate* impact on salaries for Detroit employees). An indication of the cumulative effect of this policy can be seen in a comparison of salaries for comparable administrative positions in the three cities, twenty-five years later. (See Table IX-1, p. 157.)

We have already discussed in some detail in Chapter VIII, how well the model performs in describing incremental decision processes. A more detailed investigation of the ways the model responded to systematic changes in parameters and revenue trends will be found in Chapter X. Particular attention will be placed there on the cumulative effects of these parameter and revenue shifts.

Non-Incremental Change—Unprogrammed Decisions

If we assume, for the moment, that our model adequately describes the programmed part of the municipal budgetary process, we can now direct our attention to the unprogrammed decisions or decisions representing policy shifts. Using model deviations (predicted appropriations minus

[9] Budget Bureau, city of Detroit, *Official Compensation Schedule (1964-65)*, p. ii.

TABLE IX-1

Comparative Salaries, 1965

Position	Detroit	Cleveland	Pittsburgh
Police Commissioner	$23000	$18072*	$14909*
Deputy Superintendent	$15812–$17383	$ 9500–$10000	$ 9153
Director of City Planning	$19245	$14394	$14909
Commissioner of			
Public Works	$23000	$18594	$14909
Superintendent of Motor			
Transportation	$14175	$13458	$11125
Superintendent of Street			
Construction and			
Maintenance	$14724	$13485	$10596
Draftsman	$ 6245	$ 5000–$ 5500	$ 4623
Clerk	$ 4981	$ 4000	$ 3400–$ 4400
Junior Clerk	$ 4116	$ 3500	$ 3400

* Director of Public Safety, supervising bureaus of police, fire, etc.

actual appropriations) as our guide, unprogrammed decisions for each city will be identified. Based on a set of assumed rationales for deviations, we will then attempt to discover systematic deviations. If, in fact, the model fails to explain certain kinds of decisions, it may be possible to suggest model modifications that would lead to increased predictive power.

MODEL DEVIATIONS TO BE EXAMINED. Deviations analyzed will be those associated with the one-period change models. The reason for using the one-period change rather than simulation models is a simple one. A simulation-model run for a single year will generate errors. To the extent some of these errors prove to be cumulative, an inaccurate picture of unprogrammed decisions[10] would result.

Of the total set of model deviations for each year in each city, we have picked a subset to examine in detail. The subset considered includes:

1. The five largest, absolute deviations in dollar amounts, and
2. The five largest, absolute deviations in percentage amounts.

The deviations are for department totals, not individual account categories.

RATIONALE FOR MODEL DEVIATIONS. We have classified deviations by their perceived *cause*. Four types of causes appear reasonable:

---

[10] For example, in one year in Detroit, an $18,000,000 deviation is observed in the welfare account—this deviation was the direct result of a change in policy by the state of Michigan. If the next year's run for the budget model did not reflect this new information, in effect, we would be requiring that the model also predict actions of the state of Michigan—an unreasonable burden.

1. Change in External Environment
   a. Inter-governmental transactions
      i. State and federal earmarked funds, subsidies, and regulations
      ii. Transfer of functions involving other governments
   b. Catastrophic event, emergency, crises, etc.—reaction to focus of public attention and widely perceived local problems
2. Changes in Internal Environment
   a. New administration (new actors in system of interrelationships)
   b. Change in departments or functions
      i. Transfers of activities—change in organizational structure
      ii. Changes in programs, functions
3. Lack of Information (by Model)
   a. Implications of capital budgeting decisions
   b. Additional revenue sources discovered
   c. Change in system of accounts
   d. Other information not part of allocation process (timing of elections, negotiated contracts, and the like)
4. Unexplained, Miscellaneous, and Other
   a. Model coding errors and missing data
   b. 'Improper' accounting procedures (Detroit only—capital items included in operating budget 1958-59 to 1961-62)
   c. Increased work load (or decreased) for department
   d. Other, unexplained

The outline above will provide the numbering scheme for cataloging model errors. For instance, *2.a.* might refer to the first budget after an election which resulted in a new administration (mayor). *1.a.i.* might be used to explain a model error which coincided with increased personnel financed with federal funds or funded through an urban renewal grant.

Those causes that represent policy shifts would be:

1.a.ii. Transfers of functions involving other governments
1.b. Catastrophic event, response to local problems
2.a. New administration
2.b.i. Transfers of activities—organizational change
2.b.ii. New programs, functions
3.b. Additional revenue sources discovered

Policy elaborations would correspond to:

1.a.i. State and federal earmarked funds, subsidies, and regulations
3.a. Implications of capital decisions
3.c. Change in system of accounts
3.d. Other information not part of allocation process (timing of elections, negotiated contracts, for example)
4.c. Increased workload

The remaining items in the outline represent things the model, ideally, should have accounted for.

Analysis of Model Deviations

Major model deviations were categorized using the classification scheme outlined above. A complete listing of deviations and causes will be found in the appendix, pp. 308-324. A summary of these findings will be discussed below.

CLEVELAND MODEL RESIDUALS. A summary of causes for Cleveland model deviations[11] is found in Table IX-2.

TABLE IX-2
Model Deviations: Cleveland

Cause	Category	No. Observed
State and Federal Funds	1.a.i.	6
Transfers of Functions—other governments	1.a.ii.	5
Response to Local Problems	1.b.	6
Reorganization of Urban Renewal Function	2.b.i.	10
New Function	2.b.ii.	1
Capital Budget Elaboration	3.a.	5
Additional Revenue Source	3.b.	7
Change in Accounting System	3.c.	2
Missing (model) Information	3.d.	4
Model Errors, Missing Data	4.a.	42
Increased Department Workload	4.c.	13
Unexplained	4.d.	10

Many of the errors in the Cleveland model involve missing data (4.a.) for the Engineering and Construction and Architecture Departments. The measurement errors or omissions, in turn, produce model errors. Missing data are used to calculate model parameters and, in some cases, generate erratic model behavior in specific departments. The net effect, of course, is to blur the revenue constraint, thus affecting the entire model. Much of this could be corrected by either tracing down the missing data or by making reasonable guesses of data values.[12] As the model was run, missing data were assumed to have a zero value.

[11] See appendix, pp. 308-315, for a complete listing of deviations and causes.
[12] Estimates of values for missing data could be obtained in a number of ways—two that are feasible:
  1. Take the average of the data values at $t - 1$ and $t + 1$ to estimate the data at t.
  2. Use the model-generated estimate for the value at t.

A primary, systematic source of model deviations has to do with funding. The Cleveland accounting system presents somewhat of a special case because many contributions to the general fund are not 'general' at all. Many revenues are earmarked (1.a.i.) for particular departments. Consequently many department appropriations are dependent upon revenue estimates from a particular source (3.b.). For example, in the Division of Housing, Department of Urban Renewal and Housing, an increase was observed in departmental appropriations of over $150,000 for one year. This was a direct result of a new ordinance requiring 'certificates of occupancy.' The fee associated with the certificate was given to the Housing Division, providing $155,000 (estimated) in additional department revenue. The model ought not to be required to explain changes in special revenues. On the other hand, it may have been reasonable to include earmarked general-fund revenue estimates as part of the DEPT. submodel of some departments. If we were constructing a model of budgeting in Cleveland instead of budgeting in all large municipalities, the additional complexity would clearly be appropriate.

A second, systematic source of deviation is related to relationships with other organizations and governments. For instance, part of Cleveland's street lighting is performed by private utility companies under a contract. A major portion of the Bureau of Street Lighting's budget is tied up in the contractual negotiations with private utility companies (3.d.). The Bureau of Street Cleaning obtains a significant portion of its appropriation through state gasoline tax receipts. Urban Renewal funds (federal funds and bond issues) provide explicit portions of general fund revenues for particular departments (1.a.i. and 3.b.).

Transfer of personnel to form new administrative units provides the third major class of deviations. Examples are the Bureaus of Traffic Engineering and Parking formed from Police Department transfers and the various bureaus that were reshuffled to form the Department of Urban Renewal and Housing (2.b.i.).

In general, we note the same general kinds of responses to urban renewal and civil rights as were observed in Detroit (1.b., 2.b.i.). These will be discussed in more detail below.

We also note the effects of the transfer of the City Hospital account to the county and the Sewer Maintenance account out of the general fund to a public utility (1.a.ii.).

DETROIT MODEL RESIDUALS. A summary of causes for Detroit model deviations is found in Table IX-3.[13]

The two highest error frequencies in Detroit were those caused by changes in the state and federal shares of programs administered by the

---

[13] See appendix, pp. 315-320, for a complete listing of deviations and causes.

TABLE IX-3

Model Deviations: Detroit

Cause	Category	No. Observed
State and Federal Contributions	1.a.i.	11
Transfer of Functions	1.a.ii.	1
Response to Local Problems	1.b.	5
New Administration	2.a.	9
Reorganization	2.b.i.	1
New City Functions	2.b.ii.	6
Capital Budget Elaboration	3.a.	2
Additional Revenue Source	3.b.	2
Change in Accounting System	3.c.	1
Missing (model) Information	3.d.	6
Model Errors, Missing Data	4.a.	3
Improper Accounting Procedures	4.b.	14
Increased Department Workload	4.c.	4
Unexplained	4.d.	8

city (primarily welfare—1.a.i.), and the changing accounting practices of the city with respect to capital items (4.b.). Obviously, our model cannot predict the outcome of the long-standing feud between the state and city of Detroit over relative shares of the welfare bill and cannot predict Federal Aid-to-Dependent-Children legislation.

The effects of the welfare problem on the model's goodness-of-fit have already been noted in Chapter VI. By filtering out welfare items in the budget and only dealing with the remainder, we were able to improve the model's performance in Detroit. It would obviously pay to filter out the capital items from the equipment and improvements account in Detroit in the years before the capital budget was a completely separate document. Unfortunately detailed, item breakdowns for mayor's recommendations and department requests are not in existence. If they were, we could expect improvement in model fit for the 1958-59 to 1962-63 period.

The distribution of the causes of model errors is certainly reasonable after the welfare and capital complications are removed. In general, we observe a pattern of systematic change toward increased involvements in the areas of planning, urban renewal, industrial growth, and the like. Also noted are changes in civil rights related fields: increased police after the summer of 1963 (boycotts, demonstrations, March on Washington) and expanded community relations functions (1.b.). We would probably note the effect of the federal anti-poverty program if an additional measurement were taken in 1966, and the effects of the civil disorders if 1967 were included in the study.

Most changes, it will be observed, are routine changes, resulting from more detailed information than our model has (knowing when elections are held, for example—3.d.) and involving routine responses to emerging problems (not filling positions when times are 'tight'—1.b.), and reflecting elaborations of other decisions (3.a., 3.d., and 4.c.—people needed to arrange for collection of a new income tax). Also noted are results of a survey of police and fire operations in Detroit by the Public Administrative Service (PAS) Survey. Had the resulting changes amounted to more than a 2½ per cent wage increase, the existence of national salary norms for police and firemen might have been indicated. The PAS functions as a consulting firm and could provide a mechanism for transmitting standards.

PITTSBURGH MODEL RESIDUALS. A summary of Pittsburgh deviations is found in Table IX-4.[14]

TABLE IX-4

Model Deviations: Pittsburgh

Cause	Category	No. Observed
State and Federal funds	1.a.i.	7
Transfers of Functions—other governments	1.a.ii.	3
Response to Public Problems	1.b.	7
New Department	2.b.i.	1
New Function	2.b.ii.	4
Capital Budget Elaboration	3.a.	3
Additional Revenue Source	3.b.	2
Missing (model) Information	3.d.	7
Model Errors, Missing Data	4.a.	7
Increased Department Workload	4.c.	4
Unexplained	4.d.	15

In Pittsburgh, we experienced relatively more errors to which a cause could not be attributed (4.d.). Perhaps this is due to the fewer data points and the more completely specified system of accounts. (See Table V-3.) A more completely specified system of accounts leads to smaller account sizes, on the average. A moderate error, otherwise, will be large, percentage-wise, with small accounts.

We observe that the primary source of model error is due to the external environment. The dependence of the city on the liquid fuels program (share of state gasoline tax) for financing various public works programs leads to deviations (1.a.i.) whenever the state's contribution drops (be-

[14] See appendix, pp. 320-324, for a complete listing of deviations and causes.

cause of a declining city population relative to the rest of the state). This closely parallels the Cleveland experience. In addition, many fluctuations seem to be caused by variations in the terms of negotiated contracts (3.d.). Rubbish collection is contracted out in some areas, as is street lighting. Another source of error entered when the Recreation Department picked up, dropped, then picked up again, a summer program formerly run by the board of education (1.b. and 4.c.).

The impact of federal programs on the budget is noticeable in the civil rights, economic opportunity, and human relations areas. The responses, as highlighted by model errors (1.a.i.), consist of the formation of departments (Human Relations Commission) and the addition of personnel (1964 Mayors Office) to administer federal programs and to seek federal funds. An implied response to the civil rights problem might be the addition to the police force of 100 new patrolmen in 1965, as well as an increase in the Human Relations Commission staff in 1964 (1.b.).

General Patterns of Policy Shifts in Detroit, Cleveland, and Pittsburgh

By studying model deviations we note unusual or unprogrammed changes in the decision system—decisions that our model was unable to predict. Some of these unusual changes were dictated changes—changes the external environment imposed on the municipal government. Other unprogrammed changes represented conscious, optional policy shifts on the part of municipalities.

Although there seems to be a consistent pattern of unprogrammed change with respect to outside, contractual agreements, this is of less interest to us because the change is, within broad limits, forced upon the city. We also note that the larger the municipality, the smaller the number of unusual changes that involve contractual relations. It is not clear whether this represents an economies-of-scale kind of argument where big cities can afford to provide a service for the entire area (serving as contractor instead of consumer) while smaller cities must rely on an area-wide (and possibly private) organization to provide the service,[15] or whether this reflects the bargaining power of the bigger city to 'force' contractors to stay within incremental limits. Another common situation where the municipality is forced to react concerns revenue derived from the state. Welfare contributions in Detroit and gasoline and fuel tax shares for public works items in Cleveland and Pittsburgh provide vivid illustrations of the city at

[15] The presence or absence of contractual services as a percentage of total budget is discussed in Chapter XI in relation to the model's applicability to other sizes of municipalities.

163

the mercy of its revenue sources (the state in this case). In all cases, the municipality 'makes plenty of noise' to the legislature, but only Detroit has succeeded in convincing the state to increase its contribution to municipal activities.[16]

If there are any general patterns of unprogrammed decisions that can be classified as policy shifts in Cleveland, Detroit, and Pittsburgh, they occur in the same problem areas in which we find the federal government active. Urban renewal departments or commissions have been established as separate units in Detroit and Cleveland. In Pittsburgh, as we have noted earlier while discussing invisible changes, the growth of this kind of activity has taken place within the City Planning Department, and through a system of non-profit corporations.

The requirement of a Comprehensive Master Plan in order to participate (obtain funds) in the federal Community Renewal Program has provided a substantive change in the urban planning process as well as a level change.

The presence of federal funds has also led to the establishment of job retraining commissions in Detroit and Cleveland and a new staff position in the Mayor's Office in Pittsburgh to take advantage of the availability of funds.

The emergence of human relations commissions in all three cities is at least partially a result of federal interest in this area, and it is probably due in part to fear of racial violence on the part of the city administrations (note increases in the number of patrolmen in all three police bureaus in 1964 and 1965).

The conclusion that the federal government is having a great impact on the real allocation of resources in urban areas is as obvious as it is important. The real magnitude of the impact is not reflected in the operating budget, however. Nearly all the new departments were set up to administer and coordinate a number of federal programs and monies which do not appear in the operating budget. These observations are not new or particularly interesting. They do lead to a profound question concerning federal involvement in urban affairs, however.[17]

Urban government has been perpetually plagued by a lack of revenues. Federal funds effectively relax the severe revenue constraints in some fields of municipal activity. One important question that could be

[16] Due more to the first Democratic-controlled state legislature in many decades (because of reapportionment) than to any convincing on Detroit's part.

[17] If the Department of Housing and Urban Development and the federal Anti-Poverty Programs are to be allowed to expand, we can expect dramatic reallocations of urban resources in the near future, especially following a reduction in our Viet Nam involvement.

raised is: If federal funds came with 'no strings attached,' would municipal resources be allocated in roughly the same ways they are being allocated now—'with the strings'?

Because planning and long-range problems appear to be the target of federal monies, if we believe the 'Gresham's Law' of planning, that daily routine drives out planning,[18] then the answer to our question would probably be 'no.' March and Simon, in discussing this, cite one condition that brings about unprogrammed activity—". . . allocate resources to goals requiring unprogrammed activity, and . . . refuse to provide substitutes or alternative goals that can be reached by programmed activity."[19] The federal government has done just that in the area of urban planning and urban renewal. Federally financed projects, if they are to be approved, must be consistent with a Comprehensive Master Plan of the urban area's growth. Planning and renewal must be executed in the context of a program of activity and not as a series of *ad hoc* projects.

IMPLICATIONS FOR MODEL VALIDITY. We have argued that the decision system used to solve the municipal budgeting problem is strongly based in a system of mutual expectations. If the expectations of participants are at all accurate, then participants ought to be able, in some sense, to predict outcomes of the process and know when a particular decision satisfies expectations and when it runs counter to them. Our model generates an expectation for particular decisions as well. An analysis of model residuals is really an analysis of those decisions that run counter to (model) expectations.

If we make the reasonable assumption that the decisions people talk about are those that run counter to expectations, those that need justifying, the explicit analysis of model residuals can contribute to our knowledge of the model's goodness-of-fit and, more importantly, validity. Quite by accident, while trying to attach reasons to particular model deviations, it was discovered that the mayor's budget messages were the best sources of information, by a wide margin. Observing that the text of these budget messages refers only to a small percentage of the budgetary decisions, it became apparent that the actual decision system (mayor) was identifying nearly the same set of decisions as being 'different,' as was our formal model (by generating large errors or residuals). This observation is submitted as additional evidence that the computer model adequately describes the budgetary decision process. The large deviations that are sometimes found are not 'random' in the usual sense; they bear a strong correlation with the 'deviant cases' identified by mayors.

[18] J. G. March and H. A. Simon, *Organizations* (New York: John Wiley & Sons, 1958).
[19] March and Simon, *op. cit.*, pp. 185-186.

LONG-RUN CHARACTERISTICS OF BUDGET PROCESS

Model Drift

The formal model describes a somewhat drifting budgetary process. The sensitivity tests in Chapter X should tell us, generally, the direction of drift.

The traditional studies of public finance, by trying to couple economic, political, and population characteristics to municipal expenditure items, attempt to identify those forces that determine the direction of drift. Their contention is that the role of governmental decision-makers is that of a passive translator of environmental characteristics into expenditure items. These studies have met with only marginal success (see Chapter II, pp. 12-14, 19-21).

FIGURE IX-1

Environmental Factors in Municipal Finance

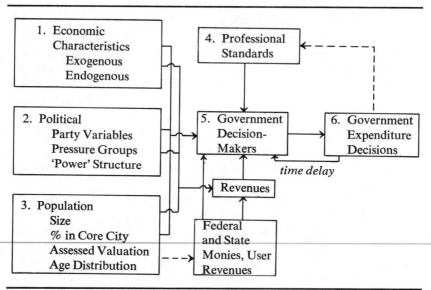

By emphasizing the short-run decision process, we have focused on internal characteristics of the governmental decision process and the relationship between current and historical decisions. In Figure IX-1 our findings are that in the short-run items 5 and 6 are the most significant. By studying the budgetary phenomena over time, others have emphasized items 1, 2, 3, and 4 almost to the exclusion of 5. The question now remains —do our short-run findings apply in the long run?

Causes of Model Drift

Model drift could be biased by external constraints. Expenditures would be permitted to drift only so far without being corrected. They would be brought back into line with national standards, party or pressure group demands, population needs or tastes, etc. If, in fact, this were the case, evidence of the use of correcting mechanisms should exist in our model deviations because our model has no provisions for these mechanisms.

Observed Environmental Corrections in Drift

In Detroit corrections in drift (model deviations) seemed to consist of establishing new departments in the urban renewal area, adjusting appropriations to correspond with state and user revenue changes, and one adjustment in police and fire salaries resulting from a Public Administration Survey report (that could be interpreted as a correction in drift to correspond to some national operating standard).

Cleveland's drift corrections consisted of new departments in the urban renewal area, adjustments in appropriations because of changes in state and user revenue contributions and costs for negotiated contracts, and special wage increases for police and firemen (corresponding to national rates?).

Pittsburgh appears much the same, with changes in state revenue contributions, the terms of negotiated service contracts (street lighting), and the emergence of city activities in areas of federal program involvement accounting for most of the environmental corrections in model drift.

It appears from an analysis of our residuals over time that environmental corrections

1. are seldom (if ever) evoked directly to bring specific expenditure items 'into line,' *and*
2. are filtered through the revenue constraint (see Figure IX-1), blurring the cause of increased (decreased) revenues and blunting possible direct impact on specific budget items.

In any event, environmental corrections appear to be more related to revenue changes than expenditure changes. Hence, their impact on expenditures appears to be a blurred one that is exercised through the administrative allocation and decision forces rather than through any direct expenditure-correcting mechanism.

The nature of this somewhat-random drift (see Chapter X, pp. 180-184, for a discussion of some non-random features of this drift) is examined under a number of revenue-change patterns in Chapter X.

Some *direct* environmental corrections were observed however. Negotiated contracts and changes in earmarked revenue (state and user) provided some clear corrections. The existence of federal monies for municipal programs also appears to have caused a change in the budgetary drift.

What seems to emerge from this study is an opportunity model of budgetary change. The broad pattern of drift is accelerated or depressed due to changes in general revenues. The drift in specific expenditure items changes in response to changes in earmarked revenues or the terms of negotiated contracts. Rapid spurts of growth are observed in those areas where the city has the opportunity to expand activities because of the presence of revenues (federal funds), *rather than in areas having rapid changes or spurts in needs.* This also could be due to the fact that needs do not change in spurts either.

From a normative standpoint, the drifting *general fund* budget has some appeal. If, in fact, we are *able* to specify desired changes in municipal expenditures as a function of environmental changes, the *system* (if we have a Darwinian view of the world) would tend to place these expenditures *outside* of the general fund. The funding of activities where we *can* logically connect environmental changes (demands, ability to pay, etc.) to expenditure (or activity) changes, is common. The extreme case results in a private good where supply equals demand and level of activity is determined by the price mechanism. Somewhere in between lie the public power and utility companies where price roughly equals cost of goods sold and supply (activity) equals demand. Public transportation companies, hospitals, community colleges, etc., all have a system of user taxes where the municipal government provides a partial subsidy. Generally, only activities where user-tax financing is not feasible or desirable receive a full municipal subsidy and hence are eligible for inclusion into the general fund. *It should not be surprising, then, that in the absence of a system of standard costs or ways of determining activity levels* (characteristics of general fund activities) *the decision systems exhibit drifting, opportunistic characteristics.*

CHAPTER X

Sensitivity Analysis

OUR COMPUTER MODEL of municipal resource allocation represents a partially tested theory of governmental decision-making. It describes a system of human behavior and makes some strong assertions about that behavior. The purpose of this chapter is to find out more about the system of behavior, the relative importance of some of the assertions, and the logical implications of the theory under differing conditions.

The model as a closed, dynamic system, where model outputs one period can serve as inputs for the next, facilitates an analysis of the model's dynamic properties.[1] Changing individual model mechanisms or parameters is a relatively simple task and allows the researcher to trace theory implications unambiguously.

The choice of alternative mechanisms and parameters to examine is not independent of the model's dynamic properties.

LENGTH OF MODEL RUNS. Our model is basically one describing the short-run decision process. An integral part of the process (although not formally a part of the model) concerns the external environment. The environmental corrections as revealed in the analysis of residuals in Chapter IX constitute an important set of variables. Although we have argued that these corrections are somewhat random and out of the control of the decision-makers, government does respond to them in fairly predictable ways. How long should we let the model run without environmental interventions? A somewhat arbitrary period of ten years was chosen as being sufficient to allow patterns and shifts to emerge, but not so long a period as to lose all relevance to the real-world process.

[1] See Figure VIII-2 for a description of different types of model runs. We will use simulation runs here.

DETROIT AS TEST MODEL. Rather than experiment with all three cities, it was decided to test the model's properties using data from just one. Detroit was chosen because it had a complete set of departmental request data. It was feared that cumulative effects of DEPT. parameter instability, due to a lack of data in Cleveland and Pittsburgh, could lead to an unstable system (if not subject to environmental corrections).

WHAT TO MEASURE? Inasmuch as preliminary-calculations parameters constitute a system of mutual expectations, they were not varied in the test runs described below. It might have made sense to change parameters in one or two departments and note the effects on resource allocation. This was not done, however. In all probability, only the one or two departments would have been affected. Also, the study has focused (rightly or wrongly) on the *total* process, not on individual, micro elements.

Presumably, we are interested in the *relative* allocation of resources rather than just dollar amounts or single departments. With this in mind, share-of-the-total-budget appears to be a reasonable dependent variable for model tests.

The formal model presented in Chapters IV-VII is generally an administrative, problem-solving model. The analysis of the model's residuals in Chapter IX revealed that the external environment enters the process either on a random ad hoc basis *or* through the revenue constraint. With this in mind, we will undertake two different kinds of analyses: one relating to administrative constraints and guidelines (internal problem environment) and the other relating to the systematic, externally-imposed revenue constraint (effects of external environment).

MODEL TEST—ADMINISTRATIVE CONSTRAINTS AND GUIDELINES

In testing the model we assumed a stable system of interaction and consequently held the preliminary-calculations parameters [see item 3 in Figure V-1b (DEPT.), item 4 in Figure VI-1b (MAYORS), item 9 in Figure VII-1b (COUNCIL)] constant, while loosening a number of constraints. In particular, effects of the following parameters and variables were investigated:

1. Tone-of-mayor's-letter or mayor's limit on increments—XL
2. Minimum salary increase—XK
3. Balanced-budget tolerance limit—$XLMT$[2]

Two model runs were undertaken to see what effect (if any) the relaxing of tight mayor's guidelines, wage increases, and solution criteria

---

[2] XL, see item 18 in Figure VI-1b (MAYORS). XK, see items 9 and 10 in Figure VI-1b (MAYORS). $XLMT$, see item 11 in Figure VI-1b (MAYORS).

(XLMT) would have on the relative allocation of community resources. Revenue was held constant (at 1964-65 levels) throughout the ten-year runs in order to isolate possible effects of the three parameters.

Parameter values used are shown in Table X-1.

TABLE X-1
Alternative Administrative-Constraint Conditions

	Run 1 *(Normal)*	*Run 2* *(Relaxed Administrative* *Constraints)*
Limit on Regular Increments, tone-of-mayor's-letter		
$XL =$	.05	.15
Salary Increment		
$XK =$	.05	.10

Tolerance Limit—
  stops search for
  balanced budget		

$XLMT =$	\$ 150,000	\$ 1,000,000
Revenue (constant)	\$153,000,000	\$153,000,000

Graphs of budget shares over time (1965-1975) implied under normal administrative-constraint conditions and shares under a looser system of constraints are found in Figures X-1 through X-3.

Although results for all accounts in all departments were plotted, only three are included here. The three are highly representative of the others.

Results

The following observations can be made, based on an analysis of all departments and accounts in Detroit:

    a. For all but a very few account categories in a very few departments, the relaxed constraints led to *no* large shifts in budget share for the ten-year model run (assuming constant revenues) relative to normal constraints.

    b. Most account categories experienced *no* change in budget share from 1965 to 1975 under a constant revenue assumption in either runs 1 or 2.

    c. The looser constraints *slightly* disadvantaged the Salary and Wage accounts. For all years (10), in all departments (48), Salary and Wage budget share was (slightly) lower than, or equal to the share under normal constraints.

FIGURE X-1

City of Detroit—Council

10-year Forecast of Appropriations
(Constant Revenues)

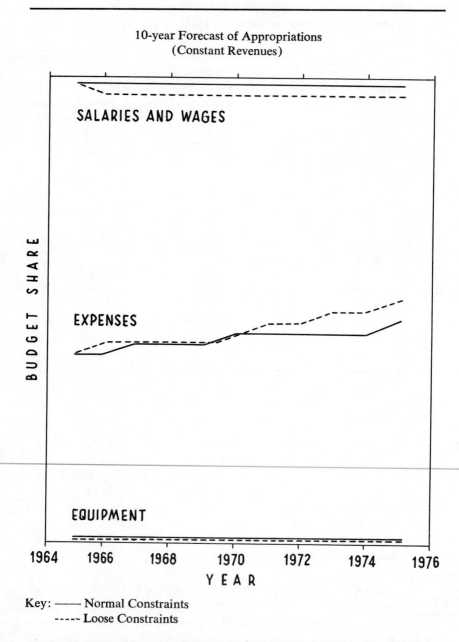

SALARIES AND WAGES

EXPENSES

EQUIPMENT

1964 1966 1968 1970 1972 1974 1976

Y E A R

B U D G E T   S H A R E

Key: ——— Normal Constraints
----- Loose Constraints

FIGURE X-2
City of Detroit—House of Correction

10-year Forecast of Appropriations
(Constant Revenues)

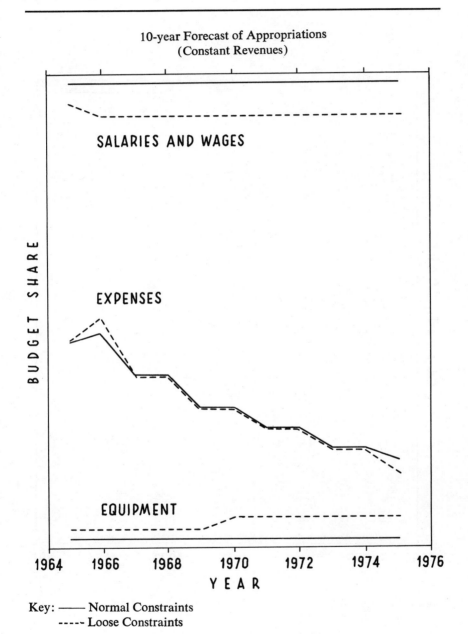

Key: —— Normal Constraints
----- Loose Constraints

FIGURE X-3
City of Detroit—Civic Center

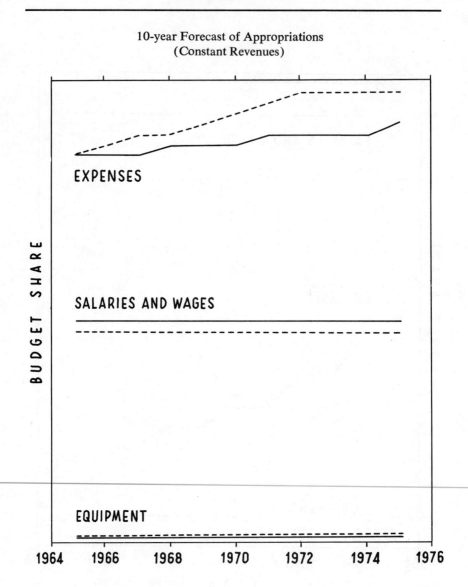

10-year Forecast of Appropriations
(Constant Revenues)

BUDGET SHARE

EXPENSES

SALARIES AND WAGES

EQUIPMENT

1964   1966   1968   1970   1972   1974   1976

Key: —— Normal Constraints
----- Loose Constraints

d. Related to c., the Expense and Equipment accounts, in a majority of departments tended to pick up the small loss in salary shares.

Some crude statistics may help identify some dynamic properties of the system at a revenue equilibrium. Three questions seem relevant:

i. How are *trends* distributed among account categories?

ii. How are trends distributed within departments? Are account *trends* cumulative for a department?

iii. How many large, discrete differences are there under the two constraint assumptions?

Table X-2 addresses itself to those departments and accounts where both normal and loose administrative constraints lead to *trends* in the same direction (but not necessarily of the same magnitude).

TABLE X-2

Trends in Budget Share with Constant Revenues

| | | Trend | |
Account type	down	stable	up
Wages and Salaries	8	40	0
Materials, Supplies, and Expenses	7	15	25
Equipment	1	44	4

Under a constant revenue assumption, relative and absolute account growth appears reasonably independent of administrative constraints and occurs in the Material, Supplies, and Expense categories at the expense of Salary and Wage accounts.

Are these *trends* cumulative? If one account in a department grows, do they all grow?

Table X-3 indicates that accounts within a department are independent of one another for the most part.

We have ascertained that budget-share trends are distributed somewhat differently between accounts, and, within departments, few cumulative effects are observed. How are the significant differences in *level* distributed?

Of the nearly 150 accounts observed, a significance difference in budget-share *level* was found only nine times. Seven involved the Materials, Supplies, and Expenses account. Two of the seven were better off under normal constraints and the remainder had better fortune with loose conditions. Two Equipment accounts experienced significantly better luck under loose administrative constraints. There are few significant level dif-

TABLE X-3

Cumulative Properties of Trends in Departments
(Constant Total Budget)

Account trends in a department	Frequency
All 3 accounts up	0
2 up—1 stable	2
1 up—2 stable	22
all 3 stable	9
1 down—2 stable	8
2 down—1 stable	1
all 3 down	0
Mixed:	
1 up, 1 down, 1 stable	5
other	0

ferences under the two constraint conditions and they are concentrated in the Expense accounts.

Conclusions—Role of Internal Constraints

The empirical observations above suggest some possibilities:

1. If the three internal constraints tested *are* important at all, they are not important under a constant-revenue assumption.
2. The model constraints investigated are deeply embedded in the empirically determined parameters and hence our test was not really a test at all.
3. External constraints (revenues) dominate internal constraints.

We know the second point has a great deal of merit because we were forced to use model outputs to estimate internal model parameters.[3]

Points one and three refer to the revenue constraint and its effect on resource allocation.

EXTERNAL ENVIRONMENT—PROBLEMS IN ANALYZING EFFECTS

We wish to analyze the impact of various environments on a model of the municipal budgetary decision process. This creates many problems

---

[3] See Chapter VI, pp. 42-47, for estimation methods, and appendix, pp. 251-253, for a discussion of the reasonableness of this approach. In Chapter VI we find the parameters tested in this section were not empirically estimated. Test results here indicate precise estimation was not crucial.

—how can we analyze the impact of the environment without also modeling that environment?

Decomposable Systems and Their External Environments

The works of Simon and Ando,[4] and Ando and Fisher[5] are relevant to our problem. To paraphrase Ando and Fisher:

Political scientists are often concerned with the stability properties of a political system or institution considered in isolation—for example, the municipal budgetary process. However, there may be a somewhat uncomfortable feeling that this may not be a meaningful problem since the models describing the political (sub-) system are themselves embedded in a far larger set of models describing the socio-economic and physical universe. It follows that the movement of the political variables toward equilibrium may itself disturb variables (such as the local economy) which are assumed by the political model to be given. Further, non-political variables which political theory admits to be influenced by political ones may, in turn, influence the latter of the assumed given non-political variables and thereby hinder the political variables from reaching equilibrium. It follows that general equilibrium of the political variables (budgetary process), which is a partial equilibrium of the larger system, may be unattainable even if it is stable when considered in isolation.

The Simon-Ando and Ando-Fisher theorems suggest a general answer to this problem in the following way. Partition the set of all non-political (socio-economic) variables into: (1) those variables which theory assumes influence the budgetary process, but are not themselves influenced thereby; (2) those variables which are assumed to be influenced by but which do not influence political or budgetary variables; and (3) those variables which are assumed to be unrelated to political or budgetary variables. We may disregard variables in the third category. Thus we visualize our budgetary theory as assuming that causal influences run from the first set to the budgetary or political variables to the second set with no feedbacks. The difficulty raised, however, is that there may in fact be weak feedbacks since the assumptions of the theory are at best only good approximations. The Ando-Fisher theorem shows that *if these feedbacks are sufficiently weak relative to direct influences*, that is if the theoretical assumptions are sufficiently good approximations, there exists a time span over which the be-

[4] Herbert A. Simon and Albert Ando, "Aggregation of Variables in Dynamic Systems," in Albert Ando, F. M. Fisher, and H. A. Simon, *Essays on the Structure of Social Science Models* (Cambridge, Mass.: The M.I.T. Press, 1963).
[5] Albert Ando and F. M. Fisher, "Near-Decomposability, Partition and Aggregation, and the Relevance of Stability Discussions," and "Two Theorems on *Ceteris Paribus* in the Analysis of Dynamic Systems," in Ando, Fisher, and Simon, *op. cit.*

havior and stability of the political (budgetary) system can be analyzed in isolation without regard for the difficulties raised by the presence of such feedbacks. The length of the time span under which this analysis is valid is dependent on the relative weakness of the feedbacks to the direct influences.

Furthermore, the Ando-Fisher theorem asserts that when the time period under consideration is long enough to make it necessary for the influence of other parts of the socio-economic and physical system on the political system (budgetary process) to be explicitly considered, there will come a time after which the political system (budgetary process) will always be in its own partial equilibrium (if, indeed, transitory outside influences ever disturb that equilibrium once it has been reached), that the variables in it (budget items) will be moving proportionately to one another, and that we can therefore represent the budgetary system as an index (total revenue or total budget) and can consider the influence of other parts of the social system on this index rather than on the political system (budgetary process) in its entire complexity.[6]

What this means for our problem is that we can meaningfully study the movement of *budget shares* (not totals) in the long run by focusing on changes in total revenue *if* we can show that relatively weak feedbacks exist between parts of the budgetary process (budget items) and the remaining socio-economic system. We have described the strong, direct influences in the internal environment of the budgetary process in Chapters IV through VII. The measures of the goodness-of-fit of a model based primarily on an internal process are offered as strong evidence for this in Chapter VIII and should not be at issue. Evidence of weak feedbacks from the external environment was offered through an analysis of residuals in Chapter IX and also will be discussed briefly here.

Weak Feedbacks Between Budgetary System and External Environment

The model of budgetary decision-making we have constructed contends that the external environment has a rather minor role to play in the *allocation* of municipal operating funds, but exerts its major influence through the revenue total. If, in fact, our model is wrong and the assumed independence of individual budget items and external environment does not exist, the inappropriateness of the independence assumption should have been reflected in the overall goodness-of-fit of our model *and* in the errors associated with individual budget items. In particular, if environ-

[6] Ando and Fisher, "Near-Decomposability . . . ," *op. cit.*, pp. 100-102.

mental corrections of the drifting bureaucratic process were an important part of the 'real' process, then at least some individual model errors ought to be associated with environmental corrections.

The careful study of model residuals in Chapter IX revealed little in the way of evidence for direct environmental corrections, other than those associated with negotiated contracts, earmarked revenues, and some federal monies. We offer these findings as evidence for the existence of only weak feedbacks between the modeled, internal environment and the external environment. Based on the strong, internal relationships in the budgetary process and the existence of only very weak feedbacks between it and the external environment, it is reasonable (using the Simon-Ando and Ando-Fisher theorems) to analyze the relative, long-run relation of budget items by treating the external environment as an aggregate index (revenues).

Model Test—External Environment (Revenue Constraint)

Through the balanced-budget requirement, the revenue constraint plays a key role in the budgetary process. It defines the primary problem for the MAYORS submodel and provides the filter through which external pressures exert their influences. Unlike internal constraints, the revenue constraint is probably not embedded in the estimated model parameters. What kinds of revenue patterns are reasonable? Which ranges of revenue behavior should be examined for possible effect on the *allocation* of resources?

Using the stable system of interaction-parameters and normal constraint values, the model was run with three patterns of revenue:

1. Constant (same as run 1—normal—in part A of this chapter),
2. Accelerating—10 per cent increase per year,
3. Fluctuating—a base revenue increasing at 5 per cent per year with a random fluctuation about this base to calculate revenue for a given year.[7]

Actual estimates using these patterns are found in Table X-4.

The model was run for a ten-year period, changing only the revenue estimate or constraint. The constant-revenue assumption defines a very tight revenue constraint, whereas the accelerating-revenue condition specifies an extremely loose or non-existent constraint. The fluctuating assumption is more realistic and provides for moderate growth (on the

---

[7] $\text{BASE}_t = 1.05(\text{BASE}_{t-1})$
$\text{REVEST}_t = \text{BASE}_t + Z$
where Z is a normally distributed random variable with mean zero and a standard deviation of $10,000,000.

TABLE X-4

Alternative Revenue Patterns

Year	Constant	Accelerating	Fluctuating
1965–66	153,000,000	153,000,000	153,000,000
1966–67	153,000,000	168,300,000	154,700,000
1967–68	153,000,000	185,200,000	160,900,000
1968–69	153,000,000	203,700,000	167,900,000
1969–70	153,000,000	224,100,000	191,000,000
1970–71	153,000,000	246,500,000	197,600,000
1971–72	153,000,000	271,100,000	184,700,000
1972–73	153,000,000	298,200,000	227,000,000
1973–74	153,000,000	328,000,000	239,900,000
1974–75	153,000,000	360,800,000	221,400,000
1975–76	153,000,000	396,900,000	249,700,000

average) with the spurts and occasional downturn common in the last decade.

Results

Figures X-4, X-5, and X-6 give time-series plots of *budget share*[8] for three departments. Again, the dynamic behavior of the model is such that each department exhibits nearly the same pattern of behavior. Although all departments were graphed, little information is lost by presenting just three.

Some general observations can be made. As the total budget size increases, the *share* (though *not* dollar amount) for Wages and Salaries nearly always decreases. The reasons for this are not entirely clear. Perhaps this is an inevitable result of automation (one policeman in a patrol car can cover many times the area that he could on foot). It could reflect the fact that city revenues have really never grown more than 2-3 per cent per year, if that. Employees are much harder to dispose of than Equipment and other standard expense items. The reluctance of the model (and city administration) to take on employees at a rate of increase the same as (or

---

[8] The use of *share* rather than dollar amounts allows us to compare outcomes under the three revenue conditions, and using the Simon-Ando and Ando-Fisher theorems on 'nearly completely decomposable subsystems' represents a theoretically defensible way of analyzing long-run system (model) dynamics. See John P. Crecine, "A Computer Simulation of Municipal Budgeting: The Impact of Problem Environment," in W. D. Coplin, ed., *Simulation and the Study of Politics* (Chicago: Markham Press, 1968), for a complete treatment of theoretical issues in analyzing the long-run dynamics of our budgetary decision model.

FIGURE X-4

City of Detroit, Buildings and Safety Engineering Department

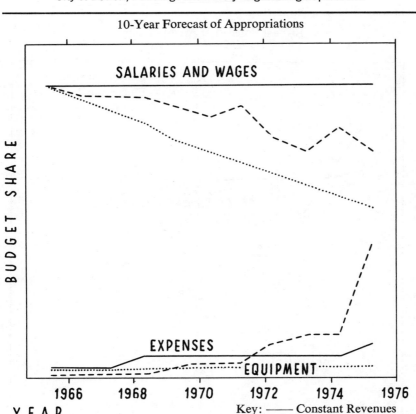

10-Year Forecast of Appropriations

SALARIES AND WAGES

BUDGET SHARE

EXPENSES

EQUIPMENT

1966   1968   1970   1972   1974   1976

Y E A R

Key: ——— Constant Revenues
----- Fluctuating Revenues
.... Accelerating Revenues

higher than) the total budget, might reflect a cautious approach to hirings. Employees involve long-run commitments of funds.

Another interesting phenomenon was noted. The constant and accelerating revenue assumptions create a kind of funnel or envelope (See Figures X-4, X-5, X-6) for appropriations, within which appropriations under fluctuating revenues usually remain. In most cases, a change in revenue growth rate accelerates or depresses the trend in budget share for an account but does not change its direction. Yet, in looking over the entire set of data, we notice some accounts break out of this envelope to obtain a larger share of the total (in the model) under fluctuating revenues than under accelerating, while some receive an even smaller share than under a constant

FIGURE X-5
City of Detroit—Civil Defense Department

10-Year Forecast of Appropriations

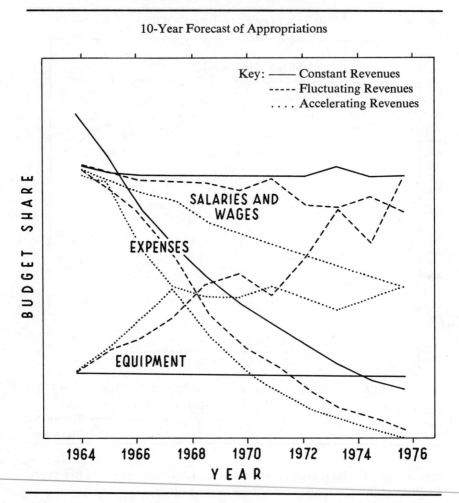

Key: —— Constant Revenues
----- Fluctuating Revenues
. . . . Accelerating Revenues

SALARIES AND WAGES

EXPENSES

EQUIPMENT

BUDGET SHARE

1964 1966 1968 1970 1972 1974 1976

Y E A R

revenue situation. Are there any regularities in this deviant behavior? No department or group of departments seemed to be helped or hurt by fluctuating, erratic revenues to the extent that they systematically fall outside the constant-accelerating limits.

Table X-5 suggests that the Expense account fluctuates with fluctuating revenue more than Salaries, for instance. The 8-4 split suggests little in the way of consistent advantage for Expense under fluctuating conditions, however. The Equipment account is a different matter. Almost a third of all departments (according to the model) were able to secure a larger share

FIGURE X-6
City of Detroit, Recorders Court—Traffic Division

10-Year Forecast of Appropriations

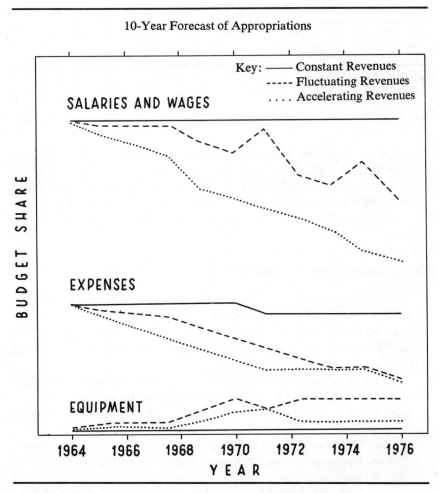

for Equipment under somewhat erratic revenue conditions than under either stable or steadily expanding conditions. Of the eleven departments that somehow managed to use fluctuating revenues to their advantage by securing an increased share for their Equipment account, *ten of the eleven* time-series plots of fluctuating revenues 'broke out of the envelope' in 1972-73. What was so unusual about that year? Looking back at fluctuating revenue levels in Table X-4, we see that after a revenue decline (of nearly $7,000,000) for 1971-72, the system received a sudden spurt in the form of an increase of more than 20 per cent. Equipment accounts, for

TABLE X-5

Fluctuating-Revenue Accounts
Outside of Constant or Accelerating Limits

	Relation to Limits		
Account type	*Above*	*Within*	*Below*
Salaries and Wages	1	44	1
Materials, Supplies, and Expenses	8	33	4
Equipment	11	36	0

some reason, were able to siphon off more than a fair share of the increase. Interestingly enough, the eleventh case 'broke out' of the constant-accelerating-revenue envelope in 1969-70. This was a year with another sudden spurt in revenues (nearly a 20 per cent increase). Once the Equipment accounts reached this new plateau, the model implied they would stay there.

Conclusions—Role of Revenue Constraint

The experiments with the revenue constraint suggest some additional dynamic properties of our model:

1. Revenue increases (decreases) seem to accelerate or depress the *rate* of change in budget share for all accounts, but do not usually change the direction of drift.
2. As the total budget increases, our model indicates that the *share* (*not* dollar amount) of wage and salary costs, declines.
3. When the decision system is 'shocked' through an unusual revenue change:
   a. Salary and Wages accounts are least responsive to the change.
   b. Expenses accounts are most responsive to the change and its direction.
   c. Some Equipment accounts are responsive to accelerating revenues and are able to maintain their new levels after revenue acceleration tapers off.

SUMMARY—IMPACTS OF INTERNAL AND EXTERNAL ENVIRONMENTS

Because the system is decomposable, and one of the systems describes the budgetary process, we were able to analyze the budgetary subsystem independently from the larger socio-economic system of which it is a part.

"[I]f a nearly completely decomposable system is analyzed as though it were completely decomposable, the results obtained will remain approximately valid even in the long run as regards the *relative* behavior of the variables within any one set."[9] Therefore our analysis of the behavior of budget *shares* in the process under various revenue assumptions, 'revenue' being the primary link between internal and external environment, is 'approximately valid' in the long run.

Experiments with our decision model have revealed some interesting behavioral characteristics of the system. The inertial qualities of the model were apparent in both sets of tests. *Analysis of budget shares by accounts over time, revealed, under changing revenue conditions, that a substantial reallocation of resources can occur.* Although this change in budget share is an inertial one for most accounts, we have noted some interesting departures.

The primacy of the revenue constraint in the reallocation of resources is the major finding of this chapter.

Implications for Future Research

In assessing the impact of the internal or problem (short-run) and external (long-run) environments on the budgetary decision process we have confronted some interesting theoretical and methodological questions. It appears as if the Simon-Ando and Ando-Fisher theorems on decomposable systems might prove exceedingly useful in the development of an integrated, positive theory of governmental resource allocation that links influences of the larger socio-economic environment with some realistic notions of how government officials reach decisions.

[9] Ando and Fisher, "Two Theorems on *Ceteris Paribus* . . . ," *op. cit.*, p. 108.

CHAPTER XI

Budgeting from Different Viewpoints

IN CHAPTERS I and II references were made to a number of works and approaches to the municipal resource allocation problem. We have studied one aspect of municipal resource allocation in great detail—the process of formulating operating (or general fund) budgets.

A rather detailed and explicit conceptualization of the process has been presented and largely confirmed (at least not disconfirmed). How does the decision process model of municipal budgeting relate to other approaches in the literature? We now turn to this question. The formal model of municipal resource allocation presented in Chapter IV will be our reference point. Other theories and findings will be examined for points of convergence and divergence with our process model, in a test for a kind of consistency.

As was pointed out in Chapter II, conceptions (or theories applicable to the problem) of municipal resource allocation roughly fall into two categories:

1. The budget as an externally determined outcome,
2. The budget as an internal bureaucratic process.

BUDGET AS AN EXTERNALLY DETERMINED OUTCOME

The more traditional social science approaches to governmental resource allocation generally describe the decision process as a particular form of response mechanism. Generally, government officials perceive pressure, influence, needs, etc., and translate these perceptions into public policy, governmental actions or inactions. There appears to be a disciplinary breakdown based on the kinds of stimuli focused on in this external influence-response conception.

186

Political scientists and sociologists generally emphasize influence groups, political decision-makers, and economic and social elite forms of stimuli, and economists and public administrators usually emphasize citizenry-demand-for-services, needs, and service standards as the stimuli leading to a budgetary response. Quite clearly, our model does not view these external events or stimuli as being particularly important in the formation of a municipal operating budget. While it is always possible, given proper assumptions concerning value distributions and subjective costs, to construct a rational explanation for any kind of behavior, the behavior reported here certainly is not in the spirit of the rational, optimizing models in Chapter II.

If we define 'influence' to be any kind of external force that impinges on the budgetary process, it is immediately apparent that our formal model accounts for only certain kinds of influence, requires that it be elaborated in well-defined ways, and permits it to enter the system at only a few points. Specification of the kinds of influence permitted by the formal model will precede a detailed comparison of our simulation model with others appearing in the literature.

Influence and the Simulation Model

Basically, external influence (either political or demand-for-services) consistent with the simulation model can enter the process in two ways:
1. Through empirically determined parameter values, or
2. As informational inputs.

Parameters and Influence or Demands

The model assumes parameters are constant over time and vary only by department and account category. As we saw in Chapters V-VII, the model is one of programmed change, subject to a set of imposed constraints. *If* we assume that pressure, external influences, or service demands are important in the budgetary process, what assumptions concerning external factors, etc., must be made in order to make an external-influence model consistent with ours? A basic relationship may be of use here:

a. $(\text{Quan}_{ij}) \times (\text{Qual}_{ij}) \times (\text{U cost}_{ij}) = \text{Budget}_{ij}$
where $\text{Quan}_{ij} = $ Quantity of service demanded from department i, expenditure category j.
   $\text{Qual}_{ij} = $ Quality of service demanded from department i, expenditure category j.
   $\text{U Cost}_{ij} = $ Unit cost of the above service.

As we saw in Chapter VIII, our model implies that budget behavior ($Budget_{ij}$) exhibits a regular programmed pattern of changes.[1] Referring to 'a,' opposite, systematic change in '$Budget_{ij}$' can result from unsystematic changes in quality, quantity, and cost of services as long as changes tend to balance one another. Systematic changes in quality, quantity, and cost of services would also produce (according to 'a') a systematic change in '$Budget_{ij}$.' These considerations have some definite implications for the way the real system would have to deal with external influences, pressures, needs, or demands for services, if it is to be consistent with our decision system.

If we remember that the budget is a plan or *a forecast of future influences or needs,* the decision-maker's assumption (implied in the simulation model) that next year's influences, demands, needs, etc., will be nearly the same as this year's, is not an unreasonable one.

To pursue this point a bit further—if the simulation model accurately portrays the budgetary process, '$Budget_{ij}$' changes systematically. Relationship 'a,' in turn, indicates a particular kind of response to pressure or needs *during* the budget period. The response is *not* to change budget levels ('$Budget_{ij}$') necessarily, but to take the budget ceiling as a given and respond to pressures or needs *within* the ceiling. Referring to relationship 'a,' our model of the budgetary process is consistent with the notion that:

    i. Changing pressures and demands are met within a fixed '$Budget_{ij}$' by:

        1. Varying the quantity of service-($Quan_{ij}$)

        2. Varying the quality of service-($Qual_{ij}$)

        3. Increasing efficiency (lowering the U $Cost_{ij}$) or increasing organizational slack[2] (raising U $Cost_{ij}$)

This means that the street maintenance department would have a stable or constantly increasing[3] budget, but might respond to an unusually 'hard' winter (resulting in more than the usual amount of pot-holes in streets) as follows:

    a. Spending less time on each pot-hole filled—fail to roll the asphalt even with the adjacent pavement, ignore small pot-holes, etc.,

    b. Pulling people out of the garage or warehouse and putting them to work filling pot-holes, and/or

    c. Using asphalt instead of bituminous concrete, etc.

---

[1] Implied by the preliminary-calculation, goal-setting, and aspiration-level functions in the submodels [item 3 in Figure V-1b (DEPT.), item 4 in Figure VI-1b (MAYORS), and item 9 in Figure VII-1b (COUNCIL)]. 'Demand' is used with its economic meaning as a measure of relative value of services.

[2] See R. M. Cyert and J. G. March, *A Behavioral Theory of the Firm* (Englewood Cliffs, N.J.: Prentice-Hall, Inc., 1963), for a discussion of "organizational slack" and its uses, pp. 36-38.

[3] Relative to other municipal departments.

In what other ways can departments respond to pressures created by community influentials, economic elites, interest groups, etc.? If model parameters are constant over time and *if* interest groups, elites, etc., have an influence on budget amounts for various departments, then it must be a constant influence and reflected in parameter values. The presence of external influence or pressure in the political sense was not detected in the budget formation process during interviews with city officials.[4] A much more likely response pattern for the department is to change the agenda in response to political or elite pressure (if, in fact, it is exerted). The relevant question for the department head is: Whose street gets repaired first? And not: How many dollars should be spent on street repair? Which neighborhood will the new park be placed in? Not: How many new parks? In the short run, the simulation model implies that responses to political, interest group, or elite pressure (*if* it exists), could also mean that:

    ii. *Response to political pressures and elite influences takes the form of a change in departmental attention rules rather than a change in budget levels.*[5]

Long-run changes in budget levels would be in response to a large number of *cumulative* short-run pressures, demands, and influences and not a relatively-immediate response to a single influential or a 'one-shot' demand. Similarly, our model is consistent with the notion that

    iii. *The decision system is responsive only to long-run, cumulative political pressures and citizenry needs or to reasonably catastrophic events in the short-run.*[6]

Informational Inputs to the Model as External Influence

Perhaps the only widely perceived *exertion* of political influence, if it can be called that, in all three cities during all the years studied was

[4] "The same groups show up at the public (budget) hearings every year. They all want more money. Employee groups want a pay raise, cultural groups want more money for their interests, and some citizen group is always ready to complain about taxes (being too high). Our costs keep rising, but revenues don't. We just don't have the revenues to satisfy them even if we wanted to." Aldo Colautti, mayor's executive secretary, Pittsburgh, Pennsylvania. Interview, October, 1964.

    "It's impossible for me to consider all the requests for increased spending. No one seems to want anything cut out of the budget." Hon. Joseph M. Barr, mayor, city of Pittsburgh, interview, December, 1964.

    "Of course, many individuals and groups come to the city with what some might term 'legitimate' requests for municipal funds. The city simply does not have the resources necessary to satisfy these requests." Alfred M. Pelham, controller, city of Detroit, interview, December, 1964.

[5] See Chapter IV, pp. 47-49, for a discussion of the budget limit as one of a series of departmental decisions.

[6] One such cumulative (or constant) pressure comes from city employees for pay increases (see Chapter VI, p. 72). See analysis of model residuals in Chapter IX for the effects of catastrophic events.

through the revenue estimate. This influence was not exerted in any direct sense or dictated by anyone. As has been indicated by the chief budget officers in all three cities, the only interest the business community has in the operating budget is that they don't want taxes increased. This, of course, is a highly general kind of interest or influence that most people in the community are aware of. Adding to this consideration is the fear on the part of the mayors in our three cities that business and industry will move to the suburbs or to a different region. This fear (especially acute during the 1958-62 period), coupled with the knowledge that the average voter takes a dim view of tax increases, conspires to keep tax rates constant, if at all possible, in light of citizenry service demands.[7]

In summary, the complexity of the problem of estimating external demands, pressures, influences, etc., for the budget period conspires to prescribe that the municipal government perceive these influences to be relatively constant while planning and to respond to variable demands and influences (when they occur) by:

1. Varying service quantity,
2. Varying service quality,
3. Varying service cost,
4. Changing attention rules,

rather than by changing the budget-level rules. In addition, the requirement of a balanced budget makes pressure appear black and white. Hold the line on taxes *versus* increase expenditures. The problem is usually mediated by financing increased expenditures through the naturally increasing tax *yields* (not rates).

Budget as Externally-Determined Event: Literature

The decision process usually cited in the literature is, briefly:

1. Different interests are present in the community.
2. These interests have different amounts of force, power, or influence.
3. The outcome is determined by the 'sum of the (exerted) forces'; the most powerful wins.

Dahl, in *Who Governs?* (a study of decision-making in New Haven, Connecticut), contends that the "influentials" are a function of the particular decision and that different influentials are found in different decision areas at different points in time. He also contends that many influence groups arise quickly in response to a problem, attempt to exert influence, and dis-

[7] Just when cumulative service demands are great enough to force a step increase in revenues (tax rise) is a question that lack of time-series data reluctantly forces us to avoid. See discussion on revenues in Chapter VI.

appear with the problem. Hunter, in a study of community decision-making in Atlanta *(Community Power Structure)* concludes that there is a single group of influentials whose influence is pervasive over all decision areas (and over time).[8] While these studies cover a much broader range of community decisions than our simulation model, the operating budget for a city covers a very significant class of community decisions and hence, will have a good deal to say about community decision-making in general. Both Dahl and Hunter emphasize the importance of extra-governmental influence as a crucial determinant of community decisions. Extra-governmental influence plays a very minor role in our simulation model, entering the process explicitly only through the revenue estimate and the model parameters.[9]

A tentative conclusion of our study, *relative to budget-level decisions,* is that influence groups are either an unimportant part of the process or that a stable influence group exists.

The works of Truman and Key also suggest that governmental decisions are the result of an interaction of interest group pressures.[10] Evidence that extra-governmental groups and individuals are important in determining municipal budgets is not an explicit part of our model. The process uncovered in this study can be characterized as a problem-solving situation involving a great deal of uncertainty. Few effective guidelines for reducing the uncertainty are found in the extra-governmental environment and hence, influentials play a very minor role in the formulation of municipal operating budgets. To the extent that budgets represent an allocation of resources between functions, influentials play a very minor role in the gross allocation of governmental resources.

External Influences—Summary

It would be naive and probably false to suggest that no extra-governmental influence exists in a community and that governments do not respond, in some fashion, to this influence. It is *not* naive or inaccurate to suggest that governments do not respond through the municipal operating

[8] R. A. Dahl, *Who Governs?* (New Haven: Yale University Press, 1961), pp. 197-198; and F. W. Hunter, *Community Power Structure* (Chapel Hill: University of North Carolina Press, 1953).
[9] While it is true that by assuming a stable group of influentials with a stable set of interests, the influence of extra-governmental groups *could* be reflected in the empirically determined model parameters, *no* indications that this might be the case were uncovered in the interviews. The only stable interest group of importance appears to be internal—municipal employees.
[10] D. B. Truman, *The Governmental Process* (New York: Alfred A. Knopf, Inc., 1960). V. O. Key, Jr., "The Lack of a Budgetary Theory," *American Political Science Review* (December, 1940).

budget.[11] Rather, response to pressure and influence appears to take place at different levels of decision-making altogether.

A Hierarchy of Disjoint Decision Processes

Our model suggests that a convergence of voter and business interests helps 'hold the line' on tax rates and hence tends to limit the total amount of resources available for governmental allocation.[12] Within this total-resource (revenue) constraint, an allocation is made among departments and expenditure categories. Effective guidelines for the allocation of total resources to departments consist of historical level and trend data. Effective cues from the environment are *not* received from community interest groups either because they are not articulated or because the cues, taken in *toto,* add up to an infeasible set of demands on the system (i.e., every interest group wants more money spent in a particular area, but no increase in taxes, etc.). The perceived incomparability of data ("Pittsburgh's hills make it impossible to compare Detroit street expenditures with ours.") also means that few cues are received from other cities. In this context, a series of decisions is made, resulting in a municipal operating budget.

Once the operating budget is formulated, it provides a set of guidelines for actual expenditure decisions. Within the budget constraints, departments are free to allocate resources as they see fit during the fiscal year. At this stage—actual expenditures *versus* planned expenditure totals —influence appears to be an important consideration. Influence groups appear to articulate their demands at this point in the process. A neighborhood pressure group may influence the location of *one* new park in a particular year, but will not have much to say about the *total* number of new parks to be opened in that year. What our model suggests is that budgets in municipal governments are reasonably abstracted documents, bearing little direct relationship to specific community pressures.

The budget provides the limits, within which the response to pressure and influence must be conducted. *The entire process could be viewed as a hierarchical system or sequence of constraints.* The revenue estimate is fixed first. Then a budget is formulated (using historical guidelines)

---

[11] A similar conclusion is reached by R. C. Martin and F. J. Munger, *Decisions in Syracuse* (Garden City, N.Y.: Anchor Books, Doubleday & Company, Inc., 1965), p. 14.
[12] Although a specification of governmental response-to-pressure-and-influence is outside the scope of·this study, the scheme reported was suggested from some of the interviews with governmental officials. Evidence in support of a stable system of community interests or power is found in the naive models (A1, A2, and A3) tested in Chapter VIII. The fact that simple models fit the data very well indicates a great deal of stability in the decision process.

within the revenue constraints. The final budget or appropriations then provides constraints for an entirely different class of expenditure decisions. We suggest that response to political pressure and citizenry needs (at least in the short run—one city administration) is almost always exercised within budgetary constraints. We suggest that the budgetary constraints are set using a procedure independent (at least consciously) of political or interest group pressure. Little or no conscious attempt is made by administrators to translate present influence into future spending plans. The only behavior observed, consistent with the theory that budgets are responses to community 'pressure,' is that departments always try to increase appropriations. It appears, then, that power, influence, and pressure are so far removed from the budget-formation decision process that they lose much of their usefulness in a positive theory of municipal budgeting.[13]

Demand for Services

Much of the literature on municipal finance consists of attempts to relate municipal expenditures, by function, to variables expressing a demand for services (population) and an ability to pay. Related attempts to define *service standards* and *unit costs* are also widespread.[14] (See discussion in Chapter II, pp. 12-14).

The implied model of budget-making focusing on demands for services is also a force model, similar to the one discussed earlier. The service standard-unit cost approach implies that budget-makers translate the sum of forces into dollar amounts. The forces in this formulation are public demands for service levels (amount of service) and for service quality (cost of services).

The discussion related to forces as community influentials and pressure groups also applies when the forces are service demands or needs. *Our model does not view the budget-maker as a passive instrument—as a person who merely translates forces, needs, demands, etc., into dollar*

[13] Wildavsky reaches much the same conclusion (implicitly) when discussing federal budgetary calculations. Aaron Wildavsky, *The Politics of the Budgetary Process* (Boston: Little, Brown and Company, 1964), Chapter II. O. A. Davis, M. A. H. Dempster, and Aaron Wildavsky, "A Theory of the Budgetary Process," *American Political Science Review* (September, 1966), provide empirical evidence in support of Wildavsky's conclusions. In a study of decision-making in Syracuse, Martin and Munger also reach this conclusion. Martin and Munger, *op. cit.*, p. 14.
[14] Seymour Sacks and W. F. Hellmuth, *Financing Government in a Metropolitan Area* (New York: The Free Press, 1961); Harvey E. Brazer, *City Expenditures in the United States* (New York: National Bureau of Economic Research, 1959); Jesse Burkhead, *Government Budgeting* (New York: John Wiley & Sons, Inc., 1956); Arthur Smithies, *The Budgetary Process in the United States* (New York: McGraw-Hill, Inc., 1955); C. E. Ridley and H. A. Simon, *Measuring Municipal Activities* (Chicago: International City Managers' Association, 1938).

budgetary amounts. The budget-maker in our model is a problem-solver who is unable (due primarily to cognitive and informational limitations and conditions of economic scarcity) to make this direct, deterministic translation of expected 'demands' and needs to budget requirements. Consequently, our model is also at variance with the service standard-unit cost approach to budgeting.

Related to the service standard-unit cost conceptualization of the budgetary process is the idea of a performance or program budget where a desired level of activity is specified (x miles of streets, y applications processed, etc.) or a particular program is expressed as a combination of personnel and materials. The activities are then multiplied by unit costs and the resulting dollar amount constitutes the budget. Obviously, our budget model first calculates dollar amounts and then transforms this into personnel and materials. The model is one of a line-item budget, not a performance budget.

BUDGET AS INTERNAL BUREAUCRATIC PROCESS

Budget as System of Precedents and Commitments

Many organizational theorists have emphasized the role of precedent in decision-making, especially in regard to the budget.[15]

Our model is heavily history-dependent and relies almost exclusively on historical data. The DEPT. submodel has, as informational inputs, current appropriations, recent trends in appropriations, and the most current expenditure data available [items 1 and 2 in Figure V-1b (DEPT.)]. Goals, constraints, and aspiration levels are based upon the relationship of preliminary calculations and problem solutions to historical appropriations data [items 5, 6, and 7 in Figure V-1b (DEPT.)]. DEPT. submodel parameters indicate that, relative to other information and influences, current appropriations are more important than anything else in determining the department budget request for the next year.[16]

The effect of historical data on the MAYORS and COUNCIL submodels is exerted through informational inputs and the providing of standards and constraints:

1. Information—previous budgets and recent appropriations trends [item 3 in Figure VI-1b (MAYORS) and item 7 in Figure VII-1b (COUNCIL)];
2. Goals, constraints, and aspiration levels stated in terms of historical standards [items 4, 16, 21, 25 in Figure VI-1b (MAYORS) and item 15 in Figure VII-1b (COUNCIL)].

[15] See Chapter II, pp. 14-21, for a discussion of this approach.
[16] In item 3 in Figure V-1b (DEPT.), the values of the parameter A_{ij} (multiplier of $APPR1_{ij}$) are generally much larger than any of the others.

In general, the historical character of the municipal budgetary process indicated above is certainly well represented in our formal model.

Budget as Result of Subunit Conflict

Another set of conceptualizations emphasize the competitive nature of a budget.[17]

Our formal model of municipal resource allocation contains no mechanisms that explicitly allow for the agency-conflict conceptualization of municipal budgeting. Features of the model could be related to subunit-conflict, however. The relative values of parameters in the preliminary-calculations mechanisms [item 4 in Figure VI-1b (MAYORS) and item 9 in Figure VII-1b (COUNCIL)] for various departments in the MAYORS and COUNCIL submodels *could* provide a measure of the differential ability of departments to secure funds. The nearest thing to evidence indicating a competition for funds discovered in the interviews was the fact that departments were perceived differentially in Detroit relative to the honesty or accuracy of their departmental request.[18] In all three cities departments were crudely differentiated by participants in the budgetary process when categorized as growing or declining departments. The assumption inherent in our model is that *if* there is conflict between subunits (departments), the relative strengths of departments in this competition are reasonably constant over time.

The agency-conflict view of budgeting is a prominent one in the literature and merits further investigation. For instance, March and Simon, commenting on "conflict centering on budget allocations," state that where funds are limited, conflict between subunits over the budget is likely to be high.[19] This hypothesis is clearly relevant to municipal resource allocation.

RAW CONFLICT. We should be able to find indications of departmental conflict in our data if conflict does, in fact, exist. Consider a raw conflict situation, where the unit or department with the most leverage, pull, resources, etc., wins. In our case, the competition for funds, if any, clearly is a fight over increases in appropriations from year to year, rather than over the total budget amount for a department. Several models of raw conflict over resources between business firms exist in the literature. It may be useful to draw an analogy between, on the one hand, (a) the conflict of many firms over sales in an industry with a fixed demand schedule for the industry's product and (b) the conflict of many departments for budget appropriations where the city has a revenue constraint. Haire cites the situ-

[17] See Chapter II, p. 15, for a discussion of this approach.
[18] See pp. 69-70.
[19] J. G. March and H. A. Simon, *Organizations* (New York: John Wiley & Sons, 1958), p. 123.

ation where larger firms (departments) in the industry find it easier to obtain bigger sales increases (appropriations increases) than the smaller firms (departments)[20]—magnitude of growth being directly proportional to size. The explanation for this phenomenon is that large firms have more resources available to aid in securing additional portions of the market. If this is the case in the municipal resource allocation process, we should expect to find a significant, positive correlation between account growth and account size.[21] An analysis of cross-sectional account data in each city should shed some light on a 'raw-conflict-for-funds' situation where success is a function of account size.

The correlations between account growth ($APPR2_{ij} - APPR1_{ij}$) and size ($APPR1_{ij}$) are found in Table XI-1.

TABLE XI-1

Relation of Budget Increases to Subunit Size

Account	*Correlation (R^2)*
Cleveland	
Salaries and Wages	.049
Other	.245
Detroit	
Salaries and Wages	.187
Expenses	−.533
Equipment	−.688
Pittsburgh	
Administrative Salaries	.242
Nonadministrative Salaries	.330
Materials, Supplies, Expenses	.139
Equipment	−.146
Maintenance	−.138
Miscellaneous	.303

[20] Mason Haire, *Modern Organizational Theory* (New York: John Wiley & Sons, Inc., 1959), p. 281. Haire's growth theory is

$$\frac{dN_t}{dt} = AN_t - BN_t^2$$

where N_t = number of employees, time t. The second term lowers the rate of increase in N as N becomes larger. We have dropped the second term ($-BN_t^2$) in our discussion because it is felt that none of the accounts have approached their maximum or limiting size.

[21] H. A. Simon and C. P. Bonini make the same assumption ("law of proportionate effect") while investigating the distribution of changes in the sizes of firms, "The Size Distribution of Business Firms," *American Economic Review*, 1958 (48), p. 610.

The findings do not support the hypothesis that large accounts in large administrative units are more able to secure increases than smaller units. In fact, the reverse seems to be true. At least in Detroit, for non-salary accounts, the larger accounts appear to be more vulnerable to cuts in appropriations. In the Cyert-March formulation of organizational decision-making, this would be explained by the visibility of large departments or accounts. In a situation where funds are scarce, search for ways to cut costs would tend to focus on the larger expenditure categories rather than small ones.[22]

LOG-ROLLING. Another form of conflict is one that features a "nego-tiated peace" rather than all-out combat. Cyert and March envision the organization as a coalition of members (departments), each having sep-arate goals (increases for a member's department). The goal conflict of coalition members (obtaining as large an appropriation as possible in our case) is being resolved by using "local rationality, acceptable-level decision rules, and sequential attention to goals."[23] Briefly, the goals of the depart-ment heads would be treated as independent constraints that the organiza-tion must satisfy (in the final appropriations bill). Quite clearly, this is the way subunit demands are dealt with in our model (see Chapter VII). For instance, one set of model constraints, or department goals, requires that there be no overall cuts in departmental appropriations from one year to the next [items 16 and 21 in Figure VI-1b (MAYORS)]. Another conflict-resolving device cited by Cyert and March is "sequential attention to goals." In the allocation of scarce municipal resources, this might imply that one year, one department gets an increase and the next year another department is chosen. Increases are passed around year after year.

An analogous situation is cited by Dexter in a study of congressional voting behavior.[24] Members of a block or voting coalition were observed

---

[22] Cyert and March contend search is triggered by a problem (estimated costs exceed estimated revenues). They also hypothesize that the search for a solution to the prob-lem is "simple-minded" and initial search is ". . . based initially on . . . simple rules: (1) search in the neighborhood of the problem symptom . . ." If the "symptom" is costs which are "too high," then Cyert and March would predict search in those de-partments having the greatest costs (size). Cyert and March, *op. cit.*, p. 121. Our model does not formally include this kind of search behavior. However, it appears that this mechanism is important only in Detroit. As the computer model now stands, this "bias in search" could be easily incorporated by reading in large departments first —the largest department (i) would be numbered 1 and the smallest would be num-bered N, so that the deficit-elimination routines (items 15, 16, 18, 19 in Figure VI-1b) in the MAYORS model would have a meaningful priority list for departments as well as for account types.

[23] Cyert and March, *op. cit.,* p. 117.

[24] R. A. Bauer, I. de S. Pool and L. A. Dexter, *American Business and Public Policy: The Politics of Foreign Trade* (New York: Atherton, 1963), pp. 431-432, 437.

to have traded votes—'you vote for my project and I'll vote for yours.' Perhaps the budget is really a set of transactions between departments where attention to one department's goals in one period is traded for attention to another department's goals in a preceding period. This way of viewing the problem implies that each department knows something about the internal operations of other departments (so department heads can demand special treatment 'this time' to make up for the special treatment another department got 'last time'). With this in mind, we would expect to find more sequential-attention-to-goals, transaction, or trade-off behavior in those account categories that are most visible[25]—administrative salaries and equipment.

If the transaction view of the world is a proper one, we would expect to find a very small or negative correlation between increases 'this year' and increases 'last year,' where total resources are rationed.

Another way of stating the above is that if a department received an (unusual) increase last year it is unlikely to receive one this year.

Correlations between 'this year's increase' ($APPR2_{ij} - APPR1_{ij}$) and 'last year's increase' ($APPR1_{ij} - APPR0_{ij}$) are calculated in Table XI-2.

The statistics cited above indicate that there is probably *some* transaction behavior in Detroit and Pittsburgh, but probably very little in Cleveland. This kind of behavior is implicitly present in our formal model through coefficients attached to the trend term ($APPR1_{ij} - APPR0_{ij}$) in some of the preliminary screening mechanisms [item 3 in Figure V-1b (DEPT.), item 4 in Figure VI-1b (MAYORS), item 9 in Figure VII-1b (COUNCIL)].

Perhaps we can summarize our discussion of conflict by noting that the data (interview and statistical) agree with our formal model in suggesting that conflict is not a particularly important feature of the budgetary problem-solving process.[26] Rather, we would generally agree with Cyert and March who contend that "[w]here resource rationing is necessary, we expect . . . a tendency to use arbitrary allocation rules that maintain the relative positions of the members of the coalition."[27] The presence of "arbitrary" rules is clearly what our model describes.

---

[25] "Organizations resolve conflict among goals, in part, by attending to different goals at different times. Just as the political organization is likely to resolve conflicting pressures to 'go left' and 'go right' by first doing one and then the other . . ." the city administration is likely to resolve conflicting pressures for budget increases by first granting one and then the other. Cyert and March, *op. cit.*, p. 118.

In the above situation, awareness of the conflict (and hence, the need to resolve it) is crucial. We would then expect more sequential-attention-to-department-demands to occur in visible accounts in visible departments.

[26] See pp. 69-70.

[27] Cyert and March, *op. cit.*, p. 270.

TABLE XI-2

Relation of Budget Increases to Previous Increases

Account	*Correlation (R^2)*
Cleveland	
Salaries and Wages	−.079
Other	.210
All Accounts	.028
Detroit	
Salaries and Wages	.028
Expenses	−.687
Equipment	−.362
Pittsburgh	
Administrative Salaries	−.237
Nonadministrative Salaries	−.278
Materials, Supplies, Expenses	.393
Equipment	−.391
Maintenance	−.119
Miscellaneous	.245
All Accounts	−.190

Budget Formation as Problem-Solving and as a Decision Process

We have spent a great deal of time elsewhere in this report, describing the model as a problem-solving routine or a decision process. Repeating these notions in their entirety would serve little purpose. Instead, we will note that the model of municipal resource allocation presented can very usefully be described as decision-making or problem-solving in the face of a great deal of uncertainty, a large number of constraints, and few cues from the extra-governmental environment, rather than as a process having a great deal of political content.

The remainder of the section will discuss the areas of agreement between this study and other theories and investigations in problem-solving and decision-making—notably those of Cyert and March,[28] March and Simon,[29] Lindblom,[30] Wildavsky,[31] Newell and Simon,[32] and Simon.[33]

[28] Cyert and March, *op. cit.,* Chapters I-VI.
[29] March and Simon, *op. cit.,* Chapters VI-VII.
[30] David Braybrooke and C. E. Lindblom, *A Strategy of Decision* (New York: The Free Press, 1963).
[31] Waldavsky, *op. cit.,* pp. 1-123.
[32] H. A. Simon and Allen Newell, "Computer Simulation of Human Thinking and Problem-Solving," in Martin Greenberger, ed., *Management and the Computer of the Future* (New York: John Wiley & Sons, Inc., 1962).
[33] H. A. Simon, "Theories of Decision-Making in Economics and Behavioral Science," *American Economic Review* (June, 1959).

BEHAVIORAL THEORY OF THE FIRM. The broad outlines of a model of internal resource allocation have been sketched by Cyert and March. Although based on research focusing on the business firm, they have contended that it is applicable to other, non-business, organizations.[34] The model of municipal resource allocation presented here is certainly consistent (though it is considerably more detailed) with the Cyert-March hypotheses.

The Cyert-March theory of organizational behavior consists of four major relational concepts.[35]

1. *Quasi-resolution of conflict* where goal conflicts are resolved by viewing goals as a set of independent constraints which an acceptable policy must satisfy; by subdividing problems and delegating them to subunits thereby insuring that subunits deal with a limited set of problems and a limited set of goals, and reducing the potential for goal conflict between subunits; by using acceptable-level decision rules, and by sequential attention to goals rather than simultaneous consideration of all goals.

Our model of municipal resource allocation clearly possesses all of the characteristics cited above. The model in its entirety can be viewed as a system of constraints, applied sequentially. Whenever a constraint is violated, a search or problem-solving procedure is evoked to correct the condition. For instance, the following is part of the MAYORS deficit elimination procedures, (a): [item 9 in Figure VI-1b (MAYORS)] Is the anticipated surplus large enough to finance a minimum salary increase? (b): [item 10 in Figure VI-1b (MAYORS)] If so, increase salary levels for all departments and reduce calculated surplus. The goal above is a subgoal of the *balanced-budget* goal. The factoring of the budgetary problem into subproblems (i.e., departments prepare budget requests independently, the mayor's office puts the solutions to the subproblems together to arrive at the solution to the overall budgetary problem) is an obvious feature of our model. This subdivision of problems is also reflected in our choice of submodels: DEPT., MAYORS, and COUNCIL.

2. *Uncertainty avoidance* where uncertainty is circumvented rather than faced by resorting to feedback-react decision rules to solve problems when they arise; and by negotiating with the environment to insure stability and predictability of the organization's surroundings through standard practices in an industry, or budgets within a firm.

The mere fact that we have been able to program the budgetary

---

[34] Cyert and March, *op. cit.*, pp. 270-288.
[35] See Chapter II, pp. 14-17, for a more complete discussion of the Cyert-March theory.

process can be cited as evidence that we are dealing with a *negotiated environment* (or at least a highly predictable one).

    3. *Problemistic search* where the search for alternatives or solutions is activated by the presence of a perceived problem and depressed by a perceived solution; where the search for solutions proceeds on the basis of a simple model of causality based on the characteristics of the problem, until failure to discover a solution forces use of a more complex model; and where search is biased and aimed in the direction of previous, successful problem solutions, existing organizational information, experience, and training.

Again, our model is very compatible with this notion of the relationship of problem characteristics and search activity. For example, one perceived problem in the MAYORS submodel occurs when the budget is not in balance. If the problem is one of a budget surplus, previous, successful surplus-elimination routines are evoked. If it is a budget deficit problem, similar deficit elimination routines are evoked. Cyert and March argue for the presence of a hierarchy of search routines which are tried sequentially until the problem is solved. This kind of behavior is most clearly present in the MAYORS submodel. For instance, in the case of a deficit, the first search routine involves checking, department by department, account by account, to see if the preliminary budget estimate is within the limits set by the mayors office [item 16 in Figure VI-1b (MAYORS)]. Even this procedure is executed sequentially, starting with the lowest priority accounts (maintenance and equipment) and progressing up the hierarchy until either a solution is reached (deficit eliminated) or all accounts have been processed [items 16, 17, 18, 19, 20 in Figure VI-1b (MAYORS)]. The next (expanded) search activity is a check to see if the preliminary budget request exceeds current appropriations [items 21, 22, 23 in Figure VI-1b (MAYORS)]. This search is also carried on sequentially, first checking low priority accounts and moving up the hierarchy of accounts until all are exhausted or the deficit has been eliminated [items 24, 25, 26, 27 in Figure VI-1b (MAYORS)]. If a deficit still exists, the model eliminates it by scaling down *all* non-salary accounts equally (i.e., the deficit is allocated proportionally to all departments). Quite clearly, our model has not exhausted the hierarchy of search routines in the real budgetary process. There are surely other ways that deficits and surpluses are eliminated in practice. We contend, however, that the principal search routines (those evoked first) have been identified by our model.

    4. *Organizational learning* where learning is perceived as the adaptation, with experience, of goals, attention rules, and search rules. Goals are changed on the basis of past experience, past goals, and the performance of comparable organizations. Attention rules are

reasonably fixed in the short run but shift in the long run towards those that generally indicate satisfactory performance for the subunit involved. Search rules change slowly in the direction of success. If an organization discovers a solution to a problem by searching in a particular way, it will be more likely to search that way in future problems of the same type.

Of the kinds of organizational learning cited by Cyert and March, we have captured only one—adaptation of goals with experience. The preliminary-calculations parts of each of our three submodels are really adjustments in goals based on past experience (expenditure data), past performance (current appropriations and trends in appropriations), but *not* on performance of comparable organizations. As we have argued elsewhere, no comparable organizations exist in the cognitive maps of our decision-makers. The absence of concrete reference points like sales, profits, price, etc., and the lack of performance and service standards means that adaptation of goals is achieved merely through the elaboration of historical data.

Because of the comparatively short period of time covered in our study, we have no hard data on the adaptation of the attention rules and search rules over time. Indeed, one of our principal findings is that there have been no substantial adaptations during our study period. Once again, we are referring only to one fragmented decision in the series of decisions comprising the municipal governing process. (See Figure XI-1.)

FIGURE XI-1
Fragmentation of Municipal Decisions

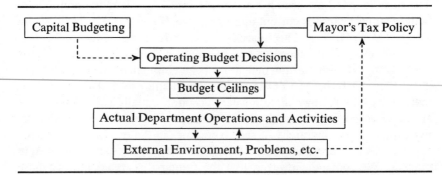

ATTENTION RULES AND SEARCH RULES. We have implicitly argued that the adaptation in attention rules is *not* a key part of the budgetary decision process. Operating budget decisions have a fixed focus of attention, such as existing administrative units and standard account categories and the balanced budget. Only rarely (as our analysis of residuals demonstrated in Chapter IX) is an event in the external environment so catastrophic as to dictate a change in attention rules at the budgetary-decision level.

On the other hand, attention rules seem to be an *extremely* important part of the decision procedures at the *operating* level. Whose street to fix first? Whom to hire to fill a particular vacancy? Where to assign social caseworkers? Operations are *within* a budget constraint, however. The *budget constraint* for the department is isolated from the external environment and subject to a very stable set of attention rules.

Organizational learning with respect to search rules is also absent from our model. Part of the reason for relatively fixed sets of search procedures undoubtedly rests with the system of legal constraints the city must operate within. The balanced-budget requirement clearly limits the scope of search activity as well as dictating the broad directions of search. The public-accountability requirement which limits fund transfers between accounts and departments while spending appropriated money, is another key factor in the limited and stable nature of search activity in the municipal budgeting decision process. Or, to put it more simply, *public accountability* leads to a relatively stable and detailed system of accounts. A detailed system of accounts and the need for tight controls limit the form of solutions to budgetary problems and hence the variety of search procedures that can be *successfully* employed in reaching a publicly accountable solution.

Cyert and March, when discussing internal resource allocation specifically, make two predictions where resource rationing is necessary. "First a tendency to use arbitrary allocation rules that maintain the relative positions of the members of the coalition [departments]; second, a tendency to re-evaluate those estimates that are relatively difficult to defend in terms of traditional organizational practice, standard accounting procedure, or immediacy of tangible return."[36] In general, our study confirms Cyert and March's expectations. 'Arbitrary'[37] allocation rules abound in our model. The rule that if there is an anticipated deficit, all departmental requests must be within a certain percentage of current appropriations [item 16 in Figure VI-1a (MAYORS)], is an arbitrary rule in at least one sense of the word. Our model 're-evaluates' (i.e., cuts) those items most difficult to defend first before moving on to other items. A key part of the deficit-elimination procedure is the hierarchy of account categories with maintenance and equipment being lowest on the list (and most subject to

[36] Cyert and March, *op. cit.*, p. 270.
[37] 'Arbitrary' in the sense that they bear little or no relationship to worth of program, department, etc., but not arbitrary in the sense that they lead to a balanced budget.

re-evaluation) and salaries being highest. The success of the alternative model cited in Chapter VIII that hypothesizes that each department and each account maintains a constant share of the total budget indicates that relative positions of coalition members tend to be maintained in the 'real world' and in our model. Whether this is caused by the arbitrary allocation rules used when resources must be rationed or by the fluctuating revenue conditions during the study period is not clear.

In summary, our findings are highly consistent with the Cyert-March theory of organizational decision-making[38] and could clearly be cited as evidence for the validity of their model in the public as well as the private sector.

ORGANIZATION THEORIES OF SIMON AND MARCH AND SIMON. Reviewing Herbert Simon's pioneering[39] work, *Administrative Behavior*, we have found that things have not changed much in twenty years. Simon writes:

> What does the typical governmental budget include? It tells how much each department will be allowed to spend during the subsequent year, and how it may spend it. How are the particular figures to be found in budgets arrived at? How is it determined that 14 per cent of the budget shall be devoted to fire protection and 11.6 per cent to highways?
>
> A different answer to this question would be given in every community in which it was asked. Some budgets are made by copying off the figures of the previous year's expenditures. Some are constructed by increasing or decreasing appropriations by a fixed percentage. Some are determined by allotting to each department a certain percentage of its request—he who shouts loudest gets most. Some have even less systematic plans.[40]

Aside from the comment that it is not obvious how one would go about improving upon these inadequate methods,[41] little more needs to be said about the consistency of Simon's view of governmental budgeting in 1947 with ours of 1967.[42] The model of municipal resource allocation presented in this report is largely a mixture of the decision rules cited, above,

---

[38] No useful role is played by the concept of "organizational slack" in our model (although the built-in-surplus feature of the Pittsburgh budget due to its detailed system of appropriations might be cited as an example). This is the only important departure of our model from theirs.

[39] 'Pioneering' in an evolutionary sense, at least. Simon's *Administrative Behavior* (1947) led, after a fashion, to March and Simon's *Organizations* (1958) followed by Cyert and March's *A Behavioral Theory of the Firm* (1963). Each work has built upon the previous ones and forms a core of a significant portion of present-day literature on organizational decision-making.

[40] H. A. Simon, *Administrative Behavior,* 2nd ed. (New York: The Free Press, 1965), p. 193.

[41] Lindblom would argue that these methods are not necessarily inadequate. Braybrooke and Lindblom, *op. cit.*

[42] Wildavsky, *op. cit.*, reports similar budget methods in use in the federal government.

by Simon. In the class of communities chosen for study (those over 500,000), it appears likely that we would get the same answer to the question: How are the particular budgetary figures determined?

In *Organizations,* March and Simon generally agree with the notions found in Simon's *Administrative Behavior* and suggest a set of relationships similar to those found in Cyert and March's work. Consequently, our findings are generally supportive of their theories. This is true, however, only if the budgetary decision process is viewed as an ordinary organizational decision process. While discussing internal resource allocation in general, and budgeting in particular, the findings here do not agree with March and Simon's theory.

> Finally, as to conflict centering on budget allocations, intensity of the pressure toward joint decision-making will depend on how limited funds are for the organization as a whole. There is no particular problem associated with dividing an unlimited pie, and so long as the available resources of the organization permit allocations as large or larger than the allocations in the preceding budget period, organizational subunits do not feel any great pressure toward coodination and discussion. So long as such a condition obtains, conflict about budget is probably considerably less than where the supply of money resources is tight.[43]

Exactly what this means in a situation where the supply of money is 'tight,' but still large enough to permit allocations as large as last period's, is not clear. We can only report our findings—'conflict' is not a meaningful concept in the budgetary decision process observed. Certainly, no conflict between departments (organizational subunits) was observed. The conflict—if it can be called that—takes place between the departments and the mayor's office, not between departments. (See pp. 50-51.)

LINDBLOM AND INCREMENTALISM. In Lindblom's works,[44] he has concentrated on the connection between potential problem complexity and decision techniques used to deal with the problem. Briefly, in problem areas where the level of understanding is low, the observed policy-making process is one involving incremental adjustments of existing policies. (Lindblom points out that most political or public policies represent a continuing attack on ever-present problems, hence there is always a precedent to follow and adjust.) He also observes that the incremental adjustments are responses to difficulties with the present policy (very similar to the Cyert-March problem-oriented search notions). Another aspect of the Lindblom view of policy-making is that policy problems are fragmented and dealt with individually, rather than comprehensively. He argues, much as we have in Chapter VI, that the decision-maker cannot deal with the problem

[43] March and Simon, *op. cit.,* p. 123.
[44] C. E. Lindblom, "The Science of 'Muddling Through,'" *Public Administration Review* (Spring, 1959) and Braybrooke and Lindblom, *op. cit.*

otherwise. The Lindblom notions could actually be viewed as a subset of the Cyert-March model of organizational decision-making.[45]

Our findings certainly exhibit the broad characteristics of incrementalism. How Lindblom would deal with the very real balanced-budget constraints and the fact that, at some level of detail, the results of initial, incremental adjustments at the department level must be modified so that the entire budget is balanced is not clear. Let it suffice to say that our findings are generally consistent with Lindblom's hypotheses.

THE FEDERAL BUDGET: WILDAVSKY, DAVIS, AND DEMPSTER. Aaron Wildavsky in *The Politics of the Budgetary Process*[46] presents a descriptive model of the decision process surrounding the formation of the federal budget. His description is similar to ours in many respects. It is also very consistent with the ideas expressed by Braybrooke and Lindblom, and Cyert and March.

Wildavsky's basic methodology was the same as ours—interview data from participants to construct a description of the decision process. Our model of municipal resource allocation was formalized, quantified, placed in the form of a computer program, and used to regenerate municipal budgetary decisions in an attempt to assess the validity of our theory. Davis, Dempster, and Wildavsky formalized part of Wildavsky's theory[47] using a series of regression models. Their results confirm many of the behavioral mechanisms described by Wildavsky.

Wildavsky has a partially verified theory of the budgetary decision process in the federal government. How does it compare with the municipal process?

Wildavsky's model attributes the traditional bureaucratic roles to participants—as does ours:

department or agency: ask for more than they expect to obtain—advocate of agency's activity

chief executive and staff: scale down agency requests

legislative body: tends to cut executive budget

[45] Lindblom has chosen to concentrate on justifying or illustrating the advantages of incrementalism as a decision procedure where knowledge is incomplete, and cognitive abilities are limited. Cyert and March, on the other hand, have approached the problem from a less philosophical viewpoint and have seen fit to place great emphasis on the empirical validity of their theory.

Lindblom's model is consistent with the Cyert-March model, but the key features of the Cyert-March model could not be derived from Lindblom.

[46] Wildavsky, *op. cit.*, p. 61.

[47] O. A. Davis, M. A. H. Dempster, and Aaron Wildavsky, "On the Process of Budgeting: An Empirical Study of Congressional Appropriation," in Gordon Tullock, ed., *Papers on Non-Market Decision-Making* (Charlottesville, Va: Thomas Jefferson Center for Political Economy, 1966).

Except for the role of the legislative body, our findings agree with Wildavsky's. As has been seen, the municipal legislative body generally serves as a 'rubber stamp' for the executive operating budget.[48] Congress, on the other hand, plays a much more important role. The primary reasons for this role differential seem to be:

1. Lack of staff in city councils (no 'congressional' committee staffs, etc.) and lack of specialization on part of individual councilmen.
2. Balanced budget requirement in city charters—Congressmen can add or subtract freely without having to arrive at a predetermined total (revenue estimate).

In a section on "aids to calculation," Wildavsky cites two that seem especially relevant:

1. Satisficing—Rather than maximize, budget officials "satisfy and suffice." Clearly, our model is centered around a series of satisfactory or acceptable-level goals or decision criterion.
2. Incrementalism—"The largest determining factor of the size and content of this year's budget is last year's budget. . . . [I]t is based on last year's budget with special attention given to a narrow range of increases or decreases."[49] The municipal budgetary process is an example of government-by-precedent, organizational inertia, and the result of a highly constrained decision process.

Closely tied in with the incrementalism concept are two widely-held notions in the federal budgetary process—base and fair share.

Base refers to the "general expectation among participants that a department's activities will be carried on at close to the going level of expenditures . . ."[50] Calculations of a base from which adjustments are made are a prominent part of each of our submodels [item 3 in Figure V-1b (DEPT.), item 4 in Figure VI-1b (MAYORS), items 5 and 9 in Figure VII-1b (COUNCIL)].

Fair share refers to the expectation that a department will receive its fair share of any increases in the total budget. If, over time, we assume that each department's fair share of the budget total increases is constant, the following relationship should be statistically significant:

$$(APPR2_{ij} - APPR1_{ij}) = d_{ij}(TBUD2 - TBUD1)$$

This, of course, corresponds to our alternative model 3 (see Chapter VIII). The relationship did not hold. Davis, Dempster, and Wildavsky also found

---

[48] On several occasions during the study periods, city councils have vetoed the mayor's *tax* policy, but not the *distribution* of expenditures within a given budget ceiling (revenue estimate).
[49] Wildavsky, *op. cit.,* pp. 11-16.
[50] Wildavsky, *op. cit.,* p. 17.

that fair share does not hold for the Congressional portion of the federal budgetary process.[51]

While the description of the federal budgetary process is extremely consistent with the municipal case, there is one very important difference. The key motivational concept or decision criterion in the MAYORS submodel is that of the balanced budget. All problem-solving activity in the MAYORS submodel is directed towards eliminating a deficit or a surplus (i.e., achieving a balanced budget). True, the President does indicate a budget ceiling for the Bureau of the Budget to follow in the federal process,[52] but according to Wildavsky, the Presidential ceiling or target does not play nearly the role in the federal process as does the balanced budget or revenue constraint in the municipal process.[53] Therefore, one might expect a somewhat different process in a Presidential-staff model (of the Bureau of the Budget) than in our MAYORS submodel. One would expect that fewer coordinating mechanisms would be found in the federal process than in the municipal, and that there would be a greater reliance on *ad hoc,* independent decision rules as opposed to the more systematic treatments in the MAYORS process.[54]

In summary, although important differences exist between the federal budgetary process as described by Wildavsky (and supported by Davis) and the municipal process, most of the decisional mechanisms (Wildavsky's "aids to calculation") are remarkably similar.

This strong similarity in resource allocation procedures suggests that there may be some global kinds of decision processes at work here. First, consider internal resource allocation in non-market organizations. As will be seen in Chapter XII, the same decision procedures found in metropolitan budget-making also seem relevant for state and local governments, universities, and school boards. Second, had we chosen the Cyert-March theory of organizational decision-making (based on private sector observations), we would have arrived at a theory much like the one we have by just "studying the process as found." Does this fact suggest a set of pervasive decision mechanisms? We now turn to another, growing body of literature which may shed some light on the latter question.

COMPUTER SIMULATION OF HUMAN THINKING AND PROBLEM-SOLVING

Recently there have been a number of attempts to simulate the thought and problem-solving processes of human subjects. The object has

[51] Davis, Dempster, and Wildavsky, *op. cit.*
[52] Wildavsky, *op. cit.*, pp. 183-4.
[53] Wildavsky, *op. cit.*, p. 37.
[54] A system of linear regression models might be a more appropriate way to formalize the federal process than the simulation model used in our municipal study.

been to construct a computer program that attempts to solve a particular problem or complete a particular task in the same way as humans. By 'in the same way' we mean the computer program uses the same symbolic information at each stage of the problem-solving sequence and manipulates the information in the same ways as human subjects.

Ignoring for the moment the question as to whether collectivities of people behave like individuals, it might be interesting to compare our model of human decisional behavior with a more general model. A computer program called the General Problem-Solver (GPS) exists that purports to contain a "system of methods—believed to be those commonly possessed by intelligent college students—that turn out to be helpful in many situations where a person confronts problems for which he does not possess special methods of attack."[55] This program, and modified versions of it, has successfully simulated human problem-solving in proving algebraic and geometric theorems, in puzzle-solving situations, in problems in symbolic logic, and in chess playing.[56] What are the general characteristics of this program, and how do they compare with the problem-solving simulation attempted in this report?

The General Problem-Solver (GPS)

STRUCTURE OF GPS. The program deals with symbolic *objects* that describe or characterize situations—the given situation, the desired situation, various intermediate possible situations. The program also deals with symbols representing *differences* between pairs of objects and with symbols representing *operators* that are capable of inducing changes in the objects to which they are applied.

Goal types. The processes of GPS are organized around *goals* of three types:

1. *Transformation* goals: to transform object *a* into object *b*,
2. *Difference Reduction* goals: to eliminate or reduce difference *d* between objects *a* and *b*,
3. *Operator Application* goals: to apply operator *q* to object *a*.

Methods. With each type of goal in GPS there is associated one or more methods, or processes, that may contribute to the attainment of the goal. The principal methods in the present version of GPS are three in number, one for each type of goal:

1. Method for transformation goals: to transform *a* into *b*,

---

[55] Simon and Newell, *op. cit.*, p. 138.
[56] Edward Feigenbaum and Julian Feldman, "Simulation of Cognitive Processes," in Edward Feigenbaum and Julian Feldman, eds., *Computers and Thought* (New York: McGraw-Hill, Inc., 1963), pp. 272-274.

    a. Notice a difference, *d,* between *a* and *b;*
    b. Establish the goal of reducing *d* between *a* and *b;*
    c. Try to attain this new goal;
    d. If successful, find a new difference and repeat.

2. Method for difference reduction goals: to reduce *d* between *a* and *b,*

    a. Recall an operator, *q,* that is relevant to differences of the type of *d;*
    b. Establish the goal of applying *q* to *a;*
    c. Try to attain this new goal;
    d. If successful, return to the previous transform goal.

3. Method for operator application goals: to apply operator *q* to *a,*

    a. Compare conditions for application of *q* with object *a;*
    b. If these are not satisfied, establish and try to attain the goal of transforming *a* into an object that meets these conditions;
    c. When the conditions are satisfied, apply *q* to *a,* and return to the previous difference reduction goal with the modified object, *a'.*

This is a rather simplified description of what goes on in GPS, but it gives the broad outline of the program. GPS, to put it simply, is a program that reasons about ends and means. It is capable of defining ends, seeking means to attain them, and, in the process of so doing, defining new subsidiary ends, or subgoals, to the original end.[57]

A reasonably detailed comparison of the features of GPS and aspects of our simulation model should prove enlightening. Because the MAYORS submodel is by far the most significant of the three and it is involved more in problem-solving than in estimating (unlike the DEPT. submodel), it will be compared in detail with the *methods* outline, above. In essence, the verbal flow chart in Chapter VI is presented with the appropriate references to the General Problem-Solver *methods.* For instance, "check of preliminary total against revenue estimate to determine if a surplus or a deficit is anticipated" is an example of method 1.a, "notice a difference, *d,* between *a* and *b.*" Since we are trying to transform *a* into *b, a* refers to the preliminary total and *b* refers to the revenue estimate. The MAYORS submodel viewed as a special case of the General Problem-Solver is found in Figure XI-2.

GPS's correspondence with the municipal resource allocation model appears to be extremely close. The *goal* is to transform preliminary budget recommendation totals to the revenue estimate total. A *difference* between anticipated expenditures and revenue is calculated and the goal of reducing

---

[57] Simon and Newell, *op. cit.,* pp. 139-141.

FIGURE XI-2

GPS and MAYORS Budget Recommendation Model*

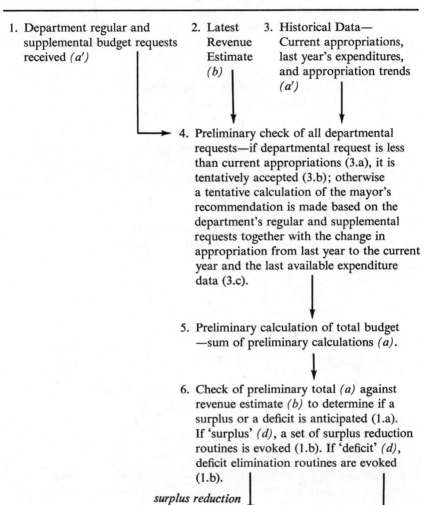

1. Department regular and supplemental budget requests received *(a')*

2. Latest Revenue Estimate *(b)*

3. Historical Data— Current appropriations, last year's expenditures, and appropriation trends *(a')*

4. Preliminary check of all departmental requests—if departmental request is less than current appropriations (3.a), it is tentatively accepted (3.b); otherwise a tentative calculation of the mayor's recommendation is made based on the department's regular and supplemental requests together with the change in appropriation from last year to the current year and the last available expenditure data (3.c).

5. Preliminary calculation of total budget —sum of preliminary calculations *(a)*.

6. Check of preliminary total *(a)* against revenue estimate *(b)* to determine if a surplus or a deficit is anticipated (1.a). If 'surplus' *(d)*, a set of surplus reduction routines is evoked (1.b). If 'deficit' *(d)*, deficit elimination routines are evoked (1.b).

surplus reduction

7.

deficit elimination

* Italicized items in parentheses refer to 'objects,' e.g., *(a')*; for code, see next paragraph. Other items in parentheses, e.g., (1.b) refer to GPS methods, pp. 209-210.

    Object Code:
        a'   department requests, other data inputs
        b   revenue estimate
        a   mayor's set of budget recommendations
        d   difference between *a* and *b*
        q   operator

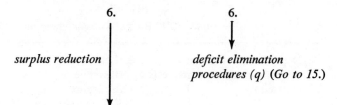

6.

surplus reduction

6.

*deficit elimination
procedures (q) (Go to 15.)*

7. Calculate magnitude of anticipated
   surplus or residual (1.a) *(d)*.

8. Find total salaries and wages for
   the city (preliminary estimates)
   (2.a) *(a')*.

9. Is the anticipated surplus *(d)* large enough
   to finance a minimum salary increase?
   (2.b), (2.c), (3.a)

   yes   *no*

10. If so, increase salary levels for
    all departments and reduce calculated
    surplus (3.c), *(a)*, (1.d), *(d)*.

11. Is there enough anticipated surplus *(d)* left
    to distribute among departments? (2.a),
    (3.a), (1.c)

    yes   *no*

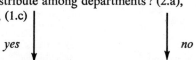

12. Consider the highest priority
    (2.a), *(q)*, (2.d), non-salary
    account category (that has not
    yet been considered) starting
    with general expense accounts and
    ending with equipment and
    maintenance accounts (2.b).

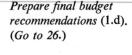

*Prepare final budget
recommendations* (1.d).
(Go to 26.)

13.

13. Increase the budget recommendation for the account category under consideration *(a)* for all departments (until the surplus *(d)* is exhausted) by granting a portion (2.c) of each department's supplemental request. When (and if) money runs out, prepare final budget recommendation *(a)*.

money runs out
(2.d), (1.d)

14. Move to next highest priority account category and go to 12. If all categories have been considered, prepare final budget recommendations (Go to 26) (3.a).

Go to 26.

Deficit Elimination Procedures *(q)*

6.

Deficit Elimination Procedures (2.a)

15. Consider accounts in reverse order (2.a) of their priority (consider equipment and maintenance first, salaries last).

16. Check, department by department, to see if the preliminary budget estimate (mayor's) *(a)* for the account category under consideration is within the limits *(b')* (% of current appropriations) implied in the mayor's budget letter to departments (3.a).

outside limits

within limits (3.b)

17. If within limits, no change in preliminary budget estimate *(a)*.

18. Decrease preliminary estimate of budget so that it falls within mayor's limits *(a')*, *(d)*, (3.c).

19.

19.

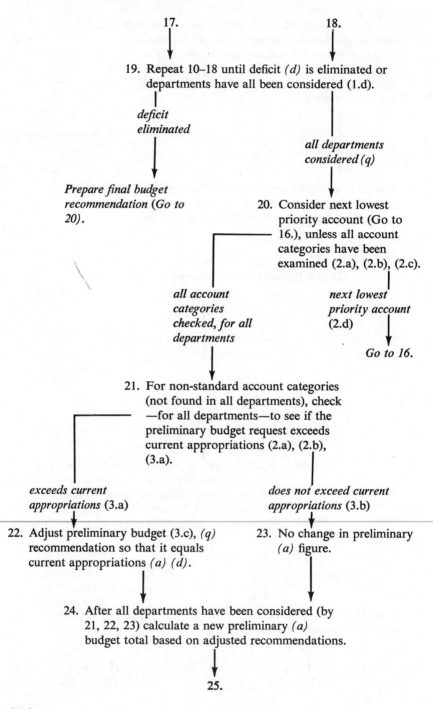

17.   18.

19. Repeat 10–18 until deficit *(d)* is eliminated or
    departments have all been considered (1.d).

deficit
eliminated

                                        all departments
                                        considered (q)

Prepare final budget
recommendation (Go to   20. Consider next lowest
20).   priority account (Go to
                                     16.), unless all account
                                     categories have been
                                     examined (2.a), (2.b), (2.c).

            all account   *next lowest*
            categories   *priority account*
            checked, for all   *(2.d)*
            departments
                                            Go to 16.

21. For non-standard account categories
    (not found in all departments), check
    —for all departments—to see if the
    preliminary budget request exceeds
    current appropriations (2.a), (2.b),
    (3.a).

exceeds current   *does not exceed current*
appropriations (3.a)   *appropriations* (3.b)

22. Adjust preliminary budget (3.c), *(q)*   23. No change in preliminary
    recommendation so that it equals   *(a)* figure.
    current appropriations *(a) (d)*.

24. After all departments have been considered (by
    21, 22, 23) calculate a new preliminary *(a)*
    budget total based on adjusted recommendations.

25.

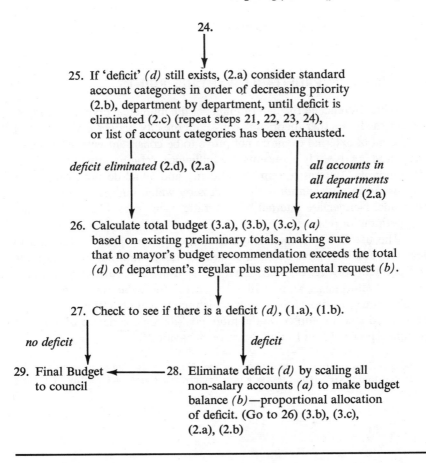

24.

25. If 'deficit' *(d)* still exists, (2.a) consider standard
account categories in order of decreasing priority
(2.b), department by department, until deficit is
eliminated (2.c) (repeat steps 21, 22, 23, 24),
or list of account categories has been exhausted.

deficit eliminated (2.d), (2.a)   *all accounts in*
                                                 all departments
                                                 examined (2.a)

26. Calculate total budget (3.a), (3.b), (3.c), *(a)*
based on existing preliminary totals, making sure
that no mayor's budget recommendation exceeds the total
(d) of department's regular plus supplemental request *(b)*.

27. Check to see if there is a deficit *(d)*, (1.a), (1.b).

no deficit   *deficit*

29. Final Budget ◄———— 28. Eliminate deficit *(d)* by scaling all
to council   non-salary accounts *(a)* to make budget
                              balance *(b)*—proportional allocation
                              of deficit. (Go to 26) (3.b), (3.c),
                              (2.a), (2.b)

this difference (i.e., eliminating the surplus or deficit) is established. A
set of operators relevant to the differences of a given type is evoked—deficit
elimination procedures or surplus reduction procedures, depending on
whether the difference is positive or negative. The various difference-
reduction routines are tested to see if the conditions for applying a particular operator are met (Is the anticipated surplus large enough to finance
a minimum salary increase?). If so, the operator (raise salaries uniformly)
is applied, and so on. Two conclusions emerge:

1. Our model of municipal resource allocation is consistent with the
   information-processing approach found in GPS.
2. A means-ends analysis of the municipal resource allocation process
   appears to be a reasonable one, where the end is a balanced
   budget and the means consists of a fixed set of residual elimination

routines (surplus reduction for positive residuals and deficit elimination for negative residuals).[58]

PROFITABLE VANTAGE POINTS

With reference to the determinants of the municipal operating budget, we can easily see that theories that assume the city budget is the result of some kind of external event do not prove to be consistent with the process uncovered in this study. Concepts like 'influence,' 'community needs,' 'service standards,' 'interest group,' 'politician,' and 'elite' do not prove to be very useful in understanding the process by which budget *level* decisions are made. Neither are internal bureaucratic phenomena like 'conflict' and 'competition for resources.'

The useful conceptualizations of the budgetary phenomena tend to deal with administrative decision processes, human information processing and problem-solving, organizational decision-making, satisficing, sequential-attention-to-goals, and the like. In general, those theories which appear to be most descriptive of the way in which municipal operating budgets are formulated tend to emphasize the more goal-directed behavior of man, his cognitive processes and administrative behavior.

[58] The questions relating to the genesis of the formal, budgeting process and how it developed into a GPS-type process are extremely interesting and worthy of further study.

CHAPTER XII

Summary, Conclusions, and Model Domain

OUR STUDY of budgetary decision processes led to the construction of a positive, formal model of individual and organizational problem-solving. This model was tested by comparing its output and characteristics with that of three municipal governments. In the process of constructing and testing the model much has been learned, both about the substantive aspects of the problem and the methodology employed.

Broadly speaking, we were able to show that a political decision process is not very much different from other organizational behaviors. By viewing the municipal operating budget as a problem to be solved, we were able to draw on several theories of organizational and individual decision-making.

CONCLUSIONS: SUBSTANTIVE

We found the same basic set of problem-solving heuristics being used in all three cities. These heuristics have evolved over time and have the same general features as many theories of individual problem-solving. The heuristics involve a type of means-ends analysis where the end for the department is increased revenues and for the mayor and the council, a balanced budget. Through a series of successive approximations, the mayor converges on the problem solution. The problem, as dealt with, is primarily one of *balancing* the budget rather than optimally allocating resources. The budget represents but one decision in a hierarchy. Generally, a particular decision provides constraints or guidelines for decisions that follow. Allocation or budget *level* decisions are made within the confines of the revenue decision; actual department activities or *mix* decisions are made *within* the constraints provided by the budget level decisions.

Budgetary Process

The principal substantive conclusions are as follows:

a. The municipal budget is but one decision process in a sequence. The sequence might be described as follows—the revenue or level decisions, the budget or allocation decisions (municipal budget), and the actual expenditure or operating decisions. The elements in this hierarchy of decisions are separated by time and partly because of this are treated as large independent problems. Each decision in the sequence forms a rigid constraint for the decision following it in the sequence. This administrative division of labor has the effect of making the municipal resource allocation problem a manageable one.

b. The structure of decision rules for formulating the municipal operating budget is basically the same, over time, in large cities, with only the parameters varying between cities. (The model functions are of the same mathematical form, contain the same variables, and differ only in the constant terms or parameters.)

c. Three institutional rules or norms appear dominant in all municipalities tested:

  1. Balanced budget requirement in city charter (revenue constraint);
  2. Physical form of budget preparation sheets for departmental budget requests (forces historical comparisons);
  3. Uniform wage policy (one group of employees does not receive a wage increase unless all municipal employees are granted one —wages account for 65-80 per cent of a city's total operating expenses); occasionally, uniformed police and fire ranks are treated separately from the other city employees.

d. The decision rules used by members of the municipal governments appear to be internalized and to a large extent insulated from external pressures.

e. The revenue constraint appears to be the only strong link between the budgetary subsystem and the larger socio-economic environment of which it is a part.

f. The decision system appears to be responsive only to special revenue opportunities, to long-run, cumulative political pressures, or to reasonably catastrophic events in the short-run.

g. Municipal operating budgets exhibit a great deal of organizational inertia.

h. The decision process can best be described as one in which the problem-solver is faced with a great deal of uncertainty about future events and must satisfy a large number of fairly restrictive constraints, rather than as a process having a great deal of political content.

i. The general hypothesis that *the more 'complex'[1] the problem, the 'simpler' the decision rules used to solve it* is supported by the findings of this study.

j. 'Last year's' budget represents a sort of equilibrium solution to the municipal resource allocation problem for city officials. 'The year's budget' represents marginal adjustments to 'last year's' solution to obtain 'this year's' solution.

k. The lack of comparable performance data *perceived* by city officials (budgets and expenditures in one city 'not the same' as 'our situation') leaves the budget-maker with little alternative but to use historical decisions as the primary reference point for current decisions.

Budgets, Pressure, and Influence

Because of the prominence of power-pressure-influence models in the literature, several conclusions of our study are worth restating:

a. While political pressure or citizen demands may determine the pattern of expenditures *within* certain accounts for certain departments, there is virtually no *direct* connection between political pressure and departmental budget or account *totals*. Such pressures may constitute an important determinant of department attention rules (whose street is repaired first), but not department budgets.

b. Negligible pressure is exerted by the business and industrial community to influence expenditure distributions or levels, directly. The only observable pressure is to keep property tax *rates* constant.

c. The nature of public demands on the council is usually such that in order to satisfy one you would have to satisfy them all. If all demands were yielded to, it would mean revision of the entire mayor's budget—including revenues—which the council is not equipped to do. Consequently, the council also ignores specific or direct pressures.

d. Relevant pressure for the system appears to be of a cumulative long-run nature which results in a very *gradual* adjustment of parameters, or is related to dramatic external events.

[1] Where complexity is indicated by a large number of interdependent, real variables, by a high degree of uncertainty attached to key variables, and by non-linear relationships between variables.

CONCLUSIONS: METHODOLOGIES IN POLITICAL RESEARCH

The findings of this study have both substantive and methodological implications for the field of political science and the study of political decision-making. Below are some differences between the approach presented here and the more familiar political science approaches:

1. Role Theory—Role has been used in this study to describe a decision process or information-processing program (three submodels illustrating three roles). Role as a position is described by a computer program. The interaction of individuals and role is defined in terms of empirically determined parameters. Individuals' cognitive maps of the decision are partially specified by the accounting system.

2. Case Study—
   a. One of the central problems with the case-study approach is the identification of *relevant* cases. The use of a process model to filter out normal or predictable decisions (similar to our analysis in Chapter IX) can help identify *relevant* cases.
   b. Another problem with case studies is that they are seldom comparable. The model presented here can easily be adapted to other cities or governments (see discussion following), and in so doing, provides an excellent organizing device for a case study.

3. Cumulative Effects of Marginal Changes—Many times a change or shift in policy is relatively minor at the time it is made, but because of cumulative effects, many actually represent a major change. A computer simulation model allows us to logically deduce the long-run or cumulative implications of such a shift (see Chapter X).

4. Institutionalists vs. Behavioralists—There has been some controversy over the proper emphasis for political research—individual behavior or institutions, etc.? What should be the unit of analysis? In our study, both elements proved important. The institutions provided constraints for the individual decision-makers and partially specified interaction patterns. For a process-oriented study, the question of the relative importance of institution and individual behavior is an empirical one, and, in the context of a particular situation, a hollow one.

For the most part, political science literature in general, and the community decision literature in particular, has focused on the identification of key variables (who makes decisions?). The use of a simulation model requires a logically complete specification of the decision units in the process as well as a precise definition of the research problem. In addition, a process model requires not only that the key variables be identified but that the *relationships between key variables* be specified.

One common argument against the formalization of political phenomena has been that political behavior is too complex and involves too many interrelationships to formalize. Given the capabilities of the computer, this argument loses much of its appeal. There are no inherent reasons why political researchers cannot realize the advantages of formalization (see Chapter III).

OTHER APPLICATIONS OF THE MODEL

The likelihood of our model's applicability in other contexts relates to the behavioral assumptions of our model (see Chapters IV-VII) and problem characteristics. Would we expect to find the same behavioral mechanisms operating in institutions with a similar budgetary structure? Smaller municipal governments? Other forms of local government (counties, townships, school boards, etc.)? At other levels of government—state or federal? In other kinds of public and semi-public institutions in our society? Naturally, the further we venture from the three data points used by the model, the less, substantively, we will be able to say.

Applicability to Other Municipal Governments

There is little reason to believe the model would not describe the budget process in most large United States cities. On the assumption that political, economic, and population characteristics represented in our sample are similar to the characteristics of other large municipalities, the model should apply.

The likelihood of the model's applicability to other levels of government, and, ultimately, to other non-market organizations, is a function of the environmental, informational, and cognitive 'assumptions' of the simulation model. We might ask what sort of decisional situation our model describes. We could then ask whether the situation is likely to be found in other contexts and is sufficiently similar to warrant the prediction that the model presented here would apply.

Briefly, our model is one where:
1. The need for a decision (appropriations bill) exists.
2. A large number of goals, programs, activities, etc., exists.
3. These goals, programs, activities, etc., cannot be reduced to a common dimension—they are incomparable.[2]

[2] In a business firm such diverse activities as production and sales can be compared (in theory at least) through their effects on profit, share of market, etc.

4. Few objective measures of goal achievement, program output, activity level, etc., exist to aid the decision-maker(s).[3] Information for the decision process is *not* provided by the market, comparable organizations, etc.
5. Little is known about relationships among variables (effect of one department's programs on those of another or the effect of a department's program on the variable in society the program is designed to affect).

Faced with the situation outlined above, the organization structures the problem (through a system of standard accounts and administrative units), separates or disengages it from other, somewhat-related decisions (operating budget takes capital budget as given, revenue as given, and largely ignores actual activities of component departments), redefines the problem and makes it more manageable (problem becomes one of balancing the budget, rather than one of optimal allocation of resources), and finally solves the problem using procedures that have worked in the past and by using available reference points and standards (historical standards—last year's budget) together with summary kinds of impressions, perceptions, and attitudes (certain departments perceived as growing, efficient, etc.).

APPLICATION OF THE MODEL TO SMALLER MUNICIPALITIES AND LOCAL GOVERNMENTS. Will the model describe budgetary decision processes in medium-sized cities (100,000 to 500,000)? The response to this question will depend on two items: 1) the extent to which the decisional situation described above corresponds to that of a medium-sized city, and 2) evidence in the form of a verbal model of budgeting in medium-sized cities.

We would expect all medium-sized cities to be faced with the same kinds of problem complexities as were found in the larger cities: large numbers of goals and variables, and largely unknown relationships between key variables. None of the *general* conditions of decision should be radically different from those 'assumed' by our model. If the city itself is the center and focal point of its own urban system, we would expect our model to apply as well as it did in the larger cities. A smaller city is faced with somewhat less complex problems involving fewer variables and interrelationships. This simplification is more than offset by the fact that the small cities also have fewer sources of information and computational abilities.[4]

---

[3] While dollar inputs can be measured, outputs cannot—hence efficiency cannot be used as an effective criteria or measure.

[4] For example, Detroit compiles the final budget and puts together departmental requests and the mayor's recommendations using electronic data processing equipment. Smaller cities, having less manpower to start with, probably would have to do the same work manually—taking much more time to complete and leaving less time for analysis.

In general, the higher the government level, the more informational and computational resources. This advantage is roughly balanced by the increased problem complexities at higher levels—leading to use of simplified decision processes.

In a report of budget-making in three medium-sized municipalities in Illinois, Anton describes a decision process remarkably similar to ours.[5] The fact that he describes an information processing procedure consistent with ours in each of the three cities is heartening, especially when it is realized that different forms of government are involved (Council-Manager and Commission), using radically different formal procedures for arriving at final appropriations because of the ambiguity of Illinois law. The same basic strategy is followed in all cases—sequential reduction of the difference between anticipated revenues and expenditure estimates. The three cities involved all form the core of the metropolitan area in which they are located, however.

If a municipal government is the central city in its region, its range of governmental activities will be reasonably well-determined and constant over time. If a municipality is really a suburb or satellite of a larger municipality, then we might expect three different kinds of budgetary behavior:[6]

1. The larger city could provide a meaningful set of service standards for the satellite. The central city would provide a comparable organization that could be relevant for the goal-setting process in the satellite—providing an alternative for historical standards and comparisons.
2. There could be a much greater tendency for the satellite government to perform a supplemental role in its community by *adding* to services provided by the central city and other area governments to bring them up to par.
3. Because of spill-over effects of central-city and metropolitan-area services, satellite governments might tend to focus on services of special interest to their residents (education in Shaker Heights, Ohio; Mt. Lebanon, Pennsylvania; and Grosse Pointe, Michigan, in our sample).

We would also expect that, because of its supplemental role, the budget of a satellite city would include a great number of contract items where the satellite would reimburse other area governments for services

[5] Thomas Anton, *Budgeting in Three Illinois Cities* (Urbana, Ill.: Institute of Government and Public Affairs, 1964).
[6] A study of budgeting in Santa Monica, California, was conducted by the author, Brent Bradley, and Hal Boren and indicated little difference between the process described here and the decision process in Santa Monica, contrary to our expectations.

performed (utilities and some forms of public works, for example). The greater the number of contract items, the fewer budget items actually under the control of the satellite government.

In the special case where the adjacent cities are of roughly equal size, we would expect a form of competition through tax rates and municipal services. Other than saying the tax rates and service levels in Dallas and Ft. Worth, Minneapolis and St. Paul, Duluth and Superior should be nearly identical, it is not clear what these levels should be. Does competition lead to lower tax rates, higher service standards, or does it just provide cities with a set of reference points for comparable organizations?

In summary, except in the special cases of twin cities and satellites, we have every reason to believe our model would apply to smaller municipalities than Cleveland, Detroit, or Pittsburgh.[7]

It would be possible to modify our model to take care of these special cases by adding a term in our model's preliminary calculations procedures [item 3 in Figure V-1b (DEPT.), item 4 in Figure VI-1b (MAYORS), item 9 in Figure VII-1b (COUNCIL)] to reflect the existence of another point of reference in addition to historical budget levels. In those activities in which the satellite assumed a supplemental role, the preliminary calculation procedure would involve a kind of two-stage process. The first stage would calculate the desired level of activity on the basis of historical and central-city standards. The second stage would subtract the central city's contribution to that activity for a particular year from the desired level to obtain the satellite's preliminary calculation or contribution.

Applicability to State and Federal Governments

In general, problem complexity is even greater at the state and federal levels than at the municipal level. There are more variables to be considered and the relationships between policy and result are even more tenuous than those in the urban area. Hence, we would expect an even greater reliance on the kinds of decisional aids and rules of thumb described in our model in state and federal resource allocation.

Two major studies contain verbal models of the budgetary process in the state and federal government. Anton's description of the state budgetary process in Illinois is nearly identical to the federal budgetary process described by Wildavsky.[8] The only difference of any significance

---

[7] Simon found that suburbs in the San Francisco area felt some obligation to maintain uniform property tax rates but no pressure to equalize service levels. H. A. Simon, *Fiscal Aspects of Metropolitan Consolidation* (Berkeley: University of California Press, 1943), pp. 2-4.

[8] Thomas Anton, *Politics of State Expenditure in Illinois* (Urbana, Ill.: University of Illinois Press, 1966). Aaron Wildavsky, *The Politics of the Budgetary Process* (Boston: Little, Brown and Company, 1964).

is that the budget constraint for the state is anticipated revenues, whereas for the federal budget, it is the figure provided by the President (based, usually, on a desire to keep the deficit less than a certain amount). The rest of the process seems nearly identical. Wildavsky's description of the federal process for non-military appropriations has been discussed in great length elsewhere (see Chapter XI) in this report. Little would be accomplished by repeating the discussion here. Anton's description is so similar that to discuss it in detail would be repetitious also.

LEGISLATIVE REVIEW. An important element of the state and federal process, as described by Anton and Wildavsky, is missing from our model of the municipal process. COUNCIL plays a very minor role in the municipal resource allocation process whereas Congress and the state legislature are key elements in this process. The reasons for differences in the legislative processes are found in two constraints imposed on municipal legislatures but not on state or federal:

1. Balanced budget—the demands on council members are one-sided (Increase expenditures or decrease taxes. With a balanced-budget constraint, the logical thing to do is nothing.);
2. Lack of staff to compile information necessary for an effective review.

If the mayor were required to leave a relatively large estimated surplus in his executive budget and council were provided with a staff, one would expect council behavior to parallel that of its state and federal counterparts.

Defense Spending

The major item in the federal budget, defense spending, has not been discussed explicitly. The Department of Defense (DOD) is an incredibly complex organization, consisting of the services—Army, Navy, Air Force, and Marine Corps—and the Office of the Secretary of Defense (OSD). Once each year this organization must submit a budget to the President and Congress. The major account categories are:

> Military Personnel (30% of total budget)
> Operation and Maintenance (25%)
> Procurement (30-35%)
> Research, Development, Testing, and Evaluation (10%)
> Military Construction (2%)

In addition, DOD administers civilian programs (Corps of Engineers) and a number of miscellaneous activities.

The budget structures within each service are unbelievably detailed. Superimposed on this appropriations-budget structure is an entire budget-based planning system.

Basically, OSD, the Joint Chiefs of Staff, and the Service Secretaries create a five-year plan based on an assumed force structure for the U.S. military. For any given year, the force structure can be read off the plan and a defense budget is implied. These budgets or plans are stated in terms of major *programs,* which are different from the appropriations categories. Coordination of the services is achieved through common force structure assumptions. As the budgeting process starts,[9] each service 'reads off' its portion of the five-year force structure plan. Each service then generates dollar amounts for the eight major DOD program categories:

> Strategic Retaliatory Forces
> Continental Air and Missile Defense Forces
> General Purpose Forces
> Airlift and Sealift Forces
> Reserve and National Guard
> Research and Development
> General Support Forces
> Military Assistance

OSD staff review these budgets, plans, etc., calling for justification of budget requests, additional analysis, etc. As budget submission time draws near, *program* amounts must be converted to *appropriations* categories. This all sounds hopelessly complicated because, in some sense, it is. Yet the requirements of the final submission somewhat simplify the pattern of outcomes.

1. *Joint Determination of Defense and Total Spending*

The entire DOD budget must add up to a total within an acceptable range. The public, the President, Congress, and the Executive Branch have a cognitive map of the federal budget characterized by a differentiation between defense and non-defense spending. How is the defense total determined? It appears to have the form of a collective opinion jointly arrived at, over time, by the President, Director of the Bureau of the Budget (BOB), and the Secretaries of State and Defense. It seems that a DOD-total decision is made at this level. Factors affecting the adjustment (from the previous year) in the DOD level appear to be things like international crises, domestic needs, and Soviet defense policies. The collective opinion of the total (not always easily arrived at) appears to have all the characteristics of a summary attitude. The environment throws up information, some of which is perceived to be relevant to defense spending. Some information causes an implicit upward adjustment in totals, some argues for a reduction. One

---

[9] In reality this process is more one of continually updating implications of changing force plans than 'beginning' the budget process for any given year.

important bit of information for the Secretary of Defense concerns service budget requests. The cumulative effects of this information (external events) specifies, in a broad sense, a new level of defense spending. Apparently a range for the total is arrived at during a meeting on the overall budget involving at least the following: the President, Director of BOB, Secretaries of Defense, State, and Treasury (for revenue estimates), and sometimes the Chairman of the Council of Economic Advisors. Secretary of Defense McNamara more or less fixed the range himself, considering the factors cited above. A bargaining session, of some sort, apparently results in filling in the components of the budget equation:

$$\begin{bmatrix} \text{Total Government} \\ \text{Revenues} \end{bmatrix} + \begin{bmatrix} \text{'Tolerable' Deficit} \end{bmatrix} =$$

$$\begin{bmatrix} \text{Defense Spending} \end{bmatrix} + \begin{bmatrix} \text{Non-Defense} \\ \text{Spending} \end{bmatrix}$$

Although none of the terms in the above equation are independent of one another, defense spending appears to have more influence over changes in total revenues (tax policy) and deficit than does non-defense spending. The two items on the right-hand side of the equation then form budgetary constraints to be administered by the Director of BOB and Secretary of Defense.

2. *Decomposition of the Defense Total*

The services have some demands to be met that appear to enter the budgetary process as somewhat independent constraints to be satisfied. Services want: a) an increase in budget total, b) an increase in numbers of military personnel, and c) a constant or increasing *share* of the total military budget. Collectively these constraints result in surprising year-to-year stability in service shares. Major changes (more than 2-5 per cent) in service shares have occurred only in wartime periods during the last thirty years.[10]

3. *Reconciliation of Program and Appropriation Budgets—Budget Trimming Time*

In spite of the change in budgetary procedures in the McNamara era, the need for a decision that satisfies some constraints on budget totals leads to arbitrary, across-the-board budget cuts similar to those in our MAYORS model. A priority of accounts also seems to exist. Vulnerable

---

[10] This is unlike our findings for the municipalities. In Chapter X we demonstrated that a substantial reallocation of resources between subunits does occur during normal revenue conditions. The budget shares in municipalities drifted, over time, whereas the defense shares appear constant. Under abnormal conditions (great jumps or drops in revenues—external events), defense budget shares behave very much like the municipal system.

accounts, when budgets must be cut, seem to be operations and maintenance and procurement. In addition, inventory and supplies which are part of the logistics policy constitute manipulable funds. Changing inventory requirements from quantities necessary to sustain 120 days of combat to ninety days represents a significant source of budgetary funds. The difficulty of measuring impacts of these expenditure cuts may account for their vulnerability.

The flexibility in procurement schedules may account for its vulnerability. Military personnel amounts, on the other hand, are pretty well fixed, once force levels have been decided. One major effect of the planning-programming-budgeting system (PPBS) in DOD seems to be to make some expenditures more defensible in the budget-cutting operation than others. This, of course, places some premium on measurability of costs and benefits.

In summary, defense budgeting seems to consist of two, related stages: the bargaining stage where the budget total is arrived at, involving the external environment to a great extent, and decomposition of the total, involving internal, bureaucratic considerations. These two stages are not dissimilar to the revenue-tax-policy and allocation-budget-balancing phases of municipal budgeting.

The crude, broad-stroke description of DOD budgeting is based on incomplete interview data and is meant to be suggestive, not definitive, in any sense.

Applicability of Model to Other Non-Market Organizations

Four major remaining categories of non-market organizations are:
1. Institutions of higher learning
2. Foundations and charities
3. Quasi-governmental or special-purpose organizations (school boards, public hospitals, private welfare agencies (local), political parties, etc.)
4. Professional societies, unions, etc.

Our model of resource allocation is predicated on multiple-goal problems dealing with intangible, diverse, and loosely related variables. To the extent that resource allocation decisions are not characterized this way, we would expect our model to be inapplicable. With this in mind, two kinds of organizations will be discussed in some detail: a local board of education and a university.

BOARD OF EDUCATION. Gerwin, in a study of internal resource allocation in the Pittsburgh Board of Education, cites:

. . . six key decisions that must be made in compiling the budget. These involve:

1. legal and contractual obligations such as prescribed salary increases and debt service on existing bond issues,
2. department requests,
3. a general salary increase,
4. debt service for a new bond issue,
5. improvements in educational services,
6. a reserve to provide additional funds for the year after next.[11]

How does this correspond to our resource allocation model? The effect of legal and contractual obligations in our model is minimal. The legal-obligation feature could easily be added to our model (and, technically, it should be added) by including the proper data inputs, and subtracting the contractual amounts from both revenues and expenditures estimates. The effect would be an accounting procedure that removed the item from budgetary negotiations. The increased descriptive power would not be worth the effort for our purposes, however.[12]

Debt service was handled by our model in much the same way Gerwin outlines his. The amount is deducted automatically from the revenue estimates and never enters into the allocation process (i.e., its allocation is taken as given).

Department requests and salary increases are parallel mechanisms in our MAYORS submodel. Gerwin indicates that departmental requests within 5 per cent of last year's appropriation are automatically given preliminary approval. Our model has an identical mechanism [items 16 and 17 in Figure VI-1b (MAYORS)]. The MAYORS submodel, like Gerwin's, grants a general salary increase as the first item on the agenda if there is an anticipated surplus and if it is large enough (item 9 in Figure VI-1b).

The 'reserve to provide additional funds for the year after next' is a key decision for Gerwin only because the Pittsburgh Board of Education's revenue supply (the Pennsylvania Legislature) meets only every other year. This means their budget must really be a two-year budget. This being the case, much of Gerwin's model consists of a description of how a 'cushion' is built up the first year as a hedge against the second. If, for example, departments were allowed to carry over unspent appropriations from one

---

[11] Donald Gerwin, "A Process Model of Budgeting in a Public Organization: Thesis Proposal," Graduate School of Industrial Administration, Carnegie-Mellon University (mimeo), 1965, p. 13.
[12] If our guesses about satellite cities and their supplemental role are correct, the legal and contractual obligations feature of the Gerwin model would be a necessary one for a model of resource allocation in a satellite city or auxiliary government.

year to the next we might find that 'slack-generation' routines were an important feature of the DEPT. submodel.

The real difference between mechanisms cited by Gerwin and ones uncovered in our investigation highlights differences we are likely to find between general governmental resource allocation (cities, states, and federal) and special-purpose organizations. That difference concerns the measurability of performance and the existence of standards. Performance measures and non-historical standards play no role at all in our model—they do not exist in the real-world for urban centers (see discussion, p. 202). In Gerwin's model, a key question is: Is department performance meeting acceptable levels? Taken literally, this implies both performance measurability and a standard of performance. Another key question that involves external standards[13] is: Has the salary scale fallen to the bottom when compared to other districts?[14]

In summary, Gerwin's model is roughly consistent with ours with the exception of key environmental differences like the existence of performance measures and standards, and a two-year, carryover budget.

A UNIVERSITY. In general, we would expect a university to exhibit great similarities to a large municipality in resource allocation. It too must deal with large numbers of loosely connected variables (physical education and physics, drama and political science, etc.), allocate resources within a budget constraint, etc. The system, like a municipal government, possesses minimal information about its component parts. In general, we would expect to find the same kind of structured problem-solving (1) with departments as DEPT., administrative vice-president as MAYOR, and board of regents as COUNCIL; (2) with academic departments as the primary administrative units; (3) with 'functions' as the account categorization scheme (teaching, research, staff, expenses). We would expect the resource allocation process to be an incremental one, exhibiting a great deal of organizational inertia, to be responsive only to long-run cumulative political pressures or to reasonably catastrophic events in the short-run.

We expect one major difference between internal resource allocation in a university and allocation in a municipality. Where external, objective

[13] In Detroit there is a regular survey of prevailing wages in the area that the city tries to match. This process, however, is loose and salary increases depend at least as much on the revenue picture as on the wage discrepancy. In addition, we have noted the differential ability of uniformed police and fire personnel to secure salary increases (see Table VI-3, p. 90). This could be explained by the existence of published *(Municipal Yearbook)* salary figures for other cities. A more likely explanation for differential pay increases, however, is that police and fire departments were unable to fill authorized positions at existing salary levels.
[14] Gerwin, *op. cit.*, pp. 22-24.

standards exist, we expect they will be used. Three general measures of performance seem to exist: (1) Number of students—budgets geared to dollars per student or average class sizes, etc., (2) Measures of student excellence, like graduate record exam scores (percentile) of both department graduates and new graduate students, and (3) measures of faculty excellence—research grants and publications. We would expect budget increases to gravitate to populous and 'successful' departments. Those departments with the largest number of outside research grants can also expect the largest budget increases.

SUMMARY. The psychological assumptions of the model are consistent with many real-world situations involving governmental and non-market organizational resource allocation.

The possibilities of the general applicability of this model of internal resource allocation to non-market organizations are highly encouraging.

FUTURE RESEARCH DIRECTIONS

Certainly, one reasonable outgrowth of this study would be the application of the model presented here, appropriately modified, to the internal resource allocation problem in other cities, governmental units, and non-market institutions.

The model itself raises many questions for the student of municipal decision-making. As only one decision process in a hierarchy of disjoint processes, attention is immediately drawn to other parts of the hierarchy: a) Revenue decision process, b) The capital budget, c) Decision on actual agency activities (within the agency's budget constraint).

Since the model has been applied only in the short run, lengthening the time dimension focuses on some interesting questions.

  a. What determines the parameter values?
  i. Parameter shifts
    —responses to crises (inability to fill positions, civil disorders, etc.)
    —responses to the availability of funds (federal and state subsidies)
  ii. Parameter drifts
    —changing population and tastes
    —emerging and disappearing problems
  b. What is the role of new department and account categories in the resource allocation process?
  c. What relations (if any) do demographic and ecological variables have on parameter values and decision structure?

d. Over time, do we find evidence of substantial taste agreements between cities? Do municipal operating standards exist in any meaningful sense?

One interesting result of this study, in light of the existing public finance studies, concerns the role of operating standards (dollars per capita) in the setting of budget levels. Over the years, scores of public finance studies have used dollars per capita, by governmental function, as a dependent variable. They have then attempted to explain the variance in per capita expenditures for these functions between cities as a function of things like income and wealth (variations in ability to pay and taste) and residential density. The point here is not a complicated one. If, in fact, such variables are meaningful and standards of sorts do exist, then the form implied in most empirical public finance studies also contains some very strong assumptions as to the kind of information available to our governmental problem-solvers and how they manipulate that information. Per capita expenditure figures are definitely not part of the cognitive maps of our decision-makers and no practitioners seem to be making the kinds of calculations implied by the public-finance formulations of the problem. The existence of municipal operating standards not only implies the existence of certain kinds of information, but also implies its transmission in some way. This entire question deserves re-examination.

Finally, the surprising similarity of certain portions of our model of organizational problem-solving to models of individual problem-solving (General Problem-Solver) raises some interesting questions in organization theory. Are organizational decision processes simple extrapolations of individual cognitive processes?

Clearly, we have raised many more questions than we have answered.

CHAPTER XIII

Normative Considerations

WE HAVE DESCRIBED in great detail a viable system of decision-making in large urban governments. We have also suggested that many of the key mechanisms in this decision system are found in other parts of society. By concentrating on a description of how municipalities *do* make resource allocation decisions, we have explicitly avoided the normative question of how they *ought to* make decisions.

The discussion in this section will be confined to two broad topics—increasing the responsiveness of the existing decision system and increasing the rationality of the system (making the system responsive to the 'right' things).

RESPONSIVENESS OF THE EXISTING BUDGET SYSTEM

In order for a decision system to function properly, it must select and respond to the 'right' things. Finally, the response ought to be an innovative one, as well as just a feasible one.

Attention-Directing Mechanisms

What sorts of problems does the system focus upon? Our model implies that the set of activities carried on next year will consist of roughly the same activities that are being carried on this year. In addition attention is focused on those areas where outside funds are *available* (i.e., federal programs). It seems reasonable to ask that our system's attention-directing mechanisms generally focus on those problems where public demands and basic needs are not being met.

Assume the following model of budgeting for programs within an agency:

$$\sum^{n}\left[\left(\begin{array}{c}\text{Unit Cost of}\\\text{Quality of Service Demanded}\end{array}\right)\times\left(\begin{array}{c}\text{Quantity of Service}\\\text{Demanded}\end{array}\right)\right]=\begin{array}{c}\text{Budget}\\\text{Level}\end{array}$$

n = all services offered by agency

The existing decision process allows for an incrementally changing, drifting budget level. *If* we assume that:

a. Quantity of service demanded changes incrementally from year to year, or
b. Unit cost of the quality of service demanded changes incrementally from year to year, or
c. The list of 'services' performed by an agency changes in such a way that new demands (services) emerge at nearly the same rate that old demands are satisfied (the *net* birth rate for services is constant within an agency)

then we can say that the existing decision system is able to respond to public demands and needs.

When one asks "Are public demands and needs being met?" a knowledge of what the demands or needs are and some criteria for deciding if they are being satisfied are implied. As has already been pointed out, assumptions a, b, and c are untestable because of our inability to measure needs and demands.

Rather we can observe municipal policy changes and see if they correspond to some public need—i.e., is the system responding to citizenry demands? The analysis of unprogrammed budgetary changes (see Chapter IX) demonstrated that most changes represented responses, not necessarily to demands of the general public but to other, more limited 'publics' in the government's environment. The unprogrammed responses seemed to be directed toward federal monies and programs, other governmental decisions (capital items, income tax necessitating collectors, etc.), and service contracts negotiated with other governments and firms. In the government's internal environment, all municipalities in our sample seemed to be continually responsive to the needs of their employees through periodic salary increases, some of which the model expected or programmed and some of which it missed.

Either the decision system is not responsive to general citizenry demands, needs, or problems, or the response is systematic, programmed, and periodic (and 'explained' in our formal model).

Let us assume that public needs are rapidly changing. Could the decision system we have described respond to fluctuating, rapidly-changing needs? Probably not. Examining the reasons why the system is a slowly responding one dealing with small adjustments, we can easily see why it *cannot* respond rapidly.

A key feature of the decision system is its stability. Stability guarantees the ability to reach a decision—to come up with a balanced budget, while upsetting a minimum number of people and programs. The balanced budget requirement forces a simultaneous consideration of all city activities, etc. This potentially difficult problem is solved by holding most of the budget constant. If public needs were fluctuating and rapidly changing, and the decision system were forced to be extremely sensitive to changing needs, sizeable changes in individual budget items would result. A great number of changes in budget items could, in turn, lead to an unsolvable problem and failure to come up with a balanced budget where the budget constraint is 'tight.'

The major problem in having a responsive system for allocating municipal resources occurs when resources are scarce. Presumably, a responsive system would take on new functions as new problems arose. This might be a feasible task if problems disappeared as rapidly as new ones came into existence (assumption 'c,' opposite). This has not been the experience in American cities, however. A responsive system could also be viable if available resources kept pace with public needs.

Responsiveness and the Revenue Constraint

Assuming we wish the government to be more responsive, and assuming this requires some relaxation of the revenue constraint, three strategies *could* bring this about:

1. Eliminate the balanced-budget requirement—allow deficit spending and operating deficits,
2. Find new revenue sources, and
3. Provide for new funding of some municipal services (through system of user taxes and fees).

A municipality could follow the example of the federal government and partially finance operations with deficit spending or borrowed money. This could lead to difficulties for the municipality, however. Unlike the federal government, municipalities cannot control either the supply of money or lending rates. While it is doubtful that deficit spending would exist for a long enough period of time to bankrupt a city, it appears as if a *long-run* policy of continuous deficit spending for operations would raise more problems than it would solve.[1]

Because municipalities must compete with one another in the money market, there are dangers of allowing one political group to pass its deficit along to its successor. It becomes apparent that the balanced budget requirement in municipal government is a reasonable substitute for the profit criteria of the business firm as a guarantee of a financially viable organization.

The three metropolitan governments in our study are at or near the taxation limits imposed by their state legislatures. This is the rule for large municipal governments, not the exception. Assuming the recent Supreme Court reapportionment guidelines (one man, one vote) result in legislatures more representative of urban populations and assuming the 'more urban' legislature is more likely to respond to urban revenue crises by raising taxation limits for municipalities, the future should bring an increased ability for cities to generate new revenues themselves.

As we observed in Chapter IX, additional sources of revenue are not confined to increased tax rates or yields. Other sources involve the transfer of municipal functions to other governments, enticing other governments to pay part of the municipal-service bill, the freeing of funds through federal credits for costs of administering federal programs, and state revenue rebates. In order for increases in these revenues to have the desired effect of creating *flexibility* (enabling the system to be more responsive) in the budget allocation process, they must result in increases in total resources available for allocation. This means that state or federal contributions should either not be earmarked for a special activity or, if earmarked, should result in the release of municipal contributions to other departments rather than just an increase in one department. As we have observed (especially in Cleveland), the net effect of increases in earmarked funds is to

---

[1] Some of these are legal problems involving state constitutions and city charters, others involve the inability to forecast needs, while others relate to participants' perceptions:

"We can only go so far in meeting these needs as is feasible within the limits of these resources without sending the city into a deficit situation. . . . [This] can only lead to ultimate trouble if you follow such a course. Now this is a dilemma which some executives will permit themselves to get into. When the pressures become so great that they will permit certain kinds of artificial budget-balancing practices such as underestimation of expenditures or overestimation of revenues . . . with the almost sure knowledge that these are not going to be met and there is going to be a resultant deficit. . . . You can do this for just so long and then you run into trouble. Eventually you get into the situation where the demands for meeting the deficit are so seriously cutting into your ability to cope with current needs that you actually find yourself in the position of having to cut back services rather than attempting to maintain them at the best possible level consistent with available revenue." Alfred M. Pelham, former controller, city of Detroit, October 6, 1964, interview.

increase the appropriations to a single department, rather than to free funds for other uses. Hence, increases in state funds to the city should not have 'strings attached' *if* the objective is to generally increase system responsiveness. The same criterion, of course, applies to federal funds (unless the city's search for earmarked funds is primarily a response to public needs rather than to the availability of funds, as appears to be the case).

Still another way of relaxing the revenue constraint exists—the refunding of municipal services. In most cities, some capital improvement and service items that directly benefit an individual are financed at least partially through a user tax or fee or a special assessment. Patients in a city hospital pay fees that help cover the costs of medical service. Property owners fronting on new or resurfaced streets must pay a portion of the cost of these improvements, etc. Without getting into the very real question of external economies and diseconomies, one possible source of additional revenue could be realized by financing as many services as possible through user fees. The transfer of activities out of the general fund, if not accompanied by a decrease in general revenues, could result in an increase in total revenue for the remaining general fund activities. By letting the price mechanism (through user fees) determine the output (level of governmental activities), we would then allow the user fee activities to be completely responsive to a form of public demand in many cases. Essentially, this argument is a variant of our discussion above, on earmarked revenues. Stated differently, activities supported by user taxes or fees should represent programs where earmarked funds are an appropriate way of measuring public needs. Hence, one might say that the way to make the system completely responsive to public needs is to place everything on a pay-as-you-go basis. This kind of funding obviously runs counter to widely-held ideas on the role of government. Essentially, the notions (however vague) of a minimum level of community services and minimum living standards are part of our political system. Certain minimum conditions ought to be available to all members of the community rather than those individuals who have an ability to pay. In those areas where services ought not to be a function of ability to pay, re-funding is not the answer to the responsiveness problem. Re-funding, under these conditions could result in a gross misallocation of resources by allowing income distribution to influence responses.[2] In addition an externality argument applies. While taxpayers or users might not be willing to purchase given service levels separately, they might be more than willing to buy the package of services. By allowing individual decisions (through the price mechanism of user taxes) to determine collective choice, the presence of externalities can lead to the wrong choice.

[2] R. A. Dahl and C. E. Lindblom, *Politics, Economics, and Welfare* (New York: Harper & Row, Publishers, 1953), pp. 430-31.

The sum of individual preferences does not always lead to the collective preference.[3]

If we assume that the government's role is to provide services in areas where:

1. Minimum acceptable social states for individuals exists, and
2. External economies and diseconomies are relatively important, then

general-fund financing is called for and resources should not be allocated via the price system.

If for no other reason than the difficulty of deciding which activities represent areas where minimum social states or externalities are relevant, re-funding of significant numbers of government services appears to be an inefficient way of increasing the flexibility of the decision system.

RELAXING REVENUE CONSTRAINT. The point has been made that additional revenues are necessary for changing the attention rules in the direction of increased responsiveness. In addition, these revenues, if they are to have maximal effect on *allocations,* must increase the entire pie, rather than individual slices. A somewhat similar position is taken by Cyert and March:

> . . . [S]lack is the difference between the payments required to maintain the organization and the resources obtained from the environment by the [organizational] coalition. In general, success [at obtaining revenues] tends to breed slack. One of the main problems of slack is a muting of problems of scarcity. Subunit demands are less likely to conflict with other demands[4] [balanced budget]. Resources are more likely to be allocated if they are sought strongly by a single subunit [trying to respond to new public needs]. Thus, distributed slack is available for projects that would not necessarily be approved in a tight budget. We have also argued that the criteria of acceptance of organizational courses of action are heavily influenced by traditional procedures and historical rules of thumb.[5] In general, therefore, the tighter the budget, the more expenditures will be controlled by essentially conservative rules [that preclude new responses to new public needs]. Slack provides a source of funds for

[3] This is true if external economies or diseconomies are present. See P. A. Samuelson, *Foundations of Economic Analysis* (New York: Atheneum Publishers, 1965), pp. 219-227 for his discussion of social welfare functions in relation to the component, individual welfare functions. Also see K. J. Arrow, *Social Choice and Individual Values* (New York: John Wiley & Sons, Inc., 1959), for a discussion of the difficulties of moving from individual to collective preferences.

[4] See mechanism item 6 in Figure VI-1b (MAYORS) in our formal model and note by-passing of departmental request reduction routines in 'deficit elimination' procedures if a surplus is anticipated.

[5] See mechanism items 16 and 21 in Figure VI-1b (MAYORS) under budget deficit conditions in the MAYORS model.

innovations that would not be approved in the face of scarcity but have strong subunit [departmental or public][6] support.[7]

Changing Attention-Directing Mechanisms

If we wish to bring about a substantial change in *attention-directing* behavior, a precondition for these innovations (perception of new problems and discovery of radically different solutions to old problems) appears to be an abundance of organization resources—a relaxation of the revenue constraint.

Before proceeding, one kind of attention-directing mechanism deserves comment. Presumably, the availability of federal funds in a given problem area represents some sort of response to public demands and needs in that area throughout the nation. If the federal government succeeds in identifying major public needs in urban affairs (as is its intention) and makes funds available in that problem area, when cities direct their attention to areas where federal funds are available, in effect they are also responding to public needs and demands. So in many cases the municipal government may be responsive to public needs, indirectly. Although this was not part of our formal model, this systematic attention-directing mechanism is clearly identified in the analysis of unprogrammed changes of Chapter IX.

The relevant information for allocation decisions appears to be primarily historical. The allocations themselves are made to historical administrative units, not to public programs. Allocations do not represent need responses. Under this kind of allocation scheme, responsiveness is left to the individual units and must be within the limits set by the inertial budget procedure. To the extent that administrative units correspond to functions or public responses to need, the present system of accounts *can* lead to a 'responsive' decision system. To the extent this is not the case, the attention-directing mechanisms (using historical guidelines) cannot lead to a 'responsive' system. Precisely this consideration makes program budgeting an appealing reform—it directs decision-makers' attention to programs and outcomes, not administrative units.[8] (See discussion of program budgeting beginning on p. 243.)

Something more is needed for a truly responsive system, however.

[6] If, in fact, the decision system is responsive to public needs, the public becomes a 'member' of the organization for the purposes of resource allocation decisions.

[7] R. M. Cyert and J. G. March, *A Behavioral Theory of the Firm* (© 1963. Reprinted by permission of Prentice-Hall, Inc., Englewood Cliffs, N.J.), pp. 278-279.

[8] Some might argue that this indicates a need to change the structure of the organization so that administrative units correspond to functions. In either case, a change in attention-directing mechanisms for the allocation decision is called for.

More rational decisions not only require more and different information, they require some cognitive abilities. We have had a reasonable degree of success in identifying the key elements of the existing set of search routines. *While additional revenues allow for a significant expansion in the number of search routines the decision system can handle* (and still 'guarantee' solutions), *revenue alone will not lead to this expansion. The presence or absence of additional search routines* (made possible by a relaxed revenue constraint) *will depend largely upon those individuals manning the decision structure.* What additional 'search routines' do public administrators and elected officials bring to their jobs?[9] *Decision systems can make innovation easier or harder, but cannot prevent or cause it.*

So far, the discussion has centered on the overall allocation of resources to departments and functions. The next issue concerns resource allocation within the administrative unit. Does our decision system allow for 'learning' within the subunit?

Does the System Allow Innovations?

By 'innovation' we refer to a particular kind of behavioral change. Our rough definition would include new problems dealt with by an administrative unit as well as new ways of dealing with old problems.

The decision system described here deals with the formation of a line-item, general-fund budget. As we have seen in Pittsburgh, where for one year over half of the City Planning Department's total budget was outside the general-fund budget,[10] the decision system does not prevent a department head from undertaking new programs, providing they are financed with outside funds.

Because the decision system generates only expenditure *ceilings* by line items, innovation or change in *actual* departmental activities is permissible *within* the historically-determined line items. The fact that a department has the same twenty men in each of two successive years does not mean they are engaged in the same activities or programs during these two years.

If innovation requires great flexibility in mix of resources (personnel, expense funds, equipment, etc.), the presence of a series of line-item appropriations really represents a series of constraints on departmental activ-

[9] Most works on role orientation *attempt* to show that different orientations of administrators 'cause' different kinds of behavior. Implicit in this approach is the notion that a given role orientation defines a given set of search routines. See Lawrence B. Mohr, "Determinants of Innovation in Organizations," *American Political Science Review* (March, 1969) for an excellent discussion of this problem.
[10] See Chapter IX, p. 152.

ities. The greater the number of constraints (standard line items or account categories), the less operating flexibility for a department or function. Cleveland with an appropriations bill containing only two account categories is *potentially* more flexible (and by our definition, potentially more innovative) than Pittsburgh with an extremely detailed appropriations bill.[11] Our model has shown that allocations to a particular account category in a given department have nearly as much historical inertia as the *total* department allocations. Anything that would increase a department's flexibility in expenditures would increase the potential for departmental innovations.

Improved conditions for innovation (other than an increase in resources) would result from:

1. Having fewer line items in the final appropriations bill,
2. Allowing department heads to transfer funds from line item to line item (within department total),
3. Allowing departments to carry over unspent appropriations from year to year

and, extending our argument to the macro allocation problem:

4. Allowing the mayor to transfer funds from one department to another in a budget period, without special council approval.

These are all marginal changes in the existing system and would be *relatively* easy to carry out. Notice, however, the changes all run counter to the public accountability function of a municipal budget.

In addition, another kind of innovative behavior is allowed within a department. Improving efficiency is itself a form of innovation. In addition, a more efficient department would be able to undertake new problems within the same budget ceiling. Detroit, in fact, has institutionalized this form of innovation through its system of budget examiners.

In summary, limited innovation is allowed in the decision system. The limiting condition is related to the rigid accounting system.

Does the System Provide Incentives for Innovation?

The conditions for innovation in macro-resource allocation (total between departments) and attention-directing mechanisms have already been discussed and related to the availability of revenues. We have emphasized what Cyert and March refer to as 'slack' innovation which depends on an excess of resources to allow the system to experiment. The subunit can accumulate 'excesses' either through a looser accounting system or increased revenues.

In conditions of scarcity, innovation is sometimes *forced*. Cyert and

[11] See Table VII-1 for a sample of Pittsburgh's appropriations bill.

March argue ". . . that failure induces search and search ordinarily results in solutions. Consequently . . . everything else being equal, relatively unsuccessful firms would be more likely to innovate than relatively successful firms . . . where 'innovation' means a new solution to a problem that currently faces the organization."[12] How do our decision systems deal with problem-oriented innovation?

Under conditions of scarcity—tight budget constraint for a department head—a subunit must innovate if it wishes to expand or add to department activities. "Low ceilings . . . can . . . *permit* several rooms."[13] Scarcity does not *result* in innovation unless there is also a strong desire for additional (replacement) activities. If the attention-directing mechanisms of municipal government are such that many *new* problems are perceived and the department and/or mayor agree on a governmental response then, and only then, will a tight budget result in a form of innovation. If the participants are not innovators or do not possess initiative, then the decision system will definitely discourage, not encourage, innovation. In short, *low ceilings do not create or foster innovative pressures but channel them*. In order to innovate and remain within the ceiling, one must eliminate activities or increase efficiency.

One way to encourage innovation is to structure attention-directing mechanisms so *new* problems are perceived. More will be said on this later in conjunction with program budgeting.

If the budgetary decision system as described in this book does not naturally encourage innovation and if there are not ways to secure additional revenues, can anything be done? Fortunately, there may be a way out of this dilemma.

> All these hypotheses about innovation rest on the assumption that the innovative process is not itself programmed. The stimuli to innovation . . . [in our model] are external.[14]

This, of course, suggests that ". . . 'natural' stimuli to innovation . . . can be supplemented by additional programmed stimuli."[15] The Budget Bureau in Detroit, discussed earlier, really functions as a set of full-time operations analysts and efficiency experts for the city government. Institutionalized innovation is clearly a feasible policy here. There is no reason to believe, for instance, that an operations research staff, or something like it, could not function just as well in city government as it does in private industry. Currently, the role of operations analyst, if performed at all, is played by

[12] Cyert and March, *op. cit.*, p. 278.
[13] T. C. Sorensen, *Kennedy* (New York: Harper & Row, Publishers, 1965), p. 414.
[14] J. G. March and H. A. Simon, *Organizations* (New York: John Wiley & Sons, 1958), p. 184.
[15] *Ibid.*

private consultants brought in by the city. The innovation of 'institutionalizing innovation' is the kind of change observed under slack conditions however, so its adoption might seem to depend on an unusually good revenue picture or a private foundation's willingness to finance the venture. We have in mind cooperative efforts similar to the arrangement between the RAND Corporation, the Ford Foundation, and New York City. It is too early to speculate on the success of this venture, begun in early 1968. Again, program budgeting is often cited as a means for programming innovative behavior.

INCREASING RATIONALITY IN BUDGETING

The budget in most cities performs many functions. The two most important are:

1. The planning function, and
2. The auditing or public accountability function.

Our purpose is to make the municipal resource allocation process (planning) in a city more rational.

A first step is the separation of planning and auditing functions. Because most accounting systems are designed to facilitate auditing or public accountability goals, most 'planning' budgets are hardly recognizable as plans. The line items in a budget refer to identifiable expenditures, not programs or activities. The extreme detail in municipal budgets (for an example, see Table VII-1) is testimony to this. Growth or change is stated in terms of changes in expenditures for specific commodities—personnel, truck rentals, maintenance contracts, etc.

Planning, Programming, Budgeting System (PPBS)[16]

The PPBS movement in the federal government has received a great deal of attention. PPBS represents a systematic attempt to increase the rationality of the budgetary process at any level of government.

> Planning, programming, and budgeting is the focus of the process of comparison and coordination . . . it involves:
> 1. Appraisals and comparisons of various government activities in terms of their contributions to [municipal] objectives.
> 2. Determination of how given objectives can be attained with minimum expenditure of resources.
> 3. Projection of government activities over an adequate time horizon.
> 4. Comparison of the relative contribution of private and public activities to [municipal] objectives.

[16] The discussion on PPBS has benefited greatly from conversations with Otto Davis, associate dean of the School of Urban and Public Affairs, Carnegie-Mellon University. The shortcomings are my own, however.

5. Revisions of objectives, programs, and budgets in the light of experience and changing circumstances.[17]

The process involves the defining of specific goals or objectives on the part of the government. Programs, activities, etc., that relate to particular objectives then become the units of analysis. Of course, the system allows for a hierarchy of objectives. For example, a city has the overall objective of ensuring the safety of its inhabitants. Subgoals might refer to protection from fire, disease, crimes of violence, theft, traffic accidents, unsafe structures, etc. The goal of protecting inhabitants from fire might be further elaborated into subgoals of fire prevention, extinguishing fires as quickly as possible, etc. Fire prevention might involve *programs* like visiting elementary schools with the view toward educating youngsters on how to prevent fires, advertisements on radio and TV, a building inspection program, liaison with fire insurance companies, etc. Then, instead of having a single budget for the Fire Department, with 'personnel,' 'expenses,' 'equipment' as line items, the line items might be 'fire prevention' and 'fire extermination,' with breakdowns for 'elementary education program,' 'public awareness (advertising) program,' 'fire inspection program,' etc. Because the budget items would relate to programs with more readily identifiable outputs, it is argued that efficiency and effectiveness of parallel or alternative programs can be measured and compared. Effectiveness can then be used as a criteria in allocating resources.

If one were convinced that the effectiveness of a fire prevention program is related to the number of people contacted weighted by the length of the contact, statistics like '$/person minute' might be used to decide whether more money should go to 'elementary education program' or 'public awareness program.' Average number of fires-per-building-per-year could be used as a criteria for deciding if additional money should go to 'fire prevention' or 'fire extermination.' By paying attention to things like average-dollar-loss-per-fire over a period of years, the city administration would at least know whether the 'fire extermination' programs in the Fire Department were doing a better or worse job than the year before. For programs that relate to similar objectives, one should be able to introduce the concept of relative efficiency into the allocation process. Given existing knowledge however, it is not clear that program budgeting will lead to more rational decision-making in the allocation of resources between dissimilar objectives. For instance, although the 'fire prevention' and 'fire extermination' programs relate to the same general objective of minimizing fire losses, how to decide how much should be spent within the total Fire Department

[17] Arthur Smithies, "Conceptual Framework for the Program Budget," *RM-4271-RC* (Santa Monica, Calif.: RAND Corporation, 1964), p. 4.

or how this total should be divided between 'prevention' and 'extermination' is not at all clear.

The comparison of the relative merits of dissimilar programs involves the existence or development of universal measures of program costs and benefits. At present, this is not possible. We simply have no way of comparing average dollar-loss-per-citizen, or crimes-per-household, with patient-days-in-hospital. Without common measures, knowing how money should be split between the criminal section of the Police Department and the City Hospital, for instance, is extremely difficult.

Program Budgeting—a Prognosis

Because program budgeting has been receiving so much attention recently, it might be useful to discuss the prospects and implications of a switch from traditional, line-item budgeting. In particular, the likelihood of comprehensive budgeting, the probable changes in decision procedures, and the importance of performance measures will be covered.

COMPREHENSIVE BUDGETING. The ultimate objective of program budgeting is to achieve a state where a complete, comprehensive, and simultaneous evaluation of all department or government programs replaces the existing, incremental approach. By consciously rejecting a program's historical base, it is hoped that each year each major program in the budget will be judged (using cost-benefit criteria) against all other existing programs and new alternatives as well. The result would be an optimum allocation of government resources, where the entire program(s) would be re-evaluated each year and not just the changes from year to year.

As Wildavsky notes in relation to the federal budget, zero-base, comprehensive or non-incremental budgeting is infeasible because it implies a completely defined system of values, a completely specified set of alternatives, and costs for achieving these alternatives.[18] He goes on to argue that the budgeting process is really a reflection of the political decision system and a drastic alteration of the budgetary process would also require a drastic alteration of the entire political system. This argument applies equally well to the urban budget.

The informational and cognitive requirements for comprehensive, normative budgeting are enormous. To reformulate an entire budget 'from scratch' each year and to compare each item (or program) in the budget with every other item implies that one know something of the relative costs and benefits of activities A versus B. To know benefits at any particular dollar level one must have some notion of the diminishing utility of the

[18] Aaron Wildavsky, *The Politics of the Budgetary Process* (Boston: Little, Brown and Company, 1964), pp. 128-129.

alternatives *relative* to all other alternatives. At the extreme, one must also know at which point it becomes more beneficial to allocate one more dollar to the private sector than to use that dollar in the public sector. The infeasibility of this kind of approach to public policy was apparent in previous discussions.

One experiment with a comprehensive budget has been reported in the literature. It concerned an attempt by the Department of Agriculture to formulate its budget request using comprehensive techniques. What happened was perfectly predictable. Participants found it impossible to calculate the relative benefits of programs within the department, let alone justify particular levels of particular programs. Instead, the department in effect reverted back to the old, incremental approach to arrive at its budget estimate.[19]

IMPACT OF PROGRAM BUDGETING ON EXISTING DECISION SYSTEM. There are two primary points to be made about the impact of PPBS on the decision process. First, although the switching from line item to program as the fundamental unit of analysis represents a basic *change in the cognitive maps* of the participants in the budgetary process, there is no reason why we should expect the *process* itself to undergo a radical change. Second, the change from a set of line items to a set of programs allows for the development of relative performance measures and, ultimately, efficiency measures (dollars-per-street-mile, etc.). The performance measures can be expected to provide another set of reference points, in addition to historical ones, that should enter the decision process described in this study at the preliminary-calculations stages [items 3 in Figure V-1b (DEPT.), 4 in Figure VI-1b (MAYORS), and 9 in Figure VII-1b (COUNCIL)]. To convert the formal line-item budget model to a model of program budgeting, two steps are necessary. First, the subscripts on model variables that represent standard account categories (the j's) should be redefined as representing the department's programs. Second, a term representing changes in recent performance measures for the programs should be included in the preliminary calculations equations.

CHANGE IN COGNITIVE MAP—NOT COGNITIVE PROCESS. As was indicated in Chapters V, VI, and VII, the absence of objective standards in municipal government leads to the use of historical standards and incremental decision procedures. Comparing dollars-per-street-mile with dollars-per-patient-day will not provide the decision-maker with any decisional cues. Comparing the changes in dollars-per-patient-day from year to year may provide some very useful information however. This historical

[19] Arthur Hammann and Aaron Wildavsky, "Comprehensive Versus Incremental Budgeting in the Department of Agriculture," *Administrative Science Quarterly* (December, 1965), pp. 321-346.

performance standard, we predict, will partially replace the historical line-item, appropriations standard in the decision process. Its role, however, will be one that has much to say about the size of particular program increments, but very little to say about the relation between increments of different programs. The behavioral antecedents underlying a model of program budgeting do not appear to be greatly different from those presented in Chapters V, VI, and VII. As others have pointed out, people cannot solve problems by considering all potential alternatives. Instead they must use heuristics or rules of thumb to narrow their area of search. It turns out that there are not very many different ways this can be done. We would be very much surprised if program budgeting, merely by changing the informational base *(inputs)* for decision-making, resulted in a *process* very much different from the existing one. The change in the cognitive map and information base may result in radical changes in system *behavior,* however.

The considerations we have presented have some clear implications for the implementation of PPBS. A change in the budget preparation procedures (i.e., budget request forms) seems to be a reasonably efficient way of changing the participants' cognitive maps.[20]

Once the system 'learns' to direct its attention to the expansion and contraction of *programs* rather than expenditure items, the next step—developing output measures for comparison with program inputs (problems or needs)—will be much easier. *Once measures of inputs and outputs are accumulated over time, the criterion of efficiency*[21] *can become meaningful.* Operative efficiency goals for administrative units can then be incorporated in the budget, presumably leading to greater efficiency in government. *The traditional approach to PPBS has been to predicate the change to program budgeting on the existence of standards, rather than to use the change to program budgeting as the means to generate standards.*

At present budgeting is only loosely related to the total revenue decision at one end and actual operations at the other. While program budgeting still provides no guarantee that it will have any impact on the total revenue decision or the total availability of public resources, it does attempt

---

[20] The particular definitions and boundaries of programs adopted as elements of the new program budget ought to be chosen with the utmost care. The same kinds of considerations (activity independence, etc.) that enter in the transfer-pricing problem ought to enter in the program-definition problem. This involves establishing a set of transfer prices within a firm so that subunits producing commodities for other subunits can optimize subunit goals and still optimize the organization's overall goal —to divide the organization in such a way that the organization optimizes (automatically) when the components suboptimize.

[21] $\text{Efficiency}_t = \left(\dfrac{\text{output in units}}{\text{input in dollars}} \right)_t$

to couple budgeting to actual activities. By changing the attention-directing mechanisms, we certainly expect different outcomes from the system.

By focusing on programs and *outputs* (fires put out by the Fire Department), attention is directed toward different features of the environment (dollars-per-fire as a cost effectiveness measure), different kinds of goals are suggested (improving fire-insurance ratings *vs.* increasing *department* revenue) and in general the *need* that the *program* was designed to respond to is more likely to be closely monitored (preventing and extinguishing fires). The response (program) draws attention to the stimulus (need). Ends draw attention to means. A system that directs attention to things like dollars-per-street-mile should produce radically different allocations, over time, than one focusing on dollars appropriated to the Department of Public Works.

The municipality would still be faced with informational and computational constraints (how would one equate dollars-per-fire with dollars-per-street-mile?). Budgeting would still focus on a series of marginal adjustments to solve the balancing problem. It makes more sense for the system to make adjustments in program or activity levels than in item expenditure classification, however.

LONG-RANGE PLANNING—A CHANGE IN PROCESS?

If budgeting is to serve as a basis for the rational allocation of expenditures, two comprehensive budgets must be substituted for the present inadequate documents: an annual budget and a long-term budget. However since the annual budget is merely a segment of the long-term budget, only the latter need be discussed.

The long-term budget will be made up of several parts: (1) long-term estimates of trends in problem-magnitude for the various departments—distribution and concentration of burnable values which must be protected against fire, mileage of streets which must be kept clean, population which must be served by libraries, etc., (2) long-term estimates of service adequacy—that is, the level of services which the city intends to provide its citizens, so many acres of park per 1,000 population, a specified fire loss, etc., (3) a long-term work program showing in work units the services which will have to be provided and facilities to be constructed to achieve the program outlined in items (1) and (2); and (4) a financial program which will relate the work program to the fiscal resources of the community.[22]

While the long-term budget is a logical necessity for rational resource allocation, it is an infeasible modification of the current system without a

[22] H. A. Simon, *Administrative Behavior,* 2nd ed. (New York: The Free Press, 1965), p. 194.

program budget. Items (1), (2), and (3) above are not available to budget decision-makers. If, for example, state legislatures were to require a Master Budget for city expenditures over a period of years similar to the Master Plan required by the federal government for participation in the Community Renewal Program, the resulting document would probably consist of linear extrapolations of department expenses by standard account category (simple extrapolation of the present, drifting system). For a dictated master budget to increase rationality, some service criteria or standards would have to be developed along with techniques for estimating needs. Histories of activities similar to those generated by a program budget are required.

By explicitly requiring a long-range forecast of needs and program levels, PPBS is, in effect, requiring that agencies and departments *plan*. By programming the planning process and forcing decision-makers to think about the future, PPBS may actually result in a significant change in the decision process itself. A significant change in process, we argue, could only be observed when methods of forecasting significantly different from the usual linear extrapolation (incremental changes from year to year) techniques are developed and used.

Importance of Output Measures

One of the principal arguments for a program budget is that by developing information concerning program inputs and outputs, we will be directing our attention to the environment the program is trying to serve. What really happens, however, is that attention is directed to changes in the measures developed and not in the environment, sets of needs, etc. If we are fortunate, the measures will correspond to proper aspects of the environment. Because statistics, once developed, seem to take on a life of their own independent of other considerations, it is imperative that great care be taken in bringing information into being. One example ought to illustrate this point.

One of the major indicators (of output) for the Bureau of Public Roads is the 'mileage of the interstate network opened during a given year.' The natural tendency then, is to, in some sense, maximize this value. That being the case, under a budget constraint one can increase mileage opened per year by building those portions of the interstate network that have the fewest design problems or are cheapest to build. If we look at a map of the interstate highway network, we see a great abundance of highways and a completed network—primarily in those areas of the country where there are no people! The highly concentrated population centers of the Northeast are hardly touched, relatively speaking, by the interstate system. Given the primacy of the urban transportation problem, one wonders if different measures of output would have led to radically different decisions by the BPR. It is probably safe to say that if average-number-of-vehicles-per-day-using-interstate-highways, for instance, had been the BPR measure of output rather than mileage-of-interstate-highways, we would have gotten different kinds of decisions and distributions of highways.

THE FUTURE—ADVANCES IN THE INFORMATION SCIENCES

The budgetary process (as well as municipal government in general) is likely to benefit from the computer age in two ways:
1. Increases in the amount and availability of information,
2. Expansion of the computational abilities of decision-makers.

Much of the rationale for the current budgetary process rests in human limitations on information and computational abilities. By relaxing these limitations, some of the marginal adjustments in the existing system presented above become easier to make, *given the motivation to change.* No real improvements in the system can be expected, however, if the same information that is collected and kept today is collected and kept tomorrow. Lacking information concerning activities and levels of government output, the net effect of the revolution in information technology will be to speed up the process, not to make it more rational. Unless the existing cognitive map of standard account categories and departments is changed, relatively little can be done to significantly improve the existing decision system. Computers make significant improvements more feasible, but they cannot guarantee them.

Appendix A

ESTIMATION OF SUBMODEL RELATIONSHIPS

DEPT.

Relationship: $\widehat{DEPR2}_{ij} = f(APPR1_{ij}, APPRO_{ij}, EXPND_{ij})$

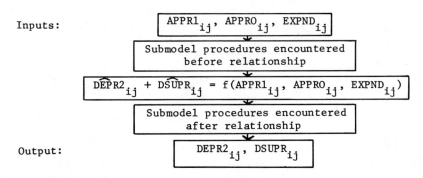

Inputs:

$APPR1_{ij}, APPRO_{ij}, EXPND_{ij}$

Submodel procedures encountered before relationship

$\widehat{DEPR2}_{ij} + \widehat{DSUPR}_{ij} = f(APPR1_{ij}, APPRO_{ij}, EXPND_{ij})$

Submodel procedures encountered after relationship

Output:

$DEPR2_{ij}, DSUPR_{ij}$

In estimating the parameters for the relationship above, the outputs of the process, $DEPR2_{ij}$ and $DSUPR_{ij}$, were used in place of the real preliminary figures $\widehat{DEPR2}_{ij}$ and $\widehat{DSUPR}_{ij}$. If we can show that the expected value of our data ($DEPR2_{ij}$ and $DSUPR_{ij}$) is equal to the true values in the relationship ($\widehat{DEPR2}_{ij}$ and $\widehat{DSUPR}_{ij}$), then our estimation procedure is reasonable. In the absence of any observations of the true values of $\widehat{DEPR2}_{ij}$ and $\widehat{DSUPR}_{ij}$, the best thing to do is to examine what happens in the DEPT. submodel to $DEPR2_{ij}$ and $DSUPR_{ij}$. By referring to Figure V-1b (DEPT.), we see that between stage 3 and the final output (stage 10), the following relations hold:

1. $(DEPR2_{ij} + DSUPR_{ij}) = \widehat{DEPR2}_{ij} + \widehat{DSUPR}_{ij}$
   and
2. $\widehat{DEPR2}_{ij} \geq DEPR2_{ij}$
3. $DSUPR_{ij} \geq \widehat{DSUPR}_{ij}$

Since the bias indicated in 2 and 3 has no effect on the estimation procedure (i.e., 1 holds), linear regression techniques using final output data instead of intermediate data are not systematically biased for calculation of the relationships in item 3 in Figure V-1b in the DEPT. submodel.

MAYORS

Relationship: $\widehat{RMAY2}_{ij} = f(DEPR2_{ij}, DSUPR_{ij}, APPR1_{ij}, APPRO_{ij}, EXPND_{ij})$

Inputs:

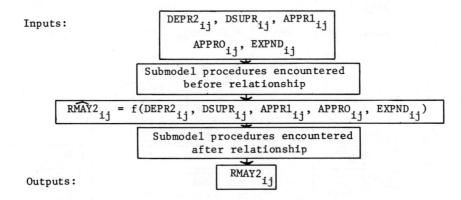

Outputs:

We are faced, here, with the same kind of problem encountered in the DEPT. submodel. Since our estimation technique, linear regression, is an unbiased estimator, we have only to show that the input data is unchanged between input and when the relationship is encountered in the submodel, and that $\widehat{RMAY2}_{ij}$ is unchanged between the time of its calculation in the submodel and the output stage, $RMAY2_{ij}$. [Between stages 4 and 29 in Figure VI-1b (MAYORS)]. Obviously, $\widehat{RMAY2}_{ij}$ is modified by the model to arrive at $RMAY2_{ij}$. The question of whether it is reasonable to use data on $RMAY2_{ij}$ as an approximation for $\widehat{RMAY2}_{ij}$ rests on the presence or absence of systematic, biased changes (changes in one direction) between the preliminary screening of applications and the mayor's recommendation to council. Three things can happen to $RMAY2_{ij}$ in the MAYORS submodel before the final mayor's decision.

1. It remains unchanged.
2. Quantity is reduced (anticipated deficit evokes deficit elimination routines).
3. Quantity is increased (anticipated surplus evokes surplus elimination routines).

If $\widehat{RMAY2}_{ij}$ goes through the process unchanged, then our use of $RMAY2_{ij}$ is reasonable. If $\widehat{RMAY2}_{ij}$ is increased as often as it is reduced, the use of $RMAY2_{ij}$ as an approximation is still justified and reasonable.

On the basis of interviews and model runs (after using $RMAY2_{ij}$ as an estimator) it appears that after preliminary screening of requests, deficit elimination procedures get evoked about as often as surplus elimination routines—in fact, much of the system of constraints the mayor places on department requests before they reach his office constitute attempts to guarantee this situation. In light of data availability and the above observations, it appears that use of $RMAY2_{ij}$ as an estimate of $\widehat{RMAY2}_{ij}$ is a reasonable procedure.

COUNCIL

The fact that council makes very few changes limits both the observations available for estimating item 9 in Figure VII-1b (COUNCIL) and the importance of this calculation. The fact that the particular branch of the program is seldom used makes almost any procedure used to estimate the relationship a relatively *reasonable* one.

Appendix B

ADMINISTRATIVE UNITS
(DEPARTMENT NUMBER AND DEPARTMENT)

Pittsburgh

100 Council	138 Lands & Bldgs.–Operating
200 Clerk	Maintenance
101 Mayor	140 Public Safety–Genl. Office
102 Police Magistrate	141 Public Safety–Traffic
202 Penn Ave. Court	142 Public Safety–Medical
302 Traffic Court	143 Public Safety–Permits
201 Service Center	144 Public Safety–Police
103 Human Relations Comm.	145 Public Safety–Youth
301 Civil Defense	244 Public Safety–Towing
401 Art Commission	146 Public Safety–Fire
104 Controller	147 Public Safety–Electricity
204 Sinking Fund Comm.	148 Public Safety–Bldg. Inspection
106 Treasurer	150 Public Works–Genl. Office
107 Law	151 Public Works–Automotive
190 Civil Service	Equipment
110 Planning	152 Public Works–Accts.
111 Board of Adjustment	250 Public Works–Photography
112 Supplies–Genl. Office	153 Public Works–Engineering
113 Supplies–Accts. & Admin.	160 Public Works–Bridges, Highways,
135 Lands & Bldgs.–Genl. Office	& Sewers
136 Lands & Bldgs.–Accts. &	167 Public Works–Refuse
Admin.	180 Parks & Recreation–Admin.
137 Lands & Bldgs.–Repairs	181 Parks & Recreation–Grounds
149 Public Safety–Traffic	183 Parks & Recreation–Recreational
Planning	Activities

Detroit

101 Art Commission	115 Public Works–Motor
145 Assessor	Transportation
149 Auditor General	117 Public Works–Permits
102 Bldgs. Fund	144 Public Works–Sanitation
182 Children & Youth Comm.	143 Public Works–Street Railway
138 Clerk	126 Purchasing
140 Controller	127 Recorder's Court–Criminal
104 Planning	Div.

141 Treasurer
175 Civic Center
111 Civil Defense
147 Civil Service
109 Council
122 Community Relations Comm.
165 Corporation Council
148 Election Comm.
106 Fire
132 Health–General
132 Health–Herman Kiefer Hospital
134 Health–Wm. H. Maybury Hospital
136 Health–Receiving Hospital
174 Historical Comm.
112 House of Correction
123 Lighting Comm.
110 Mayor's Committees
116 Parks & Recreation
118 Police
169 Public Works–Bldg. Operation & Construction
170 Public Works–Central Bldg. Maintenance
125 Public Works–Genl.

128 Recorder's Court–Traffic & Ordinance Div.
129 Recorder's Court–Psychiatric Div.
172 Recorder's Court–Jury Com.
150 Streets & Traffic
135 Welfare
146 Zoning Appeals
131 Zoological Park
124 Public Works–Sewers
181 Skid Row Problems
183 Rehabilitation of Narcotic Adults
184 Industrial & Commercial Dev.
186 Dept. Report & Information
187 Community Action for Detroit's Youth
188 Community Renewal
851 Aviation
840 Municipal Parking
450 Housing
185 Rapid Transit Com.
610 Water
800 Library

Cleveland

001 Council
003 Mayor
005 Planning
006 Building Standards
007 Zoning Appeals
008 Civil Service
009 Community Relations
010 Personnel Admin.
011 Job Retraining
015 Municipal Court–Judicial
016 Municipal Court–Clerk's Div.
017 Law
020 Public Properties–Genl. Admin.
021 City Hall Bldg.
022 City Hall Telephone Exchange
023 Bureau of Harvard Shops
025 Recreation
026 Markets, Weights & Measures

058 Welfare Institutions–Genl. Admin.
059 Camp Cleveland
065 Urban Renewal–Genl. Admin.
066 Urban Renewal–Bldgs.
067 Urban Renewal–Air & Stream Pollution
068 Urban Renewal–Housing
070 Public Safety–Genl. Admin.
071 Police
072 Police Signal System
073 Fire
074 Fire Alarm Signal System
076 Traffic Engineering
060 Health
077 Dog Pound
080 Finance–Genl. Admin.
081 Accts.
082 Assessments & Licenses

027 Street Lighting
028 Shade Trees
029 Design & Construction
030 Parks
033 Auditorium and Stadium
040 Public Service–Genl. Admin.
041 Architecture
042 Street Cleaning, Waste Coll.
      & Disposal
044 Engineering & Construction
046 Bridges & Docks
048 Public Health & Welfare
056 Correction Farm

083 Treasury
084 Purchases & Supplies
086 Employees Accident Control
090 Port Control
091 Airports
092 Harbor Div.
100 Miscellaneous Acct.
004 Boxing & Wrestling Acct.
045 Sewer Maintenance
051 Air Pollution
052 City Hospital
057 Aid to Returned Servicemen

Appendix C

MODEL PARAMETERS

NOTE—Lists of variables will be found in Chapters V, VI, and VII.

```
A. CITY OF CLEVELAND -- MAYORS SUBMODEL
   RELATIONSHIPS --
   21. RMAY2(I,J) = E(I,J)*(DEPR2(I,J)-APPR1(I,J))
                  + G(I,J)*APPR1(I,J)
                  + H(I,J)*(APPR1(I,J) - APPR0(I,J))
   22.  RMAY2(I,J) =  F(I,J)*(EXPN1(I,J) -APPR1(I,J))
                  + G(I,J)*APPR1(I,J)
                  + H(I,J)*(APPR1(I,J) - APPR0(I,J))
   23. (RMAY2(I,J)-DEPR2(I,J)) = E(I,J)*(DEPR2(I,J)-
                  APPR1(I,J)) + H(I,J)*(APPR1(I,J)-
                  APPR0(I,J))
   24. (RMAY2(I,J)-APPR1(I,J)) = F(I,J)*(EXPN1(I,J)-
                  APPR1(I,J)) + H(I,J)*(APPR1(I,J) -
                  APPR0(I,J))
```

DEPT. NO.	ACCT. NO.	MODEL NO.	E(I,J)	F(I,J)	G(I,J)	H(I,J)	DURBIN-WATSON,D	R-2
1	1	23	-1.005	.000	.000	.228	2.0994	.9893
1	2	22	.000	.180	1.117	.087	.8284	.9958
3	1	23	-1.075	.000	.000	-.600	1.1185	.9872
3	2	23	-1.209	.000	.000	-.340	2.9720	.9743
4	1	22	.000	1.397	1.004	1.304	2.4445	1.0000
4	2	24	.000	.982	.000	.198	2.8065	.8546
5	1	22	.000	.536	1.054	-.420	1.5329	.9981
5	2	22	.000	.913	1.014	-.026	1.8711	.9961
6	1	22	.000	.989	1.044	.485	1.8162	.9986
6	2	22	.000	.948	1.126	-.322	1.7089	.9912
7	1	22	.000	.758	1.012	.646	1.6566	.9993
7	2	22	.000	1.518	1.058	.431	1.1006	.9981
8	1	22	.000	.437	1.071	-.620	2.9033	.9977
8	2	22	.000	.592	1.089	-.253	2.2471	.9960
9	1	22	.000	.272	1.039	.238	1.9010	.9343
9	2	23	-1.629	.000	.000	.616	2.4267	.8266
10	1	22	.000	.558	1.113	-.946	2.4884	.9978
10	2	24	.000	1.184	.000	.135	2.2869	.4220
11	1	22	.000	2.576	1.234	.328	2.0000	.8485
11	2	22	.000	-.588	.123	.000	2.0132	.6727
15	1	22	.000	.594	1.046	-.048	2.5094	.9993
15	2	22	.000	.577	1.090	-.157	1.5519	.9939
16	1	22	.000	.994	1.066	-.732	2.1518	.9994
16	2	22	.000	.727	1.042	-.130	1.6254	.9957
17	1	22	.000	.922	1.068	-.525	2.0393	.9990
17	2	22	.000	-.212	1.058	.569	1.5629	.9918
20	1	23	-1.081	.000	.000	-.428	2.9386	.9994
20	2	22	.000	.617	1.080	-.079	.9145	.9804
21	1	22	.000	15.394	1.013	-.858	2.5176	.9444
21	2	22	.000	1.031	.991	.535	2.0711	.9992
22	1	22	.000	1.025	1.047	.000	1.7928	.9977
22	2	23	-1.125	.000	.000	-.101	2.3571	.8017
23	1	22	.000	.054	.959	.079	2.0464	.8269
23	2	23	-.465	.000	.000	.219	1.6190	.2511

DEPT.	ACCT.	MODEL	E	F	G	H	D-W	R-2
25	1	23	-1.118	.000	.000	.443	1.8961	.9942
25	2	22	.000	.579	1.036	-.200	1.7765	.9991
26	1	22	.000	-.262	1.041	-.126	2.1694	.9993
26	2	23	-1.131	.000	.000	-.621	1.5711	.9929
27	1	23	-.753	.000	.000	.000	2.0979	.7117
27	2	23	-1.006	.000	.000	.000	1.7954	.9926
28	1	23	-1.077	.000	.000	-.131	2.0941	.9939
28	2	22	.000	.695	1.020	.082	2.0472	.9992
29	1	23	-1.073	.000	.000	-.093	1.6690	.9971
29	2	23	-1.138	.000	.000	-.449	2.0902	.9913
30	1	23	-1.002	.000	.000	-.069	1.6454	.9997
30	2	22	.000	1.452	1.041	.410	2.8622	.9943
33	1	23	-1.079	.000	.000	.909	1.6245	.9923
33	2	22	.000	.512	1.063	-.146	1.4052	.9973
40	1	22	.000	-.037	1.026	-.519	2.4004	.9974
40	2	22	.000	.242	1.183	-.293	1.8888	.9902
41	1	24	.000	1.103	.000	.000	1.9572	.4763
41	2	22	.000	1.492	1.190	-.102	1.4209	.9719
42	1	23	-.625	.000	.000	1.263	1.2830	.7051
42	2	22	.000	.497	1.028	.070	3.1385	.9981
43	1	24	.000	1.217	.000	.021	1.0157	1.0000
43	2	22	.000	.000	.000	.000	.0000	1.0000
44	1	22	.000	.620	1.045	-.181	1.9617	.9972
44	2	24	.000	.379	.000	.264	2.1223	.3063
45	1	22	.000	2.683	.877	.623	1.7019	.8158
45	2	21	.000	2.559	.000	.146	2.3040	.8773
46	1	23	-1.080	.000	.000	.222	1.8780	.9922
46	2	22	.000	.569	1.092	-.205	2.1125	.9922
48	1	23	-.961	.000	.000	-.257	1.4461	.9829
48	2	22	.000	4.456	3.397	.000	.9570	.3081
50	1	22	.000	.000	.000	.000	.0000	.0024
50	2	22	.000	.000	.000	.000	.0000	.0024
51	1	22	.000	1.252	1.143	.116	2.6371	.9987
51	2	24	.000	1.001	.000	.000	1.0247	.9994
52	1	21	.000	.000	.000	.000	2.4670	1.0000
52	2	24	.000	10.961	.000	.000	2.8494	.8168
53	2	22	.000	.926	-.049	.000	2.0312	1.0000
54	1	21	.000	.000	.000	.000	2.4504	.9998
54	2	22	.000	8.990	.301	-.005	2.2414	.9970
55	1	21	.000	.000	.000	.000	2.4279	.9999
55	2	21	.000	85.499	.000	.068	.8723	.8148
56	1	22	.000	.571	1.077	-.644	2.3728	.9991
56	2	22	.000	.717	1.001	.337	1.7571	.9984
57	1	23	-1.085	.000	.000	.596	2.6782	.9928
57	2	24	.000	1.130	.000	-.179	1.6889	.8269
58	1	22	.000	.723	1.015	-.401	2.5496	.9909
58	2	22	.000	.654	1.121	-.322	2.0169	.9863
59	1	22	.000	.526	1.065	-.573	1.2073	.9987
59	2	22	.000	.882	1.065	-.096	1.0553	.9979
60	1	23	-1.069	.000	.000	.313	1.6648	.9981
60	2	22	.000	.780	1.033	-.147	2.8807	.9996
65	1	22	.000	2.146	1.164	-.141	1.8211	.9537
65	2	22	.000	1.693	1.406	-.132	1.5892	.9091
66	1	22	.000	.597	1.043	-.236	2.9781	.9282
66	2	22	.000	.577	1.061	-.241	2.9837	.9084

DEPT.	ACCT.	MODEL	E	F	G	H	D-W	R-2
67	1	22	.000	.600	1.039	.000	2.9990	.9498
67	2	22	.000	.860	1.040	.000	3.0081	.9594
68	1	22	.000	2.081	1.136	.000	1.8107	.9455
68	2	21	.000	-1.548	.000	-1.449	1.5437	.8481
70	1	23	-1.058	.000	.000	.363	2.0417	.9917
70	2	22	.000	1.093	1.071	.133	2.4956	.9974
71	1	23	-1.083	.000	.000	.383	2.3181	.9980
71	2	22	.000	1.114	.969	.510	2.5314	.9987
72	1	22	.000	.918	1.035	-.168	2.3368	.9984
72	2	22	.000	.747	1.002	-.248	2.6147	.9977
73	1	22	.000	3.820	.876	.984	2.6392	.9613
73	2	22	.000	.681	1.090	-.664	2.9903	.9971
74	1	22	.000	1.222	1.015	-.074	2.1890	.9987
74	2	22	.000	.853	1.053	-.230	1.8788	.9668
75	1	21	.000	.000	.000	.000	2.4956	.9998
75	2	22	.000	1.126	1.110	-.016	2.8430	.9979
76	1	22	.000	.248	1.057	-.201	2.3500	.9990
76	2	21	.000	1.147	.000	1.080	1.7912	.7596
77	1	22	.000	.442	1.041	.153	1.8969	.9969
77	2	22	.000	1.231	1.134	-.028	1.8911	.9964
80	1	22	.000	.904	1.023	.148	1.4964	.9893
80	2	22	.000	1.053	1.211	.770	2.0762	.9663
81	1	23	-1.217	.000	.000	-1.958	2.2565	.7741
81	2	23	-.806	.000	.000	-.378	2.1516	.4477
82	1	23	-1.110	.000	.000	-.040	1.8527	.9916
82	2	22	.000	.235	1.095	-.458	2.1789	.9992
83	1	22	.000	.893	1.065	-.112	1.5388	.9984
83	2	22	.000	.481	1.049	-.148	1.9976	.9956
84	1	22	.000	1.743	1.031	-.465	2.3178	.9990
84	2	22	.000	.291	1.047	-.669	2.6215	.9918
86	1	23	-1.106	.000	.000	-.276	2.1145	.9759
86	2	22	.000	1.212	1.148	-.104	.8488	.9834
90	1	22	.000	-.589	1.040	-.130	1.8763	.9949
90	2	23	-1.060	.000	.000	-.189	1.1401	.6483
91	1	22	.000	.461	1.113	-.196	2.0402	.9976
91	2	22	.000	1.368	1.047	-.081	2.1180	.9898
92	1	22	.000	.000	1.060	-.608	1.7147	.9988
92	2	22	.000	1.028	1.189	-.083	1.9419	.9640
100	1	22	.000	1.539	1.045	-.055	2.7702	.9982

B.1. CITY OF DETROIT -- DEPT. SUBMODEL
    RELATIONSHIPS ---
        11. DEPR2(I,J) = A(I,J)*(EXPND(I,J)-APPRO(I,J))
            + B(I,J)*(APPR1(I,J)) + C(I,J)*(APPR1(I,J)-
            APPRO(I,J))
        12. DEPR2(I,J) = B(I,J)*(APPR1(I,J)) +
            C(I,J)*(APPR1(I,J)-APPRO(I,J)) +D(I,J)*EXPND(I,J)
        13. (DEPR2(I,J)+DSUPR(I,J)) = A(I,J)*(EXPND(I,J)-
            APPRO(I,J)) + B(I,J)*(APPR1(I,J))
            + C(I,J)*(APPR1(I,J)-APPRO(I,J))
        14. (DEPR2(I,J)+DSUPR(I,J)) = B(I,J)*(APPR1(I,J))
            + C(I,J)*(APPR1(I,J)-APPRO(I,J))
            + D(I,J)*(EXPND(I,J))

DEPT. NO.	ACCT. NO.	MODEL NO.	A(I,J)	B(I,J)	C(I,J)	DURBIN-WATSON,D	R-2
101	1	13	1.157	1.005	-.083	2.5568	.9964
101	2	11	1.515	.297	-.399	1.8012	.9979
101	3	11	2.173	.376	.850	1.9940	.3170
102	1	13	1.024	.524	-.039	1.7301	.9997
102	2	11	1.121	-.088	-.027	1.7090	.9980
102	3	11	2.559	-3.352	2.205	1.6257	.9920
104	1	13	1.125	.645	-.131	2.6572	.9805
104	2	11	2.604	-2.436	2.296	1.8979	.5396
104	3	11	2.812	-1.848	1.975	1.0665	.7926
106	1	13	1.000	.684	-.050	1.6818	.9998
106	2	11	1.257	1.369	-.083	2.2255	.9896
106	3	11	.799	2.497	-2.449	1.1380	.7105
109	1	13	1.009	.000	.000	2.3506	.9998
109	2	11	1.050	-.034	.056	.8285	.9980
109	3	11	1.000	.000	.000	.0000	1.0000
110	1	13	1.063	.073	.047	1.8893	.9938
110	2	11	1.182	-.508	.300	1.9588	.9699
110	3	11	2.000	.000	.000	2.0000	.8000
111	1	13	1.058	.000	.216	2.1586	.9027
111	2	11	.756	-.317	-.320	1.5200	.9634
111	3	11	1.403	-.452	-.270	1.8596	.5246
112	1	13	1.067	.312	.000	1.8346	.9976
112	2	11	.840	-.529	-.481	1.6318	.8911
112	3	11	2.239	1.278	.457	3.1532	.7970
113	1	13	.751	.218	-.212	2.2034	.8786
113	2	11	1.030	-.532	.356	2.1692	.9197
113	3	11	.000	.000	.000	2.0000	.7970
115	1	13	1.012	.000	.000	1.3383	.9998
115	2	11	1.114	.214	-.151	2.9307	.9925
115	3	11	1.304	-1.388	1.184	2.9355	.9861
116	1	13	1.057	.686	.015	1.0997	.9980
116	2	11	1.104	.169	.016	1.7976	.9972
116	3	11	1.566	-1.487	1.587	1.5674	.3719
117	1	13	.987	-.167	-.151	1.6336	.9911
117	2	11	1.149	.000	.392	3.3264	.9085
117	3	11	.770	.016	-.971	1.4724	.9951
118	1	13	1.012	.710	-.069	1.6278	.9972
118	2	11	1.101	.437	.142	2.3757	.9961
118	3	11	1.644	.496	.088	1.0081	.9679
122	1	13	1.496	-.267	.396	3.2072	.9927
122	2	11	1.142	-.808	.576	.8825	.9430
122	3	11	1.384	1.554	.068	2.4349	.9924
123	1	13	1.042	.892	.000	1.4763	.9998
123	2	11	1.064	-.064	-.040	3.0968	.9994
123	3	11	.931	-.829	-5.167	2.1552	.9909
124	1	13	1.039	-.239	-.005	1.0409	.9992
124	2	11	1.066	.730	-.002	1.7624	.9953
124	3	12	.591	.613	.000	1.9416	.7920
125	1	13	.995	1.612	-.004	2.8707	.9996
125	2	11	1.128	1.249	-.118	2.1669	.9936
125	3	11	1.116	-.225	.479	2.3354	.7173
126	1	13	1.022	.000	.000	.9849	.9999
126	2	11	1.035	.776	-.032	2.8129	.9917
126	3	11	1.975	-1.034	.112	1.2688	.6720

DEPT.	ACCT.	MODEL	A	B	C	D-W	R-2
127	1	13	1.016	.000	.000	1.1852	.9998
127	2	11	1.063	.760	-.252	2.4151	.9963
127	3	11	43.393	227.880	-179.093	.6983	.3116
128	1	13	1.028	.332	-.030	1.7511	.9993
128	2	11	.994	-.189	-.033	2.5218	.9962
128	3	11	1.773	-1.452	1.601	2.5127	.7318
129	1	13	.994	.000	-.045	2.0037	.9999
129	2	11	1.551	-.993	1.200	1.7378	.8549
129	3	11	.915	-.223	.043	1.5378	.9333
131	1	13	1.089	-.150	.021	2.8740	.9997
131	2	11	1.055	.052	-.017	2.7838	.999
131	3	11	4.044	-1.199	2.828	.5005	.5803
132	1	13	1.003	.469	-.054	1.4489	.9995
132	2	11	1.093	.944	.047	2.0110	.9977
132	3	11	.633	1.210	-.447	1.5134	.3356
133	1	13	.983	-.158	-.056	1.4506	.9950
133	2	11	.998	.296	-.103	2.3207	.9947
133	3	11	11.593	-13.055	13.158	1.7564	.4891
134	1	13	.989	.143	-.039	1.3768	.9990
134	2	11	.982	.096	-.078	1.7777	.9986
134	3	11	2.195	-.728	.958	2.0344	.5036
135	1	13	1.328	-.703	.000	2.0683	.9406
135	2	11	1.442	-.825	.519	1.1173	.8373
135	3	11	.000	.000	-.454	1.0482	.0411
136	1	13	1.010	.486	.006	1.8301	.9987
136	2	11	1.047	.071	-.041	1.8218	.9981
136	3	11	2.050	-.795	.583	2.7140	.7781
138	1	13	1.018	.423	-.023	1.8551	.9992
138	2	11	.968	-.335	.139	3.0938	.7471
138	3	11	1.143	.241	.356	2.8264	.6288
140	1	13	1.127	-.324	.034	1.8884	.9749
140	2	11	1.154	-.122	-.107	2.9997	.9889
140	3	11	1.287	1.576	-1.144	1.3966	.9480
141	1	13	1.029	.000	.019	2.0999	.9985
141	2	11	1.149	-.375	.104	2.0722	.9810
141	3	11	3.727	-.973	-.485	.7636	.8415
143	1	11	1.005	-.700	-.022	1.6201	.9977
143	2	11	1.300	6.210	-.153	1.7534	.9787
143	3	11	1.741	-.477	.923	3.1892	.9373
144	1	13	.985	.000	.000	1.3055	.9998
144	2	11	.979	-.968	.094	1.1432	.9990
144	3	11	16.755	-7.342	11.650	2.3760	.7946
145	1	13	1.030	.747	-.013	1.4067	.9955
145	2	11	1.042	.160	-.096	2.2950	.9970
145	3	11	1.041	-.649	.254	1.8941	.6193
146	1	13	1.028	-.835	-.149	1.7606	.9991
146	2	11	1.221	-.884	.111	1.4050	.9952
146	3	11	1.662	.000	.000	2.5501	.8792
147	1	13	1.011	.645	-.034	1.2174	.9993
147	2	11	1.141	1.081	.017	1.3639	.9903
147	3	11	.779	-.059	.705	1.3844	.6337
148	1	13	1.161	-.318	.405	1.5098	.8236
148	2	11	1.032	-.941	.398	1.8878	.8436
148	3	11	.001	.000	.000	1.0168	.0081
149	1	13	1.011	-.171	-.017	2.1473	.9997

DEPT.	ACCT.	MODEL	D	E	G	H	D-W	R-2
149	2	11	1.038	-1.074	.791	.7654		.9920
149	3	11	.948	-.826	.870	1.9135		.3290
150	1	13	1.033	.000	.023	2.8157		.9996
150	2	11	1.027	.069	-.103	2.3160		.9959
150	3	11	1.397	-1.450	.501	2.4810		.6220
165	1	13	1.105	.172	.058	3.3966		.9992
165	2	11	1.177	-.088	.128	2.3779		.9913
165	3	11	2.327	-1.467	1.779	3.0118		.8899
169	1	13	.972	.177	-.097	2.8540		.9968
169	2	11	1.004	.000	-.080	2.1576		.9993
169	3	11	.000	.000	.000	1.1833		.8899
170	1	13	1.066	-.695	.104	2.5907		.9981
170	2	11	.860	-.195	-.417	1.8397		.9451
170	3	11	1.273	-.857	-.302	1.6283		.9619
172	1	13	1.017	.847	.000	1.9654		.9975
172	2	11	1.130	-.102	.254	1.8969		.9556
172	3	11	.000	.000	.000	2.0000		.9619
174	1	13	1.185	.410	-.109	.8373		.9994
174	2	11	1.190	.113	-.157	2.8012		.9907
174	3	11	5.140	-4.535	2.605	1.9467		.6493
175	1	13	1.254	-.354	.000	1.9264		.7955
175	2	11	1.035	.238	.000	1.7087		.9577
175	3	11	.397	-.473	-.399	2.0574		.8933
181	1	13	1.537	.100	.318	2.3859		.9950
181	2	11	1.161	.038	.080	2.6295		.9985
181	3	11	1.078	-1.349	.639	2.8576		.7649
182	1	13	1.088	2.230	-.070	1.8600		.9841
182	2	11	1.682	1.446	.493	1.5757		.9235
182	3	11	3.587	-.883	-.767	2.0667		.7914
183	1	13	1.000	.000	.500	.8500	1.0000	
183	2	11	.000	.000	.000	.0000		.9235
183	3	11	.000	.000	.000	.0000		.7914
184	1	13	1.151	.119	-1.083	1.6579		.9200
184	2	11	4.822	-2.184	12.322	1.9728		.1424
184	3	11	1.094	.000	5.467	2.1789		.8488
185	1	13	1.903	.647	.874	2.9573		.7289
185	2	11	1.359	-4.485	.839	1.1474		.1401
185	3	11	.000	.000	-213.400	2.0000		.9965
186	1	13	1.407	-2.598	3.398	2.0200		.9255
186	2	11	-.821	3.034	-3.542	2.0795		.7020
186	3	11	13.626	-17.498	.000	1.8821		.1684
187	1	13	.000	.000	.000	.0000		.9229
187	2	11	.000	.000	.000	.0000		.7020
187	3	11	.000	.000	.000	.0000		.1684
188	1	13	1.000	.000	.000	2.0000		.5000
188	2	11	.000	.000	.000	.0000		.7020
188	3	11	.000	.000	.000	.0000		.1684
450	1	13	1.036	-.667	.261	1.4195		.9434
450	2	11	1.154	-.084	.192	2.0360		.9911
450	3	11	.000	.000	-12.131	.9819		.8775
501	1	13	.961	.900	.000	2.5025		.8155
610	1	13	1.022	-.135	.653	1.9029		.5598
610	2	11	.042	.116	.224	1.9088		.2826
610	3	11	.000	.219	-.069	1.3193		.0804
800	1	13	.747	3.521	-3.113	2.4239		.8316

DEPT.	ACCT.	MODEL	A	B	C	D-W	R-2
800	2	11	-.060	.072	.385	2.0573	.4072
800	3	11	1.085	.004	.000	1.0388	.9923
840	1	13	.268	.000	.000	2.0050	.0763
840	2	11	.052	.043	.374	1.5683	.4558
840	3	11	.374	.272	-.030	1.8419	.8039
851	1	13	1.296	-8.251	8.631	2.1062	.6936
851	2	11	.056	.000	.786	1.3920	.4841
851	3	11	-.878	1.632	-1.453	2.1293	.6073

B.2. CITY OF DETROIT -- MAYORS SUBMODEL
RELATIONSHIPS ---

23. (RMAY2(I,J) - DEPR2(I,J)) = E(I,J)*(DSUPR(I,J))
+ G(I,J)*(DEPR2(I,J)-APPR1(I,J))
+ H(I,J)*(APPR1(I,J)-APPRO(I,J))

24. (RMAY2(I,J) - DEPR2(I,J)) = D(I,J)*(EXPND(I,J)-APPRO(I,J)) + H(I,J)*(APPR1(I,J)-APPRO(I,J))

DEPT. NO.	ACCT. NO.	MODEL NO.	D(I,J)	E(I,J)	G(I,J)	H(I,J)	DURBIN-WATSON,D	R-2
101	1	23	.000	.773	-.912	.180	2.8492	.9898
101	2	23	.000	.000	-1.027	-.336	1.7392	.9832
101	3	23	.000	.000	-.903	1.000	1.9850	.9659
102	1	23	.000	5.529	-.805	-.318	1.6598	.8654
102	2	23	.000	.000	-.851	.192	1.2497	.8849
102	3	23	.000	.000	-.947	-.240	1.5313	.9196
104	1	23	.000	-20.785	-.549	-.234	1.7323	.7816
104	2	24	-.353	.000	.000	-.701	2.0552	.3659
104	3	23	.000	.000	-.710	-.251	1.2392	.7570
106	1	23	.000	396.293	-.516	-.076	1.5585	.4518
106	2	23	.000	.000	-.904	.587	1.2567	.9541
106	3	23	.000	.000	-1.021	-.190	2.3678	.9295
109	1	24	.022	.000	.000	-.314	2.4143	.6753
109	2	23	.000	.000	-.076	-.030	1.2844	.2357
109	3	23	.000	.000	.000	.000	.0000	1.0000
110	1	23	.000	4.262	-.753	.439	1.0695	.9653
110	2	24	.140	.000	.000	-.113	2.0917	.2330
110	3	23	.000	.000	.000	1.280	.0000	1.0000
111	1	23	.000	.000	-.657	-.060	2.6870	.6116
111	2	23	.000	.000	-.452	-.181	1.6188	.2261
111	3	23	.000	.000	-.379	-.633	1.7611	.7595
112	1	23	.000	-.320	-.600	.516	2.6442	.8816
112	2	23	.000	.000	-.933	.729	.8763	.9916
112	3	24	-.335	.000	.000	.234	1.9654	.9772
113	1	24	-.247	.000	.000	-.252	1.9419	.3304
113	2	24	-.520	.000	.000	-.619	1.3611	.6823
113	3	23	.000	.000	.000	.000	.0000	1.0000
115	1	24	.038	.000	.000	-.414	2.2236	.9506
115	2	23	.000	.000	-.635	.015	2.9586	.9625
115	3	24	-.211	.000	.000	.194	1.4762	.5592
116	1	23	.000	.000	-.602	-.285	1.7310	.9360
116	2	23	.000	.000	-.828	-.221	.7909	.9083
116	3	24	-.695	.000	.000	-.680	.6749	.9512
117	1	23	.000	.000	-.355	.038	1.3443	.4716

DEPT.	ACCT.	MODEL	D	E	G	H	D-W	R-2
117	2	24	-.146	.000	.000	.471	2.7525	.7649
117	3	23	.000	.000	1.017	.438	2.5078	.8787
118	1	23	.000	-.311	-.416	.000	1.6754	.8387
118	2	24	.000	.000	.000	.808	1.3630	.4530
118	3	23	.000	.000	-1.510	.430	2.2976	.8466
122	1	23	.000	-1.472	-.535	.498	2.4383	.8500
122	2	24	-.119	.000	.000	-.559	2.2608	.3110
122	3	23	.000	.000	-1.917	1.659	2.2591	.9852
123	1	24	.012	.000	.000	.719	1.5353	.8962
123	2	23	.000	.000	-.675	-.072	2.1422	.7094
123	3	22	2.189	.000	.000	-.263	2.1620	.9465
124	1	24	-.148	.000	.000	.000	1.1895	.1249
124	2	24	-.136	.000	.000	3.544	1.3304	.2879
124	3	23	.000	.000	-.811	.158	1.3217	.8443
125	1	24	.006	.000	.000	.951	3.1852	.9715
125	2	23	.000	.000	-.632	.694	2.4566	.9667
125	3	23	.000	.000	-.011	-.023	.4498	.3296
126	1	23	.000	27.427	-2.290	-.465	1.4043	.7405
126	2	23	.000	.000	-.444	.027	1.5686	.6211
126	3	23	.000	.000	-.731	-.342	1.4503	.6946
127	1	24	.017	.000	.000	.000	1.1640	.6045
127	2	23	.000	.000	-.571	.092	3.1099	.8348
127	3	23	.000	.000	-1.001	.000	1.3469	1.0000
128	1	24	.038	.000	.000	.000	1.5852	.8245
128	2	23	.000	.000	-.066	.232	1.2965	.6766
128	3	24	-.415	.000	.000	-.134	2.1000	.3360
129	1	24	.022	.000	.000	-.380	1.2940	.3217
129	2	24	.042	.000	.000	-.236	1.6888	.0549
129	3	24	-.286	.000	.000	-.365	1.6645	.6320
131	1	23	.000	.000	-.695	.000	1.7955	.8655
131	2	23	.000	.000	-.359	-.009	1.7989	.4205
131	3	23	.000	.000	-.946	.000	1.7870	.9759
132	1	24	.038	.000	.000	-.115	2.7533	.7986
132	2	23	.000	.000	-1.021	.601	2.1191	.9088
132	3	23	.000	.000	-.711	-.542	2.1444	.9341
133	1	23	.000	-1.323	-.118	.157	2.1953	.5446
133	2	23	.000	.000	-.610	.576	1.6023	.5333
133	3	23	.000	.000	-.921	-.354	2.5959	.9827
134	1	23	.000	-.423	.568	-.039	2.2003	.3885
134	2	24	-.033	.000	.000	.295	1.3518	.4004
134	3	23	.000	.000	-.548	-.164	.7774	.8580
135	1	23	.000	.000	-.608	-.163	1.9263	.3727
135	2	23	.000	.000	-.934	-.234	1.5311	.8416
135	3	23	.000	.000	-.748	-.353	1.2263	.7311
136	1	24	.014	.000	.000	.358	1.5415	.3889
136	2	24	.037	.000	.000	.328	1.9897	.3863
136	3	23	.000	.000	-.660	.097	1.3858	.7064
138	1	24	.028	.000	.000	.134	1.1323	.4821
138	2	23	.000	.000	-.029	.139	.4543	.4572
138	3	23	.000	.000	.000	.000	.0000	.5682
140	1	24	.124	.000	.000	-.170	1.9216	.2486
140	2	23	.000	.000	.021	-.148	1.3541	.5481
14	3	23	.000	.000	.000	.000	.0000	.8165
141	1	24	.041	.000	.000	.114	1.8691	.5315
141	2	24	.122	.000	.000	-.124	2.0985	.2959

DEPT.	ACCT.	MODEL	D	E	G	H	D-W	R-2
141	3	23	.000	.000	.000	.000	.0000	.6281
143	1	22	.054	.000	.000	-.843	1.3812	.9998
143	2	22	.162	.000	.000	-1.319	1.5506	.9941
143	3	23	.000	.000	-.686	.424	2.1492	.6789
144	1	23	.000	20.148	-.887	-.179	1.6790	.8014
144	2	24	-.051	.000	.000	-.999	1.5373	.9999
144	3	23	.000	.000	-1.016	.971	3.0269	.9950
145	1	23	.000	23.769	-.220	-.511	1.3525	.7776
145	2	23	.000	.000	-.758	.209	1.0964	.5474
145	3	24	-.159	.000	.000	-.688	2.1669	.3583
146	1	23	.000	.000	-.055	-.497	.4041	.6141
146	2	23	.000	.000	-.369	.000	1.2394	.5818
146	3	23	.000	.000	.000	.000	.0000	.8792
147	1	24	.034	.000	.000	-.211	1.1001	.8124
147	2	23	.000	.000	-.569	.424	1.3063	.6644
147	3	23	.000	.000	.138	-.101	.5985	.4577
148	1	23	.000	-.764	-.343	-.280	2.0146	.9420
148	2	24	-.326	.000	.000	-.988	1.4831	.7611
148	3	23	.000	.000	.001	.000	1.6265	.9999
149	1	24	.026	.000	.000	-.062	1.3173	.4170
149	2	24	.000	.000	.000	.974	2.9583	.9716
149	3	24	-.620	.000	.000	-.116	1.7964	.8158
150	1	24	.027	.000	.000	.483	2.5244	.7933
150	2	23	.000	.000	-.228	-.093	1.3390	.3547
150	3	24	.000	.000	.000	-1.008	2.2354	.6055
165	1	23	.000	-.783	-.404	-.029	.9581	.7317
165	2	23	.000	.000	-.428	-.010	1.7026	.4639
165	3	23	.000	.000	-.666	.604	1.2032	.8054
169	1	23	.000	.000	-.156	-.202	2.1842	.6245
169	2	24	.025	.000	.000	.000	1.9661	.2817
169	3	23	.000	.000	-.961	-.465	1.7162	.9971
170	1	23	.000	310.386	-.619	-.103	2.2389	.4342
170	2	23	.000	.000	-.700	-.393	2.3390	.4091
170	3	23	.000	.000	-.773	-.085	1.6936	.6993
172	1	23	.000	-.315	-.825	.680	1.9384	.8437
172	2	23	.000	.000	.656	-.044	2.2658	.9814
172	3	23	.000	.000	-.499	-.499	2.0000	.9155
174	1	23	.000	1.563	-.834	-.186	1.9118	.9931
174	2	23	.000	.000	-1.197	-.031	1.1855	.8180
174	3	23	.000	.000	-.924	-.477	1.6152	.9480
175	1	23	.000	6.960	-.436	.124	2.1513	.9855
175	2	23	.000	.000	.080	-.137	2.1340	.3347
175	3	24	-.496	.000	.000	-.964	2.1393	.8811
181	1	23	.000	-1.265	-.896	.000	1.8092	.9900
181	2	23	.000	.000	-.819	.016	.9723	.9726
181	3	24	-.342	.000	.000	-1.177	2.6636	.8852
182	1	23	.000	-3.600	-.224	1.054	1.8453	.9845
182	2	23	.000	.000	-.864	-.146	1.1363	.9616
182	3	23	.000	.000	-.843	-.519	2.7234	.9574
183	1	23	.000	.000	.000	.000	2.0000	.7198
183	2	24	-.500	.000	.000	.000	.0000	1.0000
183	3	23	.000	.000	.000	.000	.0000	1.0000
184	1	23	.000	.000	.060	-.218	1.6893	.1439
184	2	23	.000	.000	-.993	.178	1.8749	.9824
184	3	23	.000	.000	-.005	-1.249	2.0000	.9968

DEPT.	ACCT.	MODEL	D	E	G	H	D-W	R-2
185	1	23	.000	.000	-.984	.000	2.2146	.9868
185	2	23	.000	.000	-.992	.346	2.0120	.9952
185	3	23	.000	.000	-1.054	-.988	2.1167	.9961
186	1	23	.000	-5.452	.098	.086	2.4825	.7674
186	2	23	.000	.000	-.341	-.114	.9414	.6328
186	3	23	.000	.000	-.812	-.083	1.9732	.8538
187	1	23	.000	.000	.000	.000	-.0000	.3373
187	2	23	.000	.000	.000	.000	.0000	.3373
187	3	23	.000	.000	.000	.000	.0000	.3373
188	1	23	.000	.000	-.029	.045	2.0000	1.0000
188	2	23	.000	.000	.000	.000	.0000	.0022
188	3	23	.000	.000	.000	.000	.0000	.0022
450	1	24	-.238	.000	.000	-.638	1.4645	.7397
450	2	23	.000	.000	-.583	-.774	1.9746	.1532
450	3	23	.000	.000	-.858	.121	1.8591	.9984
501	1	23	.000	.472	-.355	.328	2.0283	.8049
610	1	24	-.571	.000	.000	-.438	1.8325	.4176
610	2	24	-.910	.000	.000	-1.229	1.1778	.5766
610	3	24	-.992	.000	.000	-.821	1.0679	.5491
800	1	23	.000	.345	-.217	-.243	2.4588	.4982
800	2	23	.000	.947	.329	-1.799	1.4457	.5273
800	3	23	.000	.531	-4.714	.000	2.5647	.7914
840	1	23	.000	1.074	.325	.000	1.1661	.9997
840	2	24	-1.051	.000	.000	-.855	.9868	.8656
840	3	23	.000	.916	.075	-.428	3.0292	.9183
851	1	23	.000	.469	.000	-.215	1.2380	.6899
851	2	24	-1.049	.000	.000	-.852	.9917	.7886
851	3	23	.000	.646	-.051	-.291	2.8607	.6091

B.3. CITY OF DETROIT -- COUNCIL SUBMODEL
RELATIONSHIPS ---

31. $APPR2(I,J) = PP(I,J)*(RMAY2(I,J) + O(I,J)*(DEPR2(I,J)+DSUPR(I,J)-RMAY2(I,J))$

32. $APPR2(I,J) = PP(I,J)*(RMAY2(I,J)) + R(I,J)*(APPR1(I,J)-APPRO(I,J)) + S(I,J)*(EXPND(I,J)-APPRO(I,J))$

DEPT. NO.	ACCT. NO.	MODEL NO.	PP(I,J)	Q(I,J)	R(I,J)	S(I,J)	DURBIN-WATSON,D	R-2
101	1	31	1.003	.000	.000	.000	1.6553	1.0000
101	2	31	.986	.032	.000	.000	2.6793	.9995
101	3	31	1.001	.000	.000	.000	2.2081	.9999
102	1	31	1.005	.000	.000	.000	.5641	.9999
102	2	31	.970	.204	.000	.000	3.1671	.9996
102	3	31	1.261	-.069	.000	.000	2.5657	.8690
104	1	31	1.003	.026	.000	.000	2.5211	.9996
104	2	31	.996	.000	.000	.000	2.8147	.9999
104	3	31	1.076	-.047	.000	.000	2.4869	.9659
106	1	31	1.008	.000	.000	.000	1.4209	.9999
106	2	31	1.039	-.309	.000	.000	1.5194	.9952
106	3	31	.923	.078	.000	.000	1.3872	.9709
109	1	31	.997	.000	.000	.000	1.1529	.9999
109	2	31	.999	.000	.000	.000	2.3008	1.0000

DEPT.	ACCT.	MODEL	PP	Q	R	S	D-W	R-2
109	3	31	1.000	.000	.000	.000	2.0000	.7500
110	1	31	.997	.000	.000	.000	2.2742	1.0000
110	2	31	1.000	.000	.000	.000	.0000	1.0000
110	3	31	1.000	.000	.000	.000	.0000	1.0000
111	1	31	.963	.074	.000	.000	2.5271	.9968
111	2	31	1.018	.060	.000	.000	2.4890	.9970
111	3	31	1.000	.000	.000	.000	2.0000	.9782
112	1	31	1.001	.000	.000	.000	2.3776	1.0000
112	2	31	.989	-.008	.000	.000	2.2071	.9995
112	3	31	1.138	-.036	.000	.000	2.0212	.8765
113	1	31	1.001	.000	.000	.000	2.5345	1.0000
113	2	31	1.001	.000	.000	.000	2.5244	1.0000
113	3	31	1.000	.000	.000	.000	.0000	1.0000
115	1	31	1.001	.000	.000	.000	2.4302	1.0000
115	2	31	.683	1.566	.000	.000	2.4050	.9486
115	3	31	.276	2.954	.000	.000	2.3543	.8119
116	1	31	1.002	.000	.000	.000	2.5311	1.0000
116	2	31	.994	.000	.000	.000	2.3732	.9998
116	3	31	1.697	1.440	.000	.000	1.1692	.7905
117	1	31	1.001	.000	.000	.000	2.4337	1.0000
117	2	31	1.061	-.825	.000	.000	2.4624	.9932
117	3	31	.978	.484	.000	.000	1.9137	.4731
118	1	31	1.006	.000	.000	.000	1.4595	.9999
118	2	31	.998	-.176	.000	.000	1.8272	.9995
118	3	31	1.033	-.004	.000	.000	2.1174	.9990
122	1	31	1.001	.000	.000	.000	1.7221	1.0000
122	2	31	1.014	-.103	.000	.000	2.5978	1.0000
122	3	31	1.000	.000	.000	.000	2.0000	.5950
123	1	31	1.001	.000	.000	.000	2.5409	1.0000
123	2	31	.999	.000	.000	.000	2.3814	1.0000
123	3	32	.939	.000	-.046	-.386	2.9659	.9998
124	1	31	1.003	.000	.000	.000	3.1641	1.0000
124	2	31	.979	-.009	.000	.000	2.5596	.9990
124	3	31	1.019	-.012	.000	.093	2.7951	.9994
125	1	31	1.002	.000	.000	.000	2.2927	1.0000
125	2	31	.966	.045	.000	.000	2.5224	.9978
125	3	31	1.003	.000	.000	.000	2.7257	1.0000
126	1	31	1.000	.000	.000	.000	2.3020	1.0000
126	2	31	.994	.000	.000	.000	2.3625	.9998
126	3	31	1.123	-.067	.000	.000	2.1505	.9117
127	1	31	1.001	.000	.000	.000	2.3790	1.0000
127	2	31	.996	.000	.000	.000	2.2139	.9998
127	3	31	.999	.000	.000	.000	2.0852	.9561
128	1	31	1.003	.000	.000	.000	1.6543	1.0000
128	2	31	.999	.000	.000	.000	2.0744	1.0000
128	3	31	.937	.669	.000	.000	1.9466	.9703
129	1	31	1.001	.000	.000	.000	2.4804	1.0000
129	2	31	.971	-.038	.000	.000	2.2357	.9877
129	3	31	1.187	.000	.000	.000	2.2974	.7370
131	1	31	1.002	.000	.000	.000	2.3177	1.0000
131	2	31	.997	.000	.000	.000	2.4452	1.0000
131	3	31	1.015	.000	.000	.000	2.6765	.9995
132	1	31	1.002	.000	.000	.000	2.4562	1.0000
132	2	31	.991	.051	.000	.000	2.1327	.9997
132	3	31	1.087	.000	.000	.000	2.2708	.9213

DEPT.	ACCT.	MODEL	PP	Q	R	S	D-W	R-2
133	1	31	1.004	.000	.000	.000	1.8689	1.0000
133	2	31	.999	.136	.000	.000	1.2109	.9973
133	3	31	1.007	.000	.000	.000	2.0200	.9917
134	1	31	1.004	.000	.000	.000	1.9988	1.0000
134	2	31	1.000	.000	.000	.000	2.0014	1.0000
134	3	31	1.051	-.057	.000	.000	2.0425	.9983
135	1	31	1.017	.081	.000	.000	2.4842	.9898
135	2	31	.944	.274	.000	.000	2.3034	.8929
135	3	31	1.000	.000	.000	.000	.0000	1.0000
136	1	31	1.007	.000	.000	.000	.7927	.9999
136	2	31	1.002	.000	.000	.000	2.5735	1.0000
136	3	31	.992	-.010	.000	.000	1.9135	.9988
138	1	31	1.002	.000	.000	.000	2.1496	1.0000
138	2	31	1.055	-.162	.000	.000	2.2697	.9092
138	3	31	1.000	.000	.000	.000	.0000	1.0000
140	1	31	1.009	-2.247	.000	.000	1.4264	.9980
140	2	31	1.008	.000	.000	.000	2.6096	.9895
140	3	31	1.000	.000	.000	.000	2.0000	.9823
141	1	31	1.001	.000	.000	.000	2.0788	1.0000
141	2	31	.997	.000	.000	.000	2.2365	.9999
141	3	31	1.000	.000	.000	.000	2.0000	.8732
143	1	31	1.002	.000	.000	.000	2.6727	1.0000
143	2	31	.995	.000	.000	.000	2.2911	.9998
143	3	31	1.001	.000	.000	.000	2.4839	1.0000
144	1	31	1.000	.000	.000	.000	1.6804	.9999
144	2	31	.999	.000	.000	.000	1.7354	1.0000
144	3	31	1.001	.001	.000	.000	2.6920	.9995
145	1	31	1.001	.000	.000	.000	1.8706	1.0000
145	2	31	1.016	-.191	.000	.000	2.9162	.9995
145	3	31	1.014	-.015	.000	.000	2.3354	.9924
146	1	31	1.014	.000	.000	.000	1.2318	.9996
146	2	31	1.000	.000	.000	.000	.0400	1.0000
146	3	31	1.000	.000	.000	.000	2.0000	1.0000
147	1	31	1.002	.000	.000	.000	2.3546	1.0000
147	2	31	.986	.048	.000	.000	2.8992	.9996
147	3	31	1.000	.000	.000	.000	2.0000	.8315
148	1	31	1.002	.000	.000	.000	2.4594	1.0000
148	2	31	1.000	.000	.000	.000	1.0087	1.0000
148	3	31	1.000	.000	.000	.000	.0000	1.0000
149	1	31	1.007	.000	.000	.000	1.7984	.9999
149	2	31	.987	.000	.000	.000	2.4497	.9993
149	3	31	1.000	.000	.000	.000	.0000	1.0000
150	1	31	1.001	.000	.000	.000	2.4676	1.0000
150	2	31	1.023	-1.076	.000	.000	1.6218	.9998
150	3	31	1.004	.000	.000	.000	2.0064	.8914
165	1	31	.976	-.200	.000	.000	2.2481	.9936
165	2	32	1.202	.000	-.347	.570	2.5893	.9097
165	3	31	1.202	-.058	.000	.000	2.5434	.9233
169	1	31	1.004	.000	.000	.000	1.2937	1.0000
169	2	31	1.005	.000	.000	.000	1.2018	.9998
169	3	31	1.000	.000	.000	.000	2.0000	.9998
170	1	31	1.001	.000	.000	.000	2.4793	1.0000
170	2	31	1.000	.000	.000	.000	.0000	1.0000
170	3	31	1.000	.000	.000	.000	.0000	1.0000
172	1	31	1.008	-.092	.000	.000	2.4115	.9998

DEPT.	ACCT.	MODEL	PP	Q	R	S	D-W	R-2
172	2	31	1.000	.000	.000	.000	.0000	1.0000
172	3	31	1.000	.000	.000	.000	.0000	1.0000
174	1	31	1.003	.000	.000	.000	1.7962	1.0000
174	2	31	1.160	-.327	.000	.000	2.4193	.9840
174	3	31	1.025	-.023	.000	.000	3.2400	.9903
175	1	31	1.007	-.660	.000	.000	1.1207	.9993
175	2	31	1.061	-.994	.000	.000	.9537	.9974
175	3	31	1.000	.000	.000	.000	2.0000	1.0000
181	1	31	1.001	.000	.000	.000	2.4951	1.0000
181	2	31	.988	-1.340	.000	.000	2.0716	.9434
181	3	32	1.136	.000	.261	-.066	1.8039	.8659
182	1	31	1.024	-.012	.000	.000	1.5701	.9979
182	2	31	.972	.004	.000	.000	2.8194	.9986
182	3	31	1.000	.000	.000	.000	2.0000	.8026
183	1	31	1.000	.000	.000	.000	.0000	1.0000
183	2	31	.000	.000	.000	.000	.0000	1.0000
183	3	31	.000	.000	.000	.000	.0000	1.0000
184	1	31	1.001	.000	.000	.000	1.9320	1.0000
184	2	31	1.000	.000	.000	.000	.0000	1.0000
184	3	31	1.000	.000	.000	.000	.0000	1.0000
185	1	31	.997	.021	.000	.000	1.8685	.9999
185	2	31	.999	.003	.000	.000	2.3642	.9950
185	3	31	1.000	.000	.000	.000	.0000	1.0000
186	1	31	.997	.104	.000	.000	2.2556	.9998
186	2	31	.992	.127	.000	.000	2.0007	.9981
186	3	31	1.000	.000	.000	.000	2.0000	.9946
187	1	31	.000	.000	.000	.000	.0000	1.0000
187	2	31	.000	.000	.000	.000	.0000	1.0000
187	3	31	.000	.000	.000	.000	.0000	1.0000
188	1	31	1.018	.412	.000	.000	1.0000	1.0000
188	2	31	.000	.000	.000	.000	.0000	1.0000
188	3	31	.000	.000	.000	.000	.0000	1.0000
450	1	31	1.024	2.928	.000	.000	1.1133	.9923
450	2	31	1.001	1.132	.000	.000	2.2957	.9997
450	3	31	.993	1.000	.000	.000	1.8981	.9992
501	1	31	.948	-.880	.000	.000	2.8189	.9864
610	1	31	.721	.752	.000	.000	1.4316	.8866
610	1	31	.000	.000	.000	1.4316	.8866	
610	2	32	.000	1.069	.000	1.0930	.8254	
610	3	32	.000	-.047	.000	1.1048	.7729	
800	1	31	.000	.000	.000	.9702	.9990	
800	2	31	.000	.000	.000	1.3614	.9462	
800	3	31	.000	.000	.000	1.9392	.9997	
840	1	31	.000	.000	.000	1.8466	1.0000	
840	2	31	.000	.000	.000	2.3654	.7902	
840	3	31	.000	.000	.000	1.7006	.9384	
851	1	31	.000	.000	.000	1.6522	.9867	
851	2	32	.000	.746	.000	1.1331	.8765	

C.1. CITY OF PITTSBURGH -- MAYORS SUBMODEL
RELATIONSHIPS ---
21. RMAY2(I,J) =E(I,J)*DSUPR(I,J)
+ F(I,J)*DEPR2(I,J) + H(I,J)*(APPR1(I,J)-
APPRO(I,J))

22. RMAY2(I,J) = D(I,J)*(EXPND(I,J)−APPRO(I,J))
    + G(I,J)*APPR1(I,J) + H(I,J)*(APPR1(I,J) −
    APPRO(I,J))

DEPT. NO.	ACCT. NO.	MODEL NO.	D(I,J)	E(I,J)	F(I,J)	G(I,J)	H(I,J)	DURBIN-WATSON,D	R−2
100	1	21	.000	.000	1.003	.000	.000	2.6079	1.0000
100	2	21	.000	.410	1.020	.000	−.426	2.4497	.9990
100	3	21	.000	.000	1.051	.000	−.070	1.4898	.9999
100	4	21	.000	.000	.000	.000	.000	.0000	1.0000
100	5	21	.000	.000	.000	.000	.000	.0000	1.0000
101	1	21	.000	−1.565	1.269	.000	−.729	2.7686	.9747
101	2	21	.000	−14.276	1.819	.000	2.506	1.6417	.9997
101	3	21	.000	1.290	1.012	.000	−.444	1.6347	.9980
101	4	22	.500	.000	.000	.750	.000	1.4167	.9167
101	5	21	.000	.000	.000	.000	.000	.0000	.4000
102	1	21	.000	.000	.000	.000	.000	.0000	.4000
102	2	21	.000	−.071	1.024	.000	−.539	2.8823	.9998
102	3	21	.000	.000	1.066	.000	.000	1.9040	.9985
102	4	21	.000	.000	.000	.000	.000	.0000	1.0000
102	5	21	.000	.000	.000	.000	.000	.0000	1.0000
103	1	21	.000	114.329	.151	.000	−11.448	2.0756	.9667
103	2	21	.000	.640	.836	.000	.086	1.7483	.9532
103	3	21	.000	−.155	1.045	.000	−.279	2.2760	.9973
103	4	21	.000	.000	1.000	.000	.000	.1111	1.0000
103	5	21	.000	.000	.000	.000	.000	.0000	.2000
104	1	21	.000	17.161	.883	.000	.715	1.9571	.9997
104	2	21	.000	.839	1.010	.000	−.563	2.0746	.9992
104	3	21	.000	5.964	.966	.000	−1.438	1.4425	.9972
104	4	22	.511	.000	.000	.520	.000	.5756	.9975
104	5	21	.000	.000	.000	.000	.000	.0000	.4663
104	6	21	.000	−1.822	1.111	.000	−.145	2.0597	.9729
106	1	21	.000	.361	1.039	.000	−1.040	2.5372	.9998
106	2	21	.000	−2.062	1.120	.000	.000	2.4333	.9983
106	3	21	.000	−7.815	1.209	.000	−.708	2.3606	.9915
106	4	22	.952	.000	.000	.000	.233	.4492	.9697
106	5	21	.000	−.555	1.228	.000	−.237	.9011	.9392
107	1	21	.000	−.780	1.042	.000	−.043	2.7043	.9988
107	2	21	.000	3.167	.851	.000	−1.242	2.5900	.9997
107	3	21	.000	2.889	.984	.000	−.537	3.2203	.9993
107	4	22	1.160	.000	.000	.299	.000	1.2035	.4688
107	5	21	.000	.000	.000	.000	.000	.0000	.0987
107	6	21	.000	14.500	1.043	.000	−.028	2.5768	.9896
107	7	21	.000	−.887	1.069	.000	.000	2.1119	.9964
107	8	21	.000	3.623	1.000	.000	.000	2.0000	.8182
107	9	21	.000	.437	1.017	.000	−.264	1.8613	.9722
109	1	21	.000	.000	.998	.000	.000	2.0487	.9998
109	2	21	.000	.869	.977	.000	−1.085	1.9701	.9997
109	3	21	.000	−.131	1.035	.000	.163	1.7505	.9939
109	4	22	.187	.000	.000	.883	.000	2.3035	.9340
109	5	21	.000	.000	.000	.000	.000	.0000	.0592
110	1	21	.000	−2.397	1.093	.000	.000	1.8788	.9966
110	2	21	.000	−3.460	1.140	.000	.083	2.3843	.9905
110	3	21	.000	2.001	.696	.000	−.485	1.8645	.7011
110	4	21	.000	.198	.734	.000	.359	1.1147	.9510
110	5	21	.000	.000	.000	.000	.000	.0000	.0189

DEPT.	ACCT.	MODEL	D	E	F	G	H	D-W	R-2
110	6	21	.000	.450	.584	.000	.000	2.1994	.6805
111	1	21	.000	.000	1.010	.000	.000	2.9245	.9999
111	2	21	.000	.368	1.015	.000	-.279	2.8402	.9998
111	3	21	.000	-6.442	1.083	.000	.444	2.1283	.9728
111	4	22	1.000	.000	.000	.000	.000	.0000	1.0000
111	5	21	.000	.000	.000	.000	.000	.0000	1.0000
112	1	21	.000	-.358	1.036	.000	-.669	2.9919	.9997
112	2	21	.000	.000	1.000	.000	.392	2.7135	.9999
112	3	21	.000	-6.335	1.057	.000	.619	2.1263	.9862
112	4	21	.000	.755	-.253	.000	-.310	1.0184	.6824
112	5	21	.000	.000	.000	.000	.000	.0000	.4818
113	1	21	.000	-1.996	1.048	.000	-.120	2.4590	.9997
113	2	21	.000	.976	.985	.000	-.793	2.3669	.9997
113	3	21	.000	3.767	1.018	.000	-.638	2.3303	.9997
113	4	22	.443	.000	.000	.675	.000	2.3546	.9827
113	5	21	.000	.469	1.027	.000	-.782	2.2741	.9971
113	6	21	.000	.000	1.000	.000	.000	.0000	1.0000
135	1	21	.000	1.904	1.018	.000	-.372	2.2569	.9994
135	2	21	.000	-1.140	1.011	.000	-.184	2.1388	.9870
135	3	21	.000	.000	.000	.000	.000	.0000	.1802
135	4	21	.000	.000	.000	.000	.000	.0000	.1802
135	5	21	.000	.000	.000	.000	.000	.0000	.1802
136	1	21	.000	.000	1.030	.000	-.232	2.3017	.9959
136	2	21	.000	.144	1.005	.000	-.254	2.7793	.9996
136	3	21	.000	5.141	1.033	.000	-1.248	1.4833	.9935
136	4	21	.000	.093	.990	.000	-.976	1.9216	.9577
136	5	21	.000	2.179	.834	.000	-2.320	1.4324	.9617
137	1	21	.000	1.404	1.026	.000	-.692	2.1172	.9995
137	2	21	.000	.000	1.014	.000	.000	2.3894	.9998
137	3	21	.000	.000	.000	.000	.000	.0000	.6831
137	4	21	.000	.000	.000	.000	.000	.0000	.6831
137	5	21	.000	.000	.000	.000	.000	.0000	.6831
138	1	21	.000	-.771	1.025	.000	-.502	2.9000	.9998
138	2	21	.000	.737	.929	.000	-.508	2.6215	.9977
138	3	21	.000	.000	.000	.000	.000	.0000	.0163
138	4	21	.000	.000	.000	.000	.000	.0000	.0163
138	5	21	.000	.000	.000	.000	.000	.0000	.0163
140	1	21	.000	-.407	1.044	.000	-.496	2.4927	.9992
140	2	21	.000	.000	1.011	.000	.095	2.7082	.9996
140	3	21	.000	1.779	.992	.000	.000	1.7104	.9749
140	4	22	.374	.000	.000	.691	.000	2.7242	.9061
140	5	21	.000	.000	.833	.000	.000	2.4000	.8333
141	1	21	.000	.000	.000	.000	.000	.0000	.1667
141	2	21	.000	-.065	1.022	.000	.054	2.6267	.9996
141	3	21	.000	.000	1.005	.000	.253	2.9218	.9999
141	4	21	.000	-1.518	2.595	.000	-2.597	1.7260	.9239
141	5	21	.000	3.333	1.000	.000	.000	2.0500	.9930
142	1	21	.000	.000	1.004	.000	.000	2.4059	.9999
142	2	21	.000	.000	1.009	.000	.000	2.9975	.9999
142	3	21	.000	1.428	1.005	.000	-.856	1.9236	.9984
142	4	22	.192	.000	.000	.667	.000	2.2224	.9552
142	5	21	.000	.000	1.000	.000	.000	.0000	1.0000
143	1	21	.000	.000	.000	.000	.000	.0000	1.0000
143	2	21	.000	.000	1.000	.000	.000	2.2243	.9999
143	3	21	.000	.000	.000	.000	.000	.0000	.0977

DEPT.	ACCT.	MODEL	D	E	F	G	H	D-W	R-2
143	4	21	.000	.000	.000	.000	.000	.0000	.0977
143	5	21	.000	.000	.000	.000	.000	.0000	.0977
144	1	21	.000	1.999	1.001	.000	-.117	2.7674	.9996
144	2	21	.000	2.138	.942	.000	-.840	2.0146	.9995
144	3	21	.000	-1.936	1.134	.000	-.752	3.2010	.9989
144	4	21	.000	.048	.889	.000	-.180	1.9642	.9870
144	5	21	.000	12.308	1.000	.000	.000	2.0500	.9207
145	1	21	.000	.000	.000	.000	.000	.0000	.2000
145	2	21	.000	.000	.999	.000	.000	1.7219	1.0000
145	3	21	.000	5.076	1.002	.000	-.861	2.2144	.9789
145	4	22	.000	.000	.000	1.000	.000	.0000	1.0000
145	5	21	.000	.000	.000	.000	.000	.0000	1.0000
146	1	21	.000	-2.481	1.068	.000	-.587	2.7044	.9991
146	2	21	.000	-.738	1.081	.000	-.498	2.5641	.9996
146	3	21	.000	.000	1.006	.000	.000	1.1282	.9999
146	4	22	.191	.000	.000	.747	.000	1.1959	.9862
146	5	21	.000	.000	1.000	.000	.000	.0000	1.0000
147	1	21	.000	.000	1.006	.000	.000	2.8060	.9999
147	2	21	.000	.000	1.006	.000	.000	2.9565	.9999
147	3	21	.000	.750	1.004	.000	.172	1.8824	.9996
147	4	22	.000	.000	.000	1.061	-.361	1.8966	.7777
147	5	21	.000	.000	.000	.000	.000	.0000	.0967
148	1	21	.000	.000	1.018	.000	-.459	2.6390	.9999
148	2	21	.000	.391	.993	.000	.000	2.3460	.9998
148	3	21	.000	.041	1.025	.000	-.777	2.8001	.9985
148	4	21	.000	.000	1.009	.000	.000	2.6976	.9200
148	5	21	.000	.000	.000	.000	.000	.0000	.2972
149	1	21	.000	-.222	1.050	.000	.135	2.4674	.9969
149	2	21	.000	.072	1.035	.000	-.598	2.1804	.9985
149	3	21	.000	-.464	1.026	.000	.204	2.0439	.9992
149	4	22	-.339	.000	.000	1.386	.000	1.7396	.9640
149	5	21	.000	3.230	.999	.000	-4.138	2.2556	.9929
150	1	21	.000	-1.641	1.047	.000	.000	2.4679	.9988
150	2	21	.000	.000	1.003	.000	.320	1.9208	.9999
150	3	21	.000	.870	1.023	.000	.000	2.0742	.9999
150	4	22	-.021	.000	.000	1.023	.000	2.0928	1.0000
150	5	21	.000	1.000	1.000	.000	.000	.0000	1.0000
150	6	21	.000	1.168	.959	.000	-.343	1.0172	.9986
150	7	21	.000	1.064	.976	.000	.000	2.4692	.9962
151	1	21	.000	-4.728	1.094	.000	-.017	2.1454	.9991
151	2	21	.000	1.067	.975	.000	-.932	2.9122	.9996
151	3	21	.000	3.570	.936	.000	-.493	1.9388	.9996
151	4	21	.000	.069	.983	.000	-.988	.9737	.9959
151	5	21	.000	.000	.000	.000	.000	.0000	.5733
152	1	21	.000	.607	1.035	.000	-.379	2.3500	.9992
152	2	21	.000	.557	1.013	.000	-.732	2.5089	.9996
152	3	21	.000	.983	1.017	.000	.000	2.4050	.9999
152	4	22	1.000	.000	.000	.000	.000	.0000	1.0000
152	5	21	.000	.000	1.000	.000	.000	.0000	1.0000
153	1	21	.000	.000	1.020	.000	.000	1.8049	1.0000
153	2	21	.000	.000	1.011	.000	.000	1.5949	.9998
153	3	21	.000	.000	1.000	.000	.000	.0000	1.0000
153	4	21	.000	.000	1.000	.000	.000	.0000	1.0000
153	5	21	.000	-1.597	1.065	.000	.000	2.2888	.9991
160	1	21	.000	.000	1.012	.000	-.418	3.0766	.9981

DEPT.	ACCT.	MODEL	D	E	F	G	H	D-W	R-2
160	2	21	.000	.731	.987	.000	.148	2.6174	.9969
160	3	21	.000	.000	1.009	.000	.000	1.6406	.9998
160	4	22	.000	.000	.000	1.007	.000	3.0419	.9999
160	5	21	.000	-5.770	1.250	.000	-.781	.7404	1.0000
160	6	21	.000	8.139	1.003	.000	.000	.5942	.9998
167	1	21	.000	.000	1.010	.000	-.410	1.9596	1.0000
167	2	21	.000	-1.060	1.081	.000	-1.546	1.5273	.9998
167	3	21	.000	.000	1.006	.000	1.046	2.9942	.9977
167	4	21	.000	-.295	1.170	.000	.093	2.1456	.9872
167	5	21	.000	.000	1.000	.000	.000	1.0026	1.0000
167	6	21	.000	.000	1.000	.000	.000	2.1483	1.0000
180	1	21	.000	1.244	1.003	.000	-1.300	2.1122	.9998
180	2	21	.000	-.776	1.098	.000	-1.162	2.4233	.9990
180	3	21	.000	.042	1.019	.000	-.122	2.8480	.9995
180	4	21	.000	-.183	1.306	.000	-1.137	2.2243	.9946
180	5	21	.000	1.458	1.065	.000	-1.165	2.4378	.9972
181	1	21	.000	.000	1.069	.000	-1.119	1.1669	1.0000
181	2	21	.000	-2.149	1.203	.000	-2.300	1.0692	.9999
181	3	21	.000	.000	1.008	.000	.000	3.1606	.9999
181	4	21	.000	.000	.000	.000	.000	.0000	1.0000
181	5	21	.000	.000	1.086	.000	-1.094	3.1534	.9991
183	1	21	.000	.000	1.021	.000	-.186	3.1368	.9997
183	2	21	.000	-3.130	1.077	.000	-.718	2.5799	.9998
183	3	21	.000	-26.526	1.170	.000	.000	1.8756	.8188
183	4	21	.000	.000	.000	.000	.000	.0000	.8862
183	5	21	.000	.000	.000	.000	.000	.0000	.8862
183	6	21	.000	.000	1.037	.000	.000	2.0006	.0637
200	1	21	.000	.238	1.028	.000	-.882	2.8449	.9997
200	2	21	.000	1.511	.979	.000	.302	2.4872	.9972
200	3	21	.000	-.608	1.010	.000	1.815	1.8132	.9993
200	4	22	.000	.000	.000	1.000	.000	.0000	1.0000
200	5	21	.000	.000	.000	.000	.000	.0000	1.0000
201	1	21	.000	.156	1.010	.000	.000	2.0000	1.0000
201	2	21	.000	.000	.999	.000	-.643	1.4992	.9999
201	3	21	.000	.000	.000	.000	.000	.0000	.6318
201	4	21	.000	.000	.000	.000	.000	.0000	.6318
201	5	21	.000	.000	.000	.000	.000	.0000	.6318
202	1	21	.000	-4.405	1.315	.000	.000	2.1275	.9995
202	2	21	.000	-2.070	1.083	.000	2.010	2.1636	.9999
202	5	21	.000	.000	.000	.000	.000	.0000	1.0000
204	1	21	.000	.000	.000	.000	.000	.0000	1.0000
204	2	21	.000	-13.887	1.434	.000	.000	1.4867	.9999
204	3	21	.000	-16.043	1.114	.000	-1.141	.2222	1.0000
204	4	21	.000	.000	.000	.000	.000	.0000	.5000
204	5	21	.000	.000	.000	.000	.000	.0000	.5000
244	1	21	.000	.000	1.002	.000	.000	1.6894	1.0000
244	2	21	.000	.000	1.008	.000	.000	3.1754	.9999
244	3	21	.000	.000	1.015	.000	.000	1.4774	.9998
244	4	21	.000	.000	.000	.000	.000	.0000	1.0000
244	5	21	.000	.000	.000	.000	.000	.0000	1.0000
250	1	21	.000	.000	1.064	.000	-1.365	1.8439	1.0000
250	2	21	.000	-3.277	1.167	.000	-.242	2.0102	.9991
250	3	22	.438	.000	.000	.694	.000	1.7279	.9787
250	4	22	.615	.000	.000	.365	.000	1.5556	.8251
250	5	21	.000	.000	1.000	.000	.000	.0000	1.0000

DEPT.	ACCT.	MODEL	D	E	F	G	H	D-W	R-2
301	1	21	.000	-3.932	1.285	.000	.000	2.2196	.9997
301	2	21	.000	.041	1.016	.000	-.679	2.6963	.9989
301	3	21	.000	.004	1.014	.000	-.094	.7937	.9992
301	4	21	.000	-.149	1.226	.000	.000	1.4240	.9729
301	5	21	.000	.000	.000	.000	.000	.0000	.3333
302	1	21	.000	-5.224	1.350	.000	.000	1.6657	1.0000
302	2	21	.000	-.542	1.044	.000	-1.049	1.9425	.9994
302	3	21	.000	.046	.996	.000	.000	1.4417	.9996
302	4	21	.000	.000	1.000	.000	-.144	1.0000	1.0000
302	5	21	.000	.000	.000	.000	.000	.0000	1.0000
401	1	21	.000	-3.796	1.341	.000	.000	2.5489	.9970
401	2	21	.000	.000	1.044	.000	-1.087	1.5663	.9999
401	3	21	.000	.000	.000	.000	.000	.0000	.8877
401	4	21	.000	.000	.000	.000	.000	.0000	.8877

C.2. CITY OF PITTSBURGH -- COUNCIL SUBMODEL
RELATIONSHIPS ---

31. $APPR2(I,J) = PP(I,J)*(RMAY2(I,J) + Q(I,J)*(DEPR2(I,J)+DSUPR(I,J)-RMAY2(I,J)))$

32. $APPR2(I,J) = PP(I,J)*(RMAY2(I,J)) + R(I,J)*(APPR1(I,J)-APPRO(I,J)) + S(I,J)*(EXPND(I,J)-APPRO(I,J))$

DEPT. NO.	ACCT. NO.	MODEL NO.	PP(I,J)	Q(I,J)	R(I,J)	S(I,J)	DURBIN-WATSON,D	R-2
100	1	31	1.001	.000	.000	.000	2.3157	1.0000
100	2	31	1.015	-.289	.000	.000	.7271	.9998
100	3	32	1.381	.000	1.577	-2.280	2.0000	.9653
100	4	31	.000	.000	.000	.000	2.0000	.9653
100	5	31	.000	.000	.000	.000	2.0000	.9653
101	1	31	.976	-.067	.000	.000	.8555	.9996
101	2	31	1.013	-.500	.000	.000	1.9133	.9966
101	3	31	.980	-.177	.000	.000	2.6848	.9981
101	4	31	.947	-.034	.000	.000	2.2903	.9803
101	5	31	.000	.000	.000	.000	.0000	.9797
102	1	31	.000	.000	.000	.000	.0000	.9797
102	2	31	1.136	-2.462	.000	.000	2.5724	.9960
102	3	31	1.066	3.708	.000	.000	2.3864	.8545
102	4	31	.000	.000	.000	.000	.0000	.8448
102	5	31	.000	.000	.000	.000	.0000	.8448
103	1	31	.982	-.030	.000	.000	2.0400	.9988
103	2	32	1.038	.000	-.187	.330	2.1743	.9517
103	3	32	.788	.000	.728	-.624	1.5960	.9890
103	4	32	.866	.000	-.014	-.690	2.4629	.9961
103	5	31	.000	.000	.000	.000	.0000	.9961
104	1	31	1.013	-.691	.000	.000	2.0886	.9978
104	2	31	.989	-.401	.000	.000	2.1695	.9995
104	3	31	.969	.288	.000	.000	1.9644	.9948
104	4	31	.948	.000	.000	.000	2.4000	.9853
104	5	31	.000	.000	.000	.000	.0000	.9855
104	6	31	.996	.185	.000	.000	2.1204	1.0000
106	1	31	1.006	.000	.000	.000	1.8843	.9999
106	2	31	1.039	-.141	.000	.000	2.0605	.9975

DEPT.	ACCT.	MODEL	PP	Q	R	S	D-W	R-2
106	3	31	1.008	-.061	.000	.000	1.9883	.9998
106	4	32	1.081	.000	.069	.273	2.5691	.9293
106	5	31	.833	.302	.000	.000	2.5671	.8769
107	1	31	.994	-.596	.000	.000	2.2541	.9994
107	2	31	.988	.000	.000	.000	3.5024	.9988
107	3	31	.952	1.350	.000	.000	2.6402	.9928
107	4	31	.604	.418	.000	.000	2.7393	.7326
107	5	31	.000	.000	.000	.000	.0000	.4933
107	6	32	.922	.000	.278	-.419	2.6872	.9386
107	7	31	.952	-.508	.000	.000	3.0318	.9910
107	8	32	.000	.000	1.500	-.750	2.2308	1.0000
107	9	31	.993	.000	.000	.000	1.6446	.9998
109	1	31	1.027	-.470	.000	.000	2.1266	.9980
109	2	32	.993	.000	1.230	.738	1.8589	.9943
109	3	32	1.269	.000	-.806	.892	1.6162	.9884
109	4	32	1.024	.000	-.121	.046	1.3561	.9381
109	5	31	.000	.000	.000	.000	.0000	.9381
110	1	32	1.011	.000	-.243	.000	1.7391	.9973
110	2	31	.986	.389	.000	.000	1.4370	.9971
110	3	31	1.038	.202	.000	.000	2.5023	.9381
110	4	32	.990	.000	-.065	.205	1.1994	.9992
110	5	31	.000	.000	.000	.000	.0000	.9992
110	6	32	1.026	.000	-.140	.018	2.4097	.9997
111	1	31	1.003	.000	.000	.000	2.4151	1.0000
111	2	32	.995	.000	.000	-.214	2.0589	1.0000
111	3	32	1.014	.000	.000	.158	1.0961	.9999
111	4	31	.833	.000	.000	.000	2.4000	.8333
111	5	31	.000	.000	.000	.000	.0000	.8346
112	1	31	1.000	.000	.000	.000	1.6649	.9999
112	2	31	1.020	-.559	.000	.000	2.1107	.9989
112	3	32	.548	.000	1.105	-.755	3.4184	.9586
112	4	32	.887	.000	.143	-.234	1.2131	.9887
112	5	31	.000	.000	.000	.000	.0000	.9887
113	1	31	1.003	.000	.000	.000	.8279	1.0000
113	2	32	.735	.000	-.459	-2.242	3.3627	.9988
113	3	32	.623	.000	.948	-.938	2.2312	.9736
113	4	31	.877	.037	.000	.000	1.3499	.9723
113	5	32	.994	.000	-5.061	.165	1.4993	.9793
113	6	31	1.000	.000	.000	.000	.0000	1.0000
135	1	31	1.000	.000	.000	.000	.0000	1.0000
135	2	31	1.005	-.301	.000	.000	.8688	.9998
135	3	31	.000	.000	.000	.000	.0000	.9991
135	4	31	.000	.000	.000	.000	.0000	.9991
135	5	31	.000	.000	.000	.000	.0000	.9991
136	1	31	1.000	.000	.000	.000	.0000	1.0000
136	2	31	.999	-.443	.000	.000	2.7710	.9985
136	3	32	.916	.000	.446	-.268	2.3365	.9942
136	4	32	.842	.000	.541	-.463	2.7313	.9722
136	5	31	.909	-.124	.000	.000	2.7335	.9734
137	1	31	.996	.000	.000	.000	1.1936	.9999
137	2	31	.970	.843	.000	.000	1.1257	.9999
137	3	31	.000	.000	.000	.000	.0000	.9998
137	4	31	.000	.000	.000	.000	.0000	.9998
137	5	31	.000	.000	.000	.000	.0000	.9998
138	1	31	1.005	.000	.000	.000	2.5620	.9999

DEPT.	ACCT.	MODEL	PP	Q	R	S	D-W	R-2
138	2	31	1.015	-.069	.000	.000	2.3267	.9998
138	3	31	.000	.000	.000	.000	.0000	.9997
138	4	31	.000	.000	.000	.000	.0000	.9997
138	5	31	.000	.000	.000	.000	.0000	.9997
140	1	31	.996	.000	.000	.000	1.1915	.9999
140	2	31	.912	1.174	.000	.000	1.4042	.9984
140	3	31	.979	-.313	.000	.000	2.0195	.9990
140	4	32	.807	.000	.332	-.209	2.2006	.9180
140	5	31	1.000	.160	.000	.000	2.0000	1.0000
141	1	31	.000	.000	.000	.000	.0000	.9988
141	2	31	.973	.045	.000	.000	2.4651	.9972
141	3	31	.981	.434	.000	.000	2.3470	.9978
141	4	32	1.049	.000	-.511	.675	1.1665	.9968
141	5	31	.905	-.543	.000	.000	2.0778	.9612
142	1	31	1.000	.000	.000	.000	1.2079	1.0000
142	2	31	1.000	.000	.000	.000	.0000	1.0000
142	3	31	.978	-.177	.000	.000	2.1496	.9974
142	4	31	.943	.015	.000	.000	2.6000	.9727
142	5	32	2.050	.000	.000	1.250	2.1000	.8400
143	1	31	.000	.000	.000	.000	.0000	.8400
143	2	32	1.052	.000	-.086	.913	2.5543	.9981
143	3	31	.000	.000	.000	.000	.0000	.9981
143	4	31	.000	.000	.000	.000	.0000	.9981
143	5	31	.000	.000	.000	.000	.0000	.9981
144	1	31	1.004	.000	.000	.000	1.1926	.9999
144	2	31	.980	-.208	.000	.000	1.5267	.9986
144	3	31	1.019	.000	.000	.000	.9392	.9989
144	4	31	.847	.098	.000	.000	2.6271	.9907
144	5	31	.991	-.019	.000	.000	2.0755	.9996
145	1	31	.000	.000	.000	.000	.0000	.9996
145	2	32	1.795	.000	-1.627	1.066	2.3317	.8440
145	3	32	.835	.000	.720	-.563	2.0243	.9908
145	4	31	.799	.227	.000	.000	2.0185	.7352
145	5	31	.000	.000	.000	.000	.0000	.6454
146	1	31	.983	-.157	.000	.000	2.2386	.9993
146	2	31	.995	.000	.000	.000	2.5030	.9999
146	3	31	1.001	-.155	.000	.000	1.8724	.9995
146	4	31	.972	.000	.000	.000	2.4077	.9960
146	5	31	1.000	-1.379	.000	.000	2.5500	.9978
147	1	31	.996	.000	.000	.000	2.4030	.9999
147	2	31	.970	.178	.000	.000	2.6747	.9984
147	3	31	.993	-.053	.000	.000	2.4523	.9997
147	4	31	.974	.000	.000	.000	1.7805	.9949
147	5	31	.000	.000	.000	.000	.0000	.9953
148	1	31	1.003	.000	.000	.000	2.4179	1.0000
148	2	31	.966	.238	.000	.000	2.0452	.9986
148	3	31	1.004	.000	.000	.000	2.4208	.9999
148	4	32	.751	.000	.052	-.612	3.0984	.9778
148	5	31	.000	.000	.000	.000	.0000	.9778
149	1	32	1.001	.000	.000	-2672.001	1.2806	1.0000
149	2	31	.998	.263	.000	.000	1.9413	.9999
149	3	31	1.003	.000	.000	.000	1.7917	1.0000
149	4	32	1.082	.000	.759	.436	2.9825	.9984
149	5	32	1.000	.000	-2.010	.000	.6429	1.0000
150	1	31	.996	.000	.000	.000	2.3654	.9999

DEPT.	ACCT.	MODEL	PP	Q	R	S	D-W	R-2
150	2	32	.957	.000	1.906	.191	2.0553	.9966
150	3	31	.942	.000	.000	.000	2.3724	.9800
150	4	32	.835	.000	-.071	.068	2.5135	.8799
150	5	31	.966	.000	.000	.000	2.1214	.9754
150	6	31	1.002	.261	.000	.000	2.7594	.9996
150	7	32	1.061	.000	1.002	-.395	3.0105	.9902
151	1	31	.915	2.978	.000	.000	2.7335	.9471
151	2	31	1.003	.261	.000	.000	1.9759	.9992
151	3	31	1.005	.000	.000	.000	2.3675	.9998
151	4	31	.953	-.009	.000	.000	2.4016	.9827
151	5	31	.000	.000	.000	.000	.0000	.9825
152	1	31	1.005	-.210	.000	.000	2.1120	.9997
152	2	31	1.001	.000	.000	.000	2.4391	1.0000
152	3	31	.943	-1.221	.000	.000	2.0418	.9823
152	4	31	.844	.009	.000	.000	2.4969	.8674
152	5	31	1.000	-20.000	.000	.000	2.5500	.8400
153	1	31	1.040	-.190	.000	.000	1.5527	.9992
153	2	31	1.032	.000	.000	.000	1.9563	.9987
153	3	32	.388	.000	.000	-.984	1.9863	.9953
153	4	31	1.013	-.193	.000	.000	2.7147	.9982
153	5	31	.945	-1.283	.000	.000	2.1729	1.0000
160	1	31	1.023	.000	.000	.000	1.7085	1.0000
160	2	31	1.009	.332	.000	.000	2.2542	.9990
160	3	32	.935	.000	.000	-.481	3.0413	.9999
160	4	31	.953	-.215	.000	.000	2.6085	.9983
160	5	32	.945	.000	-.301	.595	1.3375	1.0000
160	6	31	.999	-.531	.000	.000	1.8578	1.0000
167	1	32	1.053	.000	-.591	1.395	.2370	1.0000
167	2	31	.982	.273	.000	.000	2.0488	.9998
167	3	31	1.020	.234	.000	.000	1.4902	.9999
167	4	32	1.131	.000	-.960	.613	2.3396	.9973
167	5	32	.988	.000	.599	.000	2.9959	.9991
167	6	31	1.001	.000	.000	.000	2.8358	.9998
180	1	31	1.001	.000	.000	.000	2.4573	1.0000
180	2	31	.994	.000	.000	.000	1.0049	1.0000
180	3	32	1.047	.000	.000	1.412	1.0894	.9999
180	4	31	1.004	.000	.000	.000	1.1090	.9998
180	5	31	.992	-.319	.000	.000	.7430	.9988
181	1	32	1.001	.000	.000	.000	2.9901	1.0000
181	2	31	.998	.000	.000	.000	1.7913	.9999
181	3	31	.847	-8.320	.000	.000	1.9080	.9850
181	4	31	.000	.000	.000	.000	.0000	.9979
181	5	31	.994	.000	.000	.000	3.1623	.9999
183	1	31	1.010	.000	.000	.000	3.0900	.9998
183	2	32	1.200	.000	.000	9.412	2.7868	.9999
183	3	32	1.284	.000	.577	-2.389	.8182	1.0000
183	4	31	.000	.000	.000	.000	.0000	1.0000
183	5	31	.000	.000	.000	.000	.0000	1.0000
183	6	31	1.017	.715	.000	.000	2.5321	.9997
200	1	31	1.023	-.190	.000	.000	1.2311	.9998
200	2	31	.978	.417	.000	.000	1.0954	.9996
200	3	32	1.044	.000	.000	-.555	2.6512	.9688
200	4	32	6.580	.000	-1.046	9.423	2.8846	1.0000
200	5	31	.000	.000	.000	.000	.0000	1.0000
201	1	31	1.000	.000	.000	.000	2.0009	.6923

DEPT.	ACCT.	MODEL	PP	Q	R	S	D-W	R-2
201	2	31	.996	.000	.000	.000	1.8974	.9999
201	3	31	.000	.000	.000	.000	.0000	.9999
201	4	31	.000	.000	.000	.000	.0000	.9999
201	5	31	.000	.000	.000	.000	.0000	.9999
202	1	31	1.000	.000	.000	.000	3.1544	1.0000
202	2	32	.866	.000	2.404	-1.938	2.1768	.9989
202	3	32	.754	.000	.192	-.234	1.5707	.9885
202	4	31	.961	.004	.000	.000	1.8973	.9965
202	5	31	.000	.000	.000	.000	.0000	.9964
204	1	31	.000	.000	.000	.000	.0000	.9964
204	2	31	1.000	.000	.000	.000	.0000	1.0000
204	3	32	.000	.000	.320	-4.400	2.2201	.9999
204	4	31	.000	.000	.000	.000	.0000	.9999
204	5	31	.000	.000	.000	.000	.0000	.9999
244	1	31	1.039	.000	.000	.000	1.6174	1.0000
244	2	31	.985	.000	.000	.000	2.4731	.9999
244	3	31	1.102	29.015	.000	.000	3.1791	.9859
244	4	31	.000	.000	.000	.000	.0000	.6927
244	5	31	.000	.000	.000	.000	.0000	.6927
250	1	31	1.000	.000	.000	.000	.0000	1.0000
250	2	31	1.000	.000	.000	.000	.0000	1.0000
250	3	31	.989	-.118	.000	.000	1.0505	.9977
250	4	31	.970	.017	.000	.000	1.4310	.9995
250	5	31	1.000	-50.000	.000	.000	2.5000	.7500
301	1	31	1.017	-.322	.000	.000	1.6256	1.0000
301	2	31	1.000	.000	.000	.000	.0000	1.0000
301	3	32	.707	.000	2.841	-.561	2.7199	.9864
301	4	31	.865	.099	.000	.000	1.8046	.9932
301	5	31	.000	.000	.000	.000	.0000	.9942
302	1	31	1.001	.000	.000	.000	3.1606	1.0000
302	2	31	.996	.000	.000	.000	3.1263	1.0000
302	3	32	1.261	.000	-.518	.694	2.2295	.9991
302	4	32	1.000	.000	1.247	.000	.7576	1.0000
302	5	31	.000	.000	.000	.000	.0000	1.0000
401	1	31	1.000	.000	.000	.000	.0000	1.0000
401	2	31	1.000	.000	.000	.000	.0000	1.0000
401	3	31	.000	.000	.000	.000	.0000	1.0000
401	4	31	.000	.000	.000	.000	.0000	1.0000

Appendix D

GOODNESS-OF-FIT MEASURES

A. Cleveland

Bayesian-Induction Criteria

$$\frac{\displaystyle\sum_{i}^{n} \sum_{j}^{m_i} \frac{(APPR2_{ij} - AAPRO_{ij})^2}{AAPRO_{ij}}}{\displaystyle\sum_{i}^{n} m_i}$$

Year	One-period Change	Simulation	A1	A2
1956	8.330×10^3		2.051×10^4	2.507×10^5
1957	3.825×10^3		3.256×10^4	2.8033×10^5
1958	1.618×10^4		5.895×10^4	2.385×10^4
1959	4.742×10^4		6.395×10^3	1.421×10^4
1960	1.881×10^3	1.881×10^3	2.817×10^3	1.401×10^4
1961	2.160×10^3	4.070×10^3	5.092×10^3	1.485×10^4
1962	1.515×10^3	6.650×10^3	5.912×10^3	1.481×10^4
1963	9.840×10^2	6.920×10^3	1.077×10^4	1.702×10^4
1964	4.380×10^3	2.096×10^4	1.203×10^4	2.005×10^4
1965	3.170×10^3	2.135×10^4	3.565×10^4	6.763×10^4

$APPR2_{ij}$ = model estimate, department i, account j.
$AAPRO_{ij}$ = observed appropriations, department i, account j.
m_i = number of accounts, department i.
n = total number of departments.

χ^2-*Criteria*

$$\dfrac{\displaystyle\sum_i^n \sum_j^{m_i} \dfrac{(APPR2_{ij} - AAPRO_{ij})^2}{APPR2_{ij}}}{\displaystyle\sum_i^n m_i}$$

Year	One-period Change	Simulation	A1	A2
1956	2.920×10^3		1.799×10^4	6.487×10
1957	6.690×10^4		1.349×10^4	5.974×10^3
1958	7.940×10^4		2.750×10^4	2.168×10^3
1959	3.440×10^4		1.414×10^4	5.033×10^3
1960	1.430×10^3	1.430×10^3	3.486×10^3	5.119×10^3
1961	4.975×10^3	4.910×10^3	3.500×10^3	3.390×10^3
1962	6.001×10^2	7.210×10^3	4.20×10^3	3.40×10^3
1963	8.540×10^3	1.622×10^4	4.095×10^3	2.922×10^3
1964	5.299×10^3	3.221×10^4	8.903×10^3	4.745×10^3
1965	6.170×10^3	3.530×10^4	2.336×10^5	3.569×10^5

$APPR2_{ij}$ = model estimate, department i, account j.
$AAPRO_{ij}$ = observed appropriations, department i, account j.
m_i = number of accounts, department i.
n = total number of departments.

Goodness-of-Fit Measure: R_c^2

$$R_c^2 = 1.0 - \dfrac{\displaystyle\sum_i^n \sum_j^{m_i} (AAPRO_{ij} - APPR2_{ij})^2}{\displaystyle\sum_i^n \sum_j^{m_i} (AAPRO_{ij} - APPR1_{ij})^2}$$

Year	One-period Change	Simulation	A3
1956	$-.9469$	—	.188
1957	.7507	—	.4793
1958	.0378	—	-16.8
1959	$-.4422$	—	.011
1960	.9302	.9302	.2179
1961	.8631	.1730	.2999
1962	$-.2527$	-5.254	-3.74
1963	$-.0048$	$-.2537$	-14.4
1964	.3510	$-.0301$	.4129
1965	$-.2707$	.0021	-1.12

$APPR1_{ij}$ = previous appropriations, department i, account j.
$APPR2_{ij}$ = model estimate, department i, account j.
$AAPRO_{ij}$ = observed appropriations, department i, account j.
m_i = number of accounts, department i.
n = total number of departments.

Goodness-of-Fit Measure: $R_o{}^2$

$$R_o{}^2 = 1.0 - \frac{\sum_{i}^{n} \sum_{j}^{m_1} (AAPRO_{ij} - APPR2_{ij})^2}{\sum_{i}^{n} \sum_{j}^{m_1} (AAPRO_{ij} - \overline{AAPRO})^2}$$

Year	One-period Change	Simulation	A1	A2
1956	.9971	—	.9730	.9191
1957	.9993	—	.9792	.9150
1958	.8953	—	.9515	.9927
1959	.9926	—	.9987	.9952
1960	.9998	.9998	.9981	.9953
1961	.9996	.9968	.9941	.9950
1962	.9999	.9966	.9929	.9954
1963	.9985	.9944	.9918	.9947
1964	.9939	.9778	.9797	.9931
1965	.9992	.9770	.9464	.8729

$APPR2_{ij}$ = model estimate, department i, account j.
$AAPRO_{ij}$ = observed appropriations, department i, account j.
m_1 = number of accounts, department i.
n = total number of departments.
$\overline{AAPRO}$ = average of all observed appropriations.

B. Detroit*

Bayesian-Induction Criteria

$$\frac{\sum_{i}^{n} \sum_{j}^{m_1} \dfrac{(APPR2_{ij} - AAPRO_{ij})^2}{AAPRO_{ij}}}{\sum_{i}^{n} m_i}$$

Year	One-period Change	Simulation	A1	A2
1958–59	8.45×10^8		1.856×10^5	2.206×10^5
1959–60	4.033×10^5		3.099×10^5	3.324×10^5
1960–61	2.319×10^4	2.319×10^4	1.470×10^5	1.204×10^5
1961–62	1.725×10^5	1.763×10^5	1.036×10^6	6.675×10^5
1962–63	4.371×10^5	6.267×10^5	2.458×10^5	1.872×10^5
1963–64	3.572×10^5	1.504×10^6	6.630×10^5	2.837×10^5
1964–65	4.040×10^4	2.303×10^6	1.262×10^5	3.482×10^5

$APPR2_{ij}$ = model estimate, department i, account j.
$AAPRO_{ij}$ = observed appropriations, department i, account j.
m_1 = number of accounts, department i.
n = total number of departments.
* including Welfare Department

χ^2-*Criteria*

$$\frac{\sum\limits_{i}^{n}\sum\limits_{j}^{m_i}\dfrac{(APPR2_{ij}-AAPRO_{ij})^2}{APPR2_{ij}}}{\sum\limits_{i}^{n}m_i}$$

Year	One-period Change	Simulation	A1	A2
1958–59	5.826×10^5		5.711×10^5	5.635×10^5
1959–60	6.988×10^4		5.536×10^5	9.868×10^5
1960–61	7.664×10^4	7.644×10^4	7.357×10^5	9.631×10^5
1961–62	1.172×10^6	1.614×10^6	3.136×10^5	4.459×10^5
1962–63	1.492×10^5	1.383×10^6	4.112×10^6	9.932×10^6
1963–64	7.400×10^4	1.595×10^6	2.749×10^6	3.854×10^6
1964–65	6.085×10^4	9.350×10^5	9.453×10^5	2.909×10^6

$APPR2_{ij}$ = model estimate, department i, account j.
$AAPRO_{ij}$ = observed appropriations, department i, account j.
m_i = number of accounts, department i.
n = total number of departments.

Goodness-of-Fit Measure: R_c^2

$$R_c^2 = 1.0 - \frac{\sum\limits_{i}^{n}\sum\limits_{j}^{m_i}(AAPRO_{ij}-APPR2_{ij})^2}{\sum\limits_{i}^{n}\sum\limits_{j}^{m_i}(AAPRO_{ij}-APPR1_{ij})^2}$$

Year	One-period Change	Simulation	A3
1958–59	.8755		1.0
1959–60	−.4764		−11.1
1960–61	.9631	.9631	−24.0
1961–62	−.2731	.0525	−4.6
1962–63	.7389	.3136	−2.94
1963–64	.6949	.045	−4.39
1964–65	.1035	−.0194	−31.36

$APPR2_{ij}$ = model estimate, department i, account j.
$AAPRO_{ij}$ = observed appropriations, department i, account j.
m_i = number of accounts, department i.
n = total number of departments.
$APPR1_{ij}$ = 'last-year's' appropriation.

Goodness-of-Fit Measure: R_0^2

$$R_0^2 = 1.0 - \frac{\sum_i^n \sum_j^{m_i} (AAPRO_{ij} - APPR2_{ij})^2}{\sum_i^n \sum_j^{m_i} (AAPRO_{ij} - \overline{AAPRO})^2}$$

Year	One-period Change	Simulation	A1	A2
1958–59	.8863		.9761	.9541
1959–60	.9621		.9429	.9257
1960–61	.9980	.9980	.9765	.9601
1961–62	.9439	.9560	.8851	.8698
1962–63	.9401	.9126	.8668	.8919
1963–64	.9880	.9200	.8467	.9057
1964–65	.9761	.9331	.8345	.8925

$APPR2_{ij}$ = model estimate, department i, account j.
$AAPRO_{ij}$ = observed appropriations, department i, account j.
m_i = number of accounts, department i.
n = total number of departments.
$\overline{AAPRO}$ = average of all observed appropriations.

Detroit*

Bayesian-Induction Criteria

$$\frac{\sum_i^n \sum_j^{m_i} \dfrac{(APPR2_{ij} - AAPRO_{ij})^2}{AAPRO_{ij}}}{\sum_i^n m_i}$$

Year	One-period Change	Simulation	A1	A2
1958–59	3.715×10^5		1.856×10^5	2.206×10^5
1959–60	3.981×10^5		3.099×10^5	3.324×10^5
1960–61	2.098×10^4	2.098×10^4	1.470×10^5	1.204×10^5
1961–62	3.648×10^5	1.171×10^5	1.036×10^6	6.675×10^5
1962–63	1.861×10^5	9.470×10^4	2.458×10^5	1.972×10^5
1963–64	4.395×10^5	5.956×10^5	6.630×10^5	2.837×10^5
1964–65	1.906×10^4	1.157×10^6	1.262×10^5	3.483×10^5

$APPR2_{ij}$ = model estimate, department i, account j.
$AAPRO_{ij}$ = observed appropriations, department i, account j.
m_i = number of accounts, department i.
n = total number of departments.
* not including Welfare Department

χ^2-*Criteria*

$$\frac{\displaystyle\sum_{i}^{n}\sum_{j}^{m_i} \frac{(APPR2_{ij} - AAPRO_{ij})^2}{APPR2_{ij}}}{\displaystyle\sum_{i}^{n} m_i}$$

Year	One-period Change	Simulation	A1	A2
1958–59	7.449×10^4		5.711×10^5	5.635×10^5
1959–60	6.199×10^4		5.536×10^5	9.866×10^5
1960–61	4.928×10^4	4.928×10^4	7.357×10^5	9.631×10^5
1961–62	1.634×10^6	1.416×10^6	3.136×10^5	4.459×10^5
1962–63	4.584×10^4	1.489×10^6	4.112×10^6	9.932×10^6
1963–64	6.886×10^4	1.778×10^6	2.749×10^6	3.845×10^6
1964–65	4.406×10^4	1.261×10^6	9.453×10^5	2.909×10^6

$APPR2_{ij}$ = model estimate, department i, account j.
$AAPRO_{ij}$ = observed appropriations, department i, account j.
m_i = number of accounts, department i.
n = total number of departments.

Goodness-of-Fit Measure: R_c^2

$$R_c^2 = 1.0 - \frac{\displaystyle\sum_{i}^{n}\sum_{j}^{m_i} (AAPRO_{ij} - APPR2_{ij})^2}{\displaystyle\sum_{i}^{n}\sum_{j}^{m_i} (AAPRO_{ij} - APPR1_{ij})^2}$$

Year	One-period Change*	Simulation	A3**
1958–59	.9120		1.0
1959–60	−.0787		−11.1
1960–61	.9649	.9649	−24.0
1961–62	−.0669	.0856	−4.6
1962–63	.7906	.0594	−2.94
1963–64	.4822	.2959	−4.39
1964–65	.3902	−.2785	−31.36

$APPR2_{ij}$ = model estimate, department i, account j.
$AAPRO_{ij}$ = observed appropriations, department i, account j.
m_i = number of accounts, department i.
n = total number of departments.
$APPR1_{ij}$ = 'last-year's' appropriation.

* not including Welfare Department
** including Welfare Department

Goodness-of-Fit Measure*: $R_o{}^2$

$$R_o{}^2 = 1.0 - \frac{\displaystyle\sum_i^n \sum_j^{m_i} (\text{AAPRO}_{ij} - \text{APPR2}_{ij})^2}{\displaystyle\sum_i^n \sum_j^{m_i} (\text{AAPRO}_{ij} - \overline{\text{AAPRO}})^2}$$

Year	One-period Change	Simulation	A1	A2
1958–59	.9128		.9761	.9541
1959–60	.9770		.9427	.9257
1960–61	.9979	.9979	.9765	.9601
1961–62	.9738	.9757	.8851	.8698
1962–63	.9963	.9898	.8668	.9818
1963–64	.9893	.9719	.8467	.9057
1964–65	.9970	.9574	.8345	.8925

APPR2_{ij} = model estimate, department i, account j.
AAPRO_{ij} = observed appropriations, department i, account j.
m_i = number of accounts, department i.
n = total number of departments.
$\overline{\text{AAPRO}}$ = average of all observed appropriations.
* not including Welfare Department

C. Pittsburgh

Bayesian-Induction Criteria

$$\frac{\displaystyle\sum_i^n \sum_j^{m_i} \dfrac{(\text{APPR2}_{ij} - \text{AAPRO}_{ij})^2}{\text{AAPRO}_{ij}}}{\displaystyle\sum_i^n m_i}$$

Year	One-period Change	Simulation	A1	A2
1960	4.095×10^3		9.430×10^4	1.671×10^8
1961	2.207×10^3		2.466×10^4	1.601×10^8
1962	2.254×10^3	2.254×10^3	1.134×10^4	1.366×10^8
1963	6.498×10^3	8.755×10^3	4.514×10^5	3.164×10^8
1964	2.177×10^3	4.939×10^3	1.274×10^5	1.130×10^8
1965	1.749×10^3	1.498×10^4	8.415×10^4	4.877×10^8

APPR2_{ij} = model estimate, department i, account j.
AAPRO_{ij} = observed appropriations, department i, account j.
m_i = number of accounts, department i.
n = total number of departments.
APPR1_{ij} = 'last-year's' appropriation.

$$\chi^2\text{-}Criteria$$

$$\dfrac{\displaystyle\sum_{i}^{n}\sum_{j}^{m_i}\dfrac{(APPR2_{ij} - AAPRO_{ij})^2}{APPR2_{ij}}}{\displaystyle\sum^{n} m_i}$$

Year	One-period Change	Simulation	A1	A2
1960	2.137×10^3		6.588×10^4	2.064×10^3
1961	2.373×10^3		6.578×10^5	1.985×10^3
1962	3.824×10^3	3.824×10^3	6.387×10^5	1.96×10^3
1963	8.000×10^3	7.520×10^3	7.885×10^4	5.459×10^3
1964	1.975×10^3	5.342×10^3	1.239×10^4	8.603×10^2
1965	8.951×10^2	8.24×10^3	4.152×10^3	1.970×10^3

$APPR2_{ij}$ = model estimate, department i, account j.
$AAPRO_{ij}$ = observed appropriations, department i, account j.
m_i = number of accounts, department i.
n = total number of departments.

Goodness-of-Fit Measure: R_c^2

$$R_c^2 = 1.0 - \dfrac{\displaystyle\sum_{i}^{n}\sum_{j}^{m_i}(AAPRO_{ij} - APPR2_{ij})^2}{\displaystyle\sum_{i}^{n}\sum_{j}^{m_i}(AAPRO_{ij} - APPR1_{ij})^2}$$

Year	One-period Change	Simulation	A3
1960	.0305		−.0872
1961	.7392		−.1961
1962	−.1079	−.1079	−57.17
1963	−.1210	−.0613	−93.7
1964	.8415	.5001	.8977
1965	.0178	.0117	−.4619

$APPR2_{ij}$ = model estimate, department i, account j.
$AAPRO_{ij}$ = observed appropriations, department i, account j.
m_i = number of accounts, department i.
n = total number of departments.
$APPR1_{ij}$ = 'last-year's' appropriation.

Goodness-of-Fit Measure: R_o^2

$$R_o^2 = 1.0 - \frac{\sum\limits_{i}^{n} \sum\limits_{j}^{m_1} (AAPRO_{ij} - APPR2_{ij})^2}{\sum\limits_{i}^{n} \sum\limits_{j}^{m_1} (AAPRO_{ij} - \overline{AAPRO})^2}$$

Year	One-period Change	Simulation	A1	A2
1960	.9989		.6269	.9994
1961	.9988		.7544	.9992
1962	.9948	.9948	.7321	.9974
1963	.9951	.9950	.6969	.9981
1964	.9996	.9979	.6231	.9997
1965	.9980	.9943	.7554	.9984

$APPR2_{ij}$ = model estimate, department i, account j.
$AAPRO_{ij}$ = observed appropriations, department i, account j.
m_1 = number of accounts, department i.
n = total number of departments.
$\overline{AAPRO}$ = average of all observed appropriations.

Appendix E

SAMPLE OF MODEL PROGRAMS—CITY OF DETROIT
ALL PROGRAMS WERE WRITTEN IN·"FORTRAN II'

A. MAIN CALLING PROGRAM FOR ONE-PERIOD CHANGE MODEL

```
CDETMAI
      DIMENSION DEPR2(60,5),APPR1(60,5),RMAY2(60,5),EXPND(60,5),
     1TEXPN(60),TAPR1(60),TDEP2(60),TSUPR(60),DSUPR(60,5),NCODE(60),
     2NACCT(60),A(60,5),B(60,5),C(60,5),D(60,5),E(60,5),F(60,5),
     3G(60,5),H(60,5),PP(60,5),Q(60,5),R(60,5),S(60,5),DREQ2(60,5),
     4DSREQ(60,5),TMAY2(60),ARMAY(60,5),ATMAY(60),TAPR2(60),APPR2(60,5),
     5AAPRO(60,5),STOR1(60,5),STOR2(60,5),DEVT(60),DEVTP(60),ANAME(999),
     6ACTNM(5),STR11(60,5),STR22(60,5),CHNGLY(60,5),NRCD(999),
     7NRCM(999),NRCC(999),NMOD(999),NNMOD(999,5)
      COMMON DEPR2,APPR1,RMAY2,EXPND,TEXPN,TAPR1,TDEP2,TSUPR,DSUPR,
     1NCODE,NACCT,A,B,C,D,E,F,G,H,PP,Q,R,S,DREQ2,DSREQ,ANAME,ACTNM,
     2STR11,STR22,CHNGLY,NRCD,NRCM,NRCC,COUNT,DEVR,DEVS,TBUD,REVEST,
     3TMAY2,ARMAY,ATMAY,TAPR2,APPR2,AAPRO,STOR1,STOR2,DEVT,DEVTP,
     4RESID,XK,P,XLMT,XL,N,NSTD,TOT,TOTT,BLANK,TOTAL,UNCALC,GG,TSAL1,YR,
     5FLAG,NMOD,NNMOD
  220 FORMAT(1X,/////////////)
      READ 222,BLANK,TOTAL,UNCALC
  222 FORMAT(1X,A5,A5,A6)
      NSTD = 3
      XK = 0.05
      P = 0.05
      XLMT = 150000.
      GG = 0.5
      XL = 1.05
      DO 554 I=1,60
      DO 554 J=1,5
      A(I,J) = 0.0
      B(I,J) = 0.0
      C(I,J) = 0.0
      D(I,J) = 0.0
      E(I,J) = 0.0
      G(I,J) = 0.0
      H(I,J) = 0.0
        PP(I,J) = 0.0
      Q(I,J) = 0.0
      R(I,J) = 0.0
      S(I,J) = 0.0
  554 CONTINUE
   60 FORMAT(2X,I3,I2,2X,7(1X,F9.3),/)
   61 FORMAT(2X,I3,I2,I2,7(1X,F9.3),/)
      K = 0
      KDX=0
      DO 400 KK=1,172
      READ 60,KD,KA,X1,X2,X3,X4,X5,X6,X7
      IF (KDX-KD) 401,402,401
  401 K=K+1
      KDX=KD
  402 NRCD(KD)=K
      KA = KA - 1
      A(K,KA) = X5
      B(K,KA) = X6
      C(K,KA) = X1
```

```
      WRITE OUTPUT TAPE 6,60,KD,KA,A(K,KA),B(K,KA),C(K,KA)
      WRITE OUTPUT TAPE 6,60,K ,KA,A(K,KA),B(K,KA),C(K,KA)
      WRITE OUTPUT TAPE 6,66,NRCD(KD)
  400 CONTINUE
      K=0
      KDX =0
      DO   70 KK=1,172
      READ 61,KD,KA,KX,X1,X2,X3,X4,X5,X6,X7
      IF (KDX-KD) 71,72,71
   71 K=K+1
      KDX = KD
   72 NRCM(KD) = K
      NMOD(KD) = K
      KA = KA - 1
      D(K,KA)=X1
      E(K,KA)=X3
      G(K,KA) = X2
      H(K,KA)=X6
      NNMOD(K,KA) = KX
      WRITE OUTPUT TAPE 6,61,KD,KA,NNMOD(K,KA),D(K,KA),E(K,KA),G(K,KA),
     1 H(K,KA)
      WRITE OUTPUT TAPE 6,61,KD,KA,KX        ,D(K,KA),E(K,KA),G(K,KA),
     1 H(K,KA)
      WRITE OUTPUT TAPE 6,66,NRCM(KD)
   70 CONTINUE
      K=0
      KDX=0
      DO 80 KK=1 ,171
      READ 60,KD,KA,X1,X2,X3,X4,X5,X6,X7
      IF (KDX-KD) 81,82,81
   81 K = K+1
      KDX=KD
   82 NRCC(KD) = K
      KA = KA - 1
      PP(K,KA) = X2
      Q(K,KA) = X3
      R(K,KA) = X6
      S(K,KA) = X7
      WRITE OUTPUT TAPE 6,60,KD,KA,PP(K,KA),Q(K,KA),R(K,KA),S(K,KA)
      WRITE OUTPUT TAPE 6,60,K ,KA,PP(K,KA),Q(K,KA),R(K,KA),S(K,KA)
      WRITE OUTPUT TAPE 6,66     , NRCC(KD)
   80 CONTINUE
   66 FORMAT(1X,I5)
   26 CONTINUE
      FLAG = 0.
      READ 50,REVEST
   50 FORMAT(F15.0)
      N=0
      I=0
   15 FORMAT(1X,I3,I2,7F8.0,A6,1X,A6,1X,A4)
      NXX=0
   19 READ 15,N1,N2,X1,X2,X3,X4,X5,X6,X7,ALPHA1,ALPHA2,YR
      IF (N1 - NXX) 20,21,20
   20 IF (N1 - 999) 22,23,23
   22 NXX = N1
      I = I + 1
      NCODE(I) = N1
```

```
      N = I
      J=0
 21   J = J+1
      NACCT(I) = J
      ANAME(N1) = ALPHA1
      ACTNM(J) = ALPHA2
      AAPRO(I,J)=X1
      ARMAY(I,J) = X2
      DSREQ(I,J)= X3
      DREQ2(I,J)= X4
      APPR1(I,J)=X5
      CHNGLY(I,J)=X6
      EXPND(I,J)=X7
      IF (EXPND(I,J)) 2,2,3
  2   EXPND(I,J) =-0.98*(CHNGLY(I,J) - APPR1(I,J))
  3   CONTINUE
      GO TO 19
 23   CONTINUE
      TBUD = 0.0
      DO 1 I=1,N
      CALL DEPRO(I)
  1   CONTINUE
      WRITE OUTPUT TAPE 6,220
      WRITE OUTPUT TAPE 6,90
      WRITE OUTPUT TAPE 6,300,YR
300   FORMAT(30H DETROIT GENERAL FUND BUDGET            , A4)
 90   FORMAT(1X,29HREGULAR DEPARTMENTAL REQUESTS,/)
      CALL RESULT (DEPR2,DREQ2)
      CALL ORDER(0)
      CALL ORDER(1)
      CALL ORDER(2)
      CALL ORDER(3)
      WRITE OUTPUT TAPE 6,220
      WRITE OUTPUT TAPE 6,100
      WRITE OUTPUT TAPE 6,300,YR
100   FORMAT (1X,21HSUPPLEMENTAL REQUESTS,/)
      CALL RESULT (DSUPR,DSREQ)
      CALL ORDER(1)
      WRITE OUTPUT TAPE 6,220
      WRITE OUTPUT TAPE 6,110
      WRITE OUTPUT TAPE 6,300,YR
110   FORMAT (1X,34HREGULAR PLUS SUPPLEMENTAL REQUESTS,/)
      DO 14 I=1,N
      NN = NACCT(I)
      DO 14 J=1,NN
      STR11(I,J) = DEPR2(I,J) + DSUPR(I,J)
 14   STR22(I,J) = DREQ2(I,J) + DSREQ(I,J)
      CALL RESULT(STR11,STR22)
      CALL ORDER(0)
      CALL ORDER(1)
      CALL ORDER(2)
      CALL ORDER(3)
      CALL MAYREC
      WRITE OUTPUT TAPE 6,220
      WRITE OUTPUT TAPE 6,120
      WRITE OUTPUT TAPE 6,300,YR
120   FORMAT(1X,23HMAYORS RECCOMMENDATIONS,/)
```

```
      CALL RESULT(RMAY2,ARMAY)
      CALL ORDER(0)
      CALL ORDER(1)
      CALL ORDER(2)
      CALL ORDER(3)
      CALL CAPRO
      WRITE OUTPUT TAPE 6,220
      WRITE OUTPUT TAPE 6,130
      WRITE OUTPUT TAPE 6,300,YR
  130 FORMAT(1X,28HFINAL COUNCIL APPROPRIATIONS,/)
      CALL RESULT(APPR2,AAPRO)
      CALL ORDER(0)
      CALL ORDER(1)
      CALL ORDER(2)
      CALL ORDER(3)
      GO TO 26
      END
              B. MAIN CALLING PROGRAM FOR SIMULATION RUNS

CDETMAI
      DIMENSION DEPR2(60,5),APPR1(60,5),RMAY2(60,5),EXPND(60,5),
     1TEXPN(60),TAPR1(60),TDEP2(60),TSUPR(60),DSUPR(60,5),NCODE(60),
     2NACCT(60),A(60,5),B(60,5),C(60,5),D(60,5),E(60,5),F(60,5),
     3G(60,5),H(60,5),PP(60,5),Q(60,5),R(60,5),S(60,5),DREQ2(60,5),
     4DSREQ(60,5),TMAY2(60),ARMAY(60,5),ATMAY(60),TAPR2(60),APPR2(60,5),
     5AAPRO(60,5),STOR1(60,5),STOR2(60,5),DEVT(60),DEVTP(60),ANAME(999),
     6ACTNM(5),STR11(60,5),STR22(60,5),CHNGLY(60,5),NRCD(999),
     7NRCM(999),NRCC(999),NMOD(999),NNMOD(999,5)
      COMMON DEPR2,APPR1,RMAY2,EXPND,TEXPN,TAPR1,TDEP2,TSUPR,DSUPR,
     1NCODE,NACCT,A,B,C,D,E,F,G,H,PP,Q,R,S,DREQ2,DSREQ,ANAME,ACTNM,
     2STR11,STR22,CHNGLY,NRCD,NRCM,NRCC,COUNT,DEVR,DEVS,TBUD,REVEST,
     3TMAY2,ARMAY,ATMAY,TAPR2,APPR2,AAPRO,STOR1,STOR2,DEVT,DEVTP,
     4RESID,XK,P,XLMT,XL,N,NSTD,TOT,TOTT,BLANK,TOTAL,UNCALC,GG,TSAL1,YR,
     5FLAG,NMOD,NNMOD
  220 FORMAT(1X,////////////)
      READ 222,BLANK,TOTAL,UNCALC
  222 FORMAT(1X,A5,A5,A6)
      NTIMES = 0
      NSTD = 3
      XK = 0.05
      P = 0.05
      XLMT = 150000.
      GG = 0.5
      XL = 1.05
      DO 554 I=1,60
      DO 554 J=1,5
      A(I,J) = 0.0
      B(I,J) = 0.0
      C(I,J) = 0.0
      D(I,J) = 0.0
      E(I,J) = 0.0
      G(I,J) = 0.0
      H(I,J) = 0.0
      PP(I,J) = 0.0
      Q(I,J) = 0.0
      R(I,J) = 0.0
```

```
      S(I,J) = 0.0
 554  CONTINUE
  60  FORMAT(2X,I3,I2,2X,7(1X,F9.3),/)
  61  FORMAT(2X,I3,I2,I2,7(1X,F9.3),/)
      K = 0
      KDX=0
      DO 400 KK=1,172
      READ 60,KD,KA,X1,X2,X3,X4,X5,X6,X7
      IF (KDX-KD) 401,402,401
 401  K=K+1
      KDX=KD
 402  NRCD(KD)=K
      KA = KA - 1
      A(K,KA) = X5
      B(K,KA) = X6
      C(K,KA) = X1
      WRITE OUTPUT TAPE 6,60,KD,KA,A(K,KA),B(K,KA),C(K,KA)
      WRITE OUTPUT TAPE 6,60,K ,KA,A(K,KA),B(K,KA),C(K,KA)
      WRITE OUTPUT TAPE 6,66,NRCD(KD)
 400  CONTINUE
      K=0
      KDX =0
      DO  70 KK=1,172
      READ 61,KD,KA,KX,X1,X2,X3,X4,X5,X6,X7
      IF (KDX-KD) 71,72,71
  71  K=K+1
      KDX = KD
  72  NRCM(KD) = K
      NMOD(KD) = K
      KA = KA - 1
      D(K,KA)=X1
      E(K,KA)=X3
      G(K,KA) = X2
      H(K,KA)=X6
      NNMOD(K,KA) = KX
      WRITE OUTPUT TAPE 6,61,KD,KA,NNMOD(K,KA),D(K,KA),E(K,KA),G(K,KA),
     1 H(K,KA)
      WRITE OUTPUT TAPE 6,61,KD,KA,KX          ,D(K,KA),E(K,KA),G(K,KA),
     1 H(K,KA)
      WRITE OUTPUT TAPE 6,66,NRCM(KD)
  70  CONTINUE
      K=0
      KDX=0
      DO 80 KK=1 ,171
      READ 60,KD,KA,X1,X2,X3,X4,X5,X6,X7
      IF (KDX-KD) 81,82,81
  81  K = K+1
      KDX=KD
  82  NRCC(KD) = K
      KA = KA - 1
      PP(K,KA) = X2
      Q(K,KA) = X3
      R(K,KA) = X6
      S(K,KA) = X7
      WRITE OUTPUT TAPE 6,60,KD,KA,PP(K,KA),Q(K,KA),R(K,KA),S(K,KA)
      WRITE OUTPUT TAPE 6,60,K ,KA,PP(K,KA),Q(K,KA),R(K,KA),S(K,KA)
      WRITE OUTPUT TAPE 6,66   , NRCC(KD)
```

```
 80 CONTINUE
 66 FORMAT(1X,I5)
 26 CONTINUE
    FLAG = 0.
    READ 50,REVEST
 50 FORMAT(F15.0)
    N=0
    I=0
 15 FORMAT(1X,I3,I2,7F8.0,A6,1X,A6,1X,A4)
    NXX=0
 19 READ 15,N1,N2,X1,X2,X3,X4,X5,X6,X7,ALPHA1,ALPHA2,YR
 20 IF (N1 - 999) 22,23,23
    IF (N1 - NXX) 20,21,20
 22 NXX = N1
    I = I + 1
    NCODE(I) = N1
    N = I
    J=0
 21 J = J+1
    NACCT(I) = J
    ANAME(N1) = ALPHA1
    ACTNM(J) = ALPHA2
    AAPRO(I,J)=X1
    ARMAY(I,J) = X2
    DSREQ(I,J)= X3
    DREQ2(I,J)= X4
    IF (NTIMES) 522,522,566
522 APPR1(I,J) = X5
    CHNGLY(I,J)=X6
    EXPND(I,J)=X7
    IF (EXPND(I,J)) 2,2,3
  2 EXPND(I,J) =-0.98*(CHNGLY(I,J) - APPR1(I,J))
  3 CONTINUE
566 CONTINUE
    GO TO 19
 23 CONTINUE
    TBUD = 0.0
    DO 1 I=1,N
    CALL DEPRO(I)
  1 CONTINUE
    WRITE OUTPUT TAPE 6,220
    WRITE OUTPUT TAPE 6,90
    WRITE OUTPUT TAPE 6,300,YR
300 FORMAT(30H DETROIT GENERAL FUND BUDGET        , A4)
 90 FORMAT(1X,29HREGULAR DEPARTMENTAL REQUESTS,/)
    CALL RESULT (DEPR2,DREQ2)
    CALL ORDER(0)
    CALL ORDER(1)
    CALL ORDER(2)
    CALL ORDER(3)
    WRITE OUTPUT TAPE 6,220
    WRITE OUTPUT TAPE 6,100
    WRITE OUTPUT TAPE 6,300,YR
100 FORMAT (1X,21HSUPPLEMENTAL REQUESTS,/)
    CALL RESULT (DSUPR,DSREQ)
    CALL ORDER(1)
    WRITE OUTPUT TAPE 6,220
```

```
      WRITE OUTPUT TAPE 6,110
      WRITE OUTPUT TAPE 6,300,YR
  110 FORMAT (1X,34HREGULAR PLUS SUPPLEMENTAL REQUESTS,/)
      DO 14 I=1,N
      NN = NACCT(I)
      DO 14 J=1,NN
      STR11(I,J) = DEPR2(I,J) + DSUPR(I,J)
   14 STR22(I,J) = DREO2(I,J) + DSREQ(I,J)
      CALL RESULT(STR11,STR22)
      CALL ORDER(0)
      CALL ORDER(1)
      CALL ORDER(2)
      CALL ORDER(3)
      CALL MAYREC
      WRITE OUTPUT TAPE 6,220
      WRITE OUTPUT TAPE 6,120
      WRITE OUTPUT TAPE 6,300,YR
  120 FORMAT(1X,23HMAYORS RECCOMMENDATIONS,/)
      CALL RESULT(RMAY2,ARMAY)
      CALL ORDER(0)
      CALL ORDER(1)
      CALL ORDER(2)
      CALL ORDER(3)
      CALL CAPRO
      WRITE OUTPUT TAPE 6,220
      WRITE OUTPUT TAPE 6,130
      WRITE OUTPUT TAPE 6,300,YR
  130 FORMAT(1X,28HFINAL COUNCIL APPROPRIATIONS,/)
      CALL RESULT(APPR2,AAPRO)
      CALL ORDER(0)
      CALL ORDER(1)
      CALL ORDER(2)
      CALL ORDER(3)
      DO 131 I=1,N
      NN = NACCT(I)
      DO 131 J=1,NN
      CHNGLY(I,J) = APPR2(I,J) - APPR1(I,J)
      EXPND(I,J) = .98*APPR1(I,J)
  131 APPR1(I,J) = APPR2(I,J)
      NTIMES = NTIMES + 1
      GO TO 26
      END
```

                C. MAIN CALLING PROGRAM FOR 10-YEAR FORECASTS

```
CDETMAI
      DIMENSION DEPR2(60,5),APPR1(60,5),RMAY2(60,5),EXPND(60,5),
     1TEXPN(60),TAPR1(60),TDEP2(60),TSUPR(60),DSUPR(60,5),NCODE(60),.
     2NACCT(60),A(60,5),B(60,5),C(60,5),D(60,5),E(60,5),F(60,5),
     3G(60,5),H(60,5),PP(60,5),Q(60,5),R(60,5),S(60,5),DREQ2(60,5),
     4DSREQ(60,5),TMAY2(60),ARMAY(60,5),ATMAY(60),TAPR2(60),APPR2(60,5),
     5AAPRO(60,5),STOR1(60,5),STOR2(60,5),DEVT(60),DEVTP(60),ANAME(999),
     6ACTNM(5),STR11(60,5),STR22(60,5),CHNGLY(60,5),NRCD(999),
     7NRCM(999),NRCC(999),NMOD(999),NNMOD(999,5)
      COMMON DEPR2,APPR1,RMAY2,EXPND,TEXPN,TAPR1,TDEP2,TSUPR,DSUPR,
     1NCODE,NACCT,A,B,C,D,E,F,G,H,PP,Q,R,S,DREQ2,DSREQ,ANAME,ACTNM,
     2STR11,STR22,CHNGLY,NRCD,NRCM,NRCC,COUNT,DEVR,DEVS,TBUD,REVEST,
```

```
      3TMAY2,ARMAY,ATMAY,TAPR2,APPR2,AAPRO,STOR1,STOR2,DEVT,DEVTP,
      4RESID,XK,P,XLMT,XL,N,NSTD,TOT,TOTT,BLANK,TOTAL,UNCALC,GG,TSAL1,YR,
      5FLAG,NMOD,NNMOD
  220 FORMAT(1X,////////////)
      READ 222,BLANK,TOTAL,UNCALC
  222 FORMAT(1X,A5,A5,A6)
      NSTD = 3
      DO 554 I=1,60
      DO 554 J=1,5
      A(I,J) = 0.0
      B(I,J) = 0.0
      C(I,J) = 0.0
      D(I,J) = 0.0
      E(I,J) = 0.0
      G(I,J) = 0.0
      H(I,J) = 0.0
        PP(I,J) = 0.0
      O(I,J) = 0.0
      R(I,J) = 0.0
      S(I,J) = 0.0
  554 CONTINUE
   60 FORMAT(2X,I3,I2,2X,7(1X,F9.3),/)
   61 FORMAT(2X,I3,I2,I2,7(1X,F9.3),/)
      K = 0
      KDX=0
      DO 400 KK=1,172
      READ 60,KD,KA,X1,X2,X3,X4,X5,X6,X7
      IF (KDX-KD) 401,402,401
  401 K=K+1
      KDX=KD
  402 NRCD(KD)=K
      KA = KA - 1
      A(K,KA) = X5
      B(K,KA) = X6
      C(K,KA) = X1
      WRITE OUTPUT TAPE 6,60,KD,KA,A(K,KA),B(K,KA),C(K,KA)
      WRITE OUTPUT TAPE 6,60,K ,KA,A(K,KA),B(K,KA),C(K,KA)
      WRITE OUTPUT TAPE 6,66,NRCD(KD)
  400 CONTINUE
      K=0
      KDX =0
      DO  70 KK=1,172
      READ 61,KD,KA,KX,X1,X2,X3,X4,X5,X6,X7
      IF (KDX-KD) 71,72,71
   71 K=K+1
      KDX = KD
   72 NRCM(KD) = K
      NMOD(KD) = K
      KA = KA - 1
      D(K,KA)=X1
      E(K,KA)=X3
      G(K,KA) = X2
      H(K,KA)=X6
      NNMOD(K,KA) = KX
      WRITE OUTPUT TAPE 6,61,KD,KA,NNMOD(K,KA),D(K,KA),E(K,KA),G(K,KA),
     1 H(K,KA)
      WRITE OUTPUT TAPE 6,61,KD,KA,KX          ,D(K,KA),E(K,KA),G(K,KA),
```

```
   1 H(K,KA)
     WRITE OUTPUT TAPE 6,66,NRCM(KD)
  70 CONTINUE
     K=0
     KDX=0
     DO 80 KK=1 ,171
     READ 60,KD,KA,X1,X2,X3,X4,X5,X6,X7
     IF (KDX-KD) 81,82,81
  81 K = K+1
     KDX=KD
  82 NRCC(KD) = K
     KA = KA - 1
     PP(K,KA) = X2
      Q(K,KA) = X3
      R(K,KA) = X6
      S(K,KA) = X7
     WRITE OUTPUT TAPE 6,60,KD,KA,PP(K,KA),Q(K,KA),R(K,KA),S(K,KA)
     WRITE OUTPUT TAPE 6,60,K ,KA,PP(K,KA),Q(K,KA),R(K,KA),S(K,KA)
     WRITE OUTPUT TAPE 6,66    , NRCC(KD)
  80 CONTINUE
  66 FORMAT(1X,I5)
     READ 777,XK,P,XLMT,GG,   XL
 777 FORMAT (5F10.0)
     READ 196,YRINC
 196 FORMAT(F8.0)
  26 CONTINUE
     FLAG = 0.
     READ 50,REVEST
  50 FORMAT(F15.0)
     RVEST = REVEST
     SIGMA = 10000000.
     RNO = .5
     N=0
     I=0
  15 FORMAT(1X,I3,I2,7F8.0,A6,1X,A6,1X,A4)
     NXX=0
  19 READ 15,N1,N2,X1,X2,X3,X4,X5,X6,X7,ALPHA1,ALPHA2,YR
     IF (N1 - NXX) 20,21,20
  20 IF (N1 - 999) 22,23,23
  22 NXX = N1
     I = I + 1
     NCODE(I) = N1
     N = I
     J=0
  21 J = J+1
     NACCT(I) = J
     ANAME(N1) = ALPHA1
     ACTNM(J) = ALPHA2
     AAPRO(I,J)=X1
     ARMAY(I,J) = X2
     DSREQ(I,J)= X3
     DREQ2(I,J)= X4
     APPR1(I,J)=X5
     CHNGLY(I,J)=X6
     EXPND(I,J)=X7
     IF (EXPND(I,J)) 2,2,3
   2 EXPND(I,J) =-0.98*(CHNGLY(I,J) - APPR1(I,J))
```

```
      3 CONTINUE
        GO TO 19
     23 CONTINUE
        YR = 1965.
    523 CONTINUE
        TRUD = 0.0
        DO 1 I=1,N
        CALL DEPRQ(I)
      1 CONTINUE
        WRITE OUTPUT TAPE 6,220
        WRITE OUTPUT TAPE 6,90
        WRITE OUTPUT TAPE 6,300,YR
    300 FORMAT(35H DETROIT GENERAL FUND BUDGET          , F6.0)
     90 FORMAT(1X,29HREGULAR DEPARTMENTAL REQUESTS,/)
        WRITE OUTPUT TAPE 6,220
        WRITE OUTPUT TAPE 6,100
        WRITE OUTPUT TAPE 6,300,YR
    100 FORMAT (1X,21HSUPPLEMENTAL REQUESTS,/)
        WRITE OUTPUT TAPE 6,220
        WRITE OUTPUT TAPE 6,110
        WRITE OUTPUT TAPE 6,300,YR
        WRITE OUTPUT TAPE 6,195,YRINC
    110 FORMAT (1X,34HREGULAR PLUS SUPPLEMENTAL REQUESTS,/)
        DO 14 I=1,N
        NN = NACCT(I)
        DO 14 J=1,NN
        STR11(I,J) = DEPR2(I,J) + DSUPR(I,J)
     14 STR22(I,J) = DREQ2(I,J) + DSREQ(I,J)
        CALL SUMR(STR11)
    195 FORMAT(23H REVENUES INCREASED BY ,F7.3,22H  OVER PREVIOUS YEAR   )
        CALL MAYREC
        WRITE OUTPUT TAPE 6,220
        WRITE OUTPUT TAPE 6,120
        WRITE OUTPUT TAPE 6,300,YR
        WRITE OUTPUT TAPE 6,195,YRINC
    120 FORMAT(1X,23HMAYORS RECCOMMENDATIONS,/)
        CALL SUMR(RMAY2)
        CALL CAPRO
        WRITE OUTPUT TAPE 6,220
        WRITE OUTPUT TAPE 6,130
        WRITE OUTPUT TAPE 6,300,YR
        WRITE OUTPUT TAPE 6,195,YRINC
    130 FORMAT(1X,28HFINAL COUNCIL APPROPRIATIONS,/)
        CALL SUMR(APPR2)
        DO 666 I=1,N
        NN=NACCT(I)
        DO 666 J=1,NN
        CHNGLY(I,J)= APPR2(I,J) - APPR1(I,J)
        APPR1(I,J) = APPR2(I,J)
        EXPND(I,J)= 0.98*APPRI(I,J)
    666 CONTINUE
        YR = YR +1.0
        FLAG = 0.
        RVEST = (1.0 + YRINC)*RVEST
        REVEST = (1.0 + YRINC)*RVEST
        REVEST = RANDND(RVEST,SIGMA,RNO)
        IF (YR - 1975.)    523,523,27
```

297

```
   27 CONTINUE
      END
```

D. SUBROUTINE FOR DEPT. SUBMODEL

```
CDEPRO
      SUBROUTINE DEPRO(I)
      DIMENSION DEPR2(60,5),APPR1(60,5),RMAY2(60,5),EXPND(60,5),
     1TEXPN(60),TAPR1(60),TDEP2(60),TSUPR(60),DSUPR(60,5),NCODE(60),
     2NACCT(60),A(60,5),B(60,5),C(60,5),D(60,5),E(60,5),F(60,5),
     3G(60,5),H(60,5),PP(60,5),Q(60,5),R(60,5),S(60,5),DREQ2(60,5),
     4DSREQ(60,5),TMAY2(60),ARMAY(60,5),ATMAY(60),TAPR2(60),APPR2(60,5),
     5AAPRO(60,5),STOR1(60,5),STOR2(60,5),DEVT(60),DEVTP(60),ANAME(999),
     6ACTNM(5),STR11(60,5),STR22(60,5),CHNGLY(60,5),NRCD(999),
     7NRCM(999),NRCC(999),NMOD(999),NNMOD(999,5)
      COMMON DEPR2,APPR1,RMAY2,EXPND,TEXPN,TAPR1,TDEP2,TSUPR,DSUPR,
     1NCODE,NACCT,A,B,C,D,E,F,G,H,PP,Q,R,S,DREQ2,DSREQ,ANAME,ACTNM,
     2STR11,STR22,CHNGLY,NRCD,NRCM,NRCC,COUNT,DEVR,DEVS,TBUD,REVEST,
     3TMAY2,ARMAY,ATMAY,TAPR2,APPR2,AAPRO,STOR1,STOR2,DEVT,DEVTP,
     4RESID,XK,P,XLMT,XL,N,NSTD,TOT,TOTT,BLANK,TOTAL,UNCALC,GG,TSAL1,YR,
     5FLAG,NMOD,NNMOD
      CALL FTRAP
      TDEP2(I)=0
      NN = NACCT(I)
      KD = NCODE(I)
      K = NRCD(KD)
      DO 1 J=1,NN
      DEPR2(I,J) = A(K,J)*APPR1(I,J) + B(K,J)*CHNGLY(I,J)
    1   + C(K,J)*(EXPND(I,J)+CHNGLY(I,J)-APPR1(I,J))
      IF (DEPR2(I,J)) 11,1,1
   11 DEPR2(I,J) = 0.0
    1 TDEP2(I) = TDEP2(I) + DEPR2(I,J)
      IF (TDEP2(I) - TAPR1(I)) 5,2,2
    2 DO 8 J=1,NN
      IF (DEPR2(I,J) - APPR1(I,J) )        4,4,3
    3 DSUPR(I,J) = DEPR2(I,J) - APPR1(I,J)
      DEPR2(I,J) = APPR1(I,J)
      GO TO 8
    4 DSUPR(I,J) = 0.0
    8 CONTINUE
      GO TO 17
    5 IF (DEPR2(I,1) - APPR1(I,1)) 7,7,6
    6 DSUPR(I,1) = DEPR2(I,1) - APPR1(I,1)
      DEPR2(I,1) = APPR1(I,1)
      DO 16 J=2,NN
   16 DSUPR(I,J) = 0.0
      GO TO 17
    7 DO 15 J=1,NN
   15 DSUPR(I,J) = 0.0
   17 CONTINUE
      NN = NACCT(I)
      DO 21 J=1,NN
      IF (DEPR2(I,J) - 1.0) 20,20,21
   20 DEPR2(I,J) = 0.0
   21 CONTINUE
      RETURN
      END
```

E. SUBROUTINE FOR MAYORS SUBMODEL

```
C.MAYREC
      SUBROUTINE MAYREC
      DIMENSION DEPR2(60,5),APPR1(60,5),RMAY2(60,5),EXPND(60,5),
     1TEXPN(60),TAPR1(60),TDEP2(60),TSUPR(60),DSUPR(60,5),NCODE(60),
     2NACCT(60),A(60,5),B(60,5),C(60,5),D(60,5),E(60,5),F(60,5),
     3G(60,5),H(60,5),PP(60,5),Q(60,5),R(60,5),S(60,5),DREQ2(60,5),
     4DSREQ(60,5),TMAY2(60),ARMAY(60,5),ATMAY(60),TAPR2(60),APPR2(60,5),
     5AAPRO(60,5),STOR1(60,5),STOR2(60,5),DEVT(60),DEVTP(60),ANAME(999),
     6ACTNM(5),STR11(60,5),STR22(60,5),CHNGLY(60,5),NRCD(999),
     7NRCM(999),NRCC(999),NMOD(999),NNMOD(999,5)
      COMMON DEPR2,APPR1,RMAY2,EXPND,TEXPN,TAPR1,TDEP2,TSUPR,DSUPR,
     1NCODE,NACCT,A,B,C,D,E,F,G,H,PP,Q,R,S,DREQ2,DSREQ,ANAME,ACTNM,
     2STR11,STR22,CHNGLY,NRCD,NRCM,NRCC,COUNT,DEVR,DEVS,TBUD,REVEST,
     3TMAY2,ARMAY,ATMAY,TAPR2,APPR2,AAPRO,STOR1,STOR2,DEVT,DEVTP,
     4RESID,XK,P,XLMT,XL,N,NSTD,TOT,TOTT,BLANK,TOTAL,UNCALC,GG,TSAL1,YR,
     5FLAG,NMOD,NNMOD
      CALL FTRAP
      LOOP = 1
      M=1
      DO 3 I=1,N
      KD = NCODE(I)
      K=NRCM(KD)
      K1 = NMOD(KD)
      NN = NACCT(I)
      DO 3 J=1,NN
      IF (DEPR2(I,J) - APPR1(I,J)) 1,1,2
    1 RMAY2(I,J) = DEPR2(I,J)
      GO TO 3
    2 RMAY2(I,J) =D(K,J)*(EXPND(I,J)+CHNGLY(I,J)-APPR1(I,J))+E(K,J)*
     1 DSUPR(I,J)   + H(K,J)*CHNGLY(I,J) +G(K,J)*(DEPR2(I,J)-APPR1(I,J))
      IF (NNMOD(K1,J) - 23) 131,130,131
  130 RMAY2(I,J) = RMAY2(I,J) + DEPR2(I,J)
      GO TO 134
  131 IF (NNMOD(K1,J) - 24) 133,132,133
  132 RMAY2(I,J) = RMAY2(I,J) + APPR1(I,J)
      GO TO 134
  133 WRITE OUTPUT TAPE 6,135,KD,J
  135 FORMAT(11H DEPT. NO.  ,I4,11H ACCT. NO.  ,I2,18H  HAS NO MODEL NO
     1.  )
  134 CONTINUE
      IF (RMAY2(I,J)) 111,3,3
  111 RMAY2(I,J) = 0.
    3 CONTINUE
    4 TBUD = 0.0
      DO 5 I=1,N
      NN = NACCT(I)
      DO 5 J=1,NN
    5 TBUD = TBUD + RMAY2(I,J)
      IF (TBUD - REVEST) 6,6,15
    6 RESID = REVEST - TBUD
      TSAL1 = 0.0
      TSAL2 = 0.0
      DO 7 I=1,N
    7 TSAL1 = TSAL1 + RMAY2(I,1)
```

```
      IF (RESID - XK*TSAL1) 10,8,8
   8 DO 88 I=1,N
  88 RMAY2(I,1) = (1.0 + XK)*RMAY2(I,1)
      RESID = RESID - XK*TSAL1
      TSAL1 = (1.0 + XK)*TSAL1
      TBUD = 0.0
  10 M = M + 1
  21 IF (RESID - XLMT) 50,50,11
  11 TBUD = 0.0
      ADDED = 0.0
      DO 13 I=1,N
      IF (M-NACCT(I)) 12,12,121
  12 RMAY2(I,M)=RMAY2(I,M)+ GG*DSUPR(I,M)
      ADDED = ADDED + GG*DSUPR(I,M)
      IF (ADDED - RESID) 121,122,122
 122 RMAY2(I,M) = RMAY2(I,M) - GG*DSUPR(I,M)
      M = 5
 121 NN = NACCT(I)
      DO 13 J=1,NN
      TBUD = TBUD + RMAY2(I,J)
  13 CONTINUE
      RESID = REVEST - TBUD
      IF (M - 5) 10,50,50
  15 CONTINUE
      J = NSTD
 150 DO 17 I=1,N
      IF (RMAY2(I,J) - XL*APPR1(I,J)) 17,17,16
  16 RESID = RESID + RMAY2(I,J) - XL*APPR1(I,J)
      RMAY2(I,J) = XL*APPR1(I,J)
  17 CONTINUE
      J = J - 1
      IF (J) 170,170,151
 151 IF (RESID) 117,170,170
 117 GO TO 150
 170 ZCNT = 0.0
      M = NSTD
  18 TBUD = 0.0
      DO 19 I=1,N
      NN = NACCT(I)
      DO 19 J=1,NN
  19 TBUD = TBUD + RMAY2(I,J)
      RESID = REVEST - TBUD
      IF(RESID) 22,22,20
  20 GO TO 21
  22 IF (ZCNT - 0.0)  26,26,23
  23 ZCNT = 1.0
      DO 24 I=1,N
      NN = NACCT(I)
      DO 24 J=NSTD,NN
      IF (RMAY2(I,J) - APPR1(I,J)) 24,24,25
  25 RMAY2(I,J) = APPR1(I,J)
  24 CONTINUE
      GO TO 18
  26 M = M - 1
      DO 29 I=1,N
      IF (RMAY2(I,M) - APPR1(I,M)) 29,29,28
  28 RESID = RESID  + (RMAY2(I,M) - APPR1(I,M))
```

```
      RMAY2(I,M) = APPR1(I,M)
      IF (RESID) 29,18,18
   29 CONTINUE
      IF (M- 1) 31,31,30
   30 GO TO 18
   31 TBUD = 0.0
      DO 32 I=1,N
      NN = NACCT(I)
      DO 32 J=1,NN
   32 TBUD = TBUD + RMAY2(I,J)
      IF (TBUD - REVEST)  21,33,33
   33 SUM = 0.0
      LOOP = -1
      SUMW = 0.0
      SCALE = 0.0
      DO 35  I=1,N
      NN = NACCT(I)
      SUMW = SUMW + RMAY2(I,1)
      DO 35 J=2,NN
   35 SUM = SUM + RMAY2(I,J)
      SCALE = (REVEST - SUMW)/SUM
      DO 36 I=1,N
      NN = NACCT(I)
      DO 36 J=2,NN
   36 RMAY2(I,J) = SCALE*RMAY2(I,J)
   50 CONTINUE
      TBUD = 0.0
      DO 51 I=1,N
      NN = NACCT(I)
      DO 51 J=1,NN
      IF (RMAY2(I,J) - 1.0) 52,53,53
   52 RMAY2(I,J) = 0.0
   53 IF (RMAY2(I,J) - DEPR2(I,J) - DSUPR(I,J)) 51,51,54
   54 RMAY2(I,J) = DEPR2(I,J) + DSUPR(I,J)
   51 TBUD = TBUD + RMAY2(I,J)
      RESID = REVEST - TBUD
      IF (RESID) 33,501,501
  501 IF (LOOP) 502,502,33
  502 CONTINUE
      RETURN
      END
```

F. SUBROUTINE FOR COUNCIL SUBMODEL

```
CCAPROP
      SUBROUTINE CAPRO
      DIMENSION DEPR2(60,5),APPR1(60,5),RMAY2(60,5),EXPND(60,5),
     1TEXPN(60),TAPR1(60),TDEP2(60),TSUPR(60),DSUPR(60,5),NCODE(60),
     2NACCT(60),A(60,5),B(60,5),C(60,5),D(60,5),E(60,5),F(60,5),
     3G(60,5),H(60,5),PP(60,5),Q(60,5),R(60,5),S(60,5),DREQ2(60,5),
     4DSREQ(60,5),TMAY2(60),ARMAY(60),ATMAY(60),TAPR2(60),APPR2(60,5),
     5AAPRO(60,5),STOR1(60,5),STOR2(60,5),DEVT(60),DEVTP(60),ANAME(999),
     6ACTNM(5),STR11(60,5),STR22(60,5),CHNGLY(60,5),NRCD(999),
     7NRCM(999),NRCC(999),NMOD(999),NNMOD(999,5)
      COMMON DEPR2,APPR1,RMAY2,EXPND,TEXPN,TAPR1,TDEP2,TSUPR,DSUPR,
     1NCODE,NACCT,A,B,C,D,E,F,G,H,PP,Q,R,S,DREQ2,DSREQ,ANAME,ACTNM,
     2STR11,STR22,CHNGLY,NRCD,NRCM,NRCC,COUNT,DEVR,DEVS,TBUD,REVEST,
```

```
    3TMAY2,ARMAY,ATMAY,TAPR2,APPR2,AAPRO,STOR1,STOR2,DEVT,DEVTP,
    4RESID,XK,P,XLMT,XL,N,NSTD,TOT,TOTT,BLANK,TOTAL,UNCALC,GG,TSAL1,YR,
    5FLAG,NMOD,NNMOD
      CALL FTRAP
      FLAG=1.0
      RESID =   REVEST - TBUD
      TBUD = 0.0
      TAPRO = 0.0
      DO 9 I=1,N
      TAPR2(I) = 0.0
      NN = NACCT(I)
      KD=NCODE(I)
      K=NRCC(KD)
      DO 8 J=1,NN
      APPR2(I,J) = RMAY2(I,J)
      IF (DEPR2(I,J) + DSUPR(I,J) - RMAY2(I,J)) 2,2,3
    2 GO TO 6
    3 IF (RESID - XLMT) 5,4,4
    4 STOR = APPR2(I,J)
      APPR2(I,J) = PP(K,J)*RMAY2(I,J) + Q(K,J)*(DEPR2(I,J)+DSUPR(I,J)
    1 - RMAY2(I,J)) + R(K,J)*CHNGLY(I,J) + S(K,J)*(EXPND(I,J)+CHNGLY(I,
    2J) - APPR1(I,J))
      IF (STOR - APPR2(I,J)) 13,13,14
   14 APPR2(I,J) = STOR
   13 RESID = RESID - (APPR2(I,J) -STOR)
      GO TO 38
    5 CONTINUE
    6 IF (RESID) 7,38,38
    7 IF (APPR2(I,J) - APPR1(I,J)) 38,38,17
   17 STOR = APPR2(I,J)
      APPR2(I,J) = APPR1(I,J)
      RESID = RESID + STOR - APPR2(I,J)
   38 IF (APPR2(I,J) - 1.0) 28,18,18
   28 STOR = APPR2(I,J)
      APPR2(I,J) = 0.0
      RESID = RESID + STOR
   18 CONTINUE
    8 CONTINUE
    9 CONTINUE
      RETURN
      END
```

G. SUBROUTINE TO PRINT AND PUNCH RESULTS

```
CRESULT
      SUBROUTINE RESULT (EMATR,AMATR)
      DIMENSION DEPR2(60,5),APPR1(60,5),RMAY2(60,5),EXPND(60,5),
    1TEXPN(60),TAPR1(60),TDEP2(60),TSUPR(60),DSUPR(60,5),NCODE(60),
    2NACCT(60),A(60,5),B(60,5),C(60,5),D(60,5),E(60,5),F(60,5),
    3G(60,5),H(60,5),PP(60,5),Q(60,5),R(60,5),S(60,5),DREQ2(60,5),
    4DSREQ(60,5),TMAY2(60),ARMAY(60,5),ATMAY(60),TAPR2(60),APPR2(60,5),
    5AAPRO(60,5),STOR1(60,5),STOR2(60,5),DEVT(60),DEVTP(60),ANAME(999),
    6ACTNM(5),STR11(60,5),STR22(60,5),CHNGLY(60,5),NRCD(999),
    7NRCM(999),NRCC(999),NMOD(999),NNMOD(999,5)
      COMMON DEPR2,APPR1,RMAY2,EXPND,TEXPN,TAPR1,TDEP2,TSUPR,DSUPR,
    1NCODE,NACCT,A,B,C,D,E,F,G,H,PP,Q,R,S,DREQ2,DSREQ,ANAME,ACTNM,
    2STR11,STR22,CHNGLY,NRCD,NRCM,NRCC,COUNT,DEVR,DEVS,TBUD,REVEST,
```

```
      3TMAY2,ARMAY,ATMAY,TAPR2,APPR2,AAPRO,STOR1,STOR2,DEVT,DEVTP,
      4RESID,XK,P,XLMT,XL,N,NSTD,TOT,TOTT,BLANK,TOTAL,UNCALC,GG,TSAL1,YR,
      5FLAG,NMOD,NNMOD
       DIMENSION EMATR(60,5),AMATR(60,5)
       CALL FTRAP
       WRITE OUTPUT TAPE 6,140
  140 FORMAT(1X,66HDEPT.    ACCT.      ESTIMATED     ACTUAL       DEV.
      1 PERCENT DEV.   )
       SM2 = 0.0
       SUMRR = 0.0
       AT2 = 0.0
       SUM = 0.0
       R2 = 0.0
       R1 = 0.
       COUNT = 0.0
       ND = 0
       BAYES = 0.
       NBD = 0
       NND = 0
       CETOT = 0.0
       CATOT = 0.0
       CDEV = 0.0
       DO 1 I=1,N
       EDTOT = 0.0
       DTOT = 0.0
       TDEV = 0.0
       TALPH = TOTAL
       NN = NACCT(I)
       NMBR = NCODE(I)
       DO 11 J=1,NN
       DEV = EMATR(I,J) - AMATR(I,J)
       IF(ABS(AMATR(I,J)) - 20.0) 2,2,3
    2 PDEV = 0.0
       WRITE OUTPUT TAPE 6,5,ANAME(NMBR),ACTNM(J),EMATR(I,J),AMATR(I,J),
      1 DEV,PDEV,UNCALC
       STOR1(I,J) = 999.
       STOR2(I,J) = 999999.
       GO TO 4
    3 PDEV= DEV/AMATR(I,J)
       IF (FLAG) 98,98,99
   99 WOT 5,97,NCODE(I),J,EMATR(I,J),AMATR(I,J),DEV,APPR1(I,J),
      1 ANAME(NMBR),ACTNM(J),YR
   97 FORMAT(1X,1H1,I4,I2,3(2X,E11.4),2X,E11.4,A6,1X,A6,1X,A4)
       GO TO 98
   98 CONTINUE
       WRITE OUTPUT TAPE 6,5,ANAME(NMBR),ACTNM(J),EMATR(I,J),AMATR(I,J),
      1 DEV,PDEV,BLANK
       STOR1(I,J) = PDEV
       STOR2(I,J) = DEV
    4 CONTINUE
       EDTOT = EDTOT + EMATR(I,J)
       DTOT = DTOT + AMATR(I,J)
       TDEV = TDEV + DEV
       SUMRR = SUMRR + (AMATR(I,J)-APPR1(I,J))*(AMATR(I,J)-APPR1(I,J))
       SM2 = SM2 + DEV*DEV
       AT2 = AT2 + AMATR(I,J)*AMATR(I,J)
       SUM = SUM + ABS(DEV)
```

```
       IF (ABS(EMATR(I,J)) - 20.0) 111,111,10
   10 R2 = R2 + (DEV*DEV)/EMATR(I,J)
      ND = ND + 1
  111 IF (ABS(AMATR(I,J)) - 20.0) 1010,1010,1011
 1011 BAYES = BAYES + (DEV*DEV)/AMATR(I,J)
      NBD = NBD + 1
 1010 IF ( ABS(EMATR(I,J) - AMATR(I,J)) - 20.0) 11,11,1111
 1111 R1 = R1 + (DEV*DEV)/(EMATR(I,J)-APPR1(I,J))
      NND = NND + 1
   11 COUNT = COUNT + 1.0
      TPDEV = TDEV/DTOT
      DEVTP(I) = TPDEV
      DEVT(I) = TDEV
      WRITE OUTPUT TAPE 6,12
   12 FORMAT(1X,/)
      WRITE OUTPUT TAPE 6,5,ANAME(NMBR),BLANK,EDTOT,DTOT,TDEV,TPDEV,
     1 TOTAL
      WRITE OUTPUT TAPE 6,13
   13 FORMAT(1X,//)
      CETOT = CETOT + EDTOT
      CATOT = CATOT + DTOT
      CDEV = CDEV + TDEV
    1 CONTINUE
    5 FORMAT(1X,A6,2X,A6,3(   E12.4),5X,E12.4,2X,A6)
      WRITE OUTPUT TAPE 6,20,YR
   20 FORMAT(1X,11HCITY TOTALS,4X,A4,/ )
      WRITE OUTPUT TAPE 6,140
      CPDEV = CDEV/CATOT
      NX = 0
      WRITE OUTPUT TAPE 6,55,BLANK,BLANK,CETOT,CATOT,CDEV,CPDEV,TOTAL
   55 FORMAT(1X,A6,2X,A6,3(E12.4),5X,E12.4,2X,A6)
      RESID = REVEST - CETOT
      WRITE OUTPUT TAPE 6,50,REVEST,CETOT,RESID
   50 FORMAT(1X,/,21H ESTIMATED REVENUES = ,E15.4,/,18H BUDGET ESTIMATE
     1= ,3X,E15.4,/,18H PLANNED SURPLUS = ,3X,E15.4)
      RCHNG = 1.0 - (SM2/SUMRR)
      RAPROM = 1.0  - (SM2/AT2)
      WDV = SUM/CATOT
      DOFN = FLOAT(ND)
      DOFNN = FLOAT(NND)
      DOFNBD = NBD
      WRITE OUTPUT TAPE 6,80
   80 FORMAT (1X,15HGOODNESS OF FIT,/)
      WRITE OUTPUT TAPE 6,85,RAPROM,RCHNG
   85 FORMAT(1H0,87H R-SQUARED EQUIVALENT   - 1.0 MINUS (SUM OF DEVIATION
     1S SQUARED / ACTUAL VALUES SQUARED)   ,E10.4,/,
     242H R-SQUARED EQUIVALENT ON BUDGET CHANGES --,/,10X,88H1.0 MINUS (
     3SUM OF PREDICTED MINUS AVTUAL CHANGES SQUARED/SUM OF ACTUAL CHANGE
     4S SQUARED) ,/,20X, 2H =, E10.4)
      WRITE OUTPUT TAPE 6,81,WDV,R2,DOFN,R1,DOFNN
   81 FORMAT(1H ,38HWEIGHTED AVERAGE ABSOLUTE DEVIATION = ,E13.4,/,
     1/,55HCHI-SQUARED STATISTIC BASED ON ESTIMATED BUDGET LEVEL =,E13.4
     2,/,34HDEGREES OF FREEDOM CONTRIBUTION = ,E13.5,/,/,
     357HCHI-SQUARED STATISTIC BASED ON ESTIMATED BUDGET CHANGE = ,E13.4
     4,/,34HDEGREES OF FREEDOM CONTRIBUTION = ,E13.5)
      WOT 6,83,BAYES,DOFNBD
   83 FORMAT(1H0,67HBAYESIAN INDUCTION STATISTIC = SUM( DEVIATIONS SQUAR
```

```
   1ED/ACTUAL)                     ,E13.4,/,34HDEGREES OF FREEDOM CONTRIBUT
   2ION =   , E13.5,//)
     WRITE OUTPUT TAPE 6,82
82 FORMAT (1X,////////////////////)
     TBUD = CATOT
     RETURN
     END
     SUBROUTINE FLOAT(N)
     FLOAT = FLOATF(N)
     RETURN
     END
     SUBROUTINE ABS(X)
     ABS = ABSF(X)
     RETURN
     END
```

H. SUBROUTINE TO PLACE MODEL RESIDUALS IN ORDER

```
CORDER
     SUBROUTINE ORDER(IDENT)
     DIMENSION DEPR2(60,5),APPR1(60,5),RMAY2(60,5),EXPND(60,5),
   1TEXPN(60),TAPR1(60),TDEP2(60),TSUPR(60),DSUPR(60,5),NCODE(60),
   2NACCT(60),A(60,5),B(60,5),C(60,5),D(60,5),E(60,5),F(60,5),
   3G(60,5),H(60,5),PP(60,5),Q(60,5),R(60,5),S(60,5),DREQ2(60,5),
   4DSREQ(60,5),TMAY2(60),ARMAY(60,5),ATMAY(60),TAPR2(60),APPR2(60,5),
   5AAPRO(60,5),STOR1(60,5),STOR2(60,5),DEVT(60),DEVTP(60),ANAME(999),
   6ACTNM(5),STR11(60,5),STR22(60,5),CHNGLY(60,5),NRCD(999),
   7NRCM(999),NRCC(999),NMOD(999),NNMOD(999,5)
     COMMON DEPR2,APPR1,RMAY2,EXPND,TEXPN,TAPR1,TDEP2,TSUPR,DSUPR,
   1NCODE,NACCT,A,B,C,D,E,F,G,H,PP,Q,R,S,DREQ2,DSREQ,ANAME,ACTNM,
   2STR11,STR22,CHNGLY,NRCD,NRCM,NRCC,COUNT,DEVR,DEVS,TBUD,REVEST,
   3TMAY2,ARMAY,ATMAY,TAPR2,APPR2,AAPRO,STOR1,STOR2,DEVT,DEVTP,
   4RESID,XK,P,XLMT,XL,N,NSTD,TOT,TOTT,BLANK,TOTAL,UNCALC,GG,TSAL1,YR,
   5FLAG,NMOD,NNMOD
     DIMENSION VECTR(60),VECTRP(60),VSAV(60),VSAVP(60),SAVE(60),
   1 SAVEP(60)
     IF (IDENT) 1,1,3
   1 WRITE OUTPUT TAPE 6,2
   2 FORMAT(1X,48HORDERED DEVIATIONS FOR TOTAL DEPARTMENT EXPENSES,//)
     DO 6 I=1,N
     VECTR(I)=DEVT(I)
   6 VECTRP(I)=DEVTP(I)
     GO TO 5
   3 WRITE OUTPUT TAPE 6,4,ACTNM(IDENT)
   4 FORMAT(1X,58HORDERED DEVIATIONS FOR DEPARTMENT EXPENSES, ACCOUNT T
   1YPE   ,A6,//)
     DO 7 I=1,N
     VECTR(I)=STOR2(I,IDENT)
   7 VECTRP(I)=STOR1(I,IDENT)
   5 CONTINUE
     ISAVE = 1
     ISAVEP = 1
     NLEFT = N
  12 CONTINUE
     DO 11 I=1,N
     IF (VECTR(I)-VECTR(ISAVE)) 9,9,8
   8 ISAVE = I
```

```
      VSAV(NLEFT) = VECTR(ISAVE)
      SAVE(NLEFT)=ISAVE
   9  IF (VECTRP(I) - VECTRP(ISAVEP)) 11,11,10
  10  ISAVEP=I
      VSAVP(NLEFT)=VECTRP(ISAVEP)
      SAVEP(NLEFT)=ISAVEP
  11  CONTINUE
      VECTRP(ISAVEP) = -.99E+07
      VECTR(ISAVE) = -.99E+08
      NLEFT = NLEFT - 1
      IF (NLEFT) 13,13,12
  13  CONTINUE
      DO 14 I=1,N
      K = SAVE(I)
      KP = SAVEP(I)
      NMBRP = NCODE(KP)
      NMBR = NCODE(K)
      WRITE OUTPUT TAPE 6,15,ANAME(NMBRP),VSAVP(I),ANAME(NMBR),VSAV(I)
  15  FORMAT(1X,A6,5X,E10.4,15X,A6,5X,E10.4)
  14  CONTINUE
      RETURN
      END
```

I. SUBROUTINE TO PRINT AND PUNCH FORECAST RESULTS

```
C SUMR
      SUBROUTINE SUMR(EMATR)
      DIMENSION DEPR2(60,5),APPR1(60,5),RMAY2(60,5),EXPND(60,5),
     1TEXPN(60),TAPR1(60),TDEP2(60),TSUPR(60),DSUPR(60,5),NCODE(60),
     2NACCT(60),A(60,5),B(60,5),C(60,5),D(60,5),E(60,5),F(60,5),
     3G(60,5),H(60,5),PP(60,5),Q(60,5),R(60,5),S(60,5),DREQ2(60,5),
     4DSREQ(60,5),TMAY2(60),ARMAY(60,5),ATMAY(60),TAPR2(60),APPR2(60,5),
     5AAPRO(60,5),STOR1(60,5),STOR2(60,5),DEVT(60),DEVTP(60),ANAME(999),
     6ACTNM(5),STR11(60,5),STR22(60,5),CHNGLY(60,5),NRCD(999),
     7NRCM(999),NRCC(999),NMOD(999),NNMOD(999,5)
      DIMENSION EMATR(60,5)
      COMMON DEPR2,APPR1,RMAY2,EXPND,TEXPN,TAPR1,TDEP2,TSUPR,DSUPR,
     1NCODE,NACCT,A,B,C,D,E,F,G,H,PP,Q,R,S,DREQ2,DSREQ,ANAME,ACTNM,
     2STR11,STR22,CHNGLY,NRCD,NRCM,NRCC,COUNT,DEVR,DEVS,TBUD,REVEST,
     3TMAY2,ARMAY,ATMAY,TAPR2,APPR2,AAPRO,STOR1,STOR2,DEVT,DEVTP,
     4RESID,XK,P,XLMT,XL,N,NSTD,TOT,TOTT,BLANK,TOTAL,UNCALC,GG,TSAL1,YR,
     5FLAG,NMOD,NNMOD
      CALL FTRAP
      WRITE OUTPUT TAPE 6,140
 140  FORMAT(1X,49HDEPT.    ACCT.        ESTIMATED        BUDGET SHARE   )
      CETOT = 0.0
      DO 111 I=1,N
      NN = NACCT(I)
      DO 111 J=1,NN
 111  CETOT = CETOT + EMATR(I,J)
      DO 1 I=1,N
      EDTOT = 0.0
      TALPH = TOTAL
      NN = NACCT(I)
      NMBR = NCODE(I)
      DO 11 J=1,NN
      BSHARE = EMATR(I,J)/CETOT
```

```
      WOT 6,5,ANAME(NMBR),ACTNM(J), EMATR(I,J),BSHARE,BLANK
      IF (FLAG) 4,4,555
  555 WOT 5,55,NMBR,J,EMATR(I,J),BSHARE,ANAME(NMBR),ACTNM(J),YR
    4 CONTINUE
    5 FORMAT(1X,A6,2X,A6,E10.4,15X,E10.4,5X,A6)
   55 FORMAT(1X,1H ,I4,I2,2(2X,E11.4),26X,A6,1X,A6,F5.0)
      EDTOT = EDTOT + EMATR(I,J)
   11 CONTINUE
      WRITE OUTPUT TAPE 6,12
   12 FORMAT(1X,/)
      BSHARE = EDTOT/CETOT
      WOT 6,5,ANAME(NMBR), BLANK,EDTOT,BSHARE,TOTAL
      WRITE OUTPUT TAPE 6,13
   13 FORMAT(1X,//)
    1 CONTINUE
      WRITE OUTPUT TAPE 6,20,YR
   20 FORMAT (1X,11HCITY TOTALS,4X,F5.0,/   )
      WRITE OUTPUT TAPE 6,140
      NX = 0
      BSHARE = CETOT/CETOT
      WOT 6,5,BLANK,BLANK,CETOT,BSHARE,TOTAL
      RESID = REVEST - CETOT
      WRITE OUTPUT TAPE 6,50,REVEST,CETOT,RESID
   50 FORMAT(1X,/,21H ESTIMATED REVENUES = ,E10.4,/,18H BUDGET ESTIMATE
     1= ,3X,E10.4,/,18H PLANNED SURPLUS = ,3X,E10.4)
      WRITE OUTPUT TAPE 6,82
   82 FORMAT (1X,/////////////////////)
      RETURN
      END
```

Appendix F

CLEVELAND MODEL RESIDUALS

Cleveland (one-period change model)

1956 Budget: Cleveland

Department	Error*	% Error	Cause	Type
Traffic Engineering	−$596,500	−100.0%	New department—mostly transfers from Police Dept.	2.b.i.
Street Cleaning	−$261,600	−39.6%	Part due to pay increase—remainder missing data	4.a. 4.d.
City Hospital	−$177,500	−3.3%	General wage increase	4.d.
Recreation	−$148,700	−10.8%	Wage increase, eight new playgrounds	4.d. 3.a.
Public Service—General Admin.	−$15,480	−39.6%	Some due to salary increase—most is model error	4.d.
Boxing and Wrestling Comm.	−$4,016	−28.0%	Small error?	
Finance—General Admin.	−$7,222	−22.3%	One new secretary (at $7,218)	4.d.
Port—General Admin.	+$17,980	+27.1%	Dept. new in 1954—growth slowing down	4.d.
Police	+$430,500	+4.3%	Transfers to new Traffic Engineering and Parking Dept.	2.b.i.

* (Model Predictions-Observed)

1957 Budget: Cleveland

Department	Error	% Error	Cause	Type
Public Service— Gen. Admin.	− $36,420	−92.4%	Addition of consulting engineer model error	4.d.
Personnel	− $111,500	−76.8%	Bad data, causing unstable model parameters	4.a.
Traffic Engineering	− $148,100	−23.9%	Department new in 1956, so 'normal' data missing	2.b.i. 4.a.
Port— Gen. Admin.	− $25,070	−29.1%	Doubled engineering staff (Seaway?)	1.b. 2.b.ii.
Police	− $161,900	−1.5%	10% uniformed personnel salary increase, 50 new policemen	4.d.
Street Cleaning	− $143,000	−2.4%	8% general salary increase and 50 new people due to increase in state gasoline tax receipts	1.a.i. 3.d.
Engineering and Construction	− $137,900	−23.5%	8% general salary increase and dept. model error	4.d.
City Hospital	− $104,000	−1.8%	Increase in hospital receipts (Patient charges)	3.b.

1958 Budget: Cleveland

Department	Error	% Error	Cause	Type
Miscellaneous	− $23,990	−85.7%	Bad data	4.a.
City Hospital	+ $5,275,000	—	Transferred to County	1.a.ii.
Architecture	− $84,950	−82.4%	Bad DEPT. parameters	4.a.
Public Service— General Admin.	− $24,140	−54.3%	Bad DEPT. parameters	4.a.

Urban Renewal —General Admin.	− $38,660	− 100.0%	New dept. (transfers from Public Safety)	2.b.i. 1.a.ii.
Harvard Yards	− $47,900	− 100.0%	New unit of Parks Department	2.b.i. 3.c.
Police	− $1,368,000	− 11.7%	5% pay increase for uniform ranks plus 122 new patrolmen	4.c. 3.c.
Fire	− $795,700	− 11.1%	5% pay increase for uniform ranks plus 34 new firemen	5.c. 4.d.
Street Cleaning	− $747,000	− 11.4%	80 new people, (hourly) rental of lake-front crane, increased receipts from state gasoline tax	1.a.i. 3.b. 4.c.
Street Lighting	− $543,000	− 32.7%	Bad DEPT. parameters	4.a.

1959 Budget: Cleveland

Department	Error	% Error	Cause	Type
Personnel	+ $110,000	+ 258.4%	Unstable model parameters	4.a.
City Hospital	+ $1,115,000	—	Transferred to county	1.a.ii.
Urban Renewal —Housing	− $201,000	− 100.0%	Building and Housing split	3.c.
Urban Renewal —Building	+ $138,200	+ 23.9%	Building and Housing split	2.b.i. 4.a.
Urban Renewal —General Admin.	− $22,080	− 60.4%	Dept. new in 1958	2.b.i. 4.a.
Sewer Maintenance	− $478,700	− 64.5%	Bad data	4.a.
Police	− $446,600	− 3.5%	5% salary increase for uniformed personnel	4.a.

Community Relations	− $36,320	− 60.5%	9 new clerks	1.b.

1960 Budget: Cleveland

Department	Error	% Error	Cause	Type
Finance —Treasurer	+ $58,680	+ 110.3%	Bad Data	4.a.
Harvard Yards	+ $8,962	+ 34.6%	Department of Park Streets and Roads function transferred	2.b.i.
Police	− $155,600	− 1.2%	14 new school guards, model error	4.a.
Recreation	− $115,100	− 5.7%	2 new ice rinks opened (land issue), 4 new playgrounds, 3 new recreation centers (buildings) opened	3.a.
Urban Renewal —Housing	− $24,380	− 11.0%	Personnel increase paid for out of bonds (capital item)	1.a.i. 3.b.
Street Cleaning	− $86,010	− 1.2%	Increase in state gasoline tax receipts, opening of new city incinerator (capital item) with increase of 50 people	1.a.i.
Safety —General Admin.	− $8,897	− 27.4%	New secretary to director	4.a.
Community Relations	− $1,046	− 1.2%	New research director	4.a.

1961 Budget: Cleveland

Department	Error	% Error	Cause	Type
Finance —Treasurer	− $51,910	− 47.9%	Bad 1960 data	4.a.
Architecture	− $43,540	− 36.5%	Bad DEPT. model parameters	4.a.

Urban Renewal —Housing	− $95,280	−26.7%	Need for 'certificate of occupancy permit' produced $150,000 in extra dept. revenue	1.a.i. 3.b.
Fire	− $310,800	−3.6%	5% salary increase, shortened work week (55 new men added)	4.a.
Sewer Maintenance	− $76,140	−9.9%	Missing data	4.a.
Finance —General Admin.	+ $6,343	+25.9%	Secretary to director dropped	4.a.
Auditorium and Stadium	+ $60,260	+5.1%		4.a.
Personnel	− $9,753	−18.2%	Bad data	4.a.
Engineering and Construction	− $127,800	−17.6%	Model error	4.d.

1962 Budget: Cleveland

Department	Error	% Error	Cause	Type
Street Cleaning	+ $64,020	+9.8%	New employees starting at bottom of pay scale	1.a.i.
Job Retraining	− $17,500	−100.0%	New department	1.a.i. 2.b.ii.
Harbor	− $63,470	−14.7%	Model error (dept.)	4.a.
Fire	− $54,920	−0.6%		
Urban Renewal —Housing	+ $54,740	+15.1%	'Unusual' increase last year carried over	4.a.
Council	− $61,730	−12.5%	Councilmen salary increases (+$1500/ yr., 32 councilmen)	4.a.
Community Relations	+ $21,340	+40.8%	Office staff reduction	4.c.
Welfare Institutions —Gen. Admin.	+ $8,472	+42.4%	Commissioner's job made part time during 1961 (new Commissioner)	4.c.

| Architecture | −$24,130 | →21.3% | Bad model parameters (DEPT.) | 4.a. |

1963 Budget: Cleveland

Department	Error	% Error	Cause	Type
Welfare Institutions	−$10,830	−37.4%	Commissioner's job reinstated to full time (see 1962)	4.c.
Job Retraining	−$4,631	−21.7%	Consultants hired	4.c.
Urban Renewal— Housing	−$50,090	−12.9%	Increase in payroll support from urban renewal bonds (for capital items)	3.b.
Dog Pound	−$4,691	−11.4%	Open one more day per week after one year experiment	3.b.
Street Lighting	−$133,900	−7.4%	Rise in cost of contractual services —street lighting by privately-owned utility	3.d.
Airport	−$101,500	−8.2%		
Engineering Construction	−$56,640	−7.7%	14 new employees— engineers	4.a. 4.c.
Sewer Maintenance	+$751,400	—	Transferred out of Gen. Fund	1.a.ii.
Building Standards	−$4,112	−9.7%	2 part-time employees added	4.a.
Health	−$52,870	−3.5%	Opening of new health center (capital item)	3.a.

1964 Budget: Cleveland

Department	Error	% Error	Cause	Type
Police	−$1,177,000	−7.6%	10% salary increase ($200,000 for additional men)	4.a. 1.b.

Fire	−$654,100	−6.9%	10% salary increase	4.a.
Street Cleaning	−$640,800	−7.5%	10% salary increase	4.a.
Engineering Construction	−$250,700	−30.9%	10% salary increase, additional personnel to help administer a $5M increase on contracts (capital items)	4.a.
Docks and Bridges	−$101,400	−30.5%	Increase in payroll supported by increased billings to special funds, land issues (capital items)	3.b.
Port— Gen. Admin.	−$22,640	−19.6%	Airport activity, 10% salary increase	4.a. 4.c.
Architecture	−$24,230	−19.1%	10% salary increase, increases in payroll support by billings to special funds and bond issues	4.a.
Welfare Institutions	+$5,009	+24.6%	Commissioner replaced by clerk	4.c.
Street Lighting	+$230,900	+14.3%	Carryover from last year's increase in contractual costs·	4.a.

1965 Budget: Cleveland

Department	Error	% Error	Cause	Type
Architecture	−$56,470	−44.4%	Unstable parameters	4.a.
Engineering and Construction	−$248,500	−32.8%	Missing data	4.a.
Health and Welfare— General Admin.	−$14,940	−35.2%	$15,000 additional contractual service charge (visiting doctors and nurses)	1. 3.d.

Auditorium and Stadium	− $217,600	−13.5%	Underground exhibition hall opened (capital item)	3.a.
Police	− $349,900	−2.2%	200 new policemen	1.b.
Street Cleaning	+ $132,300	+1.6%	Carryover from unusual increase in 1964.	4.a.
Urban Renewal— Housing	− $68,730	−14.0%	Error in budget book (and data)	4.a.
Welfare Institutions	− $5,058	−19.0%	Increase in contractual service totals	3.d.
Community Relations	− $11,560	−17.2%	Increase in operations (civil rights disturbances?)	1.b. 4.e.

DETROIT MODEL RESIDUALS

Detroit (one-period change model)

1958–59 Budget: Detroit

Department	Error*	% Error	Cause	Type
Mayors Industrial Development Committee	− $21,810	−100.0%	New department, declining revenues	2.b.ii. 1.b.
Welfare	− $12,040,000	−71.2%	State reduced share from 50-50 to 30-70, bad economic situation	1.a.i.
Election Commission	− $823,000	−67.7%	Spring elections	3.d.
Recorders Court Criminal Division	+ $6,384,000	+151.9%	Capital expenses included in budget in previous periods	4.b.
Civic Center	+ $5,032,000	+92.0%	Capital items— new building	4.b.
Police	+ $1,473,000	+5.0%	Missing data in trend term	4.a.

* (Model Predictions-Observed)

Public Works	− $1,041,000	−8.4%	Capital items included in budget	4.b.

1959–60 Budget: Detroit

Department	Error	% Error	Cause	Type
Mayors Committee on Reports and Information	− $173,700	−100.0%	New department formed	2.b.ii.
Public Works— Streets	+ $6,820,000	+69.1%	Carryover from capital item in last year's budget	4.b.
Community Relations	− $38,250	−47.7%	New accounts established	3.c.
Welfare	− $4,564,000	−33.4%	State reduced share, continued 'bad times'	1.a.i. 4.c.
Parks and Recreation	− $1,143,000	−11.8%	Capital item included in budget	4.b.
Civic Center	− $1,056,000	−10.3%	Capital items included in budget	4.b.
Public Works —Sanitation	− $1,167,000	−6.5%	4% wage increase, capital items in budget	4.d. 4.b.

1960–61 Budget: Detroit

Department	Error	% Error	Cause	Type
Mayors Committee on Rehabilitation of Narcotics Addicts	− $2,000	−100.0%	New department formed	2.b.ii. 1.b.
Civic Center	− $1,355,000	−73.9%	Civic Center building opened —result of capital decision	3.a.
Election Commission	− $741,500	−63.0%	Election year	3.d.
Loyalty Investigation Committees	− $4,808	−19.7%	One new clerk	4.d.

Civil Defense	+$115,600	+53.0%	Curtailment, federal reimbursement for past expenses	1.a.i.
Police	+$890,000	+2.9%	Because of budget deficits, city not filling empty positions	1.b.
Welfare	+$771,300	+5.4%	Aftermath of buildup due to reduction in state share	1.a.i.
Public Works —Sanitation	+$569,300	+3.1%	Capital items, model error	4.b.

1961–62 Budget: Detroit

Department	Error	% Error	Cause	Type
Welfare	+$9,617,000	+137.3%	State increased share to 50-50	1.a.i.
Public Works —Streets	+$422,300	+4.0%	Part of mayor's $3M cut in capital improvements	3.a.
Community Relations	−$43,450	−34.4%	Conscious program expansion	2.b.ii. 4.c.
Parks and Recreation	−$4,620,000	−29.5%	Capital item to finance new parks	4.b.
Civic Center	−$666,700	−26.7%	Capital expenditures item	4.b.
Election Commission	−$177,000	−23.3%	Election year	3.d.

1962–63 Budget (new mayor): Detroit

Department	Error	% Error	Cause	Type
Welfare	−$14,190,000	−42.7%	Appropriation to pay off $8.5M deficit for 61–62 and *additional* $8.3M for current needs, new mayor	1.a.i. 2.a.

Mayor's Committee on Industrial Development	−$14,540	−36.2%	Opening of Washington lobby office	2.a. 1.b.
Loyalty Investigating Committee	−$7,531	−31.2%		4.d.
Planning	−$196,500	−25.4%	Carryover from capital item, fluctuations	4.a. 4.b.
Fire	−$799,700	−5.8%	2% wage increase +$100 per uniformed employee, full staffing, 25 new positions	4.a.
Zoo	+$379,700	+25.0%	Re-funding of capital items	2.a. 4.b.
Public Works —Sanitation	+$984,800	+15.2%	Re-funding of capital items	2.a. 4.b.
Health Department —Kiefer Hospital	+$828,900	+15.2%	Re-funding of capital items, decline in TB cases	2.a. 4.b. 4.c.

1963–64 Budget: Detroit

Department	Error	% Error	Cause	Type
Community Renewal	−$25,500	−100.0%	New department	2.a. 1.a.i.
Police	−$1,363,000	−3.9%	Wage increases as result of Public Administration Service survey and 125 new positions for EDP, patrolmen, school guards —civil rights?	1.b. 2.b.ii.
Health—Receiving Hospital	−$978,800	−9.0%	Patient revenue increase, city increase because of heavier case loads	3.b. 4.c.

	Error	% Error	Cause	Type
Controller's Office	− $965,300	−35.6%	People to collect new city income tax, etc.	3.d. 2.b.ii. 4.c.
Mayor's Committee on Industrial Development	− $21,780	−35.5%	New mayor	2.a.
Election Commission	+ $245,600	+61.1%	No election	3.d.
Public Works— Streets	+ $3,033,000	+71.1%	Re-funding of capital items	2.a.
Welfare	+ $3,241,000	+12.8%	Federal aid covers part of aid to dependent children with unemployed fathers	1.a.i. 3.b.

1964–65 Budget: Detroit

Department	Error	% Error	Cause	Type
Election Commission	− $666,500	−62.6%	Election year	3.d.
Public Works— Streets	− $1,606,000	−35.2%	Includes payments to general fund under state and federal agreements	1.a.i.
Police	− $2,145,000	−5.8%	2½ % wage increase and implementation of Public Administration Service survey recommendations	4.d.
Assessors	− $204,200	−13.8%	Property reassessment required by new State Constitution	1.a.i.
Fire	− $794,600	−5.2%	Wage increase and implementation of Public Administration Service survey recommendations	4.a.

Mayors Committee on Industrial Development	+$13,610	+28.9%	Rapid department growth tapers off	4.a. 4.d.
Welfare	+$7,070,000	+39.4%	Aid to dependent children with unemployed fathers legislation	1.a.i.
Public Works— Sewers	+$1,953,000	—	Transferred to Water Dept.—no longer in general fund	2.b.i. 1.a.ii.

PITTSBURGH MODEL DEVIATIONS

Pittsburgh (one-period change model)

1960 Budget: Pittsburgh

Department	Error*	% Error	Cause	Type
Public Works— Refuse	−$282,400	−6.0%	Contract for rubbish collection	3.d.
Public Works— Bridges & Highways	−$235,400	−5.0%	Street lighting cost	3.d.
Public Works— Auto Equipment	−$148,100	−11.0%	Mechanization of dept. function (increase in police fleet—step up coverage without adding men)	1.b. 2.b.ii.
Treasurer	+$52,490	+3.8%	Unfilled positions due to poor economic conditions in area	1.b.
Land & Building— Accounts & Admin.	+$46,890	+9.0%		4.a. 4.d.
Service Center	−$34,400	−100.0%	New department	2.b.ii.

* (Model Predictions-Observed)

Human Relations	−$11,260	−15.4%	2 staff positions to implement federal Fair Housing Bill	1.a.i.
Public Safety— Youth Bureau	+$13,210	+51.8%	Transfer from Police Dept.	1.a.ii.
Civil Defense	+$6,136	+27.4%	Carryover from capital item in 1959	3.a.

1961 Budget (new mayor): Pittsburgh

Department	Error	% Error	Cause	Type
Public Safety— Police	−$287,800	−3.0%	Part of wage increase financed by income tax increase	4.d. 3.b.
Lands & Buildings Accounts & Admin.	−$174,500	−29.5%		4.d.
Public Works— Gen. office	+$159,800	+7.7%	Reduction in liquid fuels tax reimbursement from state (reflects city's loss in population)	1.a.i.
Public Works— Refuse	−$154,100	−3.4%		4.d.
Public Safety —Fire	−$93,970	−1.4%	Part of wage increase financed by income tax increase	4.a. 3.b.
Public Safety —Youth Bureau	−$19,660	−71.6%	New department in 1961	4.d.
Art Commission	−$5,064	−11.8%	Small error	—
Police Magistrates	+$6,872	+13.5%		4.d.
Mayor	−$12,870	−10.3%	Personnel officer to administer job classification and pay plan program	2.b.ii. 3.d. 4.c.

1962 Budget: Pittsburgh

Department	Error	% Error	Cause	Type
Public Works— Gen. Office	−$206,000	−9.5%	Street lighting contract and liquid fuels tax program— increased responsi- bilities— inter-governmental decision	1.a.ii. 3.d.
Public Safety— Police	+$749,800	+8.5%	Carryover from last year's increase, moratorium on step increases	4.d.
Public Safety —Fire	−$115,100	−1.7%	Increments for 1st, 2nd, and 3rd year men and new men	4.d.
Public Safety —Youth Bureau	−$100,600	−78.6%	New dept. in 1961	2.b.i.
Public Works —Automotive Equipment	−$67,580	−4.9%	Increased parts costs	3.d.
Council	−$10,500	−8.6%		4.d.
Public Works —Engineering	−$8,827	−8.3%		4.d.

1963 Budget: Pittsburgh

Department	Error	% Error	Cause	Type
Public Works —Gen. Office	−$611,100	−22.3%	Liquid fuels (state) program	1.a.i.
Public Safety —Police	−$548,300	−5.9%	Social security increases, service increments	1.a.i.
Public Safety —Fire	+$212,500	+3.2%	Moratorium on hirings	1.b.
Parks & Recreation —Recreation	+$144,900	+19.3%	Took over school board's recreation program in 1954– now 'forced' to drop it	1.b.

Public Works —Auto Equip.	+$134,300	+10.9%	Carryover from previous budgets	4.a.
Public Works —Engineering	+$85,490	+4.4%	Contract schedules	3.a.
Public Safety —Youth Bureau	+$63,940	+100.2%	Rapid growth tapering off— 'unstable' model parameters	4.a. 4.d.
Human Relations Commission	+$21,640	+38.9%	Rapid growth tapering off	4.d.
Sinking Fund Comm.	+$1,010	+29.7%	Small error	—

1964 Budget: Pittsburgh

Department	Error	% Error	Cause	Type
Public Safety —Police	−$105,700	−1.0%	5% pay raise (step increases)	4.d.
Parks & Recreation —Grounds	−$68,620	−3.8%	Staff for new parks (capital item) and step increase	3.a.
Public Works —General Office	+$189,000	+8.1%	State liquid fuels program for street lighting (contract)	1.a.i. 3.d.
Treasurer	−$68,350	−3.9%	Step increases in wages	4.d.
Public Works —Refuse	+$62,400	+1.3%	2½% pay increase for laborers	4.a.
Human Relations	−$20,900	−21.2%	More staff, mayor notes '40 tension cases' over past summer	1.b. 4.c.
Mayors	−$21,670	−13.6%	Coordination of federal job retraining programs	1.a.i. 4.c.
Police Magistrates	+$6,775	+12.6%		4.a.
Sinking Fund Comm.	−$5,116	−10.2%	Small error	—

1965 Budget: Pittsburgh

Department	Error	% Error	Cause	Type
Public Safety —Police	−$596,900	−5.4%	Cost of 100 new patrolmen	1.b.
Public Works —Gen. Office	−$126,800	−5.2%	Outside contract— street lighting, increase in responsibility— inter-governmental decision	1.a.i.
Supplies—Accounts and Admin.	−$121,600	−46.0%	Outside contract	3.d.
Parks & Recreation —Recreation	−$109,400	−11.9%	Reinstated recreation program dropped two years ago	1.a.ii. 4.c.
Public Safety —Traffic Planning	−$86,820	−9.4%	Meter Maid program	2.b.ii.
Police Magistrates Clerk	−$12,800 −$14,850	−19.3% −13.9%		4.a. 4.a.

Appendix G

SAMPLE OUTPUT—MAYORS MODEL OUTCOMES
CITY OF DETROIT, 1964-65 BUDGET
ONE-PERIOD CHANGE MODEL

DEPT.	ACCT.	ESTIMATED	ACTUAL	DEV.	PERCENT DEV.	
ARTCOM	S,WAGE	.4852E 06	.5292E 06	-.4401E 05	-.8316E-01	
ARTCOM	M,SEXP	.9945E 05	.9984E 05	-.3879E 03	-.3885E-02	
ARTCOM	EQUIPI	.3957E 05	.3690E 05	.2671E 04	.7238E-01	
ARTCOM		.6242E 06	.6659E 06	-.4172E 05	-.6266E-01	TOTAL
BLDGSF	S,WAGE	.2379E 07	.2445E 07	-.6627E 05	-.2711E-01	
BLDGSF	M,SEXP	.1141E 06	.1213E 06	-.7204E 04	-.5939E-01	
BLDGSF	EQUIPI	.9732E 04	.9515E 04	.2165E 03	.2276E-01	
BLDGSF		.2503E 07	.2576E 07	-.7326E 05	-.2844E-01	TOTAL
PLANNG	S,WAGE	.5806E 06	.5966E 06	-.1600E 05	-.2681E-01	
PLANNG	M,SEXP	.2364E 05	.2420E 05	-.5551E 03	-.2294E-01	
PLANNG	EQUIPI	.2369E 04	.1910E 04	.4594E 03	.2405E 00	
PLANNG		.6066E 06	.6227E 06	-.1609E 05	-.2584E-01	TOTAL
FIRE	S,WAGE	.1356E 08	.1416E 08	-.5956E 06	-.4208E-01	
FIRE	M,SEXP	.6353E 06	.6551E 06	-.1974E 05	-.3013E-01	
FIRE	EQUIPI	.3219E 06	.2840E 06	.3787E 05	.1334E 00	
FIRE		.1452E 08	.1510E 08	-.5775E 06	-.3826E-01	TOTAL
COUNCL	S,WAGE	.1800E 06	.1829E 06	-.2922E 04	-.1597E-01	
COUNCL	M,SEXP	.6810E 05	.7950E 05	-.1140E 05	-.1434E 00	
COUNCL	EQUIPI	.6107E 03	.6250E 03	-.1434E 02	-.2294E-01	
COUNCL		.2487E 06	.2631E 06	-.1434E 05	-.5449E-01	TOTAL
MAYORS	S,WAGE	.1167E 06	.1230E 06	-.6229E 04	-.5066E-01	
MAYORS	M,SEXP	.2687E 04	.3250E 04	-.5631E 03	-.1733E 00	
MAYORS	EQUIPI	.6107E 03	.2050E 04	-.1439E 04	-.7021E 00	
MAYORS		.1200E 06	.1283E 06	-.8231E 04	-.6417E-01	TOTAL

CIVDEF	S,WAGE	.1347E 06	.1416E 06	-.6959E 04	-.4914E-01
CIVDEF	M,SEXP	.1644E 06	.1998E 06	-.3541E 05	-.1772E 00
CIVDEF	EQUIPI	.4104E 05	.1125E 05	.2979E 05	.2648E 01
CIVDEF		.3401E 06	.3527E 06	-.1258E 05	-.3567E-01 TOTAL
CORREC	S,WAGE	.1267E 07	.1329E 07	-.6229E 05	-.4686E-01
CORREC	M,SEXP	.6125E 06	.7453E 06	-.1328E 06	-.1781E 00
CORREC	EQUIPI	.5936E 05	.5530E 05	.4056E 04	.7335E-01
CORREC		.1939E 07	.2130E 07	-.1910E 06	-.8968E-01 TOTAL
LOYINV	S,WAGE	.0000E 00	.0000E 00	.0000E 00	.0000E 00 UNCALC
LOYINV	M,SEXP	.0000E 00	.0000E 00	.0000E 00	.0000E 00 UNCALC
LOYINV	EQUIPI	.0000E 00	.0000E 00	.0000E 00	.0000E 00 UNCALC
LOYINV		.0000E 00	.0000E 00	.0000E 00	.0000E 00 TOTAL
PW-MTR	S,WAGE	.1591E 07	.1628E 07	-.3780E 05	-.2321E-01
PW-MTR	M,SEXP	.1572E 07	.1582E 07	-.1005E 05	-.6353E-02
PW-MTR	EQUIPI	.1838E 07	.1839E 07	-.9947E 03	-.5408E-03
PW-MTR		.5001E 07	.5050E 07	-.4884E 05	-.9673E-02 TOTAL
PKSREC	S,WAGE	.7696E 07	.8069E 07	-.3730E 06	-.4623E-01
PKSREC	M,SEXP	.1872E 07	.1809E 07	.6312E 05	.3489E-01
PKSREC	EQUIPI	.1049E 06	.1566E 06	-.5164E 05	-.3298E 00
PKSREC		.9674E 07	.1004E 08	-.3616E 06	-.3603E-01 TOTAL
PW-PER	S,WAGE	.1337E 07	.1404E 07	-.6678E 05	-.4756E-01
PW-PER	M,SEXP	.6497E 05	.6885E 05	-.3875E 04	-.5629E-01
PW-PER	EQUIPI	.1174E 05	.4580E 04	.7155E 04	.1562E 01
PW-PER		.1414E 07	.1478E 07	-.6350E 05	-.4297E-01 TOTAL
POLICE	S,WAGE	.3296E 08	.3427E 08	-.1305E 07	-.3808E-01
POLICE	M,SEXP	.9750E 06	.1003E 07	-.2814E 05	-.2805E-01
POLICE	EQUIPI	.1602E 06	.2162E 06	-.5597E 05	-.2589E 00
POLICE		.3410E 08	.3549E 08	-.1389E 07	-.3915E-01 TOTAL

.
.
.
.
.

MREPIN	S,WAGE	.1696E 06	.1794E 06	-.9779E 04	-.5451E-01
MREPIN	M,SEXP	.4449E 05	.3620E 05	.8293E 04	.2291E 00
MREPIN	EQUIPI	.1564E 04	.1860E 04	-.2961E 03	-.1592E 00
MREPIN		.2157E 06	.2175E 06	-.1782E 04	-.8193E-02 TOTAL
MACTDY	S,WAGE	.0000E 00	.0000E 00	.0000E 00	.0000E 00 UNCALC
MACTDY	M,SEXP	.0000E 00	.0000E 00	.0000E 00	.0000E 00 UNCALC
MACTDY	EQUIPI	.0000E 00	.0000E 00	.0000E 00	.0000E 00 UNCALC
MACTDY		.0000E 00	.0000E 00	.0000E 00	.0000E 00 TOTAL
MCOMRE	S,WAGE	.2550E 05	.2665E 05	-.1155E 04	-.4333E-01
MCOMRE	M,SEXP	.0000E 00	.0000E 00	.0000E 00	.0000E 00 UNCALC
MCOMRE	EQUIPI	.0000E 00	.0000E 00	.0000E 00	.0000E 00 UNCALC
MCOMRE		.2550E 05	.2665E 05	-.1155E 04	-.4333E-01 TOTAL

CITY TOTALS   64-5

DEPT.	ACCT.	ESTIMATED	ACTUAL	DEV.	PERCENT DEV.	
		.1710E 09	.1699E 09	.1064E 07	.6259E-02	TOTAL

```
ESTIMATED REVENUES =      .1710E 09
BUDGET ESTIMATE =         .1710E 09
PLANNED SURPLUS =         .2200E 02
GOODNESS OF FIT
```

R-SQUARED EQUIVALENT -- 1.0 MINUS(SUM OF DEVIATIONS SQUARED/
    ACTUAL VALUES SQUARED) .9761E 00
R-SQUARED EQUIVALENT ON BUDGET CHANGES--
    1.0 MINUS (SUM OF PREDICTED MINUS ACTUAL CHANGES SQUARED/
        SUM OF ACTUAL CHANGES SQUARED) = .1035E 00
WEIGHTED AVERAGE ABSOLUTE DEVIATION =   .1125E 00

CHI-SQUARED STATISTIC BASED ON BUDGET LEVEL =   .8216E 07
DEGREES OF FREEDOM CONTRIBUTION = .13500E 03

CHI-SQUARED STATISTIC BASED ON ESTIMATED BUDGET CHANGE = .4175E 09
DEGREES OF FREEDOM CONTRIBUTION = .13800E 03

BAYESIAN INDUCTION STATISTIC = SUM(DEVIATIONS SQUARED/ACTUAL)
                  = .5454E 07
DEGREES OF FREEDOM CONTRIBUTION =   .13500E 03

Appendix H

DATA SOURCES

1. **Cleveland appropriations, expenditure, and mayor's budget recommendation data 1956-1965:**
    a. Supplement to *The City Record*, official publication of the city of Cleveland, containing the mayor's estimate for the year 1965: the annual appropriations ordinance based thereon and the amended official certificate of the county budget commission—one copy for each year, 1955-1965
    b. Departmental request data, 1960-63 and 1965, obtained from work sheets in the Department of Finance, the city of Cleveland
2. **Detroit appropriations, expenditure, mayor's budget recommendation, and departmental request data 1958-59 to 1964-65:**
    a. *1964-1965 Budget Estimates for Fiscal Year Ending June 30, 1965*, compiled by: City Controller's Office, Budget Bureau; revised by: Jerome P. Cavanaugh, Mayor—one copy for each year, 1958-59 to 1964-65
3. **Pittsburgh appropriations, expenditures, and mayor's budget estimates 1960-1965:**
    a. *City of Pittsburgh Budget—1965: Departmental Estimates*, Joseph M. Barr, Mayor—one copy 1960-1965
    b. Pittsburgh departmental request data, 1965, obtained from department request budget forms on file in office of the mayor, city of Pittsburgh

Name Index

Subject Index

Aids to calculation, 18, 207-208
  base, 18, 119, 121-137, 148-149, 207
  fair share, 18, 207-208, 122-137, 147-149, 207-208
Applicability of model, 221-228
  board of education, 228-230
  conditions for, 221-222
  Department of Defense budgeting, 225-228
  non-market organizations, 228-231
  other levels of government, 221-228
  satellite cities, 222-223
  small municipalities and local governments, 224-225
  twin cities, 224
  universities, 230-231
Appropriations, relation to expenditures, 97n, 151-152, 192, 231, 234-235
Attention-directing mechanisms,
  approaches to changing, 239-240
  changing rules, 233-235
  fixed focus of attention, 202-203
  importance of at operating level, 203
  in existing decision system, 233-235
  political pressures, 188-189
Autocorrelation, 46
  Durbin-Watson d statistic, 46, 46n

Balanced-budget constraint, 38, 67
  contribution to complexity, 38, 41
  Presidential appropriations target, 208
  system responsiveness, 235-239
  tightness of constraint, 97-98
Base,
  Bayesian-Induction Statistics. See Goodness-of-fit of budgetary model
  behavioralism in perspective, 220
  board of education, budgetary decision-making in, 228-230
  See also Aids to calculation
Budget categories,
  accounts, 36, 231
  administrative units, 30-31
    used in study, 254-256
  choice of, 30-31
  cognitive map of the process, 30-31
  expenditure categories, 30-31
  PPBS, 246-248, 247n
Budget ceiling,
  federal, 208
  increases in, outside general fund, 152-153

  due to increased efficiency, 154-155
Budget forms, 53
  as cognitive map of process, 52-53, 99-102, 218
  council's, 99-102
  department head's, 52-54
  mayor's, 70-71
  complexity of, 99-101
Budget guidelines, mayor's, 33-34, 49, 54, 62, 64, 68-69, 95-96
Budget shares,
  fair share. See Aids to calculation
  long-run dynamics of, 177-178
  observed shifts in, 163-165
Budget shares of departments, 170
  effect of revenue constant on, 179-184
  under normal and loose administrative constraints, 170-176
Budget requests, defensibility of accounts, 16
  See also Priority of accounts
Budgets,
  as limits on expenditures, 3, 97n, 192, 202
  policy changes not reflected in, 150-156, 220
  self-confirming nature, 3
  See also Budgetary decision process, Concepts of budgeting, and COUNCIL, DEPT., and MAYORS submodels
Budgetary decision process, municipal,
  characteristics of, 4-5
  different levels of government, viii, 221-228
  feedback in, 32, 32n, 34, 34n
  information flow in, 32
  mayor's budget guidelines, 34
  overview of, 32-35
  relationship to other forms of decision-making, vii
Business community and tax rates, 88-91, 153, 189-190, 189n
Business firms, resource allocation in, 14-16

Capital budgeting, 22n, 23n, 40
  effect on operating budget, 22, 40n, 158, 160, 162
  exclusion of, 3-4, 22
  future research, 231
  irregularities in Detroit, 130, 161
Carnegie-Mellon University, x

Submodel interdependence and feedback, 36-38
See also Decomposable systems
Suburbs, 223-224
Supplemental budget requests, 34, 34n, 54
portion granted, 98
Surplus elimination procedures, 72-73

Tax policy, 88-91, 92, 102n
characteristics of acceptable revenue sources, 89, 91
factors influencing tax rates, 189-190
factors influencing tax yields, 178-184
future research, 231
mayor's, 106
statutory limits, 89n
See also Wage policy, mayor's
Theory formalization, advantages of, 24-25
See also Mathematics
Transfer of functions, to increase available revenue, 153-154, 237
Turing's test. *See* Goodness-of-fit of budgetary model

Uncertainty, avoidance in organizations, 15, 200-201, 218-219

through common operating standards, 16
through model legislation, 16
Uniform wage policy, 89n
reduction of problem complexity, 41, 218
Unit costs. *See* Standard costs
Universities, budgetary decision-making in, 230-231
Unprogrammed decisions, 155-165
implications for model validity, 165
Unusual decisions. *See* Unprogrammed decisions
User charges, 168, 237-238

Validity of formal model of budgetary process. *See* Goodness-of-fit of budgetary model
Vulnerability of accounts to cuts, 42, 197-199
visibility of account, 198n
See also Precedent, role of, and Priority of accounts

Wage policy, mayor's, 88-92, 102n, 156, 218
See also Tax policy

PRINTED IN U.S.A.